PASSING TO AMÉRICA

PASSING

TO AMÉRICA

Antonio (Née María) Yta's

Transgressive, Transatlantic Life in the

Twilight of the Spanish Empire

THOMAS A. ABERCROMBIE

The Pennsylvania State University Press

University Park, Pennsylvania

Library of Congress Cataloging-in-Publication Data

Names: Abercrombie, Thomas Alan, 1951– author.
Title: Passing to América : Antonio (née María) Yta's transgressive, transatlantic life in the twilight of the Spanish empire / Thomas A. Abercrombie.
Description: University Park, Pennsylvania : The Pennsylvania State University Press, [2018] | Includes bibliographical references and index.
Summary: "A historical biography of Don Antonio Yta, denounced in 1803 as a woman masquerading as a man. Examines the sex/gender complex within the Spanish Atlantic empire"—Provided by publisher.
Identifiers: LCCN 2018026634 | ISBN 9780271081182 (cloth : alk. paper)
Subjects: LCSH: Yta, Antonio, 1770 or 1771– | Gender-nonconforming People—Bolivia—Biography. | Gender-nonconforming People—Spain—Biography. | Gender nonconformity—Bolivia—History—19th century. | Gender nonconformity—Spain—History—19th century.
Classification: LCC HQ77.8.Y8 A24 2018 | DDC 305.30984—dc23
LC record available at https://lccn.loc.gov/2018026634

TITLE PAGE: Unknown artist, detail from *Perfecto currutaco*, ca. 1795–1800. Museo de Historia de Madrid.

✕

For Don Antonio Yta

and all those who have paid

a high price for confounding

or transgressing

cisgender heteronormativity

CONTENTS

ILLUSTRATIONS

PREFACE AND ACKNOWLEDGMENTS

This book provides a portrait and analysis of the life of Don Antonio, née María Yta, drawing particularly on documents ensuing from judicial procedures instituted against him beginning in 1803 but also on what I have been able to track down of his prior life as María. Appendixes to the book provide a selection of those sources, in English translation and the original Spanish texts, drawn from a number of archives and publications. Readers may find the complete transcriptions of those sources with full translations at the Passing to América (PTA) website: https://wp.nyu.edu/passingtoamerica/.

I am indebted to many persons and institutions for help in researching and writing this book. But I have not been able to consult the person who might have shed the most light on the case: Don Antonio Yta himself. That is because the experiences related here took place between his birth in 1770 or 1771 and the closing of his case file in 1805, over two centuries ago. That temporality corresponds to an era of transitions: from empire to nation-state; from neoscholastic to Enlightenment-era conceptual frames; from an old regime of rigid and extreme distinctions of social estate, marked by equally rigid sartorial codes, to a capitalist fashion system, dressing up the new and more fluid distinctions of class and race, particularly within an urban bourgeoisie, accompanied by the "moral panic" such fluidity produced, a panic exacerbated by imagining the consequences of a fully realized popular sovereignty. The period's in-between, transitional temporality led me to delve into literatures of both Spain and Spanish America for the "early modern" era or "colonial" era (as the period is differently labeled by Hispanists and Latin Americanists) and the "modern" era that was just underway as the case comes to an end.

If I could have interviewed him, however, he may not have been able to satisfactorily answer a twenty-first-century reader's questions, because his frame of reference was not ours. Don Antonio could have had no recourse to the concepts used today to discuss cases like his. Terms such as gender,

gender roles, gender performance, sexual orientation, lesbian, homosexual, transsexual, transgender, and so on, did not yet exist to classify him, and concepts such as *true self* and *identity* were not yet available to diagnose a conflict between a person's inner being and the embodied outward signs by which others categorized them.

I have aimed in this book to take much care with the use of gendered pronouns (and in Spanish, gendered personal nouns), which are particularly problematic for English translations from the Spanish. Interpreting Antonio Yta's confession, given by Yta in the first person but recorded by the scribe in the third person, and others' talk about Antonio and his prior persona, María, is complicated by the rigid rules of both the Spanish and English languages with regard to pronoun usage and the gendering of things and their qualities. A first-person locution in English does not necessarily gender the speaker, while a third-person account in English does so by relentlessly repeating *he* or *she*, *him* or *her*, *his* or *hers*. A first-person account in Spanish can avoid gendering the speaker, though some circumlocution would be required to avoid self-gendering through adverbs, adjectives, and indirect pronouns. The statements "I am married" or "I am single," for example—neither of which in English implies the speaker's sex—require it in Spanish, in which one must choose between *soy casado* (making the speaker male) or *soy casada* (making the speaker female). But with some circumlocution first-person speech in Spanish *can* avoid grammatical gender (for example, *no casé*, "I did not marry"). When first-person court testimony, such as Antonio Yta's confession, is rendered in the third person by the scribe, the scribe, not the speaker, was frequently required to gender the speaker, even though pronouns are often skipped in that language: *[El/Ella] dijo que es casado/casada*. The scribe's choices, then, can profoundly mislead us as to how, or if, Antonio Yta referred to him or herself in a gender-marked way. Rendering the confession directly into English compounds the trouble, since rules of the two languages with regard to pronoun use and grammatical gender conflict. Strangely, it is English, which genders only pronouns, and not Spanish, which includes grammatical gendering (all nouns are gendered, and personal nouns gender the person), that more insistently genders *other persons* in third-person recounting. A direct translation of Don Antonio's third-person confession more than triples the number of gendered pronouns by which Yta is made into a *him* or *her*, requiring a gendered pronoun be added even in extended passages where our scribe has avoided it.

Current rules of thumb for referring pronominally to nonbinary persons are not much help in this case, for two reasons. In the first place it is standard practice today to ask college students what pronoun they prefer for themselves; *he, she,* or a singular use of *they/them* used as a neutral pronoun. But here we are reporting on a life in ways that require frequent, not occasional, use of pronouns, in the course of an extensive relation, in which the singular use of the plural becomes profoundly awkward and often confusing. We cannot ask Antonio Yta what he prefers. And even if we suppose that his insistence on maleness indicates a choice, it is complicated by the length of his account of his life as María, in which actions are in a context where they were taken for those of a *she*. Moreover, changing the scribe's (and the textualized testimony of others) to *he* or *they* when they are *she* in the text erases their choices, which, good or bad, teach us something about how they understood Don Antonio's sex.

Advice from reviewers and readers of this text about how to deal with the problem have been contradictory. My choice is to reproduce gendering in the sources as they were recorded and to translate (using as few pronouns as possible) the gender choices made by the various scribes involved in the case. Sometimes they are inconsistent. The scribe who reports Antonio's confession shifts from feminine to masculine and back in the course of the text, and Antonio's mother does the same in a letter reporting on her "son María's" history of misadventures. I aim to follow them as closely as possible. Both treat Antonio as male when he acts as Antonio and as female when acts performed as María are being reported. And so do I.

My apologies to Antonio Yta if he would have preferred it be otherwise. Exposed by a wife's denunciation and forced to disclose his prior childhood name and therefore assigned sex, he admits he once lived as a she. Clearly he had no wish to be queried or to be, like Caitlyn Jenner, notorious. If Antonio Yta were still alive and could state preferences about his name, sex (or gender), and so on, this book's references to his past as María could constitute a censurable form of involuntary disclosure. I hope that instead it can be taken as a necessary measure in the effort to understand a case of sex/gender transgression before it was nameable in contemporary terms. I use the term *passing* in the title of the book and periodically in analysis, recognizing that present-day norms recommend against using the term to describe the action of transgendered persons, since it suggests a condemnable form of deception when in reality transgendered action is about externalizing an inner reality or true self. *Passing* in this book stands both for the effort of being taken for something (almost invariably something "more") that one previously was not taken for and for the travel so often involved in the effort to leave uncomfortable pasts behind. What is more, Don Antonio was arrested for "imposture of sex" and for the poor character and possible prior crimes that deception implied. Understanding how his deeds were interpreted by others at that time requires us to consider the significance of his kind of *passing*: attending to it also makes it possible to view Don Antonio's particular efforts to be and be taken for a man comparatively, in the light of other kinds of passing then widely engaged in for social-climbing purposes and just as widely commented on and legislated about. Using the term and analyzing its use should be taken not for my support for the value systems of the period but for my efforts to understand them. Finally, it is possible that some of the Ytas of Colmenar de Oreja will find disclosure of this case an offense to their family history. In that case I hope that others among them may instead see support for their own efforts to find a place for themselves in this world.

A book over two decades in the making incurs many debts, suffers many changes, and absorbs many influences. This one began in an archival encounter in 1992 with a document mentioned to me in a seminar by history graduate student Nada Hughes at the University of Miami. It was located by the late Ana Forenza, venerable harvester of stories in the Archivo y Biblioteca Nacionales de Bolivia (ABNB), and transcribed with the help of archivist J. Judith Terán R. and late director Marcela Inch. A version of the transcription was published, with my brief analysis, in that institution's *Anuario* (Abercrombie 2009). The first of my debts, then, is to that beautifully organized and well-run archive, which owes so much to the decades of work by the sorely missed Don Gunnar Mendoza, path-breaking historian and decades-long director and indexer of the archival collections, as well as my first mentor in paleography. Outside of the ABNB, crucial help came from scores of archivists, librarians, and curators of institutions elsewhere in Bolivia and in Buenos Aires, Lima, Rome, Madrid, and Antonio Yta's hometown, Colmenar de Oreja, Spain.

Research on this project was carried out in many brief bursts of work through the support of New York University sabbaticals and the following fellowships and grants, mostly on other topics. Among others, helpful support came from Faculty Summer Research Grants from the Center for Latin American and Caribbean Studies at New York University in 1999 and 2001; an Orovitz Award from the University of Miami in 1992; a MacLamara Award from the University of Miami in 1995; a postdoctoral research grant from the Program for Cultural Cooperation Between Spain's Ministry of Education, Culture, and Sports, and United States Universities in 2003, and a Guggenheim Fellowship in 2005.

Panelists, audiences, and commentators at a number of venues where I have presented bits of the story and analysis offered here have also been instrumental, including, at the seminar of the Latin American and Caribbean Studies Center in SUNY–Stony Brook in 1999; the Latin American Studies seminar in the University of Saint Andrews in 2000; the annual meeting of the Society for Spanish and Portuguese Historical Studies in New York in 2000; a seminar of the Consejo Superior de Investigaciones Científicas (Humanidades), Madrid, in 2000; the invited session Queering Latin American Studies, Latin American Studies Association, Washington, DC, in 2001; an international conference on Crime as Culture, Texts and Contexts, organized by CNRS and the International Association for the Study of Crime and Criminality, held at the European University Institute, La Fiesole, Italy, in 2001; the Coloquio en Historia Cultural, programa doctoral, Departamento de Historia Moderna, Universidad Autónoma de Madrid, in 2002; the symposium Posgéneros y Híbridez en América Latina, at the Congreso Europeo CEISAL de Latinoamericanistas, Bratislava, Slovak Republic, in 2004; the symposium Transgressing Genders and Sexualities: (Re)-Writing and Teaching the History of the Americas, Fifty-Second International Congress of Americanists, Seville, in 2006; the Anthropology and Sociology Colloquium, Graduate Institute, Geneva, in 2017; and the Latin American History Working Group at the University of Notre Dame, in 2017.

During classroom sessions, in office hours or through email, and in meetings over food and drinks in several countries, various versions of the essay and Antonio Yta's confession have been commented on by countless students, colleagues, and friends. Drafts of the essay first published in the *Anuario* were improved from the comments of Rafael Sánchez, Alex Huerta Mercardo, and Georgina Dopico-Black; Susana Rosenbaum provided a first translation of

Yta's confession, while Rachel Lears and Kahlil Chaar-Pérez helped with translation of the entire *expediente*. A first draft of the book gained important corrections and insights from Zeb Tortorici, Nancy van Deusen, Karen Graubart, and Jane Mangan. I owe special thanks to Marta Vicente, who graciously made available to me her 2017 book in draft form and who was particularly helpful in thinking through the eighteenth-century "sex/gender system," to use the term coined by Gayle Rubin (1975). The phrase is helpful when comparing cases where "gender" is understood as a cultural construct independent of bodily sex to those where it is not and, as in Yta's era, what we call "gender" was subsumed within the concept of "sex." Ana María Presta provided help in tracking down the "Buenos Aires letter" and identifying the clothing and other possessions in Yta's list, for which I am grateful. Ignasi Clemente provided important input on the question of gender in the Spanish language. Two anonymous reviewers for Penn State University Press found weaknesses in the argument and in the writing and made many suggestions for improvement that I have tried to carry out. Of course, I have borrowed my ideas not only from people I've met or corresponded with but from the authors, living and dead, of the books and articles cited in the text and listed in the references. I thank all of them, as well. The book could not have been completed without the frequent discussion of key ideas and historiographical issues with Beth Penry, whose generosity and fine editorial sensibilities led to valuable insights in comments on its drafts, along with much-needed encouragement. All of the above, of course, are absolved from blame for my misuses of their ideas and any errors I may have committed.

CAST OF CHARACTERS

[UNNAMED]   Italian *operantas*, mother and daughter, with whom Yta traveled to Rome, according to Buenos Aires source (see chapter 2)

[UNNAMED]   Priest-confessor in Madrid who advised Yta to go to Rome

[UNNAMED]   Woman from Valencia in Los Remedios Street (Madrid, about 1792); "with whom [María's] brother-in-law caught her in the act itself *and in men's clothes*" (mother's testimony)

ALCOZER Y GUERRA, LUIS DE   Scribe in Vilvado's petition

ARIAS DE REYNA, DOÑA VICENTA   Inhabitant of Cádiz, pursues Yta for paternity about 1794, according to Yta's mother

AZAMOR Y RAMÍREZ, DON MANUEL DE   Bishop of Buenos Aires, born 1733 in Villablanca, in the archbishopric of Seville; named bishop of Buenos Aires in 1784 and died October 2, 1796; well-known Enlightenment figure with a vast book collection

BALVERDE, FRANCISCO   Second-class sergeant of garrison in charge of jail

BENEDICTO, RITA   Vecina of Corte (Madrid), pursues Yta for paternity, according to Yta's mother

BOETO, SEÑOR DR. DON ANTONIO   Regente of audiencia; another revolutionary of 1809

CAÑETE Y DOMÍNGUEZ, PEDRO VICENTE   Noted Creole Enlightenment figure (1749–1816), lieutenant adviser and scholar of intendent governor of Potosí Francisco de Paula Sanz and briefly of President García Pizarro of the Audiencia de Charcas; honorary *oidor* of Audiencia de La Plata (suspended from 1804 to 1810); prolific author and noted royalist (Roca 2007, 145; Mendoza 1954; Lorandi 2012)

CARDOZO, FELIZ   Warden of the audiencia jail

DE TAL, FRAY ÁNGEL (FRIAR ANGEL SO-AND-SO)   Franciscan who married Yta and Vilvado y Balverde in 1803; later became *procurador* of the Franciscan convent of Tarija

EUGENIO, DON (NO SURNAME GIVEN)   Yta's brother-in-law, with a post in the Madrid customs house.

GARCÍA PIZARRO, SEÑOR DON RAMÓN Born in Orán, 1729; knight of the Order of Calatrava; lieutenant general of the royal armies; president of the Audiencia de Charcas; captain general and intendant governor of the province of La Plata; intendant governor of Salta and Tucumán, 1790–97; arrested by oidores and junta, 1809 (Roca 2007)

GASCÓN, DR. ESTEBAN AGUSTÍN Don Antonio's court-appointed attorney for the poor; born in Buenos Aires in 1764; doctor of laws (Universidad Mayor Real y Pontificia San Francisco Xavier de Chuquisaca); faculty in the law school of the university and president of the Academia Carolina de Derecho, the audiencia's bar association; siding with the revolutionaries in 1809, became a judge of the Audiencia of Charcas in 1810; signer of the Argentine declaration of independence; died 1824 (Muzzio 1920, 202)

MALAVIA, JOSÉ MANUEL Court-appointed attorney for the poor; represented Don Antonio; joined Gascón in rebellion of 1809

MARIN, VICENTE JOSÉ Scribe, officer of militia; carried out inspection of conditions of jail after complaints by Don Antonio

MARZAS Friend of Yta's father in Valencia; provided money for trip to Rome

MEDINACELI, DUCHESS WIDOW OF María Petronilla Pimentel de Alcántara de Toledo y Cernesio (Seventh Marquesa de Malpica); Doña María's patroness; widowed November 24, 1789, on death of the Twelfth Duque, Pedro de Alcántara Fernández de Córdoba y Moncada ("María Petronila" 2012)

MÉNDEZ DE LA PARRA, DR. DON BERNARDINO Lawyer of the audiencia; doctoral canon of the bishopric; *comisario* of the Holy Inquisition; prosecutor and vicar general of the ecclesiastical curate; judge of the bishopric's appeals court on wills, chaplaincies, and pious works (Araujo [1803] 1908)

MONTERO, MANUEL ESTEBAN Public notary (scribe) of La Plata

MOSCOSO, MIGUEL MARIANO Scribe of His Majesty in the audiencia

ORGÁZ, SILVESTRE Lawyer of Doña Martina Vilvado y Balberde; in 1810 protector of *indios* in the audiencia and represented indigenous revolutionary movement in indigenous republic of San Agustín (Toledo) (Soux 2010)

PAZOS Resident of Buenos Aires, with whom Yta traveled from Jujuy to Potosí

PIMENTEL, JOSÉ Another of Yta's lawyers

PINTOS, JUAN ANTONIO   Cádiz businessman known to Yta's father and also (in Buenos Aires) to Bishop Azamor

PORTILLO, DR. JOSÉF EUGENIO DEL   Attorney who presented, with José Manuel Malavia, petition to audiencia seeking better jail conditions for Yta (appendix A.14); born 1760 in Salta, died 1843 in Buenos Aires; doctor of law from University of Charcas; noted writer for newspapers and independence activist; signer of Argentine constitution (Vivas 1997)

RAMOS ARAGONES, FRAY PEDRO   Franciscan; pertained to the tribunal of the penitenciaría apostólica; provided confessions and advice to speakers of Spanish who sought papal dispensations

RODRÍGUEZ ROMANO, DR. DON VICENTE   Lieutenant legal adviser to the president of the Audiencia of Charcas in 1803 (Araujo [1803] 1908, 383); in 1816 prosecutor of the Audiencia of Quito and soon after of the Audiencia of Santa Fe

SÁENZ DE JUANO, DON DIEGO   Official surgeon of the city; oversaw sixty-five-bed hospital of San Juan de Dios in 1803 (Araujo [1803] 1908, 432); elected in 1814 as representative of the Partido de Pacajes to the Cortes de Cádiz (Irurozqui 2002, 246)

SALAS, DR. DON JOSÉF GREGORIO   The city's titular physician; alcalde of the city in 1823, when he served as godfather of the son of Dr. Mariano Taborga and Ana Pizarro Zabindua, daughter of President Don Ramón García de León Pizarro (Castejón n.d.)

SÁNCHEZ, EUGENIO   Testified in place of nuns of convent of Agustinas, Colmenar de Oreja, 1803

SAN GERÓNIMO, FRAY JULIÁN DE   Discalced Carmelite of Madrid, Yta's cousin, known by bishop of Buenos Aires

SAN MIGUEL, SOR JOSEFA DE   Abbess of the convent of Santa Juana de la Cruz of Illescas in 1803

SANTÍSIMO SACRAMENTO Y ENCINA, SOR DOÑA ANA   Abbess of convent of Misericordia de la Orden de Santa Clara, outside the walls of Huete, 1803

SANZ Y ESPINOSA DE LOS MONTEROS MARTÍNEZ Y SOLER, DON FRANCISCO DE PAULA   Born 1745 in Málaga, died 1810 in Potosí; royalist Enlightenment figure and prolific polemicist; appointed intendent governor of Buenos Aires (1783–88); known for paving and lighting of public streets, improvement of drinking water, provisioning of the city, and so forth; intendent governor of Potosí (1789–1810); worked closely with Cañete in the reformation of mining operations; led royalist troops against independence militias, beginning 1809; executed in the plaza of Potosí in 1810 (Uriburu 1934, 646)

SU SANTIDAD, THE POPE   In 1771, Pius VI

TABORGA CONTRERAS, DR. MARIANO — Acted as legal adviser, taking Vilvado y Balverde's accusation against Yta; oversaw medical examination; took Yta's confession prior to being sworn-in to this post; later recused himself for this reason

USSOZ Y MOSI, DON JOSÉ AGUSTÍN DE — Oidor of Audiencia de la Plata; presided over the Academia Carolina, an association of law graduates of the university; joined revolutionary cause in 1809 in overthrow of President Pizarro

VALDA, JOSÉF CALIXTO DE — Prolix scribe in city of La Plata

VÁZQUEZ VALLESTEROS, DON JOSÉ — Oidor of Audiencia de la Plata (paperwork related to escape); another conspirator against García Pizarro in 1809.

VICENTE DE CONTRERAS, DOÑA JOAQUINA — Abbess, in 1803, of the Royal Monastery of San Vicente of nuns of the Order of San Bernardo, located outside the walls of Segovia

VILLAVA, VICTORIÁN DE — Protector of Indians (providing legal counsel to them); died before Yta arrest; author of project for reorganization of the Spanish Empire; influential among Creole revolutionaries (Villava [1797] 1822; Portillo Valdés 2007, 2009)

VILVADO Y BALVERDE, DOÑA MARTINA — Antonio Yta's young wife, native of Spain and vecina of Cochabamba; either a member of a wealthy family into which Don Antonio married or an impoverished soul rescued by Don Antonio's labors; either a naive and virginal victim of Don Antonio's deceits, meriting annulment, or a willful but back-stabbing participant in a long-term sexual relationship

YBÁÑEZ, DOÑA FELIPA (OR PHELIPA) DE — Antonio Yta's mother; after marriage to Joséf, *vecina* first of the Villa de Colmenar de Oreja and later of the corte in Madrid

YGLESIA, DON JOSÉ DE LA — Oidor of Audiencia de la Plata involved in Yta's case

YTA, DON JOSÉF (OR JOSEPH) — Yta's father, native and vecino of the Villa de Colmenar de Oreja; born into a commoner family of fruit and vegetable growers and sellers; marriage to Felipa Ybáñez seems to have prompted his eventual rise into wealth and status, finally as vecino of the Corte de Madrid

YTA, LEOCADIA — Antonio/María Yta's sister

ZAMORA Y TRIVIÑO, TENIENTE CORONEL DON MIGUEL DE — Lord governor of the province of Moxos (1792–1803) under whom Yta served as administrator of town of La Magdalena; named governor of Moxos in 1792, arrived there in 1801, accompanied by his wife the Countess of Argelejo Doña María Josefa Fontao y Losada; expelled a year later by rebel cacique (Roca 2007, 261–62)

YTA'S BIOCHRONOLOGY

[Bracketed dates are approximate; unbracketed dates are documented.]

SEPTEMBER 26, 1762 Yta's parents, Joséf Yta and Doña Felipa Ybáñez, marry, in church of Santa María la Mayor of Villa de Colmenar de Oreja (Yta's parents' marriage certificate)

[1770] María Leocadia Yta is born in Madrid (entered the Augustinian convent of Colmenar at age fourteen and declared self to be thirty-two years old in 1803)

1776 Publication in Lima of *Lazarillo de ciegos caminantes*, guide to highway between Buenos Aires and Potosí

[1779–83] From the age of nine until the age of fourteen (Yta's testimony) or seventeen (mother's testimony), Yta stayed "with powerful woman in town of his birth" (mother's testimony); with Duchess of Medinaceli (Yta's testimony)

JULY 27, 1783 At age fourteen Yta entered Convento de la Encarnación del Divino Verbo, Agustinas Recoletas, in Villa de Colmenar de Oreja (convent certification; Yta's testimony)

SEPTEMBER 22, 1783 Thrown out of Agustinas in Colmenar (convent certification; Yta's confession)

[1783–86] Yta stays with Duchess of Medinaceli, from age fourteen or seventeen (mother's testimony; Yta's confession)

1788 Baron von Nordenflycht's expedition departs Cádiz for Buenos Aires, Potosí (Helmer 1993)

1789 Duchess of Medinaceli is widowed; French revolution

[1789] Under protection of the Lady Duchess Widow of Medinaceli, placed in convent of female Franciscans, Santa Juana de la Cruz, in Cubas de la Sagra, near Illescas, for eleven months (Yta's confession; mother's chronology; convent certification estimates 1790)

[1789–90] Stayed about a year with parents after leaving Santa Juana in Illescas; Yta's confession states she next went to the convent of the Bernardas outside of Segovia, thrown out for the same reasons as from the convent of Santa Juana, but convent certifications say it was Huete next

OCTOBER 28, 1790 María Yta's parents took her to convent of Franciscas de Guet (Convento de la Misericordia de la Orden de Santa Clara, outside the city walls of Huete), staying there for about six months; thrown out (convent certification)

FEBRUARY 24, 1791 Taken from convent by parents to her sister's house, in secular clothing, for reasons unrelated to the case, according to abbess (convent certification)

NOVEMBER 21, 1791 Took habit in convent of Bernardas of Segovia (Monasterio de San Vicente el Real, outside the walls of Segovia; founded by Cister in 1156) (convent certification)

1792 *Guía de forasteros* published in Buenos Aires

JANUARY 27, 1792 Expelled from Bernardas by order of *provisor* of convent, for having taken the habit in other convents (convent certification)

[FEBRUARY–APRIL 1792] Stays with sister for a few months; works as seamstress for Rita Benedicto, who then sues for patrimony and marriage; also involved with another woman "in the street of Los Remedios" (mother's testimony); her confessor suggests she go to Rome; leaves a letter for her parents with her sister (Yta's confession)

[APRIL 1792] Leaves Madrid for Rome at about age twenty (Yta says twelve years ago in the confession)

[1792] Yta travels first to Valencia by carriage (Yta's confession); with help from friend of her father named Marzas, travels by land to Barcelona, staying there fewer than fifteen days (Yta's confession)

[MAY 1792] Goes to Genoa on a mail ship without passport or license, in company of two operantas; after twenty or twenty five days at sea . . . (Yta's confession)

[MAY–JUNE 1792] . . . arrives in Genoa, staying there about two months (Yta's confession)

[1792] With same operantas set sail for Civitavecchia and from there [by land] to Rome, always until then dressed as a woman (Yta's confession)

[JULY 1792– JANUARY 1793] Stays in Rome seven months to get pope's blessing to live as a man, from Fray Pedro Ramos Aragones; changes to men's clothing (Yta's confession)

[FEBRUARY–JUNE 1793] Returns to Civitavecchia (port of Rome) and by ship to Genoa, Barcelona (arrives late 1793), Cádiz (mother's testimony), and Málaga (Yta's confession)

[JULY 1793–FEBRUARY 13, 1794] Writes to parents from Barcelona, telling them of change to men's clothing "by order of His Holiness" (Yta's confession); detained in seclusion by bishop of Barcelona, Don Gabino Valladares Mejía, for some months, until bishop's death (mother's testimony) on February 13, 1794

[FEBRUARY–MAY 1794] Stopped in Cádiz for four months, then fled to Málaga to avoid paternity suit and marriage demand from a pregnant Doña Vicenta Arias de Reyna (mother's testimony)

[JUNE–JULY 1794] Sailed from Málaga to Montevideo (a journey of about two months) at age twenty-three (Yta's confession)

[AUGUST 1794] Took a launch to Buenos Aires (Yta's confession)

[AUGUST 1794–OCTOBER 1796] Stays in house of Bishop Azamor for three years as his page until bishop's death of October 2, 1796 (Yta's confession; bishop's biography)

OCTOBER 2, 1796 Departs for Potosí after bishop's death; four months later, because of broken leg, reaches Jujuy; then to Potosí, traveling with *porteño* named Pazos, arriving there six years ago [about March, 1797] (bishop's biography; Yta's confession)

[MARCH 1797] Presents recommendations from Buenos Aires to lord governor of Potosí (Francisco de Paula Sanz); stays in Sanz's house for two years (until 1799 marriage) (Yta's confession)

MARCH 30, 1799 Marries Doña Martina; stays another two years in Potosí (marriage certificate; Yta's confession)

[1801] Appointed administrator of La Magdalena; stays one year in the capital carrying out orders of Governor Zamora (Yta's confession; Zamora's biography dates)

[1802] Stays one year in La Magdalena as its administrator (Yta's confession) (Note: Governor Zamora and all administrators expelled from Moxos in 1802 by cacique Maraza)

1802–3 Yta and wife, Martina, in Cochabamba house after expulsion from Moxos (clothing lawsuit)

AUGUST–SEPTEMBER 1803 Don Antonio Yta in La Plata to solicit salary (Yta's confession; Buenos Aires letter)

OCTOBER 4, 1803 Arrival in La Plata of Doña Martina Vilvado y Balverde; petition for annulment presented to ecclesiastical prosecutor (Buenos Aires letter; A.9, forwarded to audiencia on October 13); jurisdiction over case ruled civil by ecclesiastical judge (A.9); asks audiencia to carry out medical inspection (A.10)

OCTOBER 7, 1803 *Denuncia* by Doña Martina Vilvado y Balverde to civil judges in audiencia (A.1); arrest (A.2); medical inspection (A.5); confession (A.7)

OCTOBER 10, 1803 Ecclesiastical prosecutor notified and asked whether or not annulment proceedings are underway (A.8)

OCTOBER 11, 1803 Writ quoted to Doña María Leocadia Yta in person (A.8)

OCTOBER 13, 1803 Mandated testimony delivered to the secretary; petition of Doña Martina Vilvado y Balverde (presented October 4) to ecclesiastical prosecutor, asking him to require Yta to consummate marriage or submit to medical evaluation of fitness, received by audiencia (A.9)

OCTOBER 17, 1803 Bernardino Méndez de la Parra (ecclesiastical prosecutor) responds to *audiencia*, says they have begun a hearing but want audiencia to establish that Yta is a hermaphrodite (A.10)

OCTOBER 18, 1803 Audiencia stalls to avoid repetition of the proceedings (medical examination) (A.10)

OCTOBER 19, 1803 José Manuel Malavia, criminal attorney to the poor, and Dr. Esteban Agustín Gascón, on behalf of Yta, complain that no crime has been alleged and that prison is too harsh for this unhappy man (A.11); Rodríguez Romano asks for prisoner to be moved to better cell; warden of royal jail replies that there is no other secure cell in which to hold her; García Pizarro orders warden to open windows and doors during certain hours; second sergeant of garrison, Francisco Balverde, given order (A.12)

OCTOBER 26, 1803 Letter from ecclesiastical prosecutor Parra, responding to official letter of twenty-first "of this month," notifying García Pizarro that civil testimony is being added to ecclesiastic file (A.13)

NOVEMBER 5, 1803 Yta's request for return of itemized clothing; transmitted to Doña Martina Vilvado by Rodríguez Romano (B.8, clothing lawsuit)

DECEMBER 7, 1803 Doña Martina's reply to request (B.8, clothing lawsuit)

JULY 9, 1804 Doña Martina required to account for clothing before audiencia (B.8, clothing lawsuit)

JULY 11, 1804 Doña Martina provides account of Yta's clothing (B.8, clothing lawsuit)

JULY 20, 1804 Defense attorney Jose Manuel Malavia (with Dr. Joséf Eugenio del Portillo) to president, plea for clemency for Yta's pitiful situation (A.14)

AUGUST 1, 1804 Second lieutenant of militia grenadiers Vicente José Marin (also scribe of intendency) reports unsuccessful escape attempt by Doña María Leocadia Yta (A.15)

AUGUST 3, 1804   Recusation of Taborga from case, since he took initial denunciation from Doña Martina Vilvado y Balverde before he was formally appointed as acting general legal adviser (A.16)

AUGUST 4, 1804   Case record passed to Dr. Don Francisco de Paula Moscoso (A.16)

AUGUST 22, 1804   Effort by Cañete to get Martina Vilvado y Balverde to complete complaint properly (A.17); José Pimentel, lawyer for Don Antonio Yta, begs for mercy; Cañete, the honorary audiencia judge and interim legal adviser of García Pizarro, notifies warden (A.18)

AUGUST 27, 1804   Don Feliz Cardozo, warden of jail, reports putting shackles on legs of Don Antonio Yta and Yta's subsequent illness; Cañete orders (male) prisoner to be examined by physician (A.18)

AUGUST 30, 1804   Titular physician, Don José Gregorio de Salas examines *el reo*, "the male prisoner," reports edema (A.18)

SEPTEMBER 6, 1804   Cañete orders warden to let doctor dictate conditions of treatment and to provide medicines from the apothecary of the Hospital of San Juan de Dios; Salas, Pimentel, and Don Pedro Ynsa notified (A.18)

SEPTEMBER 21, 1804   Yta's escape with *indio pongo* 9:30 or 10:00 p.m.; Warden Cardozo reports escape of Don Antonio Yta on following Monday (A.19)

OCTOBER 3, 1804   Prosecutor Lopez seeks ruling from president, regent, and judges (A.19)

OCTOBER 5, 1804   President, regent, and judges ordered into chambers by Don Agustín Muñoz (A.19)

OCTOBER 16, 18, 1804   Tribunal appointed—Don Antonio Boeto (regent); Don José de la Yglesia, Don José Agustín de Ussoz y Mosi, and Don José Vázquez Vallesteros (judges); signed by Don Agustín Muñoz (A.19)

OCTOBER 30, 31, 1804   Cañete tries to reacquire original case file, in power of Doña Martina's attorney; Cañete orders Martina Vilvado to formalize proceedings immediately (A.20)

NOVEMBER 28, 1804   Yta's lawyer, Gascón, delivers testimony from Yta's mother (A.21) and certifications from convents (A.22) sent from Madrid and recently received by him (and dated between July 29 and August, 7 1804); Dr. Don Esteban Agustín Gascón, Yta's lawyer, notifies audiencia of receipt of documents from Yta's mother and convents, proving no crime committed (A.24); Cañete orders the new documents added to the file, to be produced for first hearing (A.25)

DECEMBER 18, 1804 Scribe reports that original case documents have been in possession of Silvestre Orgáz, Doña Martina Vilvado y Balverde's attorney, since August 31 (A.25)

DECEMBER 19, 1804 Cañete orders their urgent return (A.25)

JANUARY 8, 1805 Cañete asks the lieutenant constable to report on whether Don Antonio Yta has returned to the jail or been found (A.26)

JANUARY 24, 1805 Warden reports that Yta has not returned or been found (A.26)

FEBRUARY 13, 1805 Prosecutor asks for original documents to be sent to ecclesiastical prosecutor, keeping a copy for the audiencia (A.27)

MARCH 14, 1805 Partial copy sent to curia (A.27)

MAY 4, 5, 1805 Ecclesiastical prosecutor requests originals of entire expediente (A.27)

MAY 7, 1805 Letter from Bernardino de la Parra, asking for original document (A.23)

JUNE 10, 1805 Certification that this transcript coincides with original document; order that testimony of said documents be delivered to ecclesiastical prosecutor Parra (A.23)

1808 Napoleon invades Spain, places his brother on Spanish throne (Phillips and Phillips 2010)

1809 President of audiencia, Don Ramón García Pizarro, arrested by audiencia judges and revolutionary junta (Roca 2007)

1810 Gascón, Yta's lawyer, becomes judge of the revolutionary audiencia (Muzzio 1920, 202); Francisco de Paula Sanz executed by firing squad in the plaza of Potosí (Uriburu 1934, 646)

1813 Gascón becomes governor of Salta within revolutionary Río de La Plata (Muzzio 1920, 202)

1814 Sáenz de Juano, the titular surgeon of the city, is elected as representative of the Partido de Pacajes to the Cortes de Cádiz (Irurozqui 2002, 246)

1816 Gascón, a member of the constitutional convention of Argentina, signed the declaration of Argentine independence (Muzzio 1920, 202)

1823 Dr. Don Joséf Gregorio Salas, titular physician who examined Yta, is serving as alcalde of La Plata (Castejón, n.d.)

1824 Gascón dies in battle of the Cerro de Gavilán (Muzzio 1920, 202)

INTRODUCTION

Exposure

Report of a Scandal

"I report to your mercy the strangest case to have happened since the beginning of the world, and it is that two women married each other four years and some months ago, which I will relate in detail for your amazement and diversion, and it is as follows" (Beruti 1946, fol. 188). Thus began a letter written by Dr. Mariano Taborga Contreras to a high-placed friend in the viceregal capital of Buenos Aires, reporting breathlessly on the revelations in his courtroom just a week before on October 7, 1803 (full text at the Passing to América [PTA] website, https://wp.nyu.edu/passingtoamerica/).[1] This was quite possibly his first case as legal adviser (a job he did not yet formally hold, though he acted as though he did) to the president of the Audiencia de Charcas, a regional appeals court of the Spanish Crown, located in La Plata, the capital city in the Andean highlands of Spain's South American realms.[2] Since the case was ongoing, sending the letter was an indiscretion.[3] But what lawyer could have resisted the temptation to repeat its details to a confidant? Let us continue with the details of Taborga's letter, written from the nearby mining center, the Villa de Potosí.

October 15, 1803:

On the seventh of the current month a woman presented herself to me who had just arrived in company of the mails from Cochabamba, named Doña Martina Vilvado y Balverde, presenting me with a petition against her husband, Don Antonio

Yta, explaining that he is native of the kingdoms of Spain and that she has been married to him for over four years and that they were married in this villa [Potosí] with license from V. [Don Francisco de Paula Sanz?] for being from Spain [*ultramarino*] and because he had not carried out the duties of matrimony, protesting [that he had made] a vow of chastity and other silliness, and having observed that he always urinated in a basin, always wore underpants, menstruated, and other observations, such as swollen breasts, etc., were revealed.

And for constantly disguising herself as a man and everything else, I had the accused searched for. Placed into my presence I observed a smallish and chubby man, around forty years old, and, taking his confession, I discovered that he was named Doña María Leocadia de Yta, native of Colmenar de Oreja, seven leagues from Madrid, who had come without license to this kingdom, having embarked in Málaga.[4] She had been in a convent of nuns at age fourteen, and because she fell in love with the other nuns, they threw her out of there; she went to confess, and the priest told her that it would be best to go to Rome. /188v/ She left a note for her parents and, wearing her natural clothing, made the following voyages: from Madrid to Valencia, from there to Barcelona; in that port she embarked on a mail ship for Genoa, in the company of some Italian actors from that city. She continued her voyage with them as far as Civitavecchia and, continuing with the Italians, by land to Rome, where she confessed, and the penitentiary, who was a Spanish Franciscan friar, told her to return on the third day. Doing so, she received absolution, and for penitence [she had] to climb the Jerusalem steps thirty times, to whip herself every Friday during one year, to avoid hearing mass in nuns' convents, and to put on men's clothing. Replying to the priest, the penitent asked how she could return to her home wearing such clothing. [He replied] that it was necessary to do what the Holy Father commanded but without returning to her home country. For that reason she dressed as a man and remained in Rome awhile. She returned to Civitavecchia, Genoa, and embarked there for Barcelona, and hence for Málaga, and in that port for Montevideo. She was in Buenos Aires for two or three years in the house of Lord Azamor, bishop of that city until his death, and then she determined to come to Peru. This side of Lujan she had the misfortune of breaking a leg and was detained for four months. Finally, she reached Potosí, where for some time she stayed in the house of the lord Sanz. There she dallied with love [*trato de amores*] and was living/sleeping/involved with [*amancebado con*] the above-mentioned Doña Martina Vilvado. Later they married. Afterward, she lived with her in comfort that was facilitated to them in Mojos, to which they both went, and, having returned, Vilvado was in her hometown of Cochabamba; and three or four months ago, Doña María Leocadia came here to litigate the salary owed to [Don Antonio] for serving as administrator. In all this time, both attested to the good treatment that he gave her [Martina], in which insofar as possible she lacked nothing for her decency, but she was irritated with his frequent jealousy over her. In my presence the said María Leocadia was examined, because she had said before the scribe and titular physician and surgeon that she had a man's parts. But it is all falsehood, and she is a woman like all the others, and if she shows herself to be very bold, she shows no other signs of being male. What is certain is that the whole story of her declaration is a web of lies. She is a woman of many secrets [or back rooms, or closets],[5] sick in the head, who hates her [woman's] clothing, because she is given over to a rascal's life. I have her alone in a cell. We'll see how it turns out. To be continued.[6] (Beruti 1946, fol. 188r–v; my translation)

Considering Don Antonio, in His Time and Place

What a scandal! Don Antonio Yta was truly a self-made man or, rather, a woman living *disguised* as a man, and with an astounding backstory. Perhaps it was a web of lies, made even more scandalous by his very success at passing as a man, deceiving powerful men for a decade and a wife for more than four years of marriage. One week into the case and Taborga had already reached that firm conclusion, having seen with his own eyes what looked like a female body and having heard Don Antonio confess to having been raised as Doña María Leocadia Yta (henceforward, Doña María). Don Antonio had insisted that he had a functional male member *in the act*, but Taborga's eyes told him that it was nothing but a lie. What *was* true, Taborga concluded, was that he was faced with a woman who loved women but hated being one and who preferred the adventurous life of a rascal—a social climber using devious means to obtain better fortune, in this case, a wife and a man's career.

Other jurists involved in the case were less certain than Taborga. Some took Don Antonio at his word and decided that he was a hermaphrodite. Even the physicians called in for the examination left a bit of uncertainty in their report, allowing that though what Don Antonio said was a penis was in fact an ordinary clitoris, they had not seen it in the state of arousal mentioned by Don Antonio. His legal standing as the man and husband and his continued self-presentation as a man in the weeks and months locked in jail as the case slowly progressed led some (his attorneys, some judges, and his jailors) to continue to refer to *him*, Don Antonio, while others stuck with *her*, Doña María, and a few vacillated in attributing name and sex to the prisoner.

What was going on here? What kind of person was this Don Antonio? Was he really a she, as Taborga concluded? Or was his sex ambiguous, with both male and female characteristics? Given that he was apparently raised as a girl and lived as a woman for more than twenty years before becoming a man, how was "she" able to learn how to adequately inhabit a man's clothing and social roles and at the same time conceal and keep secret the female (or ambiguous, "hermaphrodite," or intersexed) body beneath that clothing? What kinds of labors were required of Don Antonio to sustain his "imposture of sex," as his accusers called his practices? What motivated this change of sex? Was marrying Doña Martina a cover to be able to live as a man? Was it a "cover" to be able to love women and to marry one without being censured (as had happened when Don Antonio was still Doña María)? Or was it some combination of these things? How could his wife have taken more than four years to figure out that her husband was a woman in disguise? Finally, what explains the legal system's apparent inability to definitively determine his sex, to classify his sexual practices, or to name his crime?

This book aims to reveal Don Antonio's story in all its complexity, placing it fully into its historical and cultural context. Such a project is possible in this case (unlike many others sharing some of its aspects) because Don Antonio told at some length his own life story, later joined by a biographical sketch sent by his mother seeking to help him get out of trouble. To begin to understand Don Antonio, and not only to grasp what others thought of him but how he understood himself, we must read these sources very closely. For that reason the essential texts are provided in appendixes to this book.[7]

It has been said that the past is a foreign country (Lowenthal 1999). That is why serious effort is required to understand what kind of girl and young woman Doña María had been and what kind of man Don Antonio became. It takes effort, as well, to understand Doña Martina, the vexed wife, and the rest of the figures in the case. To unpack what was happening in that courtroom in La Plata, we must dig into the "taken for granted" of life in that time and place. It might seem that the central question here is rather straightforward: was he a man or a woman? But for his contemporaries, it turns out that (apart from Taborga), looking at his genitals was not enough to fully clarify even Don Antonio's sex. Can we do better?

As we shall see, determining another's sex is not in the least bit straightforward. Every scientific advance today seems only to complicate the matter, though some, then as now, prefer a cut-and-dried, no-complications world, where only binaries can exist, each granted "natural" forms of expression. Taborga was one of those. For him, Don Antonio was a masquerade, a deception carried out by the woman Doña María. Even if that were the case (and not everyone involved was as certain as Taborga), understanding how Doña María pulled off such a deception requires us to know about much more than just his or her genitals. For then, as now, there was not just one way to be a man or a woman. Doña María, and then Don Antonio, had to become expert in performing very specific kinds of woman and man, bound by cultural patterns quite different than our own. To understand Don Antonio requires us to know them too. Moreover, we must answer the question of how Doña María learned how, during her first twenty-one years as specific kinds of girl and woman, to convincingly be a specific kind of man, a transformation pulled off in a very short space of time.

The task is not easy, because the moment that Don Antonio's life was committed to paper occurred more than two centuries ago, in another time and another place. Doña María's adventures traversed Spain and major cities of the Mediterranean, while Don Antonio's passages swept him across the Atlantic into América. That is what Spaniards and their Creole descendants in the "Indies" or the "New World" called the American possessions of the Spanish Empire by the mid-eighteenth century, those earlier terms having fallen into disuse. The vast Spanish Empire, which had reached its apogee as a world power two centuries before, was now in decline, while the upstart British Empire had just lost its thirteen colonies on a small stretch of northeastern North America, in the nascent United States of America. No such thing as América Latina, "Latin America," yet existed in the minds of the inhabitants of Spain's América, and they bristled at the theft of their continent's name by the fledgling Anglo-American state. "América" serves to inflect the continent's name with the point of view of its Spanish-speaking majority.

Don Antonio's era was one of transition. It was the height of the Enlightenment and a revolutionary moment in Spain and its colonies. The people of his social milieu were keenly aware of living in a time of change. The

Spanish Crown was busy imposing reason on governmental administration, fiscal policies, public-health efforts, commerce, and industry, while aiming to tamp down the power of the church, in a series of measures called the "Bourbon reforms" (Stein and Stein 2003). A growing awareness of "natural rights" led the masses to push from below for their legal defense, as women, for example, sought divorces and retention of dowries and their share of wealth acquired during marriage (Premo 2017). Even the indigenous people of Spain's América rallied to courtrooms to defend rights infringed by reforms, drawing on an old Spanish concept of popular sovereignty to do so (Penry 2000, forthcoming). At the top of the social hierarchy, newspaper-reading elites, calling themselves "moderns," participated in the advancement of the sciences, and, through the rapid turnover of published ideas and fashions in clothing, enjoyed the fruits of this globalizing era, in which, according to pundits of the emerging newspaper and coffeehouse culture, the light of secular reason shone down to illuminate all the (colonized and globalized) world (see appendix B.6).

This was the era of the invention of "Nature" as something separate from society and morality, with logics accessible to the objective application of reason. It was a time of a ramifying obsession with classification, naming, and explanation of natural phenomena, including those of humankind and of the human body, with a host of newly objectivist anatomical works leading the way in the world of Spanish medicine (Cañizares-Esguerra 2006). A series of Crown-sponsored scientific expeditions over the last half of the eighteenth century gathered geographic, geological, and social information, aimed to improve mining engineering, and expanded the reach of innovative public-health measures.[8] It was also the era of the invention of sex, understood to be a matter of functionally reproductive organs. The groundwork was being laid in these decades for understanding nonreproductive sex (same-sex relations, masturbation, bestiality [Tortorici 2016b]) as violations not only of God's law but of natural law and hence reprehensible not (or not only) as sin but as impediments to the rational advance of the greater social good (Vicente 2017).[9]

While that rational advance raised new hopes (or fears) of equality before the law, it also promulgated celebration of the (male) individual and his rights to private property. A profound assault on collectivities defined by holding property in common was underway, forwarding the construction of the possessive individual (MacPherson 2011). Results of such reforms— pervasive forms of disempowerment and discrimination—excluded from

Enlightenment's benefits those who were then classified as being of insufficient reason (common laborers in Spain; Indians and blacks in Spanish America; and women in both places), who were then granted lesser rights.

Don Antonio's story unfolds in a judicial process involving mostly male colonial elites. Jurists indulge elites' sustained glorification of intellectual work, aristocratic manners, and peacock-like fashions, which made patent their "leisured" status, as rentier beneficiaries of the labor and tribute payments of commoners ("Indians" in Spanish America). Spanish and American-born Creole Spanish elites were deeply preoccupied with building privileged lineage through advantageous marriages, the consolidation of heritable, income-producing property as the transgenerational material bodies of the partly immaterial being called lineage (Abercrombie 1998, drawing on Reher 1996 and MacPherson 1999), and guaranteeing the legitimacy of their children's births, in part through the "cloistered" virtue of their wives and daughters. In Spain's América, this was in contrast to the collective property and personhood allotted to the laboring and tribute-paying people called Indians (Herzog 2013).

In Spain this was also the age of the bourgeoisie, the "middling" upper end of the former Spanish commoner social estate who now, less convinced that they should accept a lesser life because it was "God's plan" for them, surged forward in social-climbing mimicry of the more securely noble aristocrats, aiming to get their share. Don Antonio Yta was one such social climber. His strategies worked for a time, and in America his peninsular birth and his "Don" gave him advantages over an ordinary American-born Creole Spaniard. But this was a revolutionary era. Here the revolution would be led by the Creoles, bristling at the exclusions from power to which the Crown had subjected them and worried about the social-climbing urbanized Indians, blacks, and mixed *castas* who nipped at their heels. Just seven years after his arrest, neither of the qualities that elevated Don Antonio, his Spanishness and his aristocratic Don, would be worth much anymore in La Plata.[10]

Gender, Race, Class, Identity, or LGBTQIA?

To be true to Don Antonio and his contemporaries, this book aims to carry out analysis insofar as possible in the terms they used and to distinguish the kinds of social action they recognized (including dress and speech, acts of service and patronage, and the privileges and obligations by which social action was "read"). Apart from this introduction and chapter 6, "Truth," I avoid the analytic trilogy of gender, class, and race to bring him into focus as somehow "like us." Likewise, I do not classify Doña María or Don Antonio with the terms represented in the acronym LGBTQIA. Finally, I avoid the grounding concept of identity, by which all these terms today constitute the labels of identity politics. That is not because I am in any way opposed to such politics but because these categories were not yet possible to think in Doña María's and Don Antonio's day, much less become the banner term of a movement for collective liberation.[11]

Gender, race, and class are useful analytic and, now, "common sense" terms that name certain registers of differentiation in our day. Indeed, the well-institutionalized (if still contested) categories of gender, gender identity, and sexual orientation would seem useful to categorize and understand Doña María and Don Antonio. Thinking through the "sex/gender system" (Rubin 1975); separating gender, as a performative social construct, from "biological" sex (e.g., Reiter 1975, Kessler and McKenna 1978, Butler 1990, Ortner 1996); and recognizing the force of cultural expectations of sex/gender dimorphism and heteronormativity, the expectation of cross-sex desire and orientation; and the condemnation of same-sex practices (Warner 1991, drawing on Rich 1980) identify for us obstacles in Doña María's path to satisfy her "proclivity" for women. But they do not conform to concepts in use in 1800. To use our terms in reference to the past not only is anachronistic but blurs our understanding of the terms and concepts by which Doña María and Don Antonio understood their own actions and how others in their world understood them. So some of the work required to understand them in their own terms is to avoid falling back on our own analytic categories.

"Sex" then had not yet been fully medicalized, though that process was underway.[12] It was more than the sum of a body's parts and indeed included everything that we now distinguish from biology as a cultural construct. *Gender* as an analytic category is a creation of 1960s and 1970s feminists, who distinguished it from sex to aid in revealing the "constructedness" and therefore changeability of limitations placed on women, which were defended by those who regarded constraints on women as a product of a "naturally given" order, that is, as consequences of their sex. This book draws heavily on insights deriving from the distinction between sex and gender and from the work of gay, lesbian, queer, transgender, and intersex activists and theoreticians since then.[13] But it does not apply such terms of analysis in reconstructing the social world of Don Antonio. In 1803 sex still *included* what we now call gender, though it was expressed and "read" by others mostly through clothed performances of the "proper" ways of being certain *kinds* of girl or woman, boy or man, as these were then distinguished from one another. For now we might use Gayle Rubin's (1975) term "sex/gender system" to compare Don Antonio's world with ours.

Since gender, as a socially constructed identity or social role distinct from bodily sex, was not fully conceptualized until the 1970s, transgender, a concept of the 1990s, was even less imaginable in 1803.[14] As David Valentine argues, in a book that reveals the limitations and potential exclusions from projects of identity-based rights focusing on transgender: "to imagine historical subjects as 'gay,' 'lesbian,' or as 'transgender' ignores the radically different understandings of self and the contexts that underpinned the practices and lives of historical subjects" (2007, 30).

As with the present day, sex/gender (or in 1803, just sex) was also fully *intersectional* (Crenshaw 1989, 1991; see also Sedgwick 1990, 32). And so must be our analysis. Sexed persons, that is, were always also marked as distinct from others of their own sex along a variety of axes of distinction, none of which fully correspond to our own. Let us see what axes of distinction were available in 1803.

Socioeconomic class is a product of the breakdown of an older and differently structured order, that of social estate, which then still differentiated those accorded aristocratic birth and (by virtue of owning heritable property and verifiably legitimately engendered children) lineage—for example, people who merited the honorific Don or Doña—from those who were not accorded such social estate and who were labeled as undeserving commoners. Although early modern Spaniards recognized three social estates—commoners, clergy, and aristocrats—the first was differentiated from the last two along the most significant fracture, distinguishing those who engaged in manual labor and owed tributes to the king or nobles and those "with honor" who did not and who therefore lived from rents rather than wages or sweat. Rents were obtained by possessing heritable rent-producing property and heritable rights to the labor and tributes of commoners. Of course, since honor was guaranteed only by ensuring the virtue of wives and daughters by keeping them *recogidas* (enclosed), thereby securing the legitimacy of lineage, distinctions of social estate also rested on those of sex. A new individualism was creeping onto the scene in 1800, and a restless urban bourgeoisie sought the rights and recognition of aristocrats, but individual striving (or its lack) was not yet held to have replaced the hand of God-given providence as a source or defense of privileged or unprivileged station.[15]

Similarly, "race" had not yet taken its current form as a powerful cultural construct based on the supposition of inherited biological differences among populations classed by color linked to purported place of origin. The term *raza* was in use, but it still retained sixteenth-century denotation as a "flaw," as in a bad thread in a bolt of cloth, and connoted an assortment of kinds of disqualifying flaws for aristocratic social estate. It is true that persons with such flaws were conceptualized as not having "clean blood," which meant being a descendant within four generations from converts from Judaism or Islam, from someone sentenced by the Inquisition for heresy, or from someone within that span who had engaged in demeaning labor, which is to say, from a commoner. It went without saying that aristocrats could not be illegitimate children or slaves (or descended from slaves) or continue to enjoy aristocratic standing if, through impoverishment, they engaged in common labor.

When *race* fully came into view, it would be in the colonies (in both Spanish and British America), where being a commoner or not an Old Christian or an unfree person meant being descended from Indians or Africans. Thus *race* as it emerged in the Americas drew on elements from other registers of distinction, such as the fuzzier, nonbiological category of *nación*, the old regime version of what was to become *nation*, which distinguish populations (say, Spaniards from Indians or Africans) from one another, as well as the hierarchy of substance called *calidad* ("quality" distinguishing aristocrats from plebeians), and the category of *vecindad* (formal residency marked by holding private property that granted full civil rights in the constitution-like ordinances of municipalities).

Although Africans had long been categorized by their "blackness," and the latter associated with slave status, color was only just being more widely adopted as a phenotypical marker of race into the state's classificatory practices (censuses and the like), which began to lump Creole Spaniards with peninsular ones, and persons from other European countries, under the category of *blanco*, or "white."[16] Such classification depended heavily on social acceptance into a category, itself depending on reference to traits such as those indexed by extracorporeal *hábitos* (clothing and behavior), pointing beneath the skin to morally evaluated character traits. Race, then, was emerging as a useful alternative logic for inequitably distributing privilege. It especially served the Creole Spaniards, whose American birth made them suspect as Spaniards. But *race* as we know it today was not yet born in Don Antonio's day or fully theorized in the terms of a supposed genetic inheritance.[17]

In analogous ways our present-day LGBTQIA words (lesbian, gay, bi-, trans-, queer, intersex, and asexual) are no more helpful for reading another's life in 1803. Was Don Antonio transgendered? A butch lesbian? Queer? Or, perhaps, intersexed? Neither he nor his contemporaries could imagine transgender, as gender itself was indissolubly merged with sex. Butch, perhaps, might have translated what for them was *marimacho*, "tomboy," or *mujer varonil*, "manly woman," but "lesbian" was not yet thinkable: there was neither a category for members of a collectivity of women sexually oriented to other women nor a fully developed notion of a stable personal and individual "identity" of a sort that makes for the identity politics and the demand for rights for certain kinds of persons, the goal of LGBTQIA thinking in our own milieu. Don Antonio's peers certainly found him unusual, perhaps a freak of nature or possibly just a criminal. They made use of the term *hermaphrodite*, but not exclusively in reference to ambiguous genitalia as does *intersex*. They might have liked the word *queer* as an insult term had they known it. *Asexual* might have been what priests and nuns were supposed to be, but they were not to give up their "sex" as men and women, just the expression of their sexuality. It seems that Don Antonio might have objected to all these terms, given his insistence on being accepted as a "normal" man who had sex with women.

But let us not get ahead of ourselves. Unpacking and analyzing Don Antonio's confession and life is the work of the following chapters. Those who insist on classifying him by contemporary terms can skip to chapter 6, though they will miss all the fun. For now it will be enough to find out something about Doña Martina, the wife who brought Don Antonio's world crashing down on that fateful day in La Plata; about the medical inspection and what kind of experience such doctors had of cases of doubtful sex; and about the legal context that produced our main sources.

Doña Martina and Her Denunciations

Doña Martina's husband, Don Antonio Yta, had come to the capital city of
La Plata from Cochabamba a few months before, seeking his back pay from a
(disastrous) stint as administrator of an ex-Jesuit mission town in the distant
tropics. Doña Martina had just arrived and, without his knowledge, hired an
attorney and begun her legal assault on her husband, about which he seems
to have known nothing until his arrest.

Who was this Doña Martina? Unfortunately, there is not much to go on to
answer this question. Twenty-two years old in 1803, Doña Martina, daughter
of an apparently aristocratic couple from Spain now living in Cochabamba,
had been just sixteen when her husband began courting her and eighteen
years old when she married Don Antonio (then twenty-eight) in Potosí in the
year 1798. It is not clear how they met, though they were perhaps introduced
through Antonio's powerful patron in Potosí, Don Francisco de Paula Sanz,
the intendant governor of that city. It could also have been an arranged marriage, a deal between Don Antonio and Martina's father, though that would
also have required the intercession of powerful men such as the governor of
Potosí or the bishop of Buenos Aires.

Don Antonio had no wealth and much to hide, his only prospects being
his aristocratic Spanishness and his connections, but marrying a woman
from an honorable and perhaps wealthy (and also Spanish) family could
have helped with his situation. On the other hand, it could be that it was
Doña Martina who more urgently needed a step up and rescue. It is hard to
say. In a lawsuit brought by Don Antonio against Doña Martina, from prison
a month after his arrest, each portrays the *other* as a gold digger. Lawyers and
judges and later interpreters of the case also each shaped their own narrative
arcs according to which character, Antonio or Martina, they found to be the
rascal and which the innocent.

It was no doubt through Sanz or his legal adviser, the also powerful Pedro
Vicente Cañete y Domínguez, a man who also became one of Don Antonio's
judges, that Antonio had snagged a job in the colonial government after
spending a few years in Potosí wooing Martina while living with Sanz. He
was appointed as administrator of an indigenous town, a former Jesuit mission called Pueblo de La Magdalena, in the distant and tropical region of
Moxos. He spent a year in the city of La Plata before traveling with Doña

Martina to Moxos; then about a year there before all the administrators of the region were expelled by the indigenous governors of the place; and then a year or so in Cochabamba, Doña Martina's hometown. The marriage had been peripatetic and also, in terms of both money and children, fruitless. Don Antonio had returned from Cochabamba to La Plata a few months earlier, filing requests for his back pay as administrator of La Magdalena. Then Doña Martina quietly traveled to La Plata without her husband's knowledge to file her denunciations.

Whatever drove Doña Martina to denounce her husband, she presented herself as the innocent and aggrieved party. First, she went to the ecclesiastical prosecutor of the archbishopric and, with the help of an attorney, went a few days later (at the cleric's urging, since he hoped the secular court would carry out the medical investigation into Don Antonio's sex) to the judges of the royal audiencia.[18] Martina claimed that she had married Antonio in the good faith that he was male, since he wore a man's clothing. But in the end she had come to understand that her husband "was a woman dressed as a man, through a group of evident signs such as monthly menstruation, making water in the same manner as do women, and, in a word, for not having consummated with me the supposed matrimony" (appendix A.1, fol. 1r). Moreover, Don Antonio had almost always slept away from the conjugal bed, and when he did sleep in her company, he "took the precaution of putting on underwear." There were also other signs that honor would not allow her to specify, though in her earlier denunciation before the ecclesiastical judge, she had also affirmed that he "has very grown breasts." To make it clear to this religious authority that this failure to consummate the marriage was not her own fault, she insisted that he had avoided having sexual intercourse with her "in spite of my affections and insinuations," perhaps because, as he had insinuated to her, he had taken a vow of chastity. She continued that he has "never let his body be touched, even when he was sick" (A.9, fol. 11r). Without accepting Martina's claims of perfect innocence, we might note that he had reasons not to let his body be touched. At the same time, that does not mean that he was not doing the touching, of her. Indeed, Don Antonio's insistent masculinity would suggest that he was. Possibly, however, it was not in a manner that Doña Martina recognized as the particular sex act that was her husband's religious duty as procreator.

Don Antonio, Martina gave judges to understand, had hoodwinked her. She now sought, from the church, an annulment of her marriage (A.9, fol.

11r) and, from the state, she asked for justice, which is to say, revenge—an investigation that would not only prove her suspicions but perhaps reveal past crimes that might have motivated her husband's long-term "disguise" of sex and thus also disguise of identity (A.1, fol. 11r). It seems certain that she was hurt and angry, although we should not assume that we know just *what* had hurt and angered her. Taborga's account of her arguments adds yet another dimension to the source of her animus: she was tired of his extreme jealousy and the anger toward her that flowed from it.

Was Doña Martina the innocent victim that her denunciations purport? Love is a mystery, and innocence comes in many forms, as does victimhood. The brevity of her account and her failure to provide additional testimony (and her absence from the archival record apart from those documents presented here) give us little evidence to judge the degree of her innocence, whether sexual, anatomical, or moral. What kinds of bodily pleasures had she enjoyed with Don Antonio? For how long may she have enjoyed them while suspecting—or knowing with certainty—that her husband was a woman? For that matter, what actually motivated her to denounce Antonio after more than four years of marriage? What might have led to this change of heart toward her husband? Some hints that their relationship was strained, and not likely as innocent as Martina needed judges to believe, come from Antonio's lawsuit against her, initiated after his arrest, demanding delivery of his clothing (B.8), in which each accused the other of being a gold digger, and where he seems to have been threatening to reveal some of *her* secrets or *theirs* together. Whatever our guesses might be about the degree of her innocence or the motives for her denunciation of Antonio, it is clear that Martina—and those who helped her craft her denunciation—knew the laws of marriage.

At the time divorce was nearly impossible. Ending a marriage so as to be free to marry again was most easily accomplished through a dispensation, the clearest argument for which was *ratum sed non consummatum*, failure to consummate the marriage through the sacramental act of sexual intercourse. If either party to a marriage refused or otherwise failed to perform that act, they failed to perform the fundamental duty of married life and gave cause for declaring that the marriage had in fact not taken place (*Code of Canon Law* n.d., Canon 1698).[19] So, whatever did or did not take place between them (and about this Antonio would soon contradict his wife), Martina was wise to seek an end to the marriage by insisting that it had not been consummated.

Martina's denunciation lists no fewer than three additional grounds for annulment: deliberate deceit of the other party about some personal quality that can objectively and gravely perturb conjugal life (*Code of Canon Law* n.d., Canon 1098); impotence, or the permanent inability to carry out the fundamental duty of marriage (1084); and the existence of a prior vow of chastity taken in a religious institute (1088). If any of these conditions pertained, then a marriage could be declared never to have actually taken place, in the same way that would be null if the person performing it were not legally authorized to perform it. Of course, proving that Antonio was a woman and not a man would seem to supersede all of these, since at the time there was no possibility of a valid marriage between two women. It was not technically *illegal* to marry under false pretenses (unless it was a bigamous marriage) and, as we shall see, proving a person's sex was surprisingly difficult in 1803. Antonio's assertions, dress, and comportment, if not the apparently female body found beneath his clothing, contradicted Martina's statement, and they continued to matter a great deal.

After Martina ran back and forth between the ecclesiastical prosecutor of the archbishopric and the judges of the high court of the Audiencia de Charcas for four days, seeking swift and quiet action so that her husband might be arrested before fleeing the city, her wish was fulfilled (see A.1 and A.9).

The Medical Examination

Disguise of sex is what Don Antonio was forced to admit he had carried out, once his wife's accusation had been read to him, and standing or (or lying) naked before the city's official physician and surgeon, the fully male persona that Don Antonio had cultivated and inhabited for a decade was shattered in the eyes of those professionals. The physician and surgeon were Dr. Don Joséf Gregorio Salas, and Don Diego Sáenz de Juano (see the "Cast of Characters" in this volume). What these medical men uncovered and described was the body—in all its exterior parts, anyway—of a woman. The "cultural genitals" (Kessler 1998) that they, and the other men of La Plata, had assumed to exist under his clothes suddenly disappeared, partially and temporarily, at least.

When Don Antonio was questioned by these two professionals—not some country bumpkins but well-educated medical men charged with the care of the infirm in the Hospital San Juan de Dios, the capital city's sixty-five-bed hospital—he told them of having regular menstruation but also insisted that "in the act in certain indecent moments a kind of fleshiness similar to the virile member protrudes over the pudenda." Continuing to refer to him as *he* (in part because he stood accused as Don Antonio Yta), the doctors nonetheless noted that what they saw when they examined his genitals was "the clitoris, a proper part of a woman's pudenda and nothing foreign to its nature, *although the certifiers have not seen it in the action that **he** describes*. In addition . . . this person's configuration is that of the feminine sex: the inferior extremities, rotund; the pelvic bones, long unlike those of men; the complete breasts that in no way differ from the sex except that they are somewhat flattened through constant compression and rigid from no secretion" (appendix A.5, fol. 3v; emphasis added).

Cautious men, the doctors Salas and Sáenz de Juano then declared Don Antonio to be a woman, although they noted that they "*have not seen it* [the man's thing, the fleshiness, or the clitoris] *in the action that **he** describes*," which is to say, in a state of excitation. Leaving the smallest opening for doubt, the trace of ambiguity in their perfectly empirical report opened a door through which Don Antonio would walk.

Doubting Sex and Judging "Imposture" in 1803: Legal and Medical Precedents

The sensationalist tone of Taborga's letter responded to the most unusual aspect of the case: two women had married each other. "Ordinary" cases of imposture of sex (and imposture more broadly) and the same-sex relations known as sodomy were downright common kinds of crimes. Even cases of hermaphrodism were more familiar than what Don Antonio had done when he married Doña Martina.

Doña Martina had gone first to the church because matrimony was in its purview. She had then gone to state prosecutors because the church itself lacked the juridical apparatus and power to arrest and examine that were the state's prerogative. The Inquisition had such powers, but it was concerned with matters of the faith, with heresy. None of Don Antonio's apparent crimes were in its purview.[20] So although Doña Martina would seek first and last the church's aid in obtaining an annulment, she was directed to the state to bring about her husband's arrest and determination of his sex. That arrest required suspicion of having committed a crime. "Imposture of sex" was not one, but it suggested deceit and the possibility of prior crimes.

How well prepared were jurists and medical men for a case such as this, given all its possibilities? Not many cases of the disguise of sex came before any particular judge or physician in this era, but when they did, they made a lasting impression. All were familiar with cross-dressing in the theater and novel and in carnivalesque moments in festive life in Spain and in its América. Same-sex acts were also familiar to the judges and medical practitioners, along with hermaphrodism (sometimes involving intersex conditions).

Of course, Don Antonio could not have committed same-sex acts and was not engaged in the imposture of sex, or passing, if his body was legitimately male as well as female. That is what the physician and surgeon were called in to determine. Don Antonio claimed that he was male, his menses and visibly female anatomy notwithstanding. What was the frame of reference of these medical men for evaluating that claim? Perhaps there would not have been many cases of hermaphrodism in La Plata in 1803. But the physician and surgeon who examined Don Antonio had plenty of experience in the capital city's hospital and training in anatomy—including lessons on the varieties of "hermaphrodism"—through which they were certified for their posts through the office of the viceregal *protomedicato*, not only a certifying board, but a medical school (Lanning 1985; see also Martínez 2014). Such training, and the likelihood (given population rates of intersex conditions, over one in one thousand, according to Fausto-Sterling 2012) that they would have had prior experience with actual intersex cases, as well as plenty of medical experience with both male and female genitals, should have led to full clarity about Don Antonio's "sex," if that term were understood exclusively as a matter of the body.[21]

In other courtrooms and other physicians' tables over the previous few centuries in Spain and its América, cases for doubting sex had been pursued at trial and published (with illustrations) in journals. Some of them turned up as cases of indeterminate sex, with aspects of both sexes (though never fully functional in the manner that the full cross between Hermes and Aphrodite had been held to be). The task assigned to the doctors, then, was to make a determination of sex, to assign people to one slot or the other, and thus to reinscribe them as legal subjects. We will review some of the best-studied cases in chapter 6, in a fuller discussion of the science of sex. Some of those cases had been determined to be males masquerading as females, or females living as males, but even then a convincing performance of manliness or femininity could override the medical findings. Not necessarily about genitalia or gonads (and certainly not the as-yet-unknown sex chromosomes), *hermaphrodism* back then was a term that could cover both body and performance.[22]

Physicians and jurists also had knowledge and experience with "imposture of sex." Almost two centuries earlier Catalina de Erauso, the infamous "lieutenant nun," another apparent woman living as a man, had passed through La Plata during a life of adventure as a Spanish soldier, a life chronicled in a century-old play likely performed in La Plata. Unlike Don Antonio Yta, Antonio de Erauso, once Catalina, had not married and made no claim to have performed *the act* with an occasionally appearing male member. Indeed, her fame (and her rewards from the king and dispensation to continue living as a man from the pope) had depended on a medical inspection proving him to be a virgin female. That case was a very real one, in spite of being known to us mainly through a fictionalized autobiography including much swashbuckling, murder, and hints of same-sex ties that are not born out in Erauso's own testimony.[23] Unlike Erauso's "autobiography," a novelized story likely written by an amanuensis drawing on the conventions of the *picaresque* genre, Don Antonio's life-narrative confession is his own.

Beyond the Erauso story, cases of long- or short-term cross-dressing women were also well known to our doctors and legal men. All would have known of numerous cross-dressing historical figures, such as Joan of Arc, or religious ones, such as Saint Barbara, who had dressed as men to carry out military action to defend their people or their faith. A large percentage of the Golden Age plays performed in La Plata or Potosí included roles for cross-dressing women, generally done in order to protect loved ones or pursuing justice for them. Bartolomé Arzáns y Vela, chronicler of Potosí, wrote about many such real-world cases during his lifetime (1676–1736).

Women were known to dress in men's clothing to enable them to walk through the streets unhindered, usually in the dark (for an example in La Plata, see Abercrombie 2000). Cases of men in androgynous dress, called *maricones*, were well known in the port city of Lima in this period (Pamo Reyna 2015), though documentation of this is missing for La Plata and Potosí. Cross-dressing men were also a staple of festive life in La Plata and Potosí (as in Spain), though generally a carnivalesque variety, such as drag performances portraying burlesque versions of women. It was particularly central to the Dance of the Devils, where men portrayed lusty and vulgar female consorts of Satan and his demons, and male members of the audience were supposed to get a "creepy feeling" of being seduced into an undefinable kind of sin when those obviously cross-dressed men flirted with and touched them along the dance route.[24]

Don Antonio insisted on having performed sex acts with Doña Martina. If Don Antonio was female and not male or hermaphrodite, that would make those acts the same-sex kind. Jurists and physicians were also familiar with same-sex acts, not those of lesbians or homosexuals (since the terms did not yet exist), but those of the male "sodomites" they occasionally prosecuted and examined (for proof of anal penetration) and the suspiciously close friendships of unmarried women who lived together, not so easy to classify through the definition of sodomy. Doña Martina seems to have argued that there were no sex acts with her husband. But even if Don Antonio was a woman and sex acts had occurred with Doña Martina, they would only have *legally* constituted sodomy if judges and physicians had found evidence of "unnatural penetration," that is, use of a dildo. They do not seem to have looked for it.[25]

Don Antonio's life was lived before lesbian, homosexual, transsexual, or transgender were imaginable, much less allowable, as habitable identities. It is possible, and even likely, that certain taverns (particularly those called *chicherías*) would have been known as meeting places by men of same-sex desires, though persecution of such men would make such locales of fleeting existence. Fewer semipublic contexts were available for women. But *homosexuals* and *lesbians* as members of a category of persons had not yet been thought up or institutionalized in medicine or law as a kind of identity. Toward the end of the nineteenth century, as Michel Foucault put it, "Homosexuality appeared as one of the forms of sexuality when it was transposed from the practice of sodomy onto a kind of interior androgyny, a hermaphrodism of the soul. The sodomite had been a temporary aberration; the homosexual was now a species" ([1976] 1990, 43).

Dror Wahrman (2006; see also C. Taylor 1992) has influentially argued that it is not until the later nineteenth century, in conjunction with the emergence of psychology as a branch of science dedicated to matters of mind and self and its adoption by the state as a tool of biopolitics, that notions of "true self" or "identity," cultivated and durable over time, began to be promoted as a "public good." Such new ideas were developed in association with the medicalization of sex over the nineteenth century, which itself progressed through the systematic examination of cases of doubtful sex, which is to say, of persons labeled as hermaphrodites (Mak 2013; Vicente 2017). While Don Antonio's examination belongs to that accumulation of case histories, it was in that history's early days, and Don Antonio's sex still included his assertions, dress, and comportment. In 1803 Taborga may have been concluding that Don Antonio's hermaphrodism was indeed a matter of the soul ("sick in the head"), but others disagreed, and at any rate he had no ready category (for example, lesbian) on which to hang his suspicions.

Whether or not we accept such arguments about lacking a concept of true self or identity in Don Antonio's day, it is certainly true that many persons aimed to "pass themselves off" as a member of a different, usually higher-ranking social category than the one they were born with. Catalina de Erauso went unpunished, and indeed was rewarded, for service to the king as a military man, in a way that would be inconceivable if the imposture were the other way around (a man posing as a woman), because it was taken as an act of social climbing. Everyone could understand the urge to better oneself. And social climbing through the imposture of a higher-ranking and more privileged social category, with greater freedom of action or "agency," was extraordinarily well known in the La Plata of 1803.

Often associated with a change of clothing, such social climbing was rampant enough to have warranted new sumptuary codes and laws enabling parents to block the marriages of children to others deemed too inferior in status. Well-known illustrations (called casta paintings) of difficult-to-parse "mixtures" of Spaniards, Indians, and Africans make it appear that these were all well classified and in their proper places, but that was a desire, not a reality, of colonial officials.[26]

When social climbing involved passing, it involved not only betterment but concealment of *stigma*, as Erving Goffman defines it: "an attribute that is deeply discrediting," sufficient to lead to social rejection (1963, 3). Passing, for Goffman, is "the management of undisclosed discrediting information about self" (42). Such terms of analysis seem to fit Don Antonio's situation very well.[27]

For those engaged in transgender activism, *passing* and what it implies, acts of *deception*, are themselves stigmatizing labels for those who seek only to exteriorize an inner true identity at odds with aspects of their bodies. I nonetheless use the term in Don Antonio's case and for 1803, given that he operated in a context where there was no possibility of remaining "un-stigmatized" once the nature of his "bodily sex" was revealed to contradict his enactments of maleness. We must address the concept of passing and the deceptions it implied to understand Don Antonio's predicament, his deeds, and their "emplotment" in his confession, as well as the stances of his judges and attorneys. Moreover, doing so helps to understand Don Antonio's practices in the broader context of social climbing.

So in spite of the headway made since the 1960s in defining gender and the usefulness of insights derived from its study, it is more revealing, for now, to unravel the "sex/gender system" of the Spanish Atlantic in 1803 than to assume that our current categories solve their problems of incomprehension. It will also be more respectful of Don Antonio not to repeat judges' obsession with genitalia, which was their way of trying to explain María's transformation into Antonio. In any case that transformation, from the sex in which María was inscribed at birth to the sex attributed to Don Antonio as an adult, cannot properly be explained as a product of *bodily* sex. It involved much more than just a change of name and clothing, something that in itself requires very close attention. It involved fully and convincingly inhabiting and performing a set of social roles, attitudes, stances toward others, and ways of walking and looking, speaking and listening, embedded in and constitutive of what Don Antonio's contemporaries understood as *sex*.

The performance of sex/gender in Don Antonio's day was deeply intertwined with other kinds of social performance; it was inseparable from the performative means of indexing every other kind of social distinction that was then discursively intelligible. Surely, in her efforts to become Don Antonio, Doña María had engaged in the "stylization of the body" and a host of performative acts (concepts developed by Butler 1990, drawing on Austin 1975), beginning with binding of the breasts and dressing, walking, speaking, looking, and acting as a man, thereby pointing to or indexing (and constructing or constituting) male sex. But his clothing and comportment indexed much more than just being a man: they pointed to aristocratic, peninsular Spanish (and metropolitan), cosmopolitan, and white maleness.

Once Doña Martina denounced Don Antonio and the medical examination revealed female genitalia, breasts, and pelvic bones, however, there was the question of what laws he might have broken. Don Antonio was interrogated to that end. Disguise or imposture of sex was not itself illegal, but, as Taborga makes clear, that act of disguise suggested the character of a rascal, one who might have committed some prior crime the disguise and that travel might have sought to hide. There was no evidence of penetrative sex involving a dildo, so sodomy was not at issue, at least without further questioning of Doña Martina, which was not to take place. If Doña María had professed as a nun in one of her convents, her marriage to Martina would have been the crime of bigamy, and so jurists set about investigating that. After confessing, Don Antonio would be forced to endure a protracted period in the audiencia's jail while the court awaited such information.

Plan of the Book

In what follows I present a series of chapters querying the case in some detail. First chapter 1, "*Confession*," is an interrogation of Don Antonio's own statement, which offers much detail that Taborga did not present in his summary of the proceedings. Putting it first into the context of this courtroom proceeding, chapter 1 also aims to determine what kind of narrative the confession might be and think through how best to read it, given the scribal screen behind which Don Antonio's speech hides in the source and the involuntary form of a self-narrative produced under interrogation.

In this analysis of spoken and written narrative, I give special treatment to the use of pronouns, gendered in the third person in both English and Spanish and problematic when reporting about a person who challenged this binary as conventionally understood. *He* and *she* are both ordinary lexical items signifying one or another sex as conceptual entities and indexes that point to the sex of a particular person in the world referred to by the speaker or writer. As shifters, in the terminology of Michael Silverstein (1976), pronouns are particularly forceful, especially with iteration, in establishing the sex of *him* or *her*. I thus take great care in presenting Don Antonio's story both to point out the force of pronominal gendering, an effect he likely used to entrench his maleness in speech but that some judges used to undermine that maleness by referring to him as her, and to avoid misleading readers about how Don Antonio gendered himself in his confession, something of which we cannot be certain.

Drawing on the work of a host of literary scholars and cultural critics who have written of the period, the chapter considers the genre of Don Antonio's confession and questions the degree to which that genre was itself gendered (Cruz 2010). Locating the confession intertextually among other sorts of life narration in legal, literary, theatrical, and everyday speech contexts, it addresses their interplay and the emergence in the Spanish context of auto-biography as a well-developed form of self-narration.

The practiced self-narration of Don Antonio's time was influenced by rafts of prior judicial reportage as well as picaresque literature and by the conventions of theater as well as everyday gossip. Don Antonio crafted his story, like such sources, as a sequence of episodes anchored in a succession of places, forging a chronotopic (Bakhtin 1981) story of transformation, marked by episodic movement simultaneously through space and time.[28]

In the picaresque novel, which functions as a kind of satire both of earlier, earnest tales of honorable deeds in romances of chivalry and of the equally earnest, always dutiful, acts reported in the curriculum vitae–like letters to the king known as *relaciones de servicios y méritos* (González Echevarría 1990), self-narration is cast in the form of the confession, a statement dictated to a distant judging authority, by a potentially unreliable narrator already under accusation. *Pícaros* are identifiable for their disingenuous ways or their ingen-uous lack of self-awareness. Such satires fed back into situations such as the confession, where legal subjects were already suspected of disingenuousness and had to emplot their stories so as to craft virtuous characters to counter judges' suspicions, but also into petitions of all sorts, in which petitioners drew on the literary corpus to portray themselves as victims of others' misdeeds (Davis 1987).[29]

Of course, the charge against Don Antonio is disguise of sex and suspicion of prior illegalities perhaps committed by a deceptive character. Assessing how he narratively emplots his transformation from Doña María into Don Antonio begins to address the question of how it could be that in 1803 a medical inspection revealing female sex does not stop many case participants from continuing to doubt Don Antonio's sex, and how it is that he retains legal standing as man and husband in spite of the fact that some, but not all, judges and scribes now refer to him as María.

Chapter 2, "Habits," then enters the timeline of Don Antonio's story, wending back to his origins and complicated, peripatetic, and frequently *exposed* life as non–sex-conforming Doña María. The chapter's title points to its focus: habitual kinds of embodied practice carried out while clothed. Habits, and the Spanish *hábitos*, refer to matters of costume as well as customary action of sorts that differentiated different sorts of roles and statuses in Don Antonio's world. Constituting a kind of "social skin" (T. Turner 1980), these exteriorized communicative material signals pointed to persons' statuses and interior states in ways that link individuals to broader, well-patterned social worlds.[30]

To approach social acts, the chapter draws on frameworks for the analysis of the practices of everyday life ranging from generative structuralism (T. Turner 1980) to the dramaturgical approach to social interaction (Goffman 1959, 1963), ethnomethodology (Birdwhistell 1970; Garfinkel 1967), and performance studies and its attention to the connection between embodied performance and ritual (Roach 1996; Schechner 1985; D. Taylor 2003; V. Turner 1982). The chapter draws on notions of linguistic performativity (Austin 1975) that have been central to Judith Butler's approach to gender, which she has defined as "the repeated stylization of the body, a set of repeated acts within a highly rigid regulatory frame that congeal over time to produce the appearance of substance, of a natural sort of being" (1990, 25). Attending to clothing and embodied performance requires attention to material and embodied signs and to those that serve as indexes and icons, pointing to or exhibiting likeness to other things, sometimes qualities of persons in their immediate context, and how such signs might be systematized through a poetics of action. The chapter also then draws from practice theory and the concepts of habitus, schema, and field (Bourdieu 1985, 1990). I use *habitus* in a somewhat more expansive way than does Pierre Bourdieu or, say, Susan Stryker, for whom, drawing also on Butler's definition of gender performativity, it is "our habitual or customary way of carrying ourselves and styling our bodies" (2017, 26).

I equate *habitus* with the Spanish term *hábitos* to draw in kinds of indexical signs such as clothing and the full range of acts that mark social roles, not all of which are habitual or unconscious, and which may be taught and reflexively understood. In a society where only men are allowed to wear pants, for example, wearing them comes to index the sex of the wearer. Of course, pants also become icons of maleness (appearing to be "male"), as in the graphic signs on restroom doors portraying pants- or skirt-wearing stick figures distinguishing men's rooms from ladies' rooms. I then aim to illustrate the organizing schemas that bundle such signs together and make them comparable to one another across different fields of social action. My uses of Charles Sanders Peirce's (1931–35) terms *index* and *icon* also point to the influence here of approaches to linguistic pragmatics (Hanks 1990, 2005; Harkness 2015; Keane 2003; Silverstein 1976), which foreground the materiality of signs, as well as their production and productiveness in communicative interaction, whether in embodied and clothed interaction or in speech and writing.

I aim to clothe these sometimes abstract theoretical approaches in the readily intelligible contexts of Don Antonio's life. So the chapter follows Doña María from her tender childhood years in her parents' home to her tenure as a *criada* in the palace of one of the most powerful noble families of Madrid and her expulsion, for what she did with the nuns, from convents in Colmenar de Oreja, Huesca, Illescas, and Segovia. Drawing on fine work on the "clothing system" generally and in particular that of late eighteenth-century Spain, from nun's habits to the hábitos of everyone else, from rigid costumes of social estate to the emergence of fashion (Barthes 1983), the chapter follows the apparently failed efforts to socialize Doña María as a proper, reserved and constrained, even cloistered, female of the lower rungs of aristocracy.[31] That is, it examines the concept of *recogimiento* (van Deusen 2001), constraint of action and speech, or closure of the self to the world as the proper attitude of the woman who would be an aristocratic daughter and wife, or nun.[32] Likewise, it examines recogimiento's opposite, the unconstrained action characteristic of masculinity. In a context felicitous for our analysis, Covarrubias Orozco's dictionary ([1611] 1943, 790) gives us the Spanish term in his definition of *marimacho*, "tomboy," as *"la muger que tiene desembolturas de hombre,"* "the woman who exhibits the *desenvolturas* of a man." The range of current meanings of *desenvoltura* indeed sum up precisely the antithesis of recogimiento.[33]

Such terms compose an explicit semiotic ideology (Keane 2018) of sex/gender performativity, applicable also to grasping the performative expression of the other kinds of social ranking that sex/gender intersects. *Recogimiento* and *desenvoltura* describe situated interactional dispositions of persons toward others, located in relation to a public-versus-private classification of social space. In the introduction to his short but influential book, *The Education of a Christian Woman*, sixteenth-century author Juan Luís Vives, tutor of Princess Mary ("Queen of Scots," daughter of Henry VIII and Catherine of Aragon) accounted for its brevity by noting that women's lives, confined to the private sphere, were not as complex as those of men, whose lives were also public ([1523] 2000). The distinction has been central to gender ideologies and until the present day has plagued women, whose presumptive place, according to some men, is "in the home." Yet, as Susan Gal (2002) has shown, *public* and *private* are recursive and fractal, as well as contextually reversible (such as when two people whisper to each other in the midst of the forum). Likewise, *recogimiento* and *desenvoltura* were learned as contextually reversible dispositions. The abbess, ideally recogida as a nun, could be unconstrained and direct in speaking to novices (and as CEO of the convent when she signed contracts and directed sometimes massive business operations [Burns 1999, 2003]); likewise, the most desenvuelto aristocrat had to be submissive and circumspect before the king. Such dispositions were therefore learned in an inherently reflexive manner.

The chapter reviews available sources by which Doña María was able to develop an especially reflexive understanding of hábitos. These include the varied contexts of her life; the explicit efforts of others to socialize and discipline her, including the application of rigid rules of the convent and explanations thereof; models of such reflexivity provided (in narrative form) in speech and literature and (in enacted form) in formal training, initiation rites, and the theater, to which she was also exposed. Drawing on such sources, the chapter queries the acquisition of knowledge by which she was emboldened to transform her sex in its performative dimensions. Above all, the chapter seeks to answer the question of how Doña María learned to successfully inhabit particular kinds of maleness from among the range of kinds then available.[34]

Chapter 3, "Passages," then turns to the connection between movement in space, temporality, and self-transformation in Don Antonio's chronotopic life narrative. The episodes of his life are pegged to specific and widely contrasting life contexts (ships' quarters and decks, bishop's palace, inns, governor's palace, and on foot or in a carriage or on the back of a horse or mule, while on the highway or in the streets of Málaga, Buenos Aires, and Potosí), whether remaining unaccompanied, doing work for others, enjoying his freedom of movement, or courting a future bride. Each context posed new rewards, and new risks, and adjustments to the kind of work involved, first for Doña María to become Don Antonio and then to sustain Don Antonio through significant efforts to convince others of his manliness, to avoid exposure, and to pass as a man.[35]

Going beyond "ordinary" hábitos to consider the kinds of covering techniques Don Antonio needed to employ, the chapter tracks Don Antonio across the Atlantic to service as page to the bishop of Buenos Aires and from there along the mule-train highway to Potosí and into the household of Potosí's powerful governor, reprising his role as criada back in the duchess's palace in Madrid, but this time as a male *criado*. It considers Don Antonio's courtship of and marriage to eighteen-year-old Doña Martina Vilvado y Balverde, and his successful use of his cosmopolitan ways and status as a peninsular Spaniard and hidalgo, now joined by being a *blanco*, "white," in a frontier and industrial city filled with indigenous laborers and mixed castas.

Drawing on the inventories of Don Antonio's and Doña Martina's clothing produced when he sued her, while prisoner, for delivery of his property, the chapter imagines Don Antonio's public performance of masculinity in this vice-ridden boomtown full of taverns and brothels but also great wealth and upper-crust ostentation. Don Antonio seems to have adopted the costume of the *currutaco*, a particularly peacock-like suit of aristocratic clothing that was the height of fashion in Spanish imperial capitals during the last several years of the eighteenth century and defined the wearers as dandies. The chapter follows Don Antonio practicing the confident, wandering stroll of the flaneur in Potosí; observing with cosmopolitan disdain the striving but indigent majority of indigenous people and castas; and questioning the "Spanishness" of the city's Creole Spaniards. After all, it was for being an aristocratic, metropolitan *ultramarino* that the newly arrived Don Antonio was able to outcompete a host of more qualified candidates for Crown office, to become administrator of an indigenous town.[36]

Chapter 4, "Means and Ends," follows the newlyweds to the stately colonial capital of La Plata, with its genteel paseos, or stroll ways; its high-cultural events, or *tertulias*; and its formal balls featuring *contradanzas* (think the cotillions, or debutant balls, in the U.S. context). Such possibilities accompanied Don Antonio's uptake of a paid career as a Crown official, which finally provided him (in theory, at least) with a means of supporting himself and a wife in the style required to maintain their peninsular Spanish, aristocratic, and white pretensions while satisfying the expectations of a judging public. Necessary for a decent married life was having a home in which, secluded behind walls and a threshold, he would for more than one reason be concerned with keeping Doña Martina in recogimiento, the constrained aristocratic form of femininity from which he himself had fled. Of course, if Doña Martina's goals included having children, both Don Antonio's body and his jealous surveillance of her activities would disappoint.[37]

Following the couple as he took up his duties in distant Moxos, where he was to help rein in indigenous upward mobility, the chapter queries his duties there and examines what life might have been like for the reigning (and probably only) Spanish couple in the indigenous town of La Magdalena, a former Jesuit *reducción* in this distant tropical province. After what proved to be a disastrous tenure as administrator and the couple's humiliating expulsion, the chapter tracks them back to La Plata, by way of Doña Martina's home-town of Cochabamba, and finally to the denouement of the story, when as he sought in vain to get his pay from two years of administrative work, she stole into town to denounce him. And then followed his arrest, jail, what appears to be the end of his marriage and colonial career, and the accumulation of his *expediente* and their deposit in the audiencia's archive.

Chapter 5, "Afterlives," considers a series of prior "treatments" of Don Antonio's story, some deriving from the circulation of synopses of the early days of the case, others taking as their source a late nineteenth-century sum-mary, and a few from the original archival documents themselves. Reviewing the different ways that students of the case chose to portray Don Antonio's and Doña Martina's characters to emplot their accounts from the late nine-teenth to the twenty-first century, the chapter focuses attention on shifts in the literary topos of disguise, by which it may sometimes be excused, and deceit, which always seems to require its just deserts.

Chapter 6, "Truth," brings the contemporary analytics of sex and gender, including feminist, gay and lesbian, queer, and transgender theorizing, to bear on the accumulated facts and interpretations of the case. It aims to locate Doña María and Don Antonio vis-à-vis our contemporary terminologies (lesbian, intersex, transgender, transvestite, drag, etc.), using them to interro-gate him, and using his acts and their historical circumstances to interrogate them. The chapter provides an account of the emergence of transgender studies and the resistance by gay, lesbian, and queer-studies scholars to trans persons' apparent embrace of the heteronormativity that queer activists have regarded as their principal enemy.

Examining a series of cases of non–sex-conforming persons in the Spanish realms from the sixteenth through eighteenth centuries, the chapter reconsiders the sixteenth-to-eighteenth-century category of hermaphrodite. It asks if the term named the relatively accepted blurred sex/gender hábitos of historical figures who might well be historical ancestors of today's lesbian, gay, bi, trans, queer, and intersex persons, sometimes all at once, and wonders whether the rigid distinction between medicalized, "biological" sex and performative, cultural gender has been a boon or a bane for those who would be in between.

Turning to contemporary cases of transgender and to the discursive violence that is done to them by referring to their "dead names," their acts as passing, or their intentions as deceit, the chapter queries the apparent opposition between the creative efficacy of sex/gender performativity through enacted and clothed hábitos and narrativity, the narrative exposition of lives, which seems always to entail emplotments that end with judgments of character. Turning to enactments of character judgment, it considers the sometimes violent reprisals visited on, for example, male-to-female transgenders by male sexual partners on discovering the sex they claim they did not expect.

To sum up: chapter 1, "Confession," focuses on Don Antonio's life narration and its sources and models, while chapter 2, "Habits," turns to how he learned his embodied performances of his varied hábitos. Chapter 3, "Passages," treats his episodic movement through time and space, via roads and streets linking different sorts of architectural performance contexts significant to both his storied and lived practice, while chapter 4, "Means and Ends," turns to the values and goals that motivated his movements. Chapter 5, "Afterlives," then queries the kinds of moral judgment of character that treatments of Don Antonio's life invariably seem to carry out, while chapter 6, "Truth," questions the distinction between material, bodily sex, and the social construct called gender, where the latter is posited both as an inner, transcendent "identity" and as performative projections (let us say hábitos), which may be in harmony or in contradiction with one another and with the "sex" of the material body. Such contradictions lie at the heart of claims of both inauthenticity (for example, of persons said to be "in the closet") and of deception, such as the judgment that led to the persecution of Don Antonio. Varying kinds of identity politics, of course, aim toward a suspension of such judgments and persecutions, though their reliance on a language of surfaces and depths, appearances and inner truths, also accentuates the very contrasts on which judgments of authenticity or deception are made.

The book's conclusion then takes up the question of the apparent opposition between narrativity and performativity, where narrativity is taken to be a property of discourses of power etched into classifying and persecuting archives, and repertoires of performativity are held to be the locus of resistance to such power. Theorizing in the vein of poststructuralism and performance studies seems to equate narrative and language more broadly with power and archives, opposing to them the performative repertoires of meaningful enactments, particularly the staged kind, as modes of resistance to that power. Narrativity and performativity, the conclusion argues, are not autonomous realms that should be studied separately by distinct disciplines and methods (such as the critical reading of literary criticism or anthropology's ethnography or praxiography [Mak 2013; Mol 2003]), but are mutually constitutive, both for the deployment of coercive power and for resisting it.

Finally, we evaluate once more both Don Antonio's claim sometimes to have a penis and the efforts of jurists to determine his sex. To the degree that the presence of a penis is a product not only of discourse but of enactments and of sensation perceived as sexed activity and indeed sexed pleasure, the book concludes that Don Antonio may well have had one and that those who argued that he was a hermaphrodite may have had good reason to think so.

✕

So then, our task is multiple. It is to unravel the story in such a way that we might understand Don Antonio in the terms and unspoken life conventions of his time, but also, making use of recent approaches to sex, gender, social class, race, and the imperial and colonial interface, to understand Don Antonio and Doña María in ways that contemporaries could not, as well as to understand *why* they could not. But far from wanting to comprehend them through our contemporary concepts, I hope to immerse the reader in late eighteenth-century ways of knowing, joining in Eve Sedgwick's project to "denaturalize" the present rather than the past, "in effect to render less destructively presumable 'homosexuality [to which I add, intersex or transgender] as we know it today'" (1990, 48). Through an "archaeology" of our analytic concepts, and theirs, it also becomes possible to grasp the historical contingency and constructedness of *our own* taken-for-granted, everyday assumptions about the possibilities of human identity when it comes to sex and gender and the intersection of that binary with other categories of hierarchizing difference.

CHAPTER I

CONFESSION

*Self-Fashioning and the
Involuntary Autobiography*

Introduction

The impact of Doña Martina's betrayal came swiftly, and there is no doubt that the blow that now befell Don Antonio was the worst of his thirty-two years of life: the indignity of being stripped naked to be stared at, poked, and prodded by a physician and surgeon and to be forced to explain himself before Crown judges. Don Antonio, as the accused, would now tell his story, which would be heard by and then repeated among the very imperial elite he had managed to ingratiate himself with over the past decade. He could not have doubted that he would shortly be the most notorious figure at the center of a tremendous scandal.

It is hard to imagine how the edifice of the life and status that Don Antonio had built for himself could have withstood the earthquake of that humiliating process. But Don Antonio collected himself, admitted to having formerly been the person categorized as female and named María Leocadia Yta, and produced a detailed "confession." Not an admission of guilt per se, a confession was a statement akin to the voluntary report called an *información*, but given under duress and in response to a criminal accusation. Not denying that he had tightly wrapped his breasts so that they would not be noticed; had taken precautions so that his menses, and the female anatomy that produced them, would remain hidden; or had intentionally embarked, without passport or license, dressed as a man, on a series of journeys by land and sea to lead a man's life, under a given name that he had invented for himself, Antonio, he aimed to account for his actions and to explain himself sufficiently to excuse them.

Don Antonio had spoken to arresting officials before and while being examined by the physician and surgeon, and he spoke at considerable length during the interrogation that was called his confession. This chapter is also an interrogation: a questioning of the sources themselves, and particularly that confession. Here I offer that confession in its full detail and seek to understand what kind of statement it was, that is, to identify its genre and compare it with other genres of speaking and writing that account for a person's actions, sometimes (as in this case) doing so by telling an entire life story to explain particular actions and their motives. From prison, not long after the events of his arrest, examination, and interrogation, Don Antonio also spoke, this time in writing and in his own hand, when he sued Doña Martina for the delivery of the rest of his clothing, something he desperately needed in his cold cell.

He was not the only one to speak: some spoke *for* him, such as the attorneys for the poor who were assigned to him, and his mother, who sent a long explanatory letter on his behalf, while others spoke *against* him, such as Doña Martina in her denunciations and her responses to his suit against her over possessions. Mariano Taborga Contreras in his sensationalizing letter summarizing the confession, the ecclesiastical prosecutor Bernardino Méndez de la Parra, the physician and surgeon of the city, and the warden of the jail, along with countless wagging tongues that did not leave a record, spoke *about* him, sometimes referring to *him*, Antonio, and sometimes to *her*, María.

The confession, however, does not contain Don Antonio's actual words. It is different from the lawsuit he initiated from prison, a month after his arrest, via a brief document written and signed by him. We can be sure that the words in that autograph document demand for return of his (and her) clothing and possessions are his. One might think that his answers to the questions put to him in his interrogation—his confession—would also transmit his voice. But there is a complication. For the confession comes to us through what has been called the scribal screen. His words were not recorded exactly as he spoke them, but as the scribe wrote them according to the uses and customs of scribal practice.

Scribes (or *notarios*, as they were also called) were not stenographers and did not record a witness's speech word for word but took notes on the gist of testimony, later filling in remembered details (during silences or, sometimes, much later and in their offices at their writing desks) to provide a sensible and clean copy. Some things actually said were left out of it. Other things may have been added.[1] Taborga's letter, for example, mentioned the penitential practices Don Antonio was supposed to carry out (climbing the Jerusalem steps, whipping himself on Fridays) that are verisimilar enough to ring true but were not recorded by the scribe, just as Taborga's presence was elided from the official record and Rodríguez Romano inserted as presiding legal adviser, himself standing in for an absent president who also signed the official document, García Pizarro.

Even more changes to the witness's speech resulted from the legal tradition of transforming its written account into the third person, as a report by the scribe of *a version* of what the witness said. The confessional voice is double, ventriloquized, as it were. Since one purpose of the investigation and interrogation was to determine Don Antonio's sex, uses of gendering language that reached conclusions about that sex were prejudicial. It was also, however, unavoidable at that time. There was no convention for using, say, third-person singular *they* or *them* in place of *her* or *she*, *him* or *her*, when speaking or writing about another person. *Reading* a statement attributed to Don Antonio that attributes gender in ways that Don Antonio could have entirely avoided in first-person speech is also prejudicial, an effect multiplied threefold by the fact that English requires pronouns in the subject position, whereas Spanish does not.[2]

The scribe (officially, Valda, though the text itself might have been produced by a subordinate) is inconsistent in gendering his report of Don Antonio's speech. He is male as the accused Don Antonio Yta, female once admitting his ascribed name and sex, male again once Don Antonio begins to relate his actions as a man, female again once requestioned and when about to be forced to sign as María Leocadia Yta. The choices are instructive on their own, and readers should consult the translation or original Spanish of the confession in the expediente (see appendix A.7).

We cannot know how Don Antonio gendered himself when he answered the questions put to him. He may have avoided self-gendering or, if he did gender himself, might have used only masculine forms. To grant him approximate agency as speaker, I have lightly edited this presentation of my translation into English of Don Antonio's confessional statements, presenting what is offered by the scribe as his speech in the nongendered first person, while leaving the framing and questions in the scribe's voice and his "voicing" of the questioner's words in their original form. This hopefully also makes the confession more immediate and accessible to twenty-first-century readers.[3]

An advantage of presenting the confession in first person is that it highlights the similarity between confessional self-narrative and the literary
kind, particularly that of the picaresque novel (such as *Lazarillo de Tormes*
and Cervantes's *Quijote* but also the novelized "autobiography" of Catalina
de Erauso, likely produced by an amanuensis).[4] The picaresque genre is so
called for the qualities of its central protagonist, the *pícaro*, who, according
to the dictionary of the Real Academia Española, is a clever, tricky, and
shameless "person of lowly condition, astute, ingenious and of unsavory ways"
(*Diccionario*; my translation). That is certainly the character imputed to a
criminal suspect who has traveled to the colonies without license and in
disguise. And it is also the narrative genre of a confession admitting to these
deeds and aiming to justify them.

Of course, the downside of shifting the scribal third person into first
person is that the apparent immediacy of the text erases the scribe's interventions and conceals the hybrid character of the confession. Be aware, then,
that this is indirectly reported speech, possibly reconstructed from notes from
an actual but unsigned scribe, who then produced the clean copy signed by
Valda.

In the following text, then, I present in deeply indented text the scribe's
presentation of his questions and framing of the event as sworn testimony
(indicating with boldface the scribe's written gendering of Don Antonio
and in italics the added gendered pronouns mandatory in English but not
present in the original Spanish text document). Here and in the translation of
the expediente in appendix A, I have boldfaced instances where the original
Spanish has gendered Don Antonio through pronominal and grammatical
gender. To make the added gendered pronouns required by the English language of the translation stand out, I have italicized the added pronouns in
that translation. In those cases where it is clear which gender a writer might
have chosen, I have used italicized *he, she, him, her, himself, herself*.

Antonio Yta's Confession in the First Person

The person who is called Antonio Yta found himself present before his excellency
so that his confession might be taken: I, the scribe, received the oath in the name
of God Our Lord and, making the sign of the cross, under which *she* promised to

tell the truth about what **she** knew and was to be asked, and in accordance with the preceding decree, asked *her* true name, age, country, and state; *she* said,

My proper name is María Leocadia Yta. I am thirty-two years of age. I am a native of Colmenar de Oreja, seven leagues away from Madrid in Spain. I am single.

Asked with what license **she** came to America, which *she* should show if *she* has it at hand, *she* said,

In the year of 1794, though I do not recall the season, I embarked without license from the Port of Málaga on a commercial vessel sailing for Montevideo. I disembarked in Montevideo. I do not remember the name of the captain of the vessel, nor those of the passengers in whose company I traveled. And that answers the question.

Question: In view of the results of the previous questions, about the vehement suspicion thrown on *her* about the origin of the irregular practice of disguising *her* sex and having set sail without license and in men's clothing, **she** was asked if it results from some crime worthy of inquiry and punishment by the government, the concealment of which may have given rise to *her* practices, and to speak and give an account of what *her* occupation was in Spain before setting sail and what caused *her* to take these steps. And the witness said,

My parents placed me in an Augustinian convent in Colmenar de Oreja, where I took the habit. But before reaching the state of profession, the nuns threw me out, because they said it suited them. So my parents took me back and soon after thought to make a nun of me through the protection of the Lady Duchess Widow of Medinaceli, who placed me in the convent of Franciscans called Santa Juana de la Cruz, near Illescas, four or five leagues from Madrid. I remained there for eleven months, without ever professing. They sent me away after they surprised me with a nun and because they had become persuaded that I was a man. They were confirmed in this opinion by news of this type that had reached the convent from the town of Colmenar de Oreja, where one thing or another had happened to me from the age of fourteen years, when I had taken the habit of the Augustinian of Colmenar. About a year and a half had gone by in the interval between leaving that convent and entering the convent of Santa Juana de la Cruz, though I do not remember for now in which years all that took place.

Once returned to the power of my parents, who are residents and *vecinos* of Colmenar de Oreja, and after about a year, more or less, they disposed that I should take up the habit in Segovia, in the convent of the Bernardas. In effect I did so and stayed there for four or five months, and then I left, or was sent away by the nuns, as a precaution for the same cause that had occasioned my departure from the convent of Santa Juana.

From thence I was conducted to Madrid to the house of my married sister. After the space of about a year, my parents next sent me to the convent of the Franciscans of Huete, where I also wore the habit without ever reaching the state of profession. I stayed there for about six months, though I do not recall in which year it was. Then they too sent me away, handing me over to my sister for the same causes already mentioned, by the disposition of the nuns or, rather, of the chaplains who direct them.

So I again found myself in my sister's house in Madrid. Her name is Leocadia Yta, and she is married to Don Eugenio, whose surname I no longer recall, who is employed in the customs house of Madrid.

On the order of my confessor, I determined to go to Rome. In my sister's power I left a letter for my father giving an account of my resolution to go to Rome. To carry out my plan I took a carriage to the city of Valencia, a journey of some twelve days. On the trip I had no company whatever and traveled with the sole aid of the money I carried with me. Upon arriving in Valencia, with help given by a friend of my father, surnamed Maras, I passed by land to Barcelona. Staying there not more than fifteen days, I took passage, without government license or passport, on a mail ship proceeding from that port to Genoa. I attached myself to two female actors [*operantas*], a mother and daughter, who sailed on the same ship. The passage by sea to Genoa took some twenty or twenty-five days, and we stayed in Genoa for about two months. After that, I embarked once again, along with the same actresses, with the destination of Civitavecchia, and from there, always in the company of those same women, to Rome. Up until that time I always conserved woman's costume.

Finding myself in Rome, I practiced all the diligence that I judged conducive to the quietude of my conscience. This led me to having communicated to me through the Spanish-language penitential confessor, Fray Pedro Ramos Aragones of the Order of San Francisco, that by the command of his holiness I should dress forever afterward in the clothing of a man.

I explained to the penitentiary the difficulties that would of course ensue if I returned to my own country, where they had known me from earliest infancy as a woman. He told me to take the road for whatever place I liked best, but come what may to dress as a man. And I carried out [his command] from then on, from before I left Rome ever since. I remained in that capital about seven months, computing all the time from my arrival to my departure, although I do not remember for now what year it was. So I departed for Civitavecchia, where I embarked destined for Genoa, and from that port to Barcelona, and hence passed to Málaga, and I made all these journeys exclusively dressed as a man. Finally /7v/ in the Port of Málaga, I set out, as I have said, about nine years ago, for Montevideo, destination of that ship.

I stopped in Montevideo for only three days and then passed without license in a river launch to the capital of Buenos Ayres. There I searched for Dr. Juan Antonio Pintos, a merchant of Cádiz and acquaintance of my father. Failing to find him, I presented myself before the Most Illustrious Lord Azamor, bishop of that city, saying that I found myself destitute of help for having failed to find Dr. Juan Antonio Pintos, from whom I hoped for aid, and thus I implored his help, saying that I too was a son of Madrid. As a result of that conversation with the illustrious lordship, the bishop remembered a cousin of mine who he knew, a Discalced Carmelite in Madrid named Fray Julián de San Gerónimo. And finally he told me that I could have food and lodging in his palace. And thus it happened that I stayed in the bishop's house for about three years, until the lord bishop's death. And I made myself known then and since by the name of Antonio Yta.

Finally, I determined to go out on my own, and I departed without passport for Potosí. After the accidental delay of some four months, occasioned by a broken leg, I continued my journey, and in the vicinity of Jujuy ran into a *porteño* surnamed Pazos. In his company and that of his servant I arrived in Potosí six years ago now. There I presented the recommendations I had brought from Buenos Ayres to the lord governor of that town, and he maintained me in his house for around two years.

At the end of that time I left, on the occasion of arranging my wedding with Doña Martina Vilvado y Balverde, who was at that time in Potosí. The lord governor, for being a peninsular Spaniard [*ultramarino*], gave his license, and I contracted matrimony with that lady. After the license was conceded by Dr. Guzmán, the priest of the matrix church of that town, the banns were done there, and the wedding celebrated by the Franciscan, Friar Angel So-and-So, who is now the *procurador* of the convent of the city of Tarija. From that time I stayed two years in that town, with my wife, as a married man, working at whatever /8v/ was offered to me. And having come to this city [La Plata] to solicit some duties, I was asked to go to the province of Moxos with the post of administrator of the town called La Magdalena. I remained a year in the capital carrying out the orders of the lord governor, Zamora, and the other [year] in the town of La Magdalena, where I was administrator. At the end of that time, I returned to this court to solicit my salary, and that docket can be found in the royal audiencia.

Finally, in answer to the question, I add: that the cause that has motivated my maneuver to hide and disguise my womanly sex [*sexo de mujer*] has been to obey his holiness's command, as communicated to me by the penitentiary as I have said, as a result of the labors I practiced in Rome in order to quell my conscience. And that is my response.

> Asked if prior to being informed by the penitentiary in Rome the command said to be of his holiness, any inspection of *her* sex was done, the witness said,

No such inspection whatever preceded it, and that answers the question.

> With that, having held it best, given the difficulties presented by the context of the previous declarations, to inquire with greater punctuality into the identity of this person, who was thus asked for *her* name, *her* parents' names, and place of permanent legal residence [*vecindario*], the witness responded,

My father is called Don Joséf Yta, and my mother Doña Felipa Ybáñez, natives and legal residents [vecinos] of the town of Colmenar de Oreja, who lived at the time I sailed, although today I have no notice of them and do not know if they are alive or dead.

> With that, his excellency ordered this investigation suspended for now, to be continued when it is best suited, ordering that during the interim [the witness] remain in custody, given the decency proper to *her* sex. Having read this to the witness *she* said it is well written and then added,

Before my marriage to Doña Martina Vilvado, I had an illicit relationship with her for a year in the town of Potosí.

> His excellency signed and drew his rubric, to which I give faith.

CALIXTO DE VALDA, HIS MAJESTY'S SCRIBE FOR
THE PUBLIC AND THE CITY COUNCIL.

The Genre of Confesión: Production of an Involuntary Autobiography

Two striking aspects of these statements stand out for the reader. On the one hand, they seem to take a well-developed autobiographical form, constituting a kind of "life story" extending back into childhood of a sort that we may not now associate with legal testimony. On the other hand, what stands out is the vehemence by which Don Antonio sustains his male identity and his sexual agency, particularly since the statement was taken immediately after the medical inspection. These two impressions of the confession clarify Don Antonio's life project. On the one hand, the statement reveals a particularly early modern variety of life narration—a story of becoming, with the speaker playing the agentive role in the making of his or her own life. On the other, who speaks now is Don Antonio, insisting on the completion and success of a transformation from female into male persona that has been narratively achieved and fully embodied.

The first thing to grasp about Don Antonio's confession is its context. Not an unknown quantity in the city of Charcas, Don Antonio had powerful patrons there, including officials of the audiencia. Many knew him personally and had known him for several years, not only as administrator of the town of La Magdalena (a job requiring a formal oath taking ceremony in the audiencia itself) but before that, as the protégé of the powerful Don Francisco de Paula Sanz, intendant governor of the nearby mining center of Potosí, and as page to Bishop Azamor of Buenos Aires. Don Antonio had visited the audiencia in the months before his arrest seeking his back pay through a suit joined by other Moxos administrators. One of Don Antonio's judges, Don Pedro Vicente Cañete, had been legal adviser to Sanz, in whose home and under whose protection Don Antonio had lived for over a year before marrying Doña Martina. The rumor mills would now be asking how Sanz, Bishop Azamor, Cañete, and the other officials who protected and aided Don Antonio in Buenos Aires, Potosí, and La Plata could not have seen through his "disguise of sex." It is possible that because of all this Don Antonio received more delicate treatment than he otherwise would have done, as his interrogators, examiners, judges, and attorneys gingerly avoided smearing their superiors, allies, or opponents in public while eviscerating them in private gossip. Of course, Don Antonio also received favorable treatment from audiencia personnel. Because of his connections and his elevated status as a white, peninsular aristocrat, they allowed him to remain dressed in his male clothing, avoided crude manipulation in the medical examination, and evaded any repetition of that examination or even questioning of Doña Martina.

What kind of statement was Don Antonio's confession? With some prompting and requestioning by the official or stand-in questioners and the official or stand-in scribe, Don Antonio was led to explain himself. The scribe initially titled this document *información*, referring to a kind of elaborate, narrated curriculum vitae that almost all male migrants to the Indies from Spain produced over the course of the colonial era. But informaciones were voluntarily produced, at the instigation of their narrators, to provide an account of honorable genealogies that lead to a story of noble services to the king that might merit a hoped-for reward. Don Antonio, however, was forced to defend himself, to provide grounds for an exculpatory interpretation of the circumstances and events of his life. So then at some point before completing the clean copy of the document, the scribe crossed out *información*, and in the margin retitled the document *confesión*, the term for this sort of autobiography, prompted by the audiencia's presumption of guilt of a *reo*, an accused party. Don Antonio's narrative was not a confession in the sense of an admission of guilt, as nowadays we might interpret the term. Instead, the confesión that Don Antonio was forced to supply took the form of a narrative account of his life. It was a kind of autobiography, but an involuntary one (in Richard Kagan's 2005 phrase), colored by the specifics of the accusation, which it needed to address, whether to deny or explain them.

From the outset, Don Antonio's statement is direct, detailed, and at the same time, on some matters of fact, evasive. In the typical voluntary información (as we shall see, a particular variety of the broader category of *relación*), the statement of name, birthplace, and age are immediately followed by a more or less prolix genealogy—the naming of the speaker's parents, grandparents, and so on, generally to the end of demonstrating an honorable genealogy free from suspicion of being descended from lowly manual-laboring commoners, heretics, or converts from Judaism or Islam. But Don Antonio, perhaps still hoping to keep his parents out of the picture, does not name them until later in the statement, and then only to respond to insistent requestioning. To avoid revealing a stigmatizing genealogy, some social-climbing suspects avoided naming their actual parentage and place of birth, often by inventing them and finding corroborating witnesses to establish the lie as fact. Perhaps such motives played into Don Antonio's evasions, since it does not appear that his claim to *hidalguía* (justifying his use of the "Don") was entirely legitimate. But it is far more likely that his evasions resulted from a long-cultivated habit of obfuscating origins that would give away his former, or concealed, female identity. Of course he had not changed his surname and had used it to point to illustrious relatives and cement his identity as a native of Madrid when seeking help from distant relatives or "countrymen" such as the bishop and even Governor Sanz. But there was always the risk that someone who had actually known Doña María might read or hear of his confession. His questioners surmised that his efforts to conceal his true identity aimed to cover up some past crime. But we might also conclude that Don Antonio aimed to leave out his social origins because he was, more than most Spanish migrants to the Indies, very much a self-made man.

Attributions of Sex and Grammatical Gender

Close attention to how participants in the case gendered Don Antonio, starting with the scribe Valda, has helped reveal the impact of his wife's denunciations, the medical inspection, and the confession and of his prior and subsequent performance as a man. Such attention is aided by my use of boldface in the transcription and translation of the documents when they explicitly gender Don Antonio, whether through the use of pronouns or through personal nouns or other grammatical forms (preserved in the English translation with brackets). Such attention has revealed how participants attribute gender differently to Don Antonio, who is always male for his attorneys, the legal adviser Cañete, and even for the physician and surgeon who examine Don Antonio and find him to be a woman. The ecclesiastical prosecutor, Parra, who believes that Yta "is a hermaphrodite, in whom prevails the manly sex" (appendix A.10), consistently genders Yta male. On first taking charge of the person who has revealed himself to be Doña María Leocadia Yta, the warden of the jail genders Yta female but then switches back to male on all subsequent reports about his prisoner, who has returned to male dress and identity. Doña Martina denounces her male husband, but later (most insistently in the lawsuit over clothing) insists on foregrounding María Leocadia Yta's female sex.[5] Scribes Miguel Mariano Moscoso and Vicente José Marin gender Yta female, while the scribe Valda, who officially takes Don Antonio's confession, shifts back and forth. Don Antonio's mother is deeply inconsistent, as though her image of her child's sex/gender swings back and forth through her narrative. The nuns who certify María Leocadia's admission to, and ejection without professing from, their convents refer exclusively to *her*.[6]

What accounts for this variability? Don Antonio's statement introduces a host of ambiguities and descriptions of sex-linked actions, but even before he (or she) spoke, and while he (or she) was speaking, the scribe and judges felt the indexical force of repeatedly iterated sexed performance. First, there is his male legal personhood, under investigation but never legally changed into a female María Leocadia. Next, the power of sexed names: he remains Don Antonio to most of the judges and jailers. Then the clothing—after the medical examination revealed female sex, the prisoner returned to wearing male clothing, that of an aristocratic Spaniard. Obligatory grammatical gender then introduces *him*, before we learn that *she*, who calls herself María and dressed in women's clothing, had entered a convent. Progressing through a narrated life, *he*, the one they know, who calls himself Antonio and dresses and acts like a man, crosses the Atlantic, travels to Potosí and La Plata, and stands before them now as a man and (until the marriage might be annulled, which it never was) a husband with the rights of one. We can only imagine how Don Antonio's narrative account of these always-sexed (and gendered) actions, indexed through the use of a man's or a woman's name, clothing, and sex-linked activity, colored how the scribe actually saw him, or her, or pictured Antonio or María in his mind's eye in the past action being recounted.

Gendered Genre?

Perhaps it is that very insistence that most confounded the judges, who would have been deeply familiar with these narrative modes of self-fashioning (Greenblatt 1980; Fuchs 2003), which were staples of their profession and also the core of their fictional literature. Or perhaps they were swayed by the fact that this deeply ingrained, well-understood narrative form was *itself* gendered, that is, indicative of maleness. Many tens (or hundreds) of thousands of relaciones are to be found in the archives of the Spanish empire, and scholars would be hard-pressed to find many of them authored by women (or, at least, those dressed and living as such). Women did submit petitions (called informaciones or *pedimentos*), oftentimes portraying themselves humbly as obedient wives and dutiful mothers to gain the court's sympathy for return of stolen property or punishment of violent husbands (Burns 2003). Sometimes, as Marta Vicente has found for late eighteenth-century Barcelona, commercially active women, in the absence of the category "businesswoman," asserted legal rights by adopting the stance of the *mujer varonil*, the "manly woman" (Vicente 2006). Although at a rate many times less frequent than men, women were also accused of crimes and made to explain themselves through confession in the manner of Don Antonio. They were then faced with a choice of language and stance toward it: they might portray themselves as agents in the world, sallying forth to act in search of adventure and wealth or in service to the king, but this was very much a masculine stance. The feminine one was to depict themselves as the relatively innocent, obedient, and passive victims of others' unscrupulousness. At any rate, Don Antonio presented himself to the court as a man, even while telling a tale of a woman passing for one. He presents that passing as a result of obedience to authority, it is true: he sallied out into the world to obey the pope's command and to quiet his own conscience (and one might say, free himself from the limitations of action that it had imposed).

Confesión and Literary Genres of Early Modern Self-Fashioning

As strange as it may seem, the autobiographical life story was the standard shape of a confession in this era. The confesión was a sort of genre of legal argument delivered to a judging authority. As such it has real similarities to the genre of the early modern novel called the *picaresque*. The reader who compares the first-person reconstruction of Don Antonio's confession with the novelized confession of the seventeenth-century "lieutenant nun" Catalina de Erauso, and both with the style of the sixteenth-century quintessential picaresque work *Lazarillo de Tormes*, may note the similarities. Like the confesión, picaresque fiction, still very much in circulation in the early nineteenth century, is addressed to a powerful authority and aims to provide an exculpatory life story that accounts for the misdeeds of which their protagonists have been accused. As Roberto González Echevarría (1990) has argued, picaresque fiction can be read as a burlesque critique of the documentary "cousins" of the información, the petition-like documents titled *relación* or *probanza de méritos y servicios* (relation or proof of merits and services), the volunteered narrative curricula vitae that thousands of Spaniards, from the sixteenth century to the end of empire, submitted to the Crown as evidence, not of misdeeds, but of admirable and loyal service, meriting reward from on high (MacLeod 1998).

The autobiographical *relación de méritos y servicios* (which when accompanied by sworn testimony of witnesses became a *probanza*) were also the kind of first-person sources that the king's chroniclers used in the construction of their chronicles, which themselves were the fodder of histories (see Restall 2003, 12–14). Yesteryear's chroniclers and today's historians are aware that such documents are always self-serving, and therefore unreliable, and already at the end of the sixteenth century, ordinary Spaniards had come to the same conclusion (Folger 2011). Such CV-like works, written by or for thousands of striving individuals seeking reward from the king, were not only increasingly regarded as fictional, in the sense of containing partial truths or outright lies, but, in their adhesion to a standard form proclaiming honorable deeds, became boring and worthy of satire. To write a chronicle or a history, the relaciones or informaciones of many individuals involved in events such as the conquest of Peru were cross-compared to produce a single, purportedly more reliable and less self-interested story, not of a single individual's deeds but of the broader *events* in which they were involved. The writing and reading of picaresque fiction, drawing on the "real life" confesión, which included narration of less-than-honorable, unusual, and even criminal deeds, was one way of highlighting the interestedness and unreliability of the relación or información, which, like the literary genre that the picaresque displaced, the romance of chivalry, adheres to a predictable script of honorable deeds performed as service. Of course, the confesión was also a known genre of life narrative shaped by conventions, as were the relación and información and the romance of chivalry. But the picaresque and the confesión (no less full of fiction in the sense of untruths, as Natalie Zemon Davis [1987] has shown) foreground a more individualizing kind of self-fashioning, resistant to tradition, law, service to the king, and the God-given order of things that characterizes the romance of chivalry and the relación and *probanza de méritos*.

Foregrounding the active agency of the protagonist in service of self-making (not their adhesion to a given moral order), the confesión, like the picaresque novel, was the more "modern" genre of life narrative, one that accorded to the experience of a world full of striving, self-fashioning social climbers.[7] The confesión was nonetheless still constrained by requirements of intelligibility to its readers or audience, beginning with the need to recognize a succession of occurrences and actions as the development of a plot that will reveal a perhaps sympathetic individual emerging from the interaction of recognizable kinds of person, character, sex, occupation, career, and human possibility in a particular time and place. In other words, Don Antonio Yta confesses to be understood as a self-made agent, where the *she* who he speaks about has worked hard to become *he* who now speaks, and to do so he draws on narrative conventions that circulated among the contexts of the courtroom, literature, and everyday banter and gossip.

Readers of Cervantes's *Quijote* or the anonymous *Lazarillo de Tormes* indulged their cynicism about self-interested accounts of heroic and loyal service, now revealed as evidence, above all, of self-fashioning as social climbing, in which the undeserving rise in life owing to their connections and guile rather than their selflessness and through deeds rather than through inherited status. Social climbing as such, particularly when it included concealment of humble origins or debased condition, that is, *passing*, was roundly condemned and even feared in this era, even as the image of the striving individual was increasingly celebrated. The early nineteenth-century Spanish Empire remained essentially patrimonial, dependent on a concatenated hierarchy of proud but generous patrons and humble but striving clients, hoping through their service to patrons to rise into the very shoes of those they served. As we shall see, Doña María, and then Don Antonio, depended on service as criada or criado (servant or ward or subservient, kin-like house guest) to powerful patrons to accomplish each successive step up the social scale and across a gender divide that granted "self-fashioning" (Delbrugge 2015) agency in the world (and in sexual relations!) only to men.

Self-fashioning of the sort revealed in the narrative form of the confesión and picaresque novel was itself gendered. The vast majority of classic *pícaro* antiheroes of picaresque fiction, like the central agents of 99 percent of confesiones, relaciones, and informaciones, were men. Of course, there were women writers of fiction (Zayas y Sotomayor 1989) and autobiography (such as that of "La Santa Juana" [Surtz 1990]), and the eighteenth century was also an era of dramatically increased personal litigation, including that of women seeking divorce or protection of their financial interests. That increase in litigation has been brilliantly studied by Bianca Premo (2017), who convincingly describes it as a source of Enlightenment "from below," an unprecedented demand for recognition of individual rights, especially notable for the strength of such demands on the periphery of empire (the colonies) and for the spectacular growth of legal claims by the oppressed (women, slaves, indigenous people, castas). All the same, such textual genres describe modes of being "master of one's own life" that for elite men were deeply marked (as was the very idea of the "rights bearing subject") as Spanish, aristocratic, and male.

Women who wrote or spoke this way to male authorities stepped onto dangerous, androgynous ground, while men from the "underclasses" were tarred for their potentially seditious presumptuousness. The Crown took note of such turns and, particularly in the wake of the egalitarian language of mass rebellion and revolution, sought to clamp down on them, with reforms aiming to put such rebels against absolutism, God-given social estate, colonial subordination, and patriarchalism back in their places.

When women gave testimony or wrote in such ways, going out into the world to "make themselves," they challenged the sexual dimorphism both of social space, in the house-street divide, and of intentional action, in the division of agents from "patients." Being active agents in the world was definitive of masculinity, but for women it continued to connote something problematic. If they were themselves nonlaboring aristocrats and were demonstrably chaste, they were defined as the sometimes admirable *mujeres varoniles*, manly women. As we shall see in the next chapter, the training of novice nuns (and guidebooks for the instruction of wives) highlighted the importance of turning away from "the world," drawing up into themselves within enclosed spaces, away from material temptations, to enable them to develop spiritually, but if they were commoners engaged also in labor and commerce outside the home, they were *mujeres mundanas* or *públicas* ("worldly" or "public" women, both also euphemisms for prostitute).

Exceptions to the rule stand out in the autobiographical works of figures such as Santa Teresa de Ávila, Sor Juana Inés de la Cruz, and "la Santa Juana" (See Bilinkoff 2015; Juana de la Cruz [1509] 1982; Merrim 1999; Daza 1613; Tirso de Molina 1613–14; Surtz 1990; and Spadaccini and Talens 1991). Nuns all, their subordination of the will and mortification of the body (including renunciation of sexuality, and particularly of bodily marriage to men as opposed to a spiritual marriage to Christ) granted them just the right sort and degree of ambiguity of sex to be admired and even celebrated (after sustained suspicion and interrogation by their priest confessors and the Inquisition) as *mujeres varoniles*, manly women (McKendrick 1974; Perry 1987). Catalina de Erauso, the "transvestite nun" whose life as a male soldier in the Indies was recorded in a *probanza de méritos y servicios*, as well as a partly apocryphal autobiography (Erauso [1592] 1829, 1992, 1996, 2002), and celebrated in a play that young Doña María may well have seen (Pérez de Montalbán [1626] 1839) was also accorded such standing, honored by both king and pope after revealing that he was a woman (Velasco 2000). But such honors in Erauso's case had depended not only on performing military service for the king but also on never having married and having remained a virgin during those many swashbuckling years (Perry 1999). That was not to be Don Antonio's approach.

Speaking of the Penis: Enunciating and Performing Masculinity

After his statement was read back to him, and in full knowledge that his wife's request for an annulment on the grounds of nonconsummation might be granted were he to agree with her claim that there had been no sexual intercourse, Don Antonio chose to add only that "with Doña Martina Vilvado, before having celebrated what is called matrimony, [I] maintained an illicit friendship" [that is, a sexual one, a claim reinforced when Taborga says in his letter they were *amancebado*, suggesting that she was his concubine] for the duration of a year in the said Villa de Potosí" (appendix A.7). He then signed his confession, not as Don Antonio, but as María Leocadia Yta. Of course the circumstances under which he did so were narratively coercive: his "womanly sex" had already been established, and he had just told a life story beginning with his former female identity.

In any case it soon became clear that Don Antonio had relinquished neither his name nor his sex. Thus, a month later he would launch a lawsuit against Martina, asserting his rights as husband and signing off as Don Antonio (B.8). Much later, near the end of the case, Don Antonio's mother, in a letter to the judges in La Plata (A.21), was even more adamant about the functionality of the alleged virile member, pointing to witnesses to "the act" as well as to paternity suits, and raising the possibility of hermaphrodism, something certain of the participants in the case seemed eager to find.

Antonio Yta's final assertion of having an "illicit relationship" risked legal jeopardy (a possible further accusation of sodomy). This fact and the forcefulness of his claim, made during a medical examination, of having a functional member, paint a portrait of an abiding sense of masculinity, assumed or not. The strength of that masculinity is further underscored by his assertion of a husband's authority and rights and his maleness as Don Antonio when, after a month in a sunless jail cell, without clothing adequate to La Plata's high-altitude cold, he filed suit against Martina, on November 5, 1803, demanding return of his clothing—he had only the one suit of (male) clothing he been wearing when arrested—and also delivery of his wife's entire wardrobe and possessions.

In the lawsuit (B.8), Don Antonio's lawyer insinuates that Doña Martina came to the marriage in poverty, acquiring her considerable wardrobe and jewelry at Don Antonio's expense. Now a disappointed gold digger, unwilling to submit to the bonds of marriage, she was out for her black revenge (fols. 4r–v, 8r). Doña Martina's reply insists, to the contrary, that all his possessions had been bought with her money, suggesting that he had failed to provide for her in the manner that custom demanded and indeed had sold off her things to pay for his own (fols. 6r–v). What is more, she points to veiled insinuations and threats she found in what appear to be simple lists of articles of clothing (fol. 6v).

Outraged by the fact that Don Antonio aims to recover these marital goods through his husbandly rights and that he has signed his demand as Don Antonio, continuing to claim both male sex and male name a full month after his "womanly sex" was revealed, Martina refers to Antonio, only as *her*, María, even when slurring him as a jealous and violent husband. As Martina puts it, "this woman has been damaging to me, not only with the disguise and concealment of *her* sex and punishable simulation of matrimony but also by having nearly stripped me of all I had in order to dress herself up, keeping me in check by being an angry and violent and very jealous husband; it is astonishing that she still appears in her note speaking as if she were a man, throwing on me in a dissimulated way many challenges and threats" (B.8, fol. 6v).

A close reading of the lists of clothing and other property reveals what do appear to be threats, although it is likely that some would have been private references known only to Antonio and Martina. Most obviously threatening is a little whip with a silver tip of a sort that might have been used for urging along a horse or for flagellating a person (or one's self). But some items point to stories, known to Martina, that Don Antonio might yet tell:

Three hand cloths, two plain and one entirely of tatting, that at its time I will tell of;
   One set of tack and a sidesaddle;
   One perfume pot, which at its time I will also tell about. (appendix B.8, fol. 2r)

Presumably, the threat of telling the stories involving the handkerchief and perfume pot, and perhaps the tack and sidesaddle, is meant to compel Doña Martina to deliver the goods. Quite possibly those stories involve some sort of crime (might they be stolen?) or they might have been used in sexual acts, revelation of which would undermine Doña Martina's posture of innocence or even implicated her in the criminal act of sodomy.

Perhaps the expensive and even faddish continental fashions named in the couple's lists of clothing served their purposes well for Don Antonio, and even for Doña Martina, as they moved among elite high-society peninsular and Creole Spaniards in Potosí, La Plata, and Cochabamba, the three cities meant for Spanish occupation in the region. They would have been rather obscenely out of place, however, in the province of Moxos and in the formerly "utopian" little indigenous mission town (now converted into a system of forced manufactures for the market, without the Jesuits' lofty civilizational goals) of La Magdalena, where these two might have had a social life among peers only with the local priest, with whom, in any case, Don Antonio would have been at great odds, given his duties there.

Into Jail and the Wind

Chased out of La Magdalena after a brief year, returned to Cochabamba (probably to his in-laws' house), and then, seeking his back pay, denounced by Martina and arrested, inspected, and confessed, Don Antonio suffered from the cold and demanded his husbandly right to recover his property from his no-longer-obedient wife. According to Doña Martina, Don Antonio's fashionable clothing was tattered and worn out from use by the time he demanded it from her from his jail cell, a month after her denunciation and his arrest. Whoever provided the money to pay for the clothing, there was apparently not any left to buy more. Doña Martina's description of Antonio's hat sums up her assessment of the poverty into which they had been thrown in the wake of the unfortunate posting to La Magdalena and the lack of pay since its ending: "The hat arrived from Cochabamba all in pieces and eaten by cockroaches, and because of its uselessness she gave it to the boy who serves her" (appendix B.8, fol. 10r).

Called Antonio by some and María by others during his imprisonment, himself insisting on his male identity, Don Antonio now awaited judgment. The wheels of the law, however, turn slowly. This was especially the case because Martina and her attorneys stalled and hedged at every turn. It was also because secular judges refused to turn over key original documents from the case file to the ecclesiastical court. Part of that delay resulted from a long history of recently intensified mistrust and competition over their respective jurisdictions.[8] Another part may have been the secular judges hope to resolve the case without subjecting Don Antonio to another medical inspection and without causing further embarrassment to the highly placed officials, such as Intendant Governor Sanz, who had taken him in, or been taken in by him. There were also further questions to answer. Perhaps they hoped for further clarification from Doña Martina (never forthcoming) about the couple's sex life, perhaps revealing cause (the use of a "foreign instrument" such as a dildo for penetration) for a charge of sodomy. They more certainly hoped to learn more about Don Antonio's life, as María, back in Spain, where some previous life of crime might have explained his long-term imposture of sex and disguise of identity. If Doña María had taken final vows as a nun (thus marrying Christ), Don Antonio's marriage to Martina might be a case of bigamy. In any case, they kept Don Antonio in jail, some of that time in stocks, for almost a year without any additional questioning.

But neither church nor state prosecutors had the opportunity to proceed with legal maneuverings. For on Friday, September 21, 1804, at 9:30 or 10:00 p.m., Don Antonio Yta escaped from jail, according to the warden of the jail, with the collusion of the *indio pongo* (an indigenous servant whose job it was to guard and care for prisoners in the absence of the bailiff). We may wonder, of course, whether this was truly an escape or instead an unofficial release carried out with the collusion of a judge, for which one possible motive was sympathy with the accused, and another simply washing the audiencia's hands of an irresolvable case that was an embarrassment for powerful men, while preventing the ecclesiastical court from pressing for additional, also embarrassing and probably useless medical examinations.

After the escape, the matter of determining Don Antonio's sex, and if or how Doña Martina might now be granted an annulment, was complicated yet further by the arrival of a statement from Don Antonio's mother that served only to make the case more complicated and his or her sex more ambiguous. Well-educated, Enlightenment-era judges and lawyers continued to wrestle with the question for another year before turning the case definitively over to the ecclesiastical prosecutor of the archbishopric (also located in the city of La Plata), in the archive of which no trace of the case file appears to survive.[9]

Lawyers and judges and La Plata's gossips wrestled with the concepts at hand to understand the phenomenon of Antonio who had been, or was also María, a seeming contradiction in terms. Same-sex love was certainly well known to occur in this era and was formally condemned; expressions of affection between two unrelated men or women might become evidence in a trial that involved actual criminal acts, and indeed the existence of persons with a propensity to love another of the same rather than opposite sex was already common knowledge. Even so, as Michel Foucault ([1976] 1990) argued, "medicalized" formal terms for such persons (homosexual, lesbian) had not yet been invented to name what he termed a "hermaphrodism of the soul," and those who the label might have fit were not yet ascribed by medical or state classifications into a category of flawed identity. Doña María might have been punished for committing a same-sex act, but not (yet) for being a person of routinely same-sex desires. But it was not Doña María who stood accused. It was the well-worn legal subject, Don Antonio Yta, and it was his long-term success at convincing others of his maleness that left his lawyers and judges in confusion.

Discovering by examination his apparently female genitalia did not resolve the question of his "true sex" but only complicated it. The judges' conundrum resulted from what we might now say was their inability to distinguish (bodily) sex and (performed) gender, although some among them earnestly struggled to understand what for others was unthinkable. As we shall see, they all knew about transvestism in the theater and the possibility of impersonation as an "act." But the (quite common) theatrical impersonation of men by female actors was invariably produced in the register we now call "drag"; through obvious "tells" the audience was meant to "see through" what they were to know was a disguise (see Newton 1972 and Butler 1990), since the plots of these plays depended on such "knowing" (Bravo Villasante 1955; McKendrick 1974). Don Antonio's impersonation did not fit this model.

Imagine then the difficulty for Don Antonio's judges in 1803, without the concept of gender as a performative, cultural construct, to understand how he could convincingly live and act as a man while having an apparently female body. It then becomes more intelligible to us why some of those involved in the case, including judges, the highest ecclesiastical authority in the region, and Don Antonio's own mother, searched for clarity in the concept of hermaphrodism. Don Antonio himself took to the idea. We might explain it thus: Doña María Yta had so routinely and convincingly become Don Antonio in performance that those who knew him brought into being his male "cultural genitals," what is presumed to exist concealed beneath manly clothes, indexed by a host of coordinated performative acts, and could not give them up without falling into hopeless confusion. For Don Antonio himself, of course, the penis he experienced "in the act" had a different experiential and sensory kind of reality, reinforced by the rest of his manly acts, beginning with the agentive fact that it was he who was doing the touching.

The jurist Taborga had concluded that Don Antonio's masculinity was pure artifice, the result of a perversion of character, or being "sick in the head." If today we would resolve the apparent contradiction between appearances and underlying reality differently, not pointing to the body beneath the clothed indices of masculinity but to an even deeper underlying mental reality, Don Antonio's male mind or identity that was belied by having the wrong body and brought back into proper alignment through his costumed performativity, we still rely in our judgment on a distinction between exterior indexes of something and interior states to which they point. That distinction seems central to emplotting Don Antonio's deeds within a narrative meant to reveal his otherwise invisible moral character. Moral character, the stuff of theater, the novel, and everyday gossip, hinges on the complex issue of intentionality, a matter of mind. That is precisely what Don Antonio himself referred to as conscience.

Taborga and Doña Martina saw Don Antonio's performative maleness as an act of deception, itself indicative of poor character and bad intentions. Drawing on a dramatic topos of long literary and scriptural genealogy, they attributed to him the very flaw (or defining feature of humans) that exiled us from the Eden (or Olympus) of godly immortality. Don Antonio's confessional narrative sought to recontextualize the imputation of intentions, to make his motive in concealing his visibly female body and past into something laudable rather than suspect: to reconcile his conscience. Prior to the invention of an interior, enduring "true self" or "identity" from the state-endorsed biopolitical science of psychology (Wahrman 2006, Mak 2013), there was conscience, a concept that embraced not only the self-judgmental attribute of immaterial and immortal soul but individual reflexive consciousness more generally, the source and seat of the speaking *I*. When Don Antonio asserted not only that his dissimulation of sex had been carried out to reconcile his conscience, and then insisted that he had carried out the act with Doña Martina for a year before they were married, he may have raised the possibility that Doña María might be accused of the crime of sodomy, but he reinforced the notion that reconciliation of conscience required that he and his conscience *be* male, not just *act* like he was.

Don Antonio's dexterity in telling his life story and acting manly left his judges in a conundrum. They were left with no crime to pin on him, nor any apparent will to in fact bring him to trial, which would have forced them to make a legal determination of his sex. So that we may avoid falling into confusion ourselves we must take a much closer look at Doña María's and Don Antonio's life and begin to tease out just what kind of performance made Don Antonio convincingly male.

We need, that is, to understand how Don Antonio's contemporaries understood and properly performed their sex, life stages, roles in life, social estate or class, and so on. Don Antonio's clothing had helped to "make the man," along with an effort to speak in masculine ways (directly and in the imperative, we might imagine), adopting a proper stylization of the body—beginning with a masculine swagger and compression of the breasts with tightly wrapped cloth—and satisfactorily fulfilling the era's sex roles, themselves always intersectional.

How did he do it? To answer that question we need to explore, first, how everyone else did, that is, to examine the era's sartorial codes, the fashion system that governed the deployment of varieties of social skin (culturally elaborated resurfacings of the body) and the category and group distinctions that they cited and produced: those that distinguished male from female, children from adults, commoners from aristocrats, secular persons from the religious (priests and nuns), the free from the enslaved, legitimate from illegitimate, master from servant, patron from client or criado, and in the colonies Spaniards from Indians, mestizos, Afro-descended persons, and persons of mixed descent or culture, or castas.

To do so, we must get a bit more precise about what is meant by describing gender as a performative social construct, something to do with the wearing of clothes, the performance of habituated sex- and gender-marked enactments associated with particular sex- and gender-marked statuses and roles, and attribution to their wearers and performers of male or female kinds of identity. If in this chapter we have focused on the kinds of speech and writing called narrative, generally kinds of storytelling involving episodic deeds and the development through them of morally marked character, the following chapters turn to the kinds of meaning making that can be read from the clothed body and sometimes silent practices. We turn, that is, to hábitos.

CHAPTER 2

HABITS

*María's Apprenticeships in
a Cross-Dressing Culture*

Praxiography of the Social Skin and the Schemas of Hábitos and Habitus

When Don Antonio provided under questioning his involuntary autobiography, he spoke of his life as girl and woman as well as a man. He detailed a girlhood spent between service to a noblewoman and stints at home (in Colmenar and in Madrid) with his parents or in his sister's house, in convents, and as a traveler, sometimes accompanied and sometimes alone, across Spain and the Mediterranean (see map 1). He referred vaguely a few times to clothing, male or female or nun's style, and suggested a demeanor in convents that was unwelcome there. Similarly, Don Antonio's mother suggests that Doña María's behavior had been problematic from an early age, particularly María's inclination toward women, and ensuing behaviors such as cross-dressing as a man and engaging in "the act" with women, in at least one instance while clothed, as a man.

This chapter treats Don Antonio's life as Doña María. While the account is pieced together from narrative sources, I do not limit myself here to the texts but rather draw on many other sources to depict in greater detail the contexts of those narratives and the specifics of costumed practices in them that were elided from the narratives. Left out for being taken-for-granted aspects of everyday life well known to their contemporary interlocutors, they must be filled in for us to appreciate the story as contemporaries would have done.

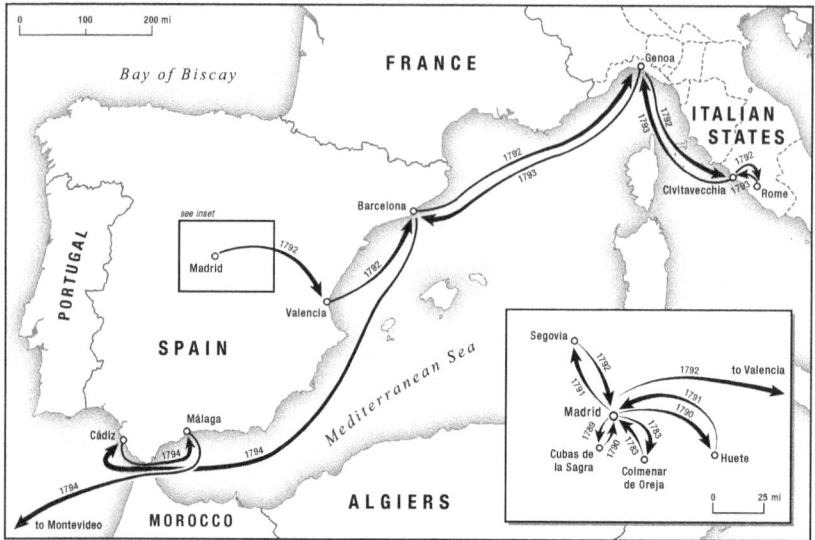

MAP 1 María Yta's itinerary of transition in the Mediterranean, age twenty to twenty-three (inset: María Yta's itineraries in the Madrid region, age nine to twenty). Map by Erin Greb Cartography.

My account gives particular attention not only to contexts, including the architectural and infrastructural forms within which described social action occurred, but to habits, or in Spanish, *hábitos*. Hábitos refers not only to the nun's costume but to a clothing system more generally and to the performances that point, along with the clothing, to certain statuses and roles. I take up the spirit of ethnography, writing about others' culture or, perhaps, of praxiography (Mol 2003; Mak 2013), writing their practices. Yet this account is not based on participant observation but on the reading of texts with an eye to contextualized action, aided by the use of visual images of clothing and experience with the kinds of still-standing built form and infrastructures through which Doña María passed. It is, then, perhaps better described as a social and cultural history informed by theoretical approaches to human action drawn from sociology, anthropology, and anthropological linguistics.

In this chapter we attend not to Don Antonio's body per se, but to the aspects of its surface and its acts that made him readable to others as a kind of person. That surface, at birth, is the skin and the hair. But as Terence S. Turner brilliantly observed, the human person "is born naked but is everywhere in clothes (or their symbolic equivalents)." "The surface of the body, as the common frontier of society, the social self, and the psycho-biological individual, becomes the symbolic stage upon which the drama of socialisation is enacted, and bodily adornment (in all its culturally multifarious forms, from body-painting to clothing and from head-dresses to cosmetics) becomes the language through which it is expressed" (1980, 112–13).

Here we focus on clothing and body modification (such as treatments of the hair) as one of the meanings of the term *habits*, or *hábitos*, but also to the other meanings of those terms, habituated acts expressing culturally significant kinds of demeanor, character, statuses, and roles.[1] Hábitos, as I shall treat them, bear striking similarity to Pierre Bourdieu's concept of *habitus*, referring to habituated practices and stances toward the world (1990).[2] Himself drawing from a philosophical and sociological tradition including Blaise Pascal and Edmund Husserl, Bourdieu defines habitus as "systems of durable, transposable dispositions, structured structures predisposed to function as structuring structures, that is, as principles which generate and organize practices and representations that can be objectively adapted to their outcomes without presupposing a conscious aiming at ends or an express mastery of the operations necessary in order to attain them" (1990, 53).

For Bourdieu, habitus gains systematicity through its organizing schemas (1990, 81–93), patterns or bundles of features of particular habitus, always understood in relation to kinds of also patterned contexts. To take a ready example, imagine someone in Doña María's day meeting an unknown person on the street. They might immediately be able to identify a member of the high nobility from their costume, not only from its cut but from its colors and materials and tailoring, exhibiting a great deal of skill and time in manufacture. They might then note the person's demeanor, their embodied attitude toward others displayed through ways of looking and speaking (or not doing so), their apparent level of ease in inhabiting their costume, and so on. Applying to the stranger a place in a system of social classification by virtue of a bundle of sensible attributes going well beyond costume, they then know how, given their own clothed and enacted place in the world, to react: whether to defer, eyes down, quickly getting out of the way of someone dangerously superior; to politely supplicate them; or to greet them as an equal. The first thing they may have noted was that person's sex, not by examining their genitals or even secondary sex characteristics, which vary so much as to be misleading, but through the rest of the costumed performance, in which sex is subsumed within other social hierarchies.

Our person's rapid evaluation was made possible by their knowledge of the organizing schemas of habituated practice, and knowing how to respond by their understanding of the relationship among organizing schemas among varied fields or contexts of social interaction, in this case, that of public inter-action on the street (other fields here being, for example, festivals versus everyday activity, public interactions in the street or square versus kinship relations in the home, the aristocratic household versus the religious convent or the university, the Crown bureaucracy versus paid manual labor, etc.).

Because Bourdieu's habitus is sufficiently close to the "native" category of hábitos, I use the two terms interchangeably. I then address the question of the systematicity of hábitos through Bourdieu's concept of organizing schemas. Given that hábitos are enactments, sometimes pointing to named statuses or roles recognized through a bundle of signaled features organized by schemas, it is important to consider what kind of signaling wearing a uni-form, for instance, might be. "Police officer" as a noun is the kind of sign that Ferdinand de Saussure (2011) treated as purely conventional: a sound pattern linked only by convention to a concept. The uniform and other elements of a police officer's hábitos, however, signal in different ways. They point to, or index, very specific aspects of the wearer's status and role; the uniform and badge (or warrant card) index "police officer" as the embodied identity of the person wearing them, while two-way radio, gun, nightstick, and handcuffs point to specific capacities for social action that person is warranted to carry out, capacities also indexed in the police officer's manner of looking and addressing one on the street. Indexes, as nonconventional kinds of signaling bound up with the material affordances of sign vehicles, are (along with icons, those signs that look like that which they represent) at the heart of hábitos, as their pragmatics.

I therefore also take up, without aiming for precision, the analytic frame-work of pragmatic linguistics (Hanks 2005; Harkness 2015; Keane 2003; Silverstein 1976) to consider just how Bourdieu's schemas are produced, through talk about talk, and action about action, at the intersection of metase-mantic and metapragmatic operations that bracket words and deeds or things out of ordinary usage to highlight and comment on or define them.[3] Bourdieu describes habitus as something acquired in the manner of riding a bicycle, accomplished without conscious understanding of the kinds of coordination involved and incorporated in a habitual form that naturalizes them. But not everyone has the inclination to easily adopt hábitos in such an unreflective manner. Doña María was a girl for whom acting as one does not appear to have come naturally. Describing the specific contexts where bracketed forms of commentary on the hábitos Doña María was supposed to inhabit should help to clarify how persons in need of stage directions for life, when lifelong experience has not directly prepared them for living at ease in chosen hábitos, might nonetheless acquire the ability to do so.

Stage directions are just what Doña María apparently needed for being a girl and woman. The term points both to dramaturgical approaches to social action as performance that complement analysis as this chapter progresses (Goffman 1959, 1963; Roach 1996; Schechner 1985; D. Taylor 2003; V. Turner 1982) and to the theater itself, a core experience in many of Doña María's life contexts. As a ritualized form of social action, bracketed by the stage itself, which served to comment on the hábitos of everyday life and particularly on the gulf that sometimes divides outward appearances and inner reality, we find theatrical performance to have been a key source of reflexive knowledge about the organization and workings of hábitos. For Doña María, theater complemented other kinds of metapragmatic training in the schemas of hábitos, such as the training and repeated correction to which she was subject when entering a convent or a grandee's palace in a new life role; following her through her initiations into such hábitos and her opportunities for gaining reflexive understanding of them as parts of a broader system integrating the performance of costumed hábitos with an equally systematic set of values will help us see how the forceful efforts of others to make her into a proper girl and woman served to teach her also how to be a man. Drawing analogies among the schemas organizing different hábitos in a series of different social fields (parent's home, grandee's house, convent, etc.) lets us see how learning to wear a dress might make pants intelligible or repeated apprenticeship as a novice nun in the recogimiento (cloistering or gathering into oneself) that was heralded as the way to be a chaste, world-renouncing nun might translate into knowledge of how to embody a man's desenvoltura (unconstrained ease of action).

The tall order for this chapter, then, is to discover what specific *kinds* of girl and woman Doña María had been, by attending to the systematicity of the

hábitos characteristic of young Spanish women from the lower end of aristocracy in the 1770s and 1780s and their place in a broader system of hábitos
embracing the roles into which Doña María would step as Don Antonio. It
means discovering how the hábitos of both were contrasted with alternative
hábitos of social estate, civil or religious status, or contrasting legal standing.
Those first twenty-one years of life were peripatetic, involving many changes
of hábitos in quite a variety of contexts. We work through them in sequence,
making use of our eclectic set of approaches to the analysis of embodied and
clothed social action.

Acquiring Feminine Hábitos: Doña María's Childhood in Colmenar de Oreja and Madrid

Don Antonio reported in his confession that his true name was Doña María
Leocadia Yta, native of Colmenar de Oreja. A search in that town's archives
turns up documents that show that Doña María's father, Joséf de Yta, was
raised in and purchased a home in that town and there married Doña María's
mother, Felipa. Yet by the time Felipa wrote her letter in support of "that son
of hers" María, Felipa, like Doña María's sister and brother-in-law, resided at
court, that is, in Madrid. Doña María's baptismal record is not to be found
in the parish archives of Colmenar de Oreja. Other evidence, such as Felipa's
statement that young María was taken in by a "powerful lady of the town
of her birth" and Don Antonio's identification of that powerful lady as the
Duchess Widow of Medinaceli, who resided in Madrid not Colmenar, suggests that Doña María was born in Madrid about the year 1771. As happened
with all newborns, her parents examined their new child and particularly
the genitals. On that basis of that examination (to be repeated with each
change of diapers), she was ascribed the female sex and was baptized and
raised as a girl.

Don Antonio claimed the honorific "Don" for himself and for Doña María
in his prior life. He also claimed that status for his parents, Don Joséf Yta and
Doña Felipa Ybañez. Being called Don or Doña at that time would have been
a sign of being among their hometown of Colmenar's small contingent of
hidalgos. In the court (that is, Madrid), they would have been among a larger
contingent so privileged but overshadowed by the presence of high and titled

nobility. *Hidalguía* was the lowest rung of the aristocracy but still a matter of considerable presumption that required distinction, even ostentation, in dress and proper expressions of disdain for commoners if one expected to be taken for a member. Until the late eighteenth century, hidalgos were exempt from the *pechos* (head tax or tribute) that the commoners (called *pecheros*) were required to pay to the king or to the noble house with jurisdiction over them.[4] Although belonging to one of these categories was a matter of descent, social mobility was also possible—one could move from pechero to hidalgo by Crown recognition of ennobling deeds or acquired wealth. One of these latter ways must have been how Joséf Yta acquired his Don, because when we first encounter him in the archival record, he was a nine-year-old child of decidedly poor and pechero parents who rented a house and grew vegetables for the market in the town of Colmenar de Oreja (see appendix B.1).

Seven leagues from Madrid (in today's measures, thirty-five miles), Colmenar de Oreja today is a short drive south of Spain's capital city. It is small (population 8,619, according to the town's website) and quaint enough to have been used as a "typically Spanish" location in many Franco-era films focusing on the customs and traditions of "deep Spain" and as a Mexican town in U.S. Westerns such as *The Magnificent Seven*.[5] For several centuries it had been a *villa*, a self-governing republic with an annually elected municipal council. Largely dedicated to agropastoral pursuits, most of those vecinos tilled fields; pastured sheep, goats, horses, donkeys, and mules; tended to olive groves and vineyards; made bread and wine and olive oil; wove cloth; and made enormous ceramic jars known as *tinajas* (for storing wine and olive oil).

Relatively prosperous by the standards of the day, Colmenar de Oreja was located on the Tajo River, giving it ample irrigated fields and extensive fruit orchards as well as significant crops of *cañamo*, hemp, and *esparto* grass; in 1751 nearly 150 of the town's poorer residents twined hemp-fiber rope and wove baskets, sandals, saddlebags, mats, and other goods using *esparto*. Extensive vineyards and olive groves produced a significant part of the olive oil, table olives, and wine consumed in the nearby capital city. On the highway that linked Madrid with Andalusia, Colmenar was also home to a significant force of transport workers, driving horse and mule carts and sometimes oxcarts. The latter were used for transport to Madrid and the royal palace there, and that of Aranjuez, of the white stone quarried by another sector of the laboring population who worked in Colmenar's quarries.

In spite of its relative prosperity as an average-sized Castilian town at the end of the eighteenth century, only a small fraction of the population used "Don" or "Doña" in front of their names in the detailed census and *catastro* (register of properties by household) conducted there in 1751 by the Marques de la Ensenada. That census lists 1,200 vecinos (heads of household) and 4,500 *almas* (total population) and provides a detailed accounting of the 750 houses they occupied, lands owned or rented, occupations, and annual income. Of 1,200 vecinos, only 56 men and women (4.6 percent of vecinos) were given a Don or Doña preceding their names. Many of these are among the town's landowning wealthy farmers, its *labradores*, and even more among the town's *forasteros*, people born and registered as vecinos elsewhere but resident in, and owning property and financial interests in, the town.

In 1751 seven vecino households were headed by someone surnamed Yta: all were engaged in humble professions, including a quarryman, a shepherd, a day laborer, and one person listed as *pobre* (poor), without possessions or income other than that gained through begging. Finally, one Yta appears in the list of *hortelanos* (vegetable gardeners and purveyors). This last person, Bernardo de Yta, rented his family's home from another man. He declared a few small properties owned outright and a few other rented fields. Among his children, the eldest, eighteen years old in 1751, was Joséf de Yta.[6] Thus Joséf de Yta would have been twenty-nine years old in 1762, when he married Felipa Ybáñez. Although they appear to have been the most well-off of the Yta families in Colmenar de Oreja, they were not counted among the town's hidalgos in 1751.

Looming over the center of town is the church of Santa María la Mayor (fig. 1), and in that church's archive a registry of marriages corresponding to the year 1762 contains the marriage certificate of Joséf and Felipa. The certificate does not prefix Don and Doña before their names, or even those of Felipa's parents, though it does provide that honorific for one of the witnesses. It seems that the family rose in social status over the next few decades. Joséf and Felipa must have come into some money by 1770, about the time of María's birth, because in that year *Joseph de Yta el Maior, yerno de Ybáñez* (the older Joseph de Yta, son-in-law of Ybáñez) purchased a house and other properties in Colmenar de Oreja.[7] Not just any house; it was the one in which he grew up, that rented by his father, Bernardo. Like the marriage certificate, the bill of sale does not grant Joséf his "Don." Whatever their true or official

FIG. 1 Church of Santa María la Mayor from plaza of Colmenar de Oreja. Photograph by author.

status, Joséf and Felipa's social pretensions seem to have had some foundation by the time their offspring María was nine years old, and by then they seem to have acquired some kind of *entré* to the royal court of Madrid.

Joséf and Felipa had found a good match for Doña María's older sister, Leocadia (who bore as first given name María's second one), who married "Don Eugenio," whose surname Don Antonio could not recall, a young man with a post in the customs' house of the royal court in Madrid. Circumstantial evidence tells us that Joséf had also gained a foothold in the royal court and resided there at the time that María was born. Felipa was a resident in Madrid at the time she writes her letter of support, in 1803–4, and it is Felipa who tells us that she placed young María, at age nine, into the care of a "powerful lady of the town of her birth." Don Antonio revealed that powerful lady to have been the Lady Duchess Widow of Medinaceli, whose palatial residence was indeed in Madrid, and not in Colmenar de Oreja. Like many of those who gained favor with, and a new home in, the royal court in Madrid, the family preserved a home and *vecindad* (legal residence with full rights) in Colmenar de Oreja. The family's connections at court are the likely source of the wealth that enabled this couple of humble origins to enlarge their social pretensions and their children's world.

Enframing Virtue and Honor: *Calidad*, Recogimiento, and *Patria Potestad*

Joséf and Felipa sought social recognition of their *calidad*, the "quality" of high-status persons meriting the honorifics they claimed for themselves. To accomplish this they would have been careful to dress the part and to strive for the proud bearing by which an elite set of clothing, made of more noble materials such as silk, was worn while engaging in elite, and not commoner, activities. While the couple's clothing, no doubt upgraded through their residence in Madrid, set them apart from the common run of person in Colmenar, Joséf's clothing was also quite distinct from Felipa's: elite styles accentuated the difference between the hábitos (clothing *and* bearing) of the sexes. Along with frilly and constraining clothing ill-suited for labor, hidalgo men, who from the perspective of laboring commoners appeared effeminate, also bore arms, indexing a potential for violent responses to slights from others as a display of *pundonór*, "point of honor." With gloves and frills and movement-constraining bindings and skirts, elite ladies' dress entrained a delicacy of movement that made their distance from demeaning labor clearer yet.

The easy elision in the term *hábitos* between clothing and demeanor, or ways of moving the body, helped to naturalize the social standing of those who wore such status-defining clothes. But more still was required to demonstrate high social standing. For both sexes, a certain haughtiness of public bearing was required to sustain their social distance from common people. For men, a hidalgo stance called for prepotent disregard for commoners and readiness to use violence or invoke the law in response to potential slights from common folk.

For aristocratic women, unlike the men, public space was to be avoided. Preserving the honor of the men in their lives required them to properly perform being recogida, "kept in": to be recogida, the condition required of daughters, sisters, and wives of hidalgo men, was to be homebound, kept away from the street, the marketplace, and the town square, except when under the supervision of a man (father, brother, husband, or perhaps another male relative). In this way men exercised patria potestad, the "power of the father" over children and women, who were thus perpetually reduced to the status of legal minor (van Deusen 2001).

Neither Don Antonio's confession, nor Felipa Ybáñez's subsequent letter, directly tell us anything about Doña María's earliest years. We learn from Felipa only that María had given her father a great deal of "worry" from an early age. But given her parents social pretensions, María would not have had the run of the town in either Madrid or Colmenar de Oreja to play with friends, unlike pechero or commoner children, who in any case were expected to work alongside both of their parents in their labors. Indeed, for pecheras, commoner women, who were the vast majority of the women of Colmenar de Oreja and of Madrid, it was their work, often enough in public places (in market stalls or as domestic workers in elite households, under the patria potestad of men *other than* their husbands and fathers) that made them, in the eyes of aristocrats, too *pública* or *mundana* (public or worldly) to be of guaranteed virtue. Virtue was defined through proper enclosure, whether in a father's or husband's house, as a criada under the protection of a higher-ranking noble family, or in a convent. The worry that María caused her father from an early age might have resulted, we must imagine, from some kind of tomboyish behavior, something Spaniards called being *marimacho*.[8] But whether or not María spoke forthrightly and ran and fought and kicked a ball like a boy, if she resisted or violated proper recogimiento and took to the streets to play (as boys were expected to do), she would already have broken with the behavior expected of good girls and have been regarded as on the path to lost virtue and ruined honor. Masculine behavior and that of unvirtuous, unruly, and worldly women had a great deal in common.

Servile Aristocracy: Doña María's Life as Criada in the Palace of the Duchess

What to do with a willful girl, one whose behavior suggested a future threat to family honor? Joséf and Felipa chose to send María to learn to submit to her superiors and to learn by example more courtly demeanor and attitudes. When María was nine (as her mother Felipa tells us), that is, in about 1780, her parents sent her to live with the Lady Duchess of Medinaceli. María stayed off and on in the duchess's household until she was seventeen years old (that is, until about 1788).

Surprisingly, Don Antonio says nothing about these eight years with the duchess, which most certainly would have been memorable. "Sent to live with" a more powerful family in this era could mean various things, from mere employment as a servant to being cared for as a ward. In either status, and more likely something in between, María would have been the duchess's criada (from *criar*, to raise), the difference being that as a paid servant, the status would confirm María's and Felipa's standing as common pecheras, while being a ward was merely recognition of a patron's higher standing. The ward-type criada's work in the palace was not to labor but to be obsequious and to serve as a mirror of the patron's grandeur, some of which was then also absorbed by the criada.[9]

As Alejandro Cañeque (2005) has pointed out, ward-like criados and criadas were sustained by their patrons within a familial, gift economy (as opposed to payment of wages), entraining them as kinds of adoptive children who thus owed their patrons filial duty. The practice was common all the way up the aristocratic hierarchy, running from poor hidalgos to middling titled nobles to grandees to the king himself, whose household included criados and criadas from among the highest levels of titled nobility. This was the norm in a patriarchal and patrimonial regime, where a criado or criada apprenticeship with high-ranking aristocrats, including service to them that recognized their patria potestad, was a measure of loyal service and filial duty meriting reward, a future leg up in social life. What was expected of a good criado or criada was loyalty and obedience and, in sum, submission to another's will, this time not parents but their stand-ins.

Doña María must not have been an impossible criada, since her service to the duchess seems to have been prolonged. But neither did it lead to an advantageous marriage, something her parents may well have hoped for. Instead, when she reached age fourteen, about the age of puberty, we might conclude, the duchess sent her away, into the convent of the Agustinas Recoletas of Colmenar de Oreja. The poorest pecheras could not hope to enter conventual life, which required an endowment be paid to the convent, as well as good character references. Even though Doña María's parents were moving up in the world, we ought still suppose that the duchess helped with both. We'll get back to the convents. For now let us concentrate on the household of the duchess and the favor that María found there, even after being expelled from her first convent.

Although Don Antonio's statement implies that his parents then sent María "right away" into the next convent, under the protection of the duchess, the convent certifications give us a gap of over six years between one convent and the next, during which time, according to Doña Felipa's testimony, María was again living in the duchess's household (see appendix A.22). We might well ask why eight years living in another's house, or six years between one convent and another, are entirely elided from Don Antonio's statement. Likewise, it is curious that Doña Felipa fails to drop one of the most famous names and titles of the era. Perhaps the elision has to do with events of which it would be "more suitable" that judges in La Plata remain unaware. But the Lady Duchess of Medinaceli again facilitated María's entrance into a convent—this time that of the Franciscas de Huete—on November 24, 1790, when María would have been not seventeen years old, but nineteen or twenty.

Not just any noblewoman, the Lady Duchess of Medinaceli was Doña María Petronilla Pimentel de Alcántara de Toledo y Cernesio, the Seventh Marquesa de Malpica prior to her marriage to Don Pedro de Alcántara Fernández de Córdoba y Moncada, the Duke of Medinaceli and one of the most powerful grandees of Spain. The duchess became *duquesa viuda*, duchess widow, and even more powerful, upon her husband's death on November 24, 1789. Only after that did the duchess widow get Doña María admitted to the convent of the Franciscas de Huete.

Where was Doña María between the ages of nine and fourteen and, again, after being expelled from the Augustinian convent of Colmenar, from age fourteen to nineteen or twenty? The duchess, who inhabited one of the great palaces of Madrid, did not reside in humble Colmenar de Oreja. At the time of Doña María's birth in 1770, the Yta/Ybañez family resided "at court" (which is to say, in Madrid, and with some connection to the royal household), as did Doña Felipa as of the writing of her letter to Don Antonio's lawyer in La Plata in 1804.

Although Doña María's role there was relatively humble, the household of the duke and duchess in Madrid was a privileged place. Their palace was a massive complex, located at the end of the eighteenth century at the inter-section of the Paseo del Prado and the Carrera de los Jerónimos (fig. 2), a familiar spot for all tourists who have visited the Museo del Prado, just

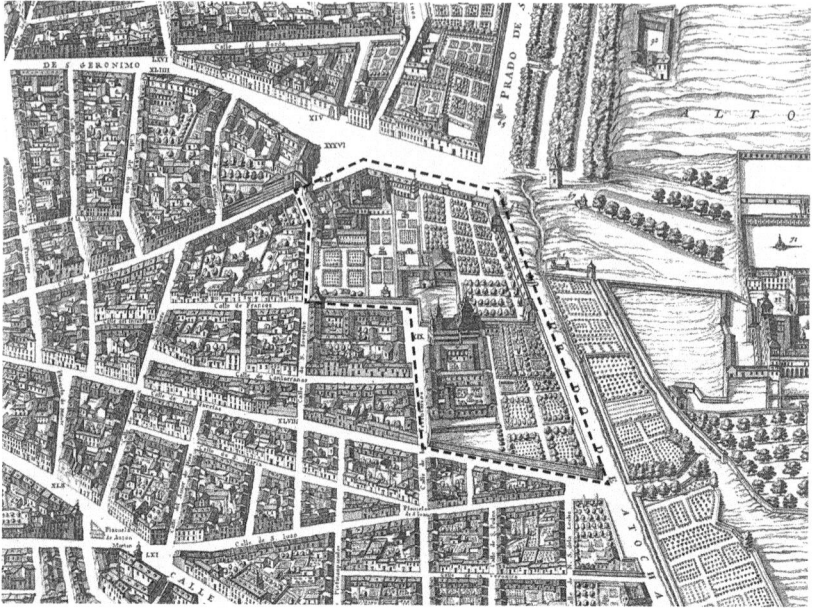

FIG. 2 Medinaceli Palace and grounds from Pedro Texeira's 1656 *Topografía de la Villa de Madrid*. Biblioteca Regional de Madrid.

across the paseo. The palace complex included two churches (one of them dedicated to Christ of Medinaceli), a convent, and a monastery, plus gardens and orchards that supplied the large household and its bakery, stables, and workshops. Apart from the monks and nuns, gardeners and bakers, stable boys and blacksmiths who occupied and worked in the separate spaces on the grounds, the palace itself was home to a minimum of some dozens of staff, ranging from slaves to servants to ladies-in-waiting and other criados and criadas, servants and retainers and protégé's and wards and hangers-on. Patrons of the arts, a succession of dukes from the sixteenth through the eighteenth centuries, hosted theatrical performances in the palace and on its grounds, where works by authors such as Lope de Rueda, Lope de Vega, Tirso de Molina, and others were regularly performed.[10]

When young María first entered the ducal household, she did so as a criada, a kind of "adopted" pseudokin but still servile member of the household. Antonio would later reprise that role, in its male version, in in the houses of the bishop of Buenos Aires and the intendant governor of Potosí. It was a position of considerable prestige, where selected members of the lower *hidalguía* could help sustain the status of the truly noble and wealthy while gaining important experience and introductions.

During all that time in the palace, Doña María would have had ample opportunity to study the ways of the high nobility and learn how criados, as well as criadas, were expected to interact with their patrons. The masked balls held there offered models for playful kinds of impersonation, which in the context of carnival turned also toward impersonation of the opposite sex as well as persons of different social estate or nation. Those kinds of impersonation, however, were meant to be "seen through," unlike the more serious attempts of the theatrical stage. It happens that the ducal palace was also host to many companies of professional actors performing works for the stage. There Doña María might not only have seen the plays but have met the players offstage, if not also backstage, where the transformation from actor's self to stage persona took place.

One wonders if young María might have seen the dramatized (and fictionalized) life story of Catalina or Antonio de Erauso, the early seventeenth-century *mujer varonil* who had fled from a convent, put on a man's clothing, and, in a manner more swashbuckling than Don Antonio's story, became a conquistador in the Americas (fig. 3). After killing a man Erauso confessed her true sex to a bishop and was sent back to Spain, where the king awarded her a lifetime pension, after which, in Rome, she received the pope's blessing to continue to live as a man (see Erauso [1592] 1829, 1992, 1996, 2002; Gómez 2009; Gunn 1999; McKendrick 1974; Miras 1992; Pancrazio 2001; and Velasco 2000, 2011).

It is not impossible that Doña María saw the play based on Catalina/Antonio's life story (written by Lope de Vega's disciple Juan Pérez de Montalbán and published in [1626] 2007). It might even have inspired young María. Indeed, one element of the play (not to be found in Erauso's life documentation) that resonates with Don Antonio's case is using a purported vow of chastity to explain (as per Doña Martina's accusation, though not Don Antonio's assertions) avoidance of "the act" during intimacy (1.2).

Even if she did not know about Erauso, if she had seen ten plays in the palace, two or three of those would have involved female-to-male cross-dressing. Female-to-male transvestism was a staple of Spanish Golden Age literature and of the stage, enough so that up to a third of Lope de Rueda's

FIG. 3 Juan van der Hamen y León (attributed), *Retrato de Doña Catalina de Erauso: La monja alferez*, ca. 1625. Oil on canvas, 57 × 46 cm. Colección Kutxa, San Sebastián, Spain.

plays include female characters who dress as men, generally temporarily, for the purposes of innocent disguise and in plots that foreground their heterosexuality (McKendrick 1974). In Spain such roles were played by women and in a manner akin to drag—the femininity "revealed" behind the male costume adding a certain *frissón* to the audience's appreciation of a female character's audacity.[11]

Changing Habits: "Manly Women" on the Spanish Stage and in the Medinaceli Palace

Reveling in cross-dressing and double-dealing, the theater was a school for scandal, where changes of costume and character carried out offstage and twists of plot and shifts of character onstage made the potential gaps between appearances and reality stand out starkly. "All the world's a stage," Shakespeare's character Jacques informs the audience in *As You Like It*, "And all the men and women merely players." That is made clear in the novel, when a character speaks to the reader behind the back of another character, and in the theater, when interactions or intentions of one character are known to the audience but not to other stage personae. The illusions, deceptions, and disillusionment of such written or performed characters were highlighted for readers and theater-goers by the knowledge that the novel's characters are inventions and the stage characters performed by actors whose own lives were other than those they more, or less, convincingly performed on stage. Revealing hábitos to be fungible and sometimes artful costumed performances rather than natural expressions of inner truths offered lessons not only in skepticism but in the covering strategies of rascals, liars, and crooks, by which they concealed their true selves and actual intentions so as to pass as honest and ingenuous persons of certain kinds.

Just such judgment is made when Spaniards cite an old saying, *El hábito no hace al monje*, or "The habit does not make the monk." A monk's habit, made in 1800 of a long, plain tunic covered by a scapular and a cowl with a hood, points toward the spiritual, world-renouncing life of a man who wears this outfit instead of pants and shirt. The saying points out that appearances do not always correspond with reality: the actual demeanor, character, or religious behavior of said monk may belie what is suggested by the habit, whether or not he is actually a monk rather than an imposter.[12] The potential gap between appearances and reality was a core theme of picaresque literature and of the Spanish stage, both of which provided models for Doña María for understanding the systematicity of the clothing system and the statuses and dispositions it helped to manifest, as well as examples of how dressing and acting a part can fail to convince and lead to exposure of inner truths.

Theatrical staging can be regarded as a ritual-like (Schechner 1985; V. Turner 1982) means by which the schemas or metapragmatic operations bracketed there in a time out of time, space out of space, observably tie particular costumes and actions to socially marked kinds of persons. Theatrical play with surfaces and depths, appearances and underlying realities, then provides the opportunity to apply moral judgment to the ennobling acts or demeaning foibles of its characters and to extend those analogically to the character of real-life persons.

The morally admirable characteristics of male characters differ from female characters, and there may be no better way to comment-in-action on such differences than cross-dressing on the stage. Unlike the novel, which is limited to words, even when describing actions, players on a stage can draw on the full and subtle repertoires of movement, timbre of voice, and allusions to the clothed and sexed body's "affordances," the kinds of action in which it might engage, in ways that written narrative cannot. As actors inhabit or "surrogate" (Roach 1996) the "others" they portray, audiences evaluate them on how convincing their surrogations might be or the degree to which their offstage or inner true identity leaks through their performance. Those are emulatable lessons in how surrogation is done and what makes it succeed or fail.

Ann Rosalind Jones and Peter Stallybrass (1991) analyze the role of clothing in theater as the fabric of identity for the making or unmaking of the self. Marjorie Garber (1992) points to the centrality of cross-dressing to theatrical mimesis, while Stallybrass and Allon White (1986) discuss the centrality of cross-dressing to the short theatrical form known as the *entremés* and the affinity of both to the world-turned-upside-down transgressiveness of the carnivalesque. As Laura R. Bass (2008, 54) concludes, "Nothing better emblematizes the wedge between the actor's seeming and her being than transvestism—How better to show off her talent than by having her seem to become that which she cannot be? Cross-dressing is cast as *the* trope for dramatic mimesis, its maximum expression and metaphor."

Cross-dressing roles develop the audacious, which is to say, masculine, qualities of the character, marking them as mujeres varoniles, "manly women," who somehow manage to illustrate the qualities of proper manly behavior as well as, or better than, the men around them (McKendrick 1974). A powerful reason for such admiration, which turned to derision when men dressed as women, was that when women dressed as men, they "dressed 'up' on the gender hierarchy . . . offer[ed] male audience members a mirror of their own privileged status" (Bass 2008, 59).

A well-known sixteenth-century female stage performer, one Maríana, spent a few years in the residence of the Medinacelis, dressed in the costume of a male page, at the invitation of the duke himself. Spending many hours with her, including forays into the countryside to hunt, Maríana's presence in the household gave rise to rumors that she was his cross-dressing mistress.[13] Perhaps what brought this relationship most fully into the light was a lawsuit filed by Lope de Rueda in 1554. Lope, who as an actor specialized in drag roles (Donnell 2003, 63), fell hard for Maríana and not only employed her in his company but married her. It was after that when he filed suit against the duke, hoping to retrieve back pay for her six years of work performing for the duke in his household. This was a household with a history of associations with transvestism, mujeres varoniles, theatrical performances of gender-crossing, and (as we shall see) androgynous nuns. Perhaps that history accounts for the duchess's long-term care for Doña María, both in her household and in convents with which she was associated as patron. Let us take a closer look at what kind of transformation in Doña María the duchess, and Doña María's parents, might have hoped for, how it was to be achieved, and how moving from secular to religious female clothing, roles, behaviors, and constraints indexed aristocracy, sex, and sexuality.

The Sex of the Suppressed Will and Mortification of the Body in the Convent

Doña María was repeatedly sent into convents, and it behooves us ask what that meant for her and for women more generally. The Medinaceli Palace compound was so large that it contained two convents and churches, so Doña María would have learned something about them while serving the duchess. While the convent shares certain characteristics with a grand noble palace—solid walls, a well-guarded entryway, long hallways connecting a multitude of rooms of different purposes, and large interior courtyards or cloisters—the convent itself differs in being an entirely homosocial space. One might imagine that a young woman discovering her desire for other women might find appealing the idea of being locked into a communal life shared exclusively with women. But although convents in the Middle Ages were notorious for the sexual escapades of their nuns, sometimes with men, and sometimes among themselves (Bass and Wunder 2009; Brown 1986; Linehan 2004), a series of reforms initiated by the Council of Trent, spurred by the Inquisition, and designed by figures such as Teresa de Ávila, had already in the sixteenth century begun to impose rules to prevent such scandals.

Convents may have been rigorously homosocial, but sexuality of any sort was just as rigorously excluded through regimes of surveillance, solitude, silence, mortification of the body, abnegation of the will, and efforts to prevent intimate contact and "special friendships" among the nuns (Bilinkoff 2015; Burns 1999; Surtz 1990). Even so, young María apparently found the opportunities conventual life offered for intimacy with young women, but, in four different convents, regimes of surveillance found out María. Let us see how María's very first convent strove to transform her and to prevent realization of the desires that led her parents to send her there.[14]

The convent of the Agustinas Recoletas of Colmenar de Oreja (fig. 4) was also known as the "Incarnation of the Divine Word." Its nuns followed a particularly severe brand of recogimiento. To be recogida meant not only to be sealed in a home with closed doors and windows but to have a well-sealed body, all its openings closed to "commerce" with the world (see van Deusen 2001, 22). Convents were places where the Doña María was to learn to make analogies, first between ordinary aristocratic womanhood and the religious kind, then between living under the power of her father and mother versus that of the duchess or the prioress, and, finally, between the architectural space of the home, palace, or convent and her own body.

As she moved through these different places, Doña María would have herself noted analogous deployments of social power in built space, a knowledge made more reflexive by theater's stagings of them. But her training in those convents included explicit analogies between building and body, which equated the ability of walls and skin or clothing to contain, and openings—doors and windows and ears, eyes, mouth, anus, and vagina—by which "commerce" between what is inside and what is outside takes place. Drawing on the writings on the training of the "perfect wife" by Fray Luís de León (1987), whose works were often read aloud in convents, Georgina Dopico-Black notes that such openings are the locus of sexual contamination as well as of sensual contamination: "It is not just the wife's chastity that must be protected from adultery, then, but her ears that must be guarded against gossip, her eyes against visual seduction, and even her nose against the corrupting vapors of cosmetic(s)." Dopico goes on to note that it is the wife's mouth that is the most critical boundary between inside and outside, following Saint Paul's condemnation of women to silence (2001, 93). As Peter Stallybrass puts it, "Silence, the closed mouth, is made a sign of chastity. And silence and chastity are, in turn, homologous to a woman's enclosure within the house" (Stallybrass 1986, 127, qtd. in Dopico-Black 2001, 93).

Yet the eyes, too, were a dangerous portal between the inside of the body and the outside world, as Saint Augustine stressed in his rules for the conventual order he founded, giving rise to the Agustinas Recoletas (the order of

FIG. 4 Convent of Augustinian nuns, Colmenar de Oreja. Photograph by author.

the convent into which Doña María was sent at age fourteen). The convent's constitution, regularly read aloud to the nuns during meals, begins with words for women written by Augustine himself:

If by chance you see [a man], do not fix your eyes onto him [*enclaveis en él los ojos*], since even though he doesn't see you, and although is not a sin to see men, it is [a sin] to desire them or to want to be desired by them. That desire is not only awakened by touching but also by looking. Do not say that you have chaste and clean hearts, while having dishonest eyes, which are a certain sign of a dishonest heart. When silencing the tongue, *unclean hearts declare themselves through the eyes and ignite base desires in each other*, so that even though their bodies do not touch, their chastity is lost. . . . for it is written: the Lord abominates those who fix their eyes on others. (Agustinas Recoletas 1648, Original Rule, item 6, fols. 6v–7r; my translation, emphasis added)[15]

Once they professed, nuns were married to Christ, and were to remain in solitude with him; just as the convent was cloistered against penetration from without, so to avoid the kind of adultery that was also apostasy, the nuns' bodily openings were to be sealed and their senses and appetites mortified: mouths were condemned to silence, ears deprived of all but religious words, stomachs subjected to fasts, eyes cast down and covered by veils, skin covered by rough woolen cloth and periodically scourged with whips. Self-abnegation, not the individual "self-fashioning" and self-regard that were keys to the narrated lives of persons whose hábitos were not the nun's habit, were the rule of the day.

If a wife's home is analogous to her body, its doors and windows like her bodily openings, then the surface of the nun's body is akin to the walls of the convent. The high and impregnable walls of the convent, its iron-grilled doors and windows, covered on the inside by a lattice of wood and opaque black cloth, were not meant to be trespassed. What made the surface of the novice's body and its openings impregnable, as visibly as did the convent's walls and closed doors, was her habit, her social skin, that was to conceal and constrain her body to foil any possible "commerce" with the world through its openings and thus help to transform her "inner state" (one that hinged on dematerialization or the foregrounding of mind and spirit) while signaling that state to whoever might see her.

On entering the convent, Doña María abandoned the costume that had marked her as an *hidalga* (or rising bourgeois) adolescent Christian and Castilian female and donned the order's *hábito de capa y coro*, a habit with a white, rather than black, veil, reserved for novice nuns prior to the act of profession (marriage to Christ and full membership in the convent). Following the rules of the order as set down in their constitution, María's hair was shorn off to the roots (so as not to require brushing), to begin the self-abnegation, the disregard for self-esteem or the esteem of others, required of nuns. Cutting off the hair, which marriageable young women elaborately styled and revealed to the world as a sign of their availability and nubility—and in its particular styling their aristocratic or commoner standing—indexed their renunciation of sexuality and procreation and also of their individuality. Since men wore their hair short, it was also a move toward androgyny.

The order's constitution called for a habit of plain, black-and-white, rough wool cloth that covered the novice's entire body, from just below the chin to the wrists and ankles (see fig. 5, the founder of the women's branch of the Augustinian order in her habit). The head covering, pulled tight across the forehead and over the ears and cheeks, left only the eyes, nose, and mouth

FIG. 5 Mariette, *Saint Clare of Montefalco* (Augustinian saint). Line engraving. Wellcome Library, University College, London.

S. CLARA de Monte falconio Celeberrima
Inter S S Moniales Eremitas S.ª Augustini
circa annum 1299.
Mariette Excu Auec Priuilegie.
52

uncovered. They were to be concealed behind a veil.[16] Lack of color, and of comfort, was also the rule for the nuns' individual cells, which were to be very small, with blank walls, no furniture but a plank bed and a mat on which to sit, a little shelf for devout books, a candle and candlestick, and no adornment other than a cross and a font for holy water. No trunk or locking box for other personal effects was permitted, as there were to be none. The cell's door was provided without a lock, so that the mistress of novices could enter for inspection at any time. No private correspondence with anyone outside the convent was permitted, unless it was read by the prioress before delivery to its recipient (Agustinas Recoletas 1648, chaps. 11, 12, fols. 42r–v, 45v–46r).

Novices were taught a strict routine, consisting of collective prayer in the choir of the church (shielded by a lattice-work screen from view by parishioners). When they arrived and departed from the choir, and whenever reprimanded by the prioress, they were to prostrate themselves on the ground. Regular fasting of three days per week and also during the feasts of vigils of the Virgin Mary, September 11 until Christmas, and Lent and harsh self-discipline (including whipping oneself three times per week) were part of the routine (Agustinas Recoletas 1648, chap. 15, fols. 45v–46r).

Most of the day, nuns and novices were to dedicate themselves to silent prayer and to tasks such as spinning thread, while sitting alone in their cells. Silence and recogimiento was the rule (Agustinas Recoletas 1648, chap. 14, fol. 44r), though it was not total: three times a week the sisters were granted a "recreational" hour. This was the only time they were allowed to speak with one another, though topics were restricted to religious themes, such as the biblical passages or writings of Santa Teresa de Ávila or Luís de León or San Juan de la Cruz, which were read aloud while dining in the refectory.

Doña María's affection for other women might not have been impeded by the rule of silence, but the rule of solitude is another matter. The convent's constitution makes it clear that they were to spend most of their time enclosed alone, each in their separate cells. They were not to enter another's cell and were essentially prevented from speaking with one another, to make sure that they would not become preoccupied by the business of others in the convent or in the world outside of it (Agustinas Recoletas 1648, chap. 7, fols. 35–36v). Even so, "special friendships" were regarded as a danger, and the constitution (which was regularly to be read aloud during "community time") ordered that any such friendships be immediately ended once detected (chap. 8, fol. 37r).

As a novice, María would have been subject not only to the prioress of the convent but, on an everyday basis, to the convent's *maestra de novicias* (teacher or mistress of novices). The constitution's instructions to this authority over the young novices leaves no room for doubt that it is not only bodily desire and attachment to worldly things that must be extinguished but individuality, self-regard, and, ultimately, the will itself: "Teach them how to live alone with God; mortify them in every possible way, even in the smallest things (Agustinas Recoletas 1648, chap. 27, fol. 63v). And they must know that *their life's work must be the abnegation of their will*, and if they truly renounce it, they will always be content. Make sure that they forget about everything they have left behind and do not allow them to speak with their relatives or about secular things [*cosas del siglo*] and teach them to forget themselves and conquer themselves. . . . Teach them to mortify their affections and pleasures" (chap. 27, fol. 65r–v; emphasis added).

Unfortunately for her parents, María was ejected from there after a few brief months. The convent reported that María Leocadia Yta entered in July 1783 and was sent away, *because it suited them*, in September of the same year.[17] What happened there? The convent's report could mean no more than that María lacked the calling to a religious life. But Don Antonio was not so reticent to explain the ejection (nor was Felipa), making it clear that it resulted from what Doña María "did with the nuns" and that they suspected that she was a man. Doing *anything* with the nuns was problematic in the convent. Scheming to actually touch them in private was cause for dismissal. Unwilling or unable to abide by the rules concerning excessive intimacy among the nuns and enacting her bodily desires rather than conquering them, Doña María exalted, rather than abnegated, her will. We might guess that she "fixed her eyes" on other sisters and perhaps even whispered to them of carnal things. Her will had its way, and in a way that was not only irreligious but positively manly.

Don Antonio expresses no regret for having been ejected from the convent of Agustinas Recoletas. Quite possibly, she found it to be a relief, in spite of being separated from the nuns on whom she had cast her eye. The words from an earlier time (1617) of the probably intersexed Spanish nun, Magdalena Muñoz, at having been declared to be a man and being sent away from the convent might have resonated with Doña María as she was stripped of her habit and sent packing. As the priest who discovered Magdalena's penis summed up the case: "*She . . . is happy because after twelve years in jail* [the convent], she knows liberty well, and *she was a woman and now a man*, which out of all things and timely events no better favor could have been paid her by nature itself" (Torres 1617, BN Mss. 2058, fols. 258–59, qtd. in Vollendorf 2005, 12; see also *Relación verdadera* 1617; and Uhagón 1896).

But it turns out that Muñoz, who had also raised suspicions among the nuns and her confessor for having "the strength and spirit and properties and conditions of a male," had been sent by her father to the convent in the first place "on account of being a closed girl and not being one who should marry" (Vollendorf 2005, 10), that is, for incomplete femaleness. Moreover, Muñoz had confessed to the priest that "she had never menstruated, but 'when she disciplined herself, in order to keep the nuns from calling her a tomboy [*marimacho*], she put blood on her nightshirts, saying that she had her period.'" The priest then inspected and palpated her body and "saw that she had grown a penis and a beard and heard the change in the register of her voice," and . . . Magdalena Muñoz was proclaimed a man" (11).

But Doña María had no such luck. Some of the nuns might have suspected that she was a man, and she might have wished to be one, but discovery of a male body and declaring her to be a man was not forthcoming. Magdalena Muñoz's father was "very happy because he is a rich man and he didn't have any heirs and now he finds himself with *a very manly son* and one who can marry" (Vollendorf 2005, 12). But Doña María's parents, and the Duchess of Medinaceli, apparently had nothing to celebrate.

After Doña María was thrown out of (or escaped from) the Agustinas Recoletas, she found herself back in the household of the duchess for some considerable time. But eventually, in 1790, the duchess, now duchess widow, used her influence to have María accepted as a novice in the convent called Santa Juana. It is quite possible that the choice was inspired by Doña María's acts and reputation.

"La Santa Juana": Androgynous Nun and Transgender Patroness

That convent, in the town of Cubas de la Sagra, near Illescas, between Madrid and Toledo and not terribly far from Colmenar de Oreja, was officially named Santa María de la Cruz, in reference to the miraculous apparition of the Virgin Mary to a young girl there while herding pigs in 1449 (Surtz 1990, 3; Christian 1989, 57–87). By the end of the sixteenth century, however, the convent was popularly referred to as that of "Santa Juana" for a famous nun who entered it in 1496, having fled home, disguised as a man, to avoid an arranged marriage.[18] Many female Christian saints were known for having changed into male costume to defend the faith (think of Jeanne d'Arc but also Saint Barbara). But Juana's temporary transvestism, which gave her freedom of movement to avoid a marriage that would have impeded her relationship with Christ, was only the first of many signs of an androgyny that brought her to the attention (and admiration) not only of the inquisitor general, Cardinal Cisneros, but of the emperor Charles V himself.

After a prolonged illness in which she lost her ability to speak, she suddenly recovered and began to exhibit an astonishing ability to preach, an ability marked in Juana's body by the presence of the Adam's apple with which she had been born. Juana's explanation for the Adam's apple, and for her manly abilities, was an unusual miracle performed on her while still in the womb. She was conceived as a boy, but the Virgin Mary prevailed on God to change her into a girl. He did so but "refused to take away the Adam's apple that she had in her throat so that it might bear witness to the miracle" (*Vida*, fol. 2v., qtd. in Surtz 1990, 6–7).

Juana's extraordinary preaching led Cardinal Cisneros to appoint her as the convent's abbess and to grant her the extraordinary privilege of the priestly function of preaching sermons (privileges seconded by papal bull), transcriptions of which were published with the cardinal's blessing (Juana de la Cruz [1509] 1982; Boon and Surtz 2016). The sermons themselves are rife with nearly erotic references to Juana's special bond with a highly feminized Christ, whose fingers played her body, which through illness was as taut as the strings of a guitar (Surtz 1990, chap. 3). What is more, the sermons highlight Christ's androgyny as well as Juana's and indeed forward arguments for the equivalence and interchangeability of the sexes (Surtz 1990, 25). More than once Juana was put forward for beatification, the first step on the way to sainthood, but the process stalled when Vatican officials closely read Juana's published sermons. A movement led by the faithful who every year repeat Juana's flight from home to the convent as a pilgrimage has recently been successful in restarting the beatification process.[19]

How much the duchess widow or nineteen-year-old María knew of the manliness of Juana or the historical link between that convent and mujeres varoniles we can only guess, although the story of Juana's cross-dressing escape from marriage to a man that was central to her story and well developed in Tirso de Molina's ([1613–14] 1948) trilogy of plays about her would have been required knowledge of novices at the convent, and it remains central to the stories told in relation to the annual pilgrimage from her hometown to the convent. But La Santa Juana's androgyny did not help María to remain in the convent. For after eleven months—María's longest stint in a convent without professing—María was thrown out of there.

The prioress reports that María was not admitted for profession because "the community did not find it appropriate for various reasons" (appendix A.22), which are not specified. But Don Antonio is less circumspect: They threw her out "after catching **her** with a nun and because they were convinced *she* [María] was a man." News from the town of Colmenar de Oreja, "where one thing or another had happened since the age of fourteen, when she took the habit in the Augustinian convent of Colmenar," says Don Antonio, confirmed the opinion of the abbess of this second convent (A.7, fol. 5v). Just what they had heard about, and whether it had happened in Colmenar or in the house of the duke and duchess, we can only guess. In any case, after this the duchess and her patronage disappear from the story.

Pitched out after eleven months in the convent of the transgendered "Santa" Juana, María was sent home to her parents. About a year later, in October 1790, the parents of this apparently willful and rebellious twenty-year-old sent Doña María into yet another of a final two convents (Don Antonio reverses the order certified by the convents), this time the convent of Franciscan sisters of Huete (Convento de la Misericordia de la Orden de Santa Clara). Thrown out four months later, in February 1791, according to Don Antonio for the same reasons as the previous convent, "by disposition of the nuns [between the lines: or of the chaplains who directed them]" (A.7, fol. 6v), Don Joséf and Doña Felipa then sent María to stay in the Madrid house of their other daughter, Leocadia.

Once again, off went the habit and on went "secular clothing," that of a young woman of aristocratic pretensions. Doña María spent nine months with her sister Leocadia and her husband, one "Don Eugenio," who worked in the customs house of Madrid. But then María's parents sent her to one final convent in November 1791, this time to that of the Bernardas de Segovia (the Monasterio de San Vicente el Real, founded by Cistercians in 1156, outside the walls of Segovia [fig. 6]). Two months later she was expelled, purportedly for having taken the habit in other convents; that is, her reputation had followed her. This was the end of the line for the conventual life: María's actions or reputation finally closed the door on the possibility of containing María's unorthodox sexuality in properly feminine recogimiento. This time her parents did not take her back into their home.

A girl's initiation into conventual life (cutting the hair, replacing a secular, unmarried girl's multicolored and estate-marked clothing with a novice's black and white religious habit, silencing the mouth, lowering the eyes, etc.) began to enact a transformation that heightened the analogy between the home and its threshold and the woman's body, as the convent's walls and heavily guarded door and the nun's body were now equally encased and surveilled. This is a procedure that Doña María went through four times. Doña María's

FIG. 6 Convent of San Vicente el Real ("Las Bernardas") outside of Segovia. Photograph by author.

repeated ritual lessons quite apparently did not lead to the transformation of the person beneath the habit that the convents hoped to achieve. The habit did not make the nun. Instead, imposing it seems to have given her lessons in the fungibility of identity, particularly with regard to sex and sexuality, on which so much attention was focused. Perhaps the iteration of these ritually portentous changes of social skin had an effect like that experienced by Dorothy facing the image of the great wizard of Oz; it led her to see the little man behind the curtain and the mere artifice behind the hoped-for ritual effect. Soon enough, Doña María would take those lessons to heart.

Almost Out, in the World

Sent from the convent to her sister's house on January 27, 1792, Doña María once more changed the nun's habit for an elite secular woman's dress, most of the time, at least. Felipa informs us that, after remaining in her sister's house for a few months, María was granted permission to visit the home of one Rita Benedicto. María had told her sister and mother that she had found work as a seamstress for this woman, thus employing one of feminine manual skills practiced in the convent. In Felipa's words: "We heard the complaint that [Rita Benedicto] was pregnant by **him** [*de este*], which surprised *his* father, my now-dead husband, and me. We heard this complaint from the aforesaid Rita when *he* [Doña María] fled to Rome without our consent and without our knowing about any of this. We later learned from her relatives that Rita died /29r/ in childbirth, as did her baby" (appendix A.21, fols. 28v–29r).

Were that not enough, Felipa reports to Don Antonio's lawyer that María had been involved with yet another woman who lived "in the street of Los Remedios, this one a Valencian woman with whom [María's] brother-in-law caught her in the act itself *and in men's clothes*" (A.21, fol. 29v). Having changed back and forth between secular woman's clothing and nun's habits, young María seems also to have rehearsed performing a man's role in male *hábitos*.

A Roman Holiday and the Pope's Dispensation

Omitting such "details" from his confession, Don Antonio returns to María's story. No doubt in response to a widening arc of scandal, as well as to the dissonance among María's desires, actions, and sense of propriety or sinfulness, María sought counsel from her priest in confession. He advised her, we learn, to go to Rome and seek the advice of the Holy Father on what to do to ease her conscience.[20] Leaving a letter for her parents at her sister's house explaining this, Doña María then left on that journey, one that María's mother explains as flight from Rita Benedicto's pregnancy, attributed to María (A.1, fol. 28v).

At age twenty, in about April 1792, eleven and a half years before Antonio was arrested, examined, and questioned in La Plata, Doña María took a carriage (a *calesa*, generally a small two- or four-wheeled vehicle pulled by one or two horses) on the long journey by land from Madrid to Valencia, a trip of over 220 miles that, according to Antonio, lasted twelve days. Seeking out a friend of her father in that town, a man named Marzas, María enlisted his help (money, we must presume, and perhaps also knowledge of that city), and after a short time traveled by land (another 220 miles) up the Spanish Mediterranean coast to Barcelona. Two weeks later María got passage on a commercial ship (the Buenos Aires source says it was a mail ship) to Genoa (a longtime Spanish possession, now putatively independent, that was to become part of Italy) traveling around the Mediterranean coast toward Rome. María was no doubt forced to bribe this ship's captain (and the next one), to secure a ticket without having the necessary travel license (equivalent, today, to a passport).

On that ship María met two women—a mother and daughter, she says—with whom she would spend the next three or four months of travel and some time in Rome. The Buenos Aires source says that they were Italians (B.7). Together they spent twenty or twenty-five days at sea before reaching the port of Genoa, where the three travelers stayed together for two months. Don Antonio identifies these women as *operantas*, a term that at the time had two different meanings. They might have been medical practitioners who operated on others, which in the case of women thus called often referred to midwives and hymen-repairers, who surgically returned girls' virginity to them. More likely, however, they were female stage performers (actors and singers, as in performers of opera); such performers were highly mobile, and the Spanish stage was replete with Italian women who specialized in the theater's female roles and the cross-dressed parts also required of them.[21]

Periodically since the end of the sixteenth century, male actors were prohibited from cross-dressing to perform female roles on the Spanish stage—it was considered an enticement to sodomy—even as the number of roles requiring female-to-male cross-dressing had grown exponentially in Spanish theater. Usually, as in Tirso de Molina's dramatic trilogy portraying the life of "Santa Juana," that cross-dressing was merely a temporary disguise by which women granted themselves freedom of movement; sometimes they used that freedom to enact "male" actions, such as the avenging of insults, sometimes to help free their male suitors or brothers from captivity. Some of the roles portrayed mujeres varoniles, "manly women," whose usually virginal feminine virtues were matched by an ability to carry out a man's most valiant deeds. Whatever their occupations, these women no doubt offered important lessons for María, above all how to survive as a woman without male escort in a world where that always led to suspicion and trouble.

Doña María arrived in Genoa with the two operantas, perhaps in May 1792, and spent two months there with them, doing we know not what. Possibly the women were contracted to perform on the stage there. María needed a place to stay and food to eat—and perhaps Marzas, the father's friend in Valencia, had given María plenty of cash to cover those expenses. Getting on another ship, again with the operantas, the three arrived by sail not long after to the port of Civitavecchia: Rome's port. Don Antonio tells us that María stayed in Rome for seven months, perhaps again in the company of the operantas. The company of actors well versed in men's clothing and cross-dressing would have been very useful to María, given what came next. Here, I again quote my first-person version of Don Antonio's confession:

Finding myself in Rome, I practiced all the diligence that I judged conducive to the quietude of my conscience. This led me to having communicated to me through the Spanish-language penitential confessor, Fray Pedro Ramos Aragones of the Order of San Francisco, that by the command of His Holiness I should dress forever afterward in the clothing of a man.

I explained to the Penitencial the difficulties that would of course ensue if I returned to my own country, where they had known me from earliest infancy as a woman. He told me to take the road for whatever place I liked best, but come what may to dress as a man. And I carried out [his command] from then on, from before I left Rome ever since.

Doña María's conscience had been bothering her. Whether it was for the attraction to women or for acting (and feeling) like a man, a combination of the two, or simply because she kept getting caught and berated, we cannot tell. It is one indication that she was aware, at least, that she could not continue to pursue women or dress episodically as man without facing serious consequences. Experience (and also, we must assume, her prior training in matters of chastity and propriety and in the proper performativity of sex) had turned her proclivities into a problem for her. Doña María apparently experienced this problem, the dissonance between how she was supposed to act and how she did, as a "bad conscience," which I take to refer not only to the self-judgment of her desires and behavior as morally wrong but to the certain knowledge that others had strenuously disapproved, causing humiliation and threatening worse consequences. María had reached an impasse, made clear to her not only by pangs of conscience but by her confessor and members of her family.

That her Madrid confessor would have recommended a pilgrimage to Rome and a consultation with the Spanish-language penitentiary may be surprising to modern readers, but it was not unusual at the time; the *penitenciaría apostólica* was the just the place for such a consultation.[22] That body had some experience in determining cases of bodily intersex and of performative sex, that is, in officially assigning a sex contrary to that assigned at birth, whether because the sexual apparatus was ambiguous or a convincing and sustained performance was contrary to the biological facts. In 1586 the penitenciaría had reviewed the case of a Spanish woman admitted to a convent at age fifteen, who two years later suddenly developed male genitalia (most likely a case of a genetically male individual with androgen insensitivity syndrome reversed at puberty; this is also the likely cause of the sudden masculinization at puberty in 1617 of the "closed" girl, Magdalena Muñoz); they reassigned her to the status of male (Tamburini 1995, 357–59). In the early seventeenth century, faced with the cross-dressing "adventurer" to the Indies, Catalina de Erauso, the same body provided a papal dispensation granting her license to live henceforth as a man (see Erauso 1996; Merrim 1994; Perry 1999; and Velasco 2000), though that did not include authorization of sexual activity.

After seeing Don Antonio's confession, La Plata's ecclesiastical prosecutor would certainly have written to the *penitenciaría apostólica*, the body to which all dispensations and annulments were referred for final decisions, since the question of such a dispensation in Yta's case affected Doña Martina's request for annulment. No records of the Don Antonio's case have been preserved in the church archives of La Plata, and I have not been able to locate any documents attesting to Doña María's meeting in Rome with the Spanish-language penitentiary (archival holdings for those years having been disrupted by Napoleon's invasion of the Vatican and their transferal to Paris and later return, during which many were lost). In any case, the ecclesiastic that Don Antonio names existed and occupied the post in the year that Doña María was in Rome.

Don Antonio does not provide details of Doña María's interactions with the penitentiary, but we must assume that they began with a confession, likely rigorous questioning by that priest, and detailed replies. Doña María must have reported her attraction to women and must also have made it clear that she believed herself to be man, to have a man's parts, and to "feel and act" like a man, as well as having been "suspected" of being a man by nuns in convents.

It is entirely consistent with the old theories of "mutable" sex still circulating in Europe and with the general conflation of bodily sex with the performative kind that the penitentiary priest would have concluded that Doña María was a hermaphrodite, something between "man" and "woman," even without any medical inspection (and Don Antonio insists there was none).[23] It is indeed likely that María gained a papal dispensation to dress and live as a man, and it is also likely that when Don Antonio told his wife that he had taken a vow of chastity, this had been a condition of such a dispensation. Doctor Mariano Taborga's letter added the details about the acts of contrition that the penitentiary purportedly also had imposed on Doña María: "to climb the Jerusalem steps thirty times, to whip *herself* every Friday of the year, never again to hear Mass in a women's convent, and to put on a man's clothing" (appendix B.7).[24] These words were not recorded by the scribe who wrote out Don Antonio's confession, but they appear apt enough to have actually been uttered. No doubt the penitentiary also advised María to stay away from women altogether. But to have reported that would be to admit to breaking a key vow.

Reflexively Inhabiting New Identities, from Rome to Buenos Aires and from Female to Male

Changing into a man's clothing, somehow acquired (perhaps from the Italian female actors or perhaps sewn by Doña María from her own clothing?), María then became a man. When she put on men's clothing in Rome, it was not for the first time. Doña Felipa testifies that María had been caught by her brother-in-law dressed in men's clothing and "in the act" with the unnamed Valencian woman on Los Remedios Street before departing from Madrid. But the experience in Rome may have been the first time that Doña María cross-dressed in public, to walk the streets and get the feel of being not a *flâneuse* but a secretly "female" flaneur, someone free to stride with purpose or to wander while looking about and fixing his eyes on others.

To do so required putting on and convincingly inhabiting men's clothing, along with a masculine hairstyle and an embodied masculine style of walking, looking at, and addressing others. It also required not only becoming a man but choosing what *kind* of man to become. At the end of the eighteenth century, this meant, to begin with, choosing an outfit (and style of inhabiting it) that marked one or another social estate: a laboring man or an hidalgo, a country person or an urbanite. And since a shift was well underway from the early modern era's relatively static estate-marked clothing styles, constrained by sumptuary codes, to frequently changing fashions tailored from industrially produced cloth, María (and her brothers) had a wider range of choices than had her grandfather or father. Like the later, French crossdresser George Sand, María appears to have chosen to strut her male stuff as a dandy. Just putting on the key elements of male garb, pants and substantial shoes, was a major step forward. The dandy outfit, however, made for an even more accentuated stride toward freedom of action.

George Sand was the pseudonym of novelist Amantine-Lucile-Aurore Dupin (1804–76). She had married and had two children before taking a break from married life and having affairs with famous men and perhaps a woman too. Rebelling against the strictures of monogamy, motherhood, and femininity, she famously described the fashionable male clothing she wore and the experience of "feeling male" when she cross-dressed as a dandy in the streets of Paris:

I had made for myself a redingote-guérite in heavy gray cloth, pants and vest to match. With a gray hat and a large woolen cravat, I was a perfect first-year student. I can't express the pleasure my boots gave me: I would gladly have slept with them, as my brother did in his young age, when he got his first pair. With those little iron-shod heels, I was solid on the pavement. I flew from one end of Paris to the other. It seemed to me that I could go around the world. And then, my clothes feared nothing. I ran out in every kind of weather, I came home at every sort of hour, I sat in the pit of the theatre. No one paid attention to me, and no one guessed at my disguise. . . . No one knew me, no one looked at me, no one found fault with me; I was an atom lost in a large crowd. (62, qtd. in Moers 2003, 9)

No doubt Doña María also put on boots along with something "passably" fashionable to head into the streets of Rome, and surely she also discovered the relative ease of movement and freedom from scrutiny that Sand describes. But there is a big difference between George Sand's transvestism, a temporary affair for experimental and professional purposes that was not fully "lived-in" (since Sand had a life and lived as a woman, as an admired author and socialite), and what Doña María was attempting to do. Had Sand accidentally revealed that she was cross-dressed while in the streets, she had a world of famous and powerful friends to bail her out of trouble. Doña María, however, was quite alone.

Leaving Rome in her new suit of clothes (we do not know what style these were), she then undertook a long journey, not home, where all had known *her*, but back to Barcelona and then to Cádiz and Málaga, then a principal Spanish port for departures to the Americas. Now Antonio, *he* would depart for the Spanish colonies of the Americas. Don Antonio's account of the journey is notably brief (again quoting from the first-person revision of the confession): "So I departed for Civitavecchia, where I embarked destined for Genoa, and from that port to Barcelona, and thence passed to Málaga, and I made all these journeys exclusively dressed as a man. Finally, in the port of Málaga, I set out, as I have said, about nine years ago, for Montevideo, destination of that ship." Don Antonio's mother provides more details: "On **her** return to Spain, **she** was discovered in Barcelona by sailors who were looking through *his* luggage and found women's clothes. For this, the last bishop kept **him** in seclusion and *he* was freed upon his death" (appendix A.21, fol. 28v).

That Doña María, now traveling as a man, had kept women's clothing (we do not know what style) suggests that she was not yet entirely certain about the permanence of the transformation. It seems likely, because of his release and continued journey as a male, that Don Antonio had been arrested on suspicion of being a male practitioner of transvestism! It was no doubt a lesson that halfway measures would not be enough to avoid trouble. The bishop who kept him in seclusion was Don Gabino Valladares Mejía, who died on February 13, 1794. Sometime during those four months, Doña María, already living as a Don Antonio, wrote to her parents to tell them of the pope's command to dress in men's clothing and of the transformation into a man and presumably to seek help in getting released from the bishop's jail. Don Antonio then traveled to Cádiz, staying there four months. Once again Felipa's words:

From Barcelona *he* traveled to Cádiz, where **he** was involved with Doña Vicenta Arias de Reyna, who, declaring that *he* had gotten her pregnant, demanded that it was *his* duty to marry her. *He* immediately disappeared and headed to Málaga, where *he* set sail for these regions, and after *he* wrote from Buenos Aires from the house of the

Illustrious Lord Azamor, I have not known *his* whereabouts until this occurrence [the arrest in La Plata], which has been announced to *her* brothers from that city, which thus shows that Your Mercy looks after **my wretched son** [ése *desgraciado mi hijo*] with interest. And with true mother's love, I am interested that you have the kindness to make use of all imaginable means to ensure that *his* case be attended by the lord president, and that he look upon **her** [*ella*] with interest, as he who is in possession of *her* destiny with respect to its good development. (appendix A.21, fol. 29r)

An astounding account, Felipa's references to her son/daughter's sexual escapades in the wake of the papal dispensation suggest, if we can believe them, that Don Antonio had no intention of keeping Doña María's vow of chastity (assuming, as is likely, that there had been such a vow, not reported by Don Antonio but by Martina) or no ability to keep it. But caution is required in reading Felipa's testimony: it is clear that she has received the gist of Don Antonio's confession, if not a complete copy. Perhaps, then, Felipa is trying to help the case by supporting Don Antonio's version of the motives driving his actions and the theory of hermaphrodism that would be exculpatory, given his insistence on maleness and sexual performance as such. Felipa also reveals that Don Antonio had been in regular communication with her mother and brothers. In service to his client, Don Antonio's lawyer had written his brothers to solicit the testimony (and attached convent certifications). Here we have evidence of a slew of communications among family members. Don Antonio is not entirely "in the closet" or on the run but has traveled far from those who knew María to give Antonio a fighting chance at passing.

Embarking, now fully in the masculine, in Málaga on a journey by sea to Montevideo, a port city across the wide Río de la Plata from the viceregal capital of Buenos Aires, American gateway to the riches of Perú, Don Antonio would have had to pay extra to do so without a license from the Crown. No doubt there was other contraband on the ship he could not name, captained by a man whose name he could not remember. Montevideo, at any rate, was an infamous smuggling port at the time. Who knows what else might have happened on that ship during the approximately five weeks the trip would have lasted, that was in Antonio's best interests to keep out of the public record?

What clothes had Don Antonio acquired in Rome or Cádiz or Málaga for five weeks at sea and a new life in América Española? By the time we have an inventory of his wardrobe, seven years later, fashions had changed, and he would have to have changed his outfits to match them, to sustain his pretenses as Don. The short period from 1789 to 1794, during which Doña María dabbled in cross-dressing in Madrid and then embarked on it as Don Antonio, saw a major shift in both men's and women's dress and the rise of a fashion industry that fueled rapid uptake of new styles, by not only aristocrats but the public at large.

Up until 1789 men's and women's costumes had remained relatively stable for a century. The ladies wore flared and sometimes pleated full-length skirts (called *polleras*—roomy enough to hide a flock of chickens), sometimes worn over a frame to enhance the diameter of the skirt's spread, and above it a tight-fitting short-waisted jacket (*jubón*, in Spanish). On her feet, the well-dressed lady wore low, slipper-like shoes that accentuated the delicacy of the foot and the stride. Men, on the other hand, wore breeches that encased the lower body from the waist to the knees, where they met knee-high stockings worn over hobnail boots, accentuating ease of motion across cobblestones and rough terrain. These would have been the styles of Doña María's youth during her years at home, in the duchess's palace, and in convents. But by the time she moved to her sister's house for nine months in 1791 and then again in early 1792, when she had her cross-dressed flings with Rita Benedicto and the Valencian woman on Los Remedios Street or in the affair, now as Don Antonio, with Doña Vicenta Arias de Reyna in Cádiz in early 1794, styles had changed.

With the French Revolution in 1789, full-length pants, often both baggy and vertically striped (the style of the sansculottes), emerged as an "egalitarian" rejection of the breeches and stockings that had ruled men's wear for the previous few centuries. And women's wide pollera-style skirts were being replaced by more form-fitting, high-waisted dresses. (The victory of reaction after the execution of Maximilien Robespierre on July 28, led to a sea change in styles, which we will take up in later chapters.)

We might imagine Don Antonio wearing the revolutionary sansculotte-style trousers and Phrygian cap from his departure from Rome until his arrival in Buenos Aires. His Madrid accent; his cosmopolitan knowledge of courtly affairs, literature, and theater; his Don and his birth in Madrid; and even the religious knowledge he must have absorbed through his former conventual life came in handy to persuade the bishop there that he would be of good service as a page in the bishop's palace. It was a good landing for a man who was wise not to go regularly carousing with other men in taverns and brothels.

Over a period of a few years, Doña María had fleetingly and occasionally, and then permanently, adopted men's clothing. She very quickly learned how to fully inhabit it and most likely to enjoy the play with its politics that came with these shifts in fashion. A change of sex-marked clothing styles was a major step forward, but to be convincing to others it had to be accompanied by a complete shift from female-to-male styles of speaking, looking, moving, and enacting aristocratic privilege, to properly index male and aristocratic hábitos in the broader sense of that term. Perhaps the Italian female actors had provided some training. But most of that knowledge must have come from taking years of scoldings for improper behavior as a girl, formal instruction in proper femininity and recogimiento endured while encased in nun's habits during her hazing as a novice in four convents, and the lessons in performance, successful and failed, that literature and theater, service in a grandee's house, and the gossip and backbiting therein had offered to Doña María.

Inverting expressed codes of behavior, looking assertively at men and women of lower social estate rather than keeping eyes averted, adopting masculine speech styles rather than feminine ones, charging into the streets and plazas and marketplaces rather than remaining safely behind the threshold home or convent cell, Doña María acted with a masculine desenvoltura (unconstrained ease) rather than a feminine recogimiento. She had acquired a more explicit and reflexive understanding than most social actors of the organizing "schemas" of located, subject-position-defining "habitus," to use Bourdieu's (1990) terms. Engaging in acts of "translation" of habitus (and hábitos), she then inhabited the clothing, sex, and social roles of a male aristocrat effectively enough to naturalize performance as an embodied male, aristocratic subject position or "identity," to use anachronistic terms for what Don Antonio, in his confession, had called an effort to resolve a problem of *conciencia* (conscience, but also consciousness, the self-knowledge of the speaking "I"). Indeed, apart from the arrest in Barcelona, where it appears that Don Antonio was suspected of being a secretly transvestite man, there is no indication that others ever doubted Don Antonio's sex until Doña Martina took him to task.

Introducing himself as Don Antonio and presenting himself to the world in a man's clothing were performative acts that, when felicitous, were recognized and accepted by others as indexes of Don Antonio's maleness, which they understood, in part, as the presence of male genitals. Such performatives were efficacious not only because Don Antonio was convincing in his performance but because he made use of a kind of name and title, and certain kinds of clothing, that had been repeatedly used by others to index maleness. His performance cited those previous uses, and a discursive chain of citations (in the terms of Derrida [1972] 1999, adopted by Judith Butler 1997) helped to crystallize in the minds of his interlocutors, a presumption of male genitalia beneath those clothes. This is what Suzanne Kessler (1998) refers to as "cultural genitals." They are the product of different but intersecting and mutually reinforcing codes and the force of their repeated performance drawing on them: a naming system that sorted names into a sexed binary, a form of grammatical gender that distinguished Don from Doña (and differentiated Juan from Juana, or Antonio from Antonia) and a fashion system (Barthes 1983) that divided male costume from female costume. As we have seen, sex/gender was also indexed by certain ways of speaking (Ochs 1992) and kinds of bodily praxis, such as walking or sitting or horseback riding, as well as ways of looking at others and doing specific kinds of things in ways that were supported or constrained by all these factors. It was not only Don Antonio's trousers but a thousand kinds of well-practiced masculine behaviors, including sexual ones, that indexed male genitalia beneath his clothing, calling them into existence for those with whom he interacted.

From a young age Doña María had begun to move from house to palace to a series of convents, returning in between to the duchess's palace, her homes in Colmenar de Oreja or Madrid, and her sister's house. In each of these moves she was invested in a new set of hábitos, associated with new strictures, new periods of training, and new opportunities to acquire a reflexive understanding of hábitos. Experiences with the theater and with the back- and offstage doings of professional actors added to such reflexivity, as did residence among strangers in Genoa and Rome, where the absence of those who had known her before and the public indifference to others typical of urban life opened the door to more fulsome exploration of becoming other than she had been.

Of course, Doña María did not try to "pass" as a man in her former haunts or to those who had known her as María. Travel to new haunts has always been the best friend of those seeking to change themselves, particularly when there is something in that past to conceal, which if revealed might be damaging to a hoped-for new social standing. That lesson had been learned, and made common knowledge, by generations of migrants from Spain to its colonies, who left behind commoner status or the stigma of a criminal past, illegitimate birth, or suspicion of being descended from Jews or Muslims to start afresh. Let us see what opportunities and risks accompanied Doña María's journey, now as Don Antonio, from Rome to Málaga, Málaga to Montevideo, and beyond, in search of a man's career in the colonial context.

CHAPTER 3

PASSAGES

The Passing Privileges of Don Antonio's Sartorial Modernity in América

Setting Sail

In previous chapters we have seen the kinds of self-narration to which Don Antonio had access and recourse to explain himself to others and the training in the logical and practical schemas of hábitos, marking every kind of social distinction, including sex and social estate, that he had received as a young girl, a criada, and a convent novice. We have reviewed the kinds of literary and stage characters, nobles, parents, nuns, and actors, who provided models for both social climbing and cross-dressing and demonstrated the "tells" of inauthenticity that Don Antonio had to avoid. Even before departing Rome, Doña María consummated the transition into Don Antonio in the time-honored manner of most coming-of-age stories and of most young Spanish social climbers: through travel (see map 2). Setting sail from Málaga (fig. 7) on a commercial vessel headed for Montevideo, he left his travails as María behind him.

Away from family and from those who knew him as *her*, Don Antonio practiced being what he had previously been scolded for, dressing and acting as a man. Lessons from his female Italian actor companions and inversion of the schemas organizing feminine hábitos, exchanging feminine recogimiento for manly desenvoltura, must have served him well enough, once he ditched the dresses that had given him away in Barcelona. We might wonder how Don Antonio managed to keep the secret of his body while thrown together

FIG. 7 Manuel Barrón y Carillo, *Port of Málaga*, 1847, detail. Oil on canvas, 45 × 84 cm. ©
Carmen Thyssen-Bornemisza Collection, on loan to the Museo Carmen Thyssen, Málaga, Spain.

with other travelers under conditions that did not allow much privacy. He
had his *Don* and the diffidence it made possible to shield him from interactions with the commoners who would have been the majority of crew and
migrants on his vessel and pants to suggest he could, like other men, urinate
while standing, though that he could not do. Perhaps seasickness gave him
an excuse to remain in his bunk most of the time at sea and some cover for
dealing with his menses.

Unlike many today who wish to radically change their lives and therefore
head to great cities where they may become unnoticeable in a generalized
urban anonymity, live in private quarters, or practice their new identities more
intimately among those more "like" them, Don Antonio not only had to share
cramped quarters over long periods with other curious passengers (see fig.
8), but went on to stay in the large households of powerful men and then to
establish his own household with a surely curious wife. Those must have been
especially stressful contexts for a person with something to conceal.

That something, in the case of Don Antonio, and Doña María before
that, was stigma. Erving Goffman defines stigma as "an attribute that is
deeply discrediting" in a manner that spoils identity, leading to social rejection
(1963, 3). For Doña María, same-sex desire was an invisible stigma, while acts

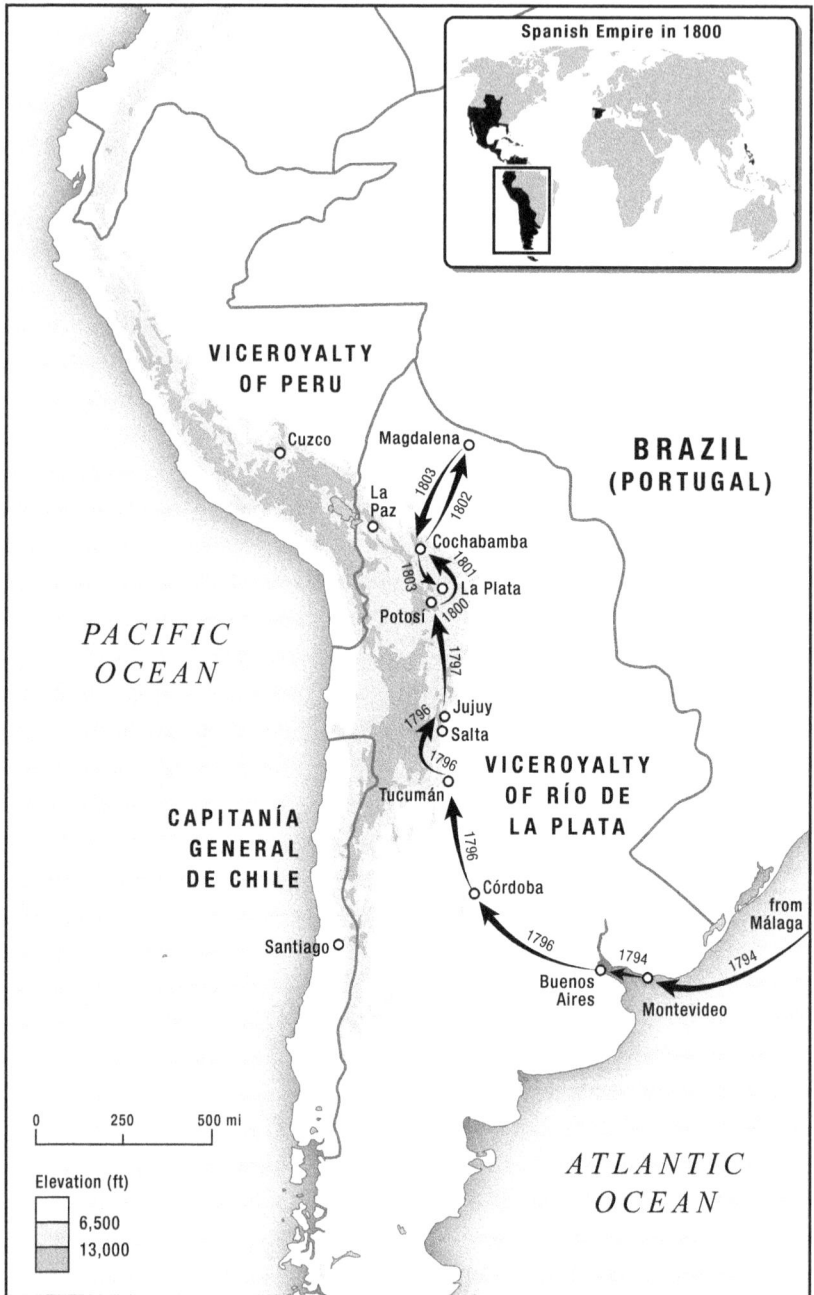

MAP 2 Antonio Yta's travels in Spanish South America, age twenty-three to thirty-two (inset: The Spanish Empire in 1800). Map by Erin Greb Cartography.

FIG. 8 Francisco Pérez, *Expedición de D. Francisco Balmís a la América*, 1846 (depicting 1803 event). Lithograph on paper, 13.5 × 22.8 cm. Lithograph by Manini, 1846. Inventory 34947. Biblioteca Nacional de España, Madrid.

that revealed it in fact stigmatized her. Becoming Don Antonio was a way to manage "discrediting information about self," which is to say, to conceal stigma, that made the stigma of Doña María's same-sex desire disappear behind Don Antonio's heterosexuality. But this covering technique required concealment of the attributes of female sex, which became *Don Antonio's* stigma. "Passing" as a man made his attraction to women acceptable, as long as the stigma of sex was concealed.

Goffman's analysis of the strain of passing is instructive: "To display or not to display; to tell or not to tell; to let on or not to let on; to lie or not to lie; and in each case, to whom, how, when, and where" (1963, 41). Moreover, those who engage in long-term passing, as opposed to momentary or temporary or situational deception, must be continuously on guard, monitoring themselves and striving to avoid situations that might lead to disclosure. They are also likely to face the prospect of having to join in with a "majority" disapproval of the stigma that might discredit them—in Don Antonio's case, of participating in jocular misogyny with male associates. It all adds up to an exhausting level of vigilance (42).

This chapter attends to the kind of "naturalized" work, of which persons may not even be aware, that Pierre Bourdieu imagines to be characteristic of habitus. It is also very much concerned with the reflexive, self-monitoring sort of work that is passing, in Harold Garfinkel's rephrasing of Goffman: "The work of achieving and making secure their rights to live in the elected sex status while providing for the possibility of detection and ruin carried out within the socially structured conditions in which this work occurred I shall call 'passing'" (1967, 118).

Don Antonio must have been very good at such work, or very lucky, because after Barcelona and until his wife "outed" him, no one was suspicious enough of the sufficiency of his maleness to denounce him to the authorities. Let us, then, follow Don Antonio's life story, from his departure from Málaga and arrival in Buenos Aires in 1794 to his posting to La Plata in 1799, to discover how migrating Spaniards made new careers in Spain's colonial possessions and, particularly, to see how Don Antonio, not the usual kind of social climber, did so under challenging new conditions, where being Spanish and aristocratic made him notably stand out from the majority of a very diverse, highly stratified population and where he had to learn a new "system" of hábitos.

Translations: Finding Privileges in Buenos Aires

The city of Buenos Aires, which had a population of about forty thousand when Don Antonio arrived (Boyer and Davies 1983), is a short journey by launch from Montevideo. Approaching Buenos Aires was a bit complicated before its harbor was dredged, since broad shallows and mudflats lay between the closest landing of the launch and dry land. Large-wheeled carts were deployed through the shallows to retrieve passengers and baggage and bring them to shore (fig. 9). Once ashore, Antonio began his colonial career.

Here in América, the term by which Spaniards called the American possessions they once had named "Las Indias," just stepping onto shore was an instant leg up in the world. Whether or not Antonio's parents were Don and Doña, and therefore Antonio could *legitimately* call himself *Don* Antonio, he was now generally free and privileged to do so. Through distance he was free from recrimination or denunciation by all those family members and

FIG. 9 Unknown artist, *Modo de desembarcar en Buenos Ayres*, ca. 1790. Watercolor on paper. Private collection. Courtesy of private collector and Roberto Amigo, agent, Buenos Aires.

accusers left back in Spain. Claiming a higher social standing than one actually possessed was much easier here. Indeed, all Spaniards in the Indies, even those who had been the lowliest of commoner pecheros back in Castile, were free from the obligation of paying tribute in these colonies, where the only tributaries and commoners were Indians.

Finally, Don Antonio was privileged by the very fact of being a Spaniard born in the peninsula, here in a new country made up predominantly of Indians, African slaves, free blacks, and the mixtures called mestizos, *mulatos*, *sambos* (these with neither the privileges of Spaniards nor the tribute and labor obligations of Indians) and *criollos* (at that time, Africans born in the Americas, Spaniards born there, and Indians acculturated to urban life who had lost their connection to rural "nations"). By the 1790s Creole Spaniards had begun to call themselves "whites" to differentiate themselves from all but other Europeans, since their "Creoleness," the fact of living among Indians in the Indies and sharing the same climate, food, and customs, had led peninsular Spaniards to doubt the Creoles' full membership in any of the nations (Castilian, Galician, Catalán, or Basque) of the home country. In spite of their doubtful "Spanishness," Creoles claimed to share the peninsular Spaniards' "whiteness," not so much a product of phenotype but of the hábitos that also indexed their shared privileged status as governing Spaniards. Such hábitos included their clothing and customary ways, including fluency in Castilian, an eagerness to own private property and to demonstrate the purity of their lineages from the taint of descent from stigmatized others, and, especially, their exemption from tributes and labor obligations to the Crown. No Spaniard in the Americas was any longer a pechero, a tributary owing a head tax to the Crown, as were, for example, over 95 percent of the inhabitants of Colmenar de Oreja.

Believably sporting a Don before one's name, along with good political contacts and family connections, also helped the newly arriving Spaniard to find his feet in the Americas. Most hoped to gain profits from the overlordship enjoyed by the small Spanish population over the indigenous majority of the population, through accessing Indian tributes or labor or gaining an administrative post where they might take advantage of both. Antonio, now assertively Don Antonio, claims to have begun his life in Buenos Aires with a search for an acquaintance of his father, one Don Juan Antonio Pintos. Not finding the man, he searched out the bishop of Buenos Aires, Don Manuel de Azamor y Ramírez. Antonio's approach to the bishop was to find a common thread apart from both being peninsular Spaniards, and he found it in the fact that both shared a *patria chica* (small fatherland): they were both Castilians. No doubt running through his mental contact list of influential men sharing biographical space with Bishop Azamor, Antonio finally named a relative of his father, another ecclesiastic, who the bishop recognized as a common tie. In Antonio's reconstructed first-person words: "As a result of that conversation with the Illustrious Lordship, the Bishop remembered a cousin of mine who he knew, a Discalced Carmelite in Madrid named Fray Julián de San Gerónimo. And finally he told me that I could have food and lodging in his palace. And thus it happened that I stayed in the Bishop's house for about three years, until the Lord Bishop's death. And I made myself known then and since by the name of Antonio Yta."

This was truly something of a coup on Antonio's part. No doubt the bishop's decision to offer Don Antonio food and lodging, implying the position of criado, which in a bishop's palace made him a page, depended on more than being Azamor's *paisano*, more than Antonio's *Don*, and more than having acquaintances in common. Don Antonio was a particularly cosmopolitan

Spaniard, with life experiences and knowledge of religion, the ways of the high nobility, theater, and literature. He was literate (an ability most likely acquired in the convents, where reading holy books was mandatory) and quite possibly also familiar with the rudiments, at least, of Enlightenment discourse (from the reading of newspapers). All these things would have made him an appealing interlocutor for the bishop, who would not have surrounded himself with mere lackeys for pages.

Landing in the bishop's palace was also advantageous for Don Antonio. Experience having to run from complications of his dalliances with the ladies in Madrid and Cádiz, and perhaps elsewhere, had forced him to keep moving in the past. Life in the bishop's palace, likely without much access to young women, at least offered some safety from the risks of acting on desire and also was an excellent cover. Having taken a vow of chastity was worth something here, and he would not have been as pressured to go carousing about town with other unmarried criados, which also entailed risky circumstances for someone who needed to keep his clothes on (drunkenness, fights, expectations that he enjoy with others the delights of the brothels, etc.).

Bishop Azamor had been named to his post in 1784, a decade before Yta arrived on his doorstep in 1794. Well liked in the viceregal court and on good terms with the viceroy and with former intendant governor of Buenos Aires Francisco de Paula Sanz (now transferred to Potosí), the bishop had made a reputation as a true Enlightenment figure, partly for his publications, such as his writings urging an end to judicial torture, and partly for amassing an enormous library full of banned works (such as Voltaire's and Denis Diderot's) that with Argentine independence in 1810 would become the heart of the new national library of Argentina (Rípodas Ardanaz 1982). The bishop's household, then, was an excellent place to gain further useful connections.

Named for the river on which Buenos Aires sits, the viceroyalty of the Río de la Plata, created in 1776 in recognition of the port's growing importance as a gateway to Peru and the silver and great markets of Potosí, had absorbed the Audiencia de Charcas and its capital city of La Plata (named for the silver production in its district and a different place altogether from Buenos Aires). In those years the Crown was busy installing a new technocratic elite in the administrative roles in the audiencias of the Indies. Upper levels of state administration were increasingly skeptical of the loyalty of Creole Spaniards, enabling newly arriving peninsulars like Antonio, even lacking the proven

FIG. 10 Emeric Essex Vidal, *Church of Santo Domingo*, 1820, detail. Lithograph. From Vidal (1820), plate following page 44.

noble genealogies and university degrees that made for truly high careers, to make something of themselves.

Whether or not Don Antonio accompanied the bishop to illustrious events and evening tertulias, as Osvaldo Bazán (2004) supposes, he would have noted the quick uptake here of the new fashions arriving from Spain (fig. 10), product of the booming textile industry in Barcelona (Vicente 2006). His own dissimulations, concealing his prior name and assigned sex behind an embodied enactment of maleness, carried off particularly through the wearing of pants and confident stride enabled by boots, was reflected in the put-on airs of a large, social-climbing population and by the concealment of individual identity that certain fashion provided, such as the wearing of the mantilla covering the face, that was all the rage among the ladies of the city.

Bishop Azamor died on October 2, 1796, almost three years after Antonio's arrival. Antonio then set out, letter of introduction from the bishop (acquired honestly or by forgery, we cannot tell) in hand, on the highway to the fortune seeker's destination of Potosí. From the coastal plain and grasslands outside of Buenos Aires, the dusty highway arcs through the pampas of Argentina for about 1,300 miles, rising gradually onto the high Andean plateau called the

FIG. 11 Emeric Essex Vidal, *Convoy of Wine Mules*, 1820. Lithograph. From Vidal (1820), plate following page 90.

altiplano, via the cities of Tucumán and Salta (in the northwestern corner of today's Argentina). The itinerary was well marked, trod by mule trains carrying silver from Potosí to Buenos Aires and all manner of merchandise to Potosí and Ciudad de la Plata, "Silver City," a few days' march farther to the north of Potosí (fig. 11). The trip from Buenos Aires to Potosí might have taken a few months on horse- or mule-back and at a good trot, but Antonio broke his leg before reaching Tucumán and took an additional four months while it healed.

Into the Maelstrom: From Buenos Aires to the Mining City of Potosí

To find his way in this vast territory, where peninsular Spaniards like himself (often called *ultramarinos*) were in a small minority and were sometimes ridiculed as *chapetones* or, in the Aymara language spoken in the region of Potosí, *puka kunkas* (red necks) for their tendency to sunburn, Antonio most likely availed himself of a pair of guidebooks. One of these, written by a mail-route inspector named Alonso Carrió de la Vandera, was published under the pseudonym Concolorcorvo (Color of the Raven) and titled *Lazarillo de ciegos caminantes* ([1773] 1908; see also the extract in English, published as *El Lazarillo: A Guide for Inexperienced Travelers Between Buenos Aires and Lima* [1773] 1965). It was not only useful (describing the highway and its way stations) but entertaining, a satire of life in the viceroyalty (see Hill 2005). The other book, José Joaquín Araujo's *Guía de forasteros* (1792, [1803] 1908) named the royal and ecclesiastical officials of all the audiencias, cities, and intendancies of the viceroyalty. Should Antonio have had to forge his own letter of introduction to Francisco de Paula Sanz, he had at hand the official titles and full names by which to do so properly. Quite possibly, the bishop had already helped him make the connection to Doña Martina through her father or through Sanz, since there was a short supply of promising young unmarried ultramarinos, and parents still sought to control their children's marriages to good political effect.

Although Antonio stopped in Potosí, the road continues from there, following a highway first built by the Incas, the Capac Ñan, over which Spaniards laid a road amenable to mules and wagons. Today the road is called the Pan-American Highway, continuing from Potosí northwest to La Paz, Cuzco, and, farther north, to Quito and Santa Fé de Bogotá. Cuzco had been the "navel of the world" and the capital of the Inca Empire, and Spaniards founded their first South American viceregal capital in the port city of Lima, also connected to this highway. But the heart and (twisted) soul of Perú, as most of South America was known, was Potosí. There in 1545 indigenous people had revealed to Spaniards the richest silver mines in the world. The region had already been considered rich before that: already under Inca rule the region of Charcas was home to a large population of indigenous people, settled in farming and herding lifeways and working elaborately terraced and irrigated maize fields as well as mines rich in precious metals.

Arriving in Potosí, Don Antonio presented his letter of introduction to that city's intendant governor, Francisco de Paula Sanz. A powerhouse of the colonial administration and right-hand man of Viceroy Juan José Vértiz, Sanz was rumored to be King Charles III's bastard son. He was also a reformer, aiming to rationalize mine labor and secularize state authority by under-cutting the church's hold on public pomp and pageantry. A well-known

Enlightenment figure, Sanz owned an impressive library (Rípodas Ardanaz 2002) and was a prodigious author of political and administrative tracts (Sanz [1794] 1970, [1779–80] 1977), although much of his work may have been written by his brilliant aide (Creole and thus lower-ranking) Pedro Vicente Cañete y Domínguez, another prodigious Enlightenment author (Cañete y Domínguez [1787] 1952, [1794] 1973–74, 1810, 1812, 1973), who would become one of Don Antonio's judges. Whether because of the bishop's letter, because Antonio shared Sanz's views, or because he was, like Sanz, a peninsular Spaniard, Sanz took Antonio under his wing, lodging him in his large Potosí household as a criado for about two years while Antonio did unknown service for Sanz and struggled to find his feet.

Potosí was known as the engine of empire for the amount of silver that flowed from its mines and was an impressively large and prosperous city (even in the 1790s, though its peak of silver production and population was long past), if a harsh and somewhat wild one. Located more than fourteen thousand feet above sea level, it was a bitterly cold place; full of fortune hunters and miners, it was also home to countless *chicherías* (taverns that served maize-based beer called *chicha*), brothels, and gambling houses, along with public theaters and a bustling marketplace where one could purchase luxury goods imported from Europe and China. Potosí was the cold heart of the Audiencia de Charcas, the colonial district that had been founded, with nearby La Plata as its capital, to administer this heavily populated Andean region. Here the majority of the population, indigenous peoples, mostly Aymara- and Quechua-speaking ones, provided tributes to the king and *encomenderos* and provided labor service in the famously rich mines of the Cerro Rico, the "rich hill" of Potosí on the very slopes of which the city of the same name was built, becoming the largest city in the hemisphere and one of the largest in the world by 1600.[1]

Although it was well past its heyday in 1797, when Don Antonio arrived, Potosí was still a major draw for young fortune hunters from Spain. Like most new arrivals, Antonio failed to make a fortune there, though he found respite and favor with Governor Sanz. Such a thing was not unusual in the households of the wealthy and powerful, whose great *casonas* ("big houses" composed of multistoried buildings surrounding a series of patios) sheltered many families and hangers-on. We don't know Antonio's role in the governor's household. Antonio's interrogators did not pursue the matter, perhaps to

FIG. 12 Unknown artist, *Retrato del Gobernador Francisco de Paula Sanz*, ca. 1790–1800. Oil on canvas. Museo Histórico Nacional, Buenos Aires, Argentina.

avoid embarrassing this powerful intendant governor. Antonio no doubt took part in some way in Sanz's activities and most certainly was more exposed to the risk of discovery of his "imposture" in Potosí than as a bishop's page.

Possibly, Antonio's work related to one of the massive reform projects that Sanz and Don Pedro Vicente Cañete were involved with during these years: the development of the Código Carolino, a new set of mining laws and procedures drawing on the expertise of a group of Polish mining engineers (members of the Nordenflycht Expedition [Buechler 1973]) who were also guests in Sanz's household at this time. A few years after his arrest, the Balmís Expedition, bringing a host of physicians and "vaccinators" to the empire's colonial reaches, would pass through, vaccinating the population against smallpox using Edward Jenner's technique (Franco-Paredes, Lammoglia, and Santos-Preciado 2005).

Apart from their scientific, engineering, and fiscal reforms, Sanz and Cañete were known for their efforts to reform—by increasing—the coercive labor system known as the *mita* of Potosí, by which indigenous people were brought en masse to work the mines for yearly turns.[2] Such reforms were needed because mine productivity had fallen. Sanz was also known at the time for his disputes with the church, since, blaming the large number of religious festivals in Indian towns for siphoning off indigenous energy and monies, he had tried to "secularize" the towns by radically reducing indigenous participation in church festivals, which meant a major loss of revenue to the church itself. And so Sanz and Cañete, as well as most judges of the audiencia, remained in an almost constant battle of jurisdictions with the church in these years, while all these officials eagerly snapped up copies of the latest gazettes and newspapers, at this time full of announcements of new production techniques, medical discoveries, and debates surrounding every sort of reform, that were published in the empire's capitals.

Governor Sanz's household was not only large but also extraordinarily lavish, helping to cement his privileged status in the viceroyalty (along with his extremely long list of surnames—he was Francisco de Paula Sanz y Espinosa de los Monteros Martínez y Soler). Reputed to have ten African slaves in livery available to serve his guests their drinks, Sanz was apparently able to spare no expense.[3] Even his "foot-warmer" little dog, waiting for cold feet under the table in Sanz's portrait, was fat (fig. 12). The household of the highest-ranking peninsular Spaniard in Potosí provided Don Antonio exceptional opportunities for the advancement of his career, of which he took good advantage.

Courtship and Marriage: Desire or Covering Strategy?

Governor Sanz introduced Antonio Yta to Martina, his wife-to-be, sometime in 1798. Antonio tells us, in the dramatic emendation to his confession, once it is read back to him, that the two had engaged in "illicit relations" for a year before their marriage in Potosí in 1799, suggesting that their courtship included a sexual relationship (or as Mariano Taborga's letter from Buenos Aires puts it, they were *amancebados*: she was his concubine). Don Antonio's confession tells us nothing of prior sexual relationships with women once he has entered his life narrative as a man, and the fact that engaging in one publicly represented considerable risk of exposure leads us to wonder why he risked such a relationship.

It is only to be expected, of course, that young people with sexual appetites will seek to satisfy them. But for Don Antonio, doing so represented a double threat. On the one hand there was the vow of chastity imposed on him by the pope as a condition for permission to dress and live as a man. On the other, there was the chance that whatever young woman he seduced would discover under his clothing the woman's parts that he worked so hard to conceal and, upon discovering them, hand him over to the authorities. That is, indeed, what ultimately happened, even though he managed the situation for over four years before it did.

Why did Don Antonio take such as risk? Was it simply the pull of desire? Was it an unstoppable urge to carry his manly life to full completion? Or was engaging in that courtship and marriage a "covering" act, meant to enhance his cover as a man? I would argue that all three motives are implicated, and no doubt also the thing called love, and what must have been, given the constant self-monitoring and avoidance of careless "reveals" that would have made his life a solitary one, a powerful need for intimacy. Courting and marrying Martina brought risks, but also rewards—among them not only intimacy, love, and sexual gratification but also another strong argument for his male-ness. A somewhat short and beardless man who avoided (we must assume) "male bonding" activities with male peers and kept mostly to himself would have invited frequent teasing by other men as an effeminate and potential sodomite or, at least, not a "manly" man. Don Antonio's potential responses to such teasing were limited. Violence was one apt reply to such insults, but brawling could leave Don Antonio unconscious and defenseless. He could not afford to lose his shirt or his pants, and treatment by a physician could spell complete disaster. Improving his covering strategies was absolutely necessary to "keep the stigma from looming large" (Goffman 1963, 102). Marriage and establishing his own household were much better choices than hypermas-culine strutting and engagement in the manly culture of *pundonor*, "point of honor." This was particularly true in the case of Don Antonio, who had plenty of practice spinning and sewing, praying and serving God and the nobility, and also, as his legal demand—written in his own hand—for return of his clothing from Martina tells us, reading and writing, but as far as we know, none in fighting. Unlike Catalina/Antonio de Erauso, who had been to Potosí and La Plata almost two centuries before Don Antonio Yta, the latter gives no evidence of familiarity with sword and dagger. He seems to have worked at becoming a bureaucrat, not a soldier.

It may be that sustaining multiple identities within a single being is "the ancestral theme of disguise, the essential attribute of gods, police, and bandits" (Barthes 1983, 256–57). Like them, the man concealing that he sleeps with other men so as to appear to be heterosexual (to remain "in the closet" or to "pass" as heterosexual) or the man disguising a female body to conceal his "trans" must develop a complex and solid cover to avoid provoking too many questions or an accidental "reveal."

It is perhaps ironic that one of the greatest threats to Don Antonio's passing would have been suspicion of having sex with (other) men and that Antonio's best cover, as an ascribed woman living disguised as a man to hide same-sex desire, was to carry out a same-sex act with another woman. Courting and marrying an aristocratic young woman would have squelched the incessant teasing and retort that is the enforcing system of mandatory heterosexuality. It would also have provided a more private life, in which socializing with his male peers and exposure to such surveillance could be reduced to a minimum without raising an eyebrow. Of course, courtship and marriage brought its own risks. He would need to find a mate herself interested in women or else a true ingenue who he could keep in the dark about the exact nature of his sex.

Doña Martina Vilvado y Balverde was sixteen or seventeen years old when Don Antonio began to court her. How did that courtship unfold? We might suppose many walks together around Potosí's central plaza (fig. 13), at least during midday hours when it is not too cold for that. Perhaps he pulled her into dark doorways for some furtive snoggling and touching (he, touching her). But we also need to picture the interactions the couple's social pretensions made possible, and required. Together they most likely attended the soirees at Governor Sanz's house, where the cosmopolitan standards of the royal court of Madrid held sway. Together Antonio and Martina shared the exclusivity of their exalted "Spanishness," now wedded (in the colonies) to whiteness and colonial privilege, in a city where every Spaniard, Creole or peninsular, lorded it over a majority population of Indians, Africans, and mixed "castes."

FIG. 13 J. Clark, *Inhabitants of Potosí, in the Great Square in Front of the Cathedral*, 1829. Engraving. From Temple (1830), plate following page 292.

Only a tiny percentage of the Spaniards in Potosí (and in the Indies more generally) actually came from noble backgrounds, and in any case the Indies had essentially been denied its own landed aristocracy. Instead, a de facto aristocracy based on the privilege of belonging to the nations of Spain, lately redefined in nascent terms of color and race, made the Americas, and Potosí in particular, into the place where lowborn ex-commoners could perform aristocratic manners and presume superiority. Such mobility was easier in the Indies than it was back in Spain, where the "commoner" majority, Spaniards all, ridiculed the social-climbing bourgeoisie by pointing out their lowly ancestry and lack of the attributes of honor and proper lineage. So here both Don Antonio and Doña Martina could put on airs and be accepted into decent high society. That meant clinging to the cosmopolitan fashions of the Spanish metropole and behaving in the "modern" ways of the imperial capital of Madrid, the more to highlight their peninsular superiority over the Creole Spaniards who, peninsulars argued, had absorbed too much of the African and Indian through an excessive intimacy in part defined through their embrace of exotic cuisine and in part merely from being born and raised in different latitudes.[4]

It is also possible to have a more visual image of the couple and what clothing they wore. It turns out that the reigning fashions of the time also

FIG. 14 Unknown artist, *Perfecto currutaco*, ca. 1795–1800. Colored engraving. Inventory 2339. Museo de Historia de Madrid.

supplied "covering" possibilities. In November 1803, while Don Antonio languished in jail, he sued Doña Martina for return of his clothing. His wardrobe (and hers) conjure up a complex picture of the absolutely latest elite Madrid fashions of the era, linked not only to specific kinds of ballroom dancing (the *contradanza*, a group dance in pairs, akin to a square dance) but to a particular style of courtship, a stance toward the world, and a self-conscious modernity that was the subject of a prodigious literature at the turn of the nineteenth century. For Don Antonio's clothing includes a complete currutaco outfit, a French-influenced faddish style that was all the rage in Madrid (and in Buenos Aires, Potosí, and Manila) (fig. 14).

Among Doña Martina's possessions Don Antonio has listed "one whole *currutaco* of fine new *zaraza* (fine, printed cotton cloth).[5] Although it is listed with her things, this particular item was associated with a very well-known male fashion of the time. It is an unusual use of the term *currutaco*; most usages of the era do not label the *outfit* as a currutaco, but name the *wearer* as one. For a currutaco, in the 1790s through 1810s, was a dandy. We might then translate the line as "a complete dandy suit of fine cotton, printed cloth." This may be just a suit of clothing, but the particular significance of wearing it, and thus being a currutaco, or dandy, during the decade coinciding with the peak of Don Antonio's career, make it worth pursuing in some depth.

Don Antonio as Currutaco: A Thoroughly Modern Dandy

The term *currutaco* is to be found relatively frequently in concordances of published works during the 1790s through 1810s, referring to a special sort of Spanish dandy, one addicted to the latest French fashions, not only to kinds of clothing but a recognizable and nameable stylization of the body and way of being by which the clothes were inhabited. A "complete" or "perfect" currutaco wore a combination of tight-fitting, knee-length breeches (*calzones*, in Don Antonio's wardrobe), closed under the knee with silver buckles, over long, also tight-fitting silk or cotton stockings (*medias*). Tucked into the calzones, a collarless shirt with a frilled lace front (*camisa, con pechera de olan*) and sometimes frilled cuffs, an underjacket (*chupezi* in Don Antonio's wardrobe) with silver buttons or clasps (*hebillas*), and a wide-colored and heavily adorned morning coat (*chaqueta*). A fashionable currutaco's chaqueta was cut back deeply at the waist, wasplike, and sported extra-long tails. For footwear, Don Antonio lists, as clothing held by Martina in Cochabamba, only a pair of boots. Perhaps when arrested he was wearing the pointy-toed, delicate slippers that made for a currutaco's mincing walk, tarred as effeminate by contemporary critics of the fashion. An extra-wide cravat covered the entire neck to the chin, and a bicorne (Napoleonic) hat accompanied the outfit, sometimes worn over a corset to achieve the desired rear-back and chest-out swayback effect. The currutaco was subject to a great deal of satire and was frequently depicted in illustrations.

One such illustration (fig. 15) includes verses of warning (my translation):

Lector mire esas figuras,	Reader, look at these figures,
que son criticas morales;	which are moral criticism;

y retratos vien cabales	and quite accurate portraits
de vanidosas locuras.	of vain insanities.
Ese Joben a infinitos	This young man represents
en el dia Representa,	an infinite number these days,
que lleban errada cuenta,	who mistakenly take great pains,
por parecer puliditos,	only to improve their appearance.
con sus locos kalendarios	from their crazy calendars
resultan muchos perjuicios;	all results are prejudicial;
pues son fomentos de vicios,	since they promote vices,
y martires boluntarios.	and voluntary martyrs.
El criado a incapie tirando	The servant sets his feet
ajusta bien el Corsé:	to tighten well the corset:
sabe muy bien el porque,	why, he knows quite well,
pero se burla callando.	but keeps the joke to himself.
A hombres afeminados	In our day all we see
miramos en nuestros dias.	are effeminized men,
pués todas sus valentias	since all their effort goes
son por berse acicalados.	to glamorize themselves.
Bestid (Jovenes Pudientes)	Dress (well-to-do young men)
sin tretas artificiales;	without artificial tricks;
y creed que prendas morales	and believe that moral outfits
son los trajes mas decentes.	are the most decent suits of clothing.

Numerous short plays, musical numbers, and no doubt scurrilous commentary accompanied such publications.

The clothing style and mannerisms of the currutaco in this late Bourbon era of Francophilia closely resemble, and were indeed copied from, those of the French *incroyables*, aristocratic young men who, following the execution of Maximilien Robespierre and the end of the Reign of Terror in July 1794, strutted back into the streets and theaters and ballrooms to assert the end of the egalitarian era and the reimposition of social difference. The social styles

FIG. 15 Unknown artist, *La armadura del buen gusto, ó, el corsé*, ca. 1795–1800. Colored engraving. Inventory 2314. Museo de Historia de Madrid.

of the incroyables and the currutacos involved a display of nonworking, lei-surely ways; disdain for servants and the poor, shown by mistreating them; and concern above all for aesthetic effect. In the currutaco, intellect and reason turned entirely to the cultivation of the (aristocratic) self as aesthetic object.

Perhaps these were "just fashions." But they were fashions marked for social estate and thus for politics, whether (as in the case of the incroyables or currutacos) a renewed display of aristocratic privilege and presumption or the antithetical fashion, which in France was that of the revolutionary Republican (plebeian and antiaristocratic) sansculottes, "without-breeches." The French *cullottes* (in Spanish called *calzones*) were the body-hugging, knee-length breeches worn by aristocrats for the previous century (and by incroyables and currutacos); sansculottes' innovation was the wearing of full-length trousers, often striped; plain white shirts without the frills and lace;

and red Phrygian caps instead of tricorn or Napoleonic-style bicorn hats. The sansculotte style, deeply antithetical to the heightened aristocratic "empire" style of the currutaco, also took off in Spain and Spanish America, where it identified a wearer's claim in the terms of social class and political philosophy.

Yet another aristocratic fashion in Spain at the turn of the nineteenth century was that of *majos* and *majas*. This fashion trend marked a specifically "national romance" (Sommer 1993) through playful social estate–crossing sexual transgression, involved "dressing down," wearing the styles of those who elites held to be the most thoroughgoingly "gender dimorphic" (maximally masculine and feminine): provincial plebeians and Gitanos (the Roma of Spain). They are also the key figures of Spain's national romances, such as Georges Bizet's *Carmen*. Currutaco ways (or *currutaquería*) also involved a swipe at this emergent Romantic flirtation with the (downward, nation-building) estate-crossing of the Romantics.[6]

The full title of one anonymous work published in Madrid in 1796 conveys the both the self-conscious embrace of Enlightened modernity and the tone of self-parody that characterized this fashion trend: *Book of Fashion at the Fair, Containing an Essay on the History of Currutacos, Pirracas, and Madamitas of the Newly Minted Kind, and the Elements or First Notions of Currutaca Science: Written by a Currutaco Philosopher, Published, Annotated, and Commented by a Little Lord Pirracas*. As this book makes very clear, to be currutaco was to be highly conscious of being "modern," a product of the Enlightenment, where what was truly new was "science," now freed of the supposition that social estate was God-given and inevitable, of self-making.

Just prior to a chapter on the "natural history" of the currutaco, the author of this tongue-in-cheek little book on what was a very recent and current fad treats its "ancient history" down to the present day, locating the figure within a sarcastic elegy to the Enlightened era that sounds every bit like the most celebratory account of twenty-first-century globalization:

We have now arrived in present history. Of the actual currutacos, let's say. In no epoch have there been so many. *Currutaquería* has never been so widespread. Lights propagate across the entire face of our terraqueous globe. Its force, its liveliness seems to grow as it spreads. Never have we known so much. Never has science been so universal. It spreads among all the classes and among all the peoples /17/. It propagates successively to the most remote regions.

O Enlightened century! Until now, even in the happiest times, science existed only among one people, the light illuminated only one horizon. Its rays did not reach the others. All the nations lay in the darkest twilight.

Today the entire globe forms a single nation, a single people, a single family. The lights have their center or focus, we know where it is, and from there they extend across the whole orbit of the wise world and reflect down in various directions on the most hidden and remote corners. Atoms of light fall both on the uncivilized Greenlanders, and the elevated Sybarites.

Let us compare, then, *currutaquería* to a reciprocity machine [*máquina de resortes*]. Everything is tied together. The most distant wheel freely communicates with the center. They all turn in the same direction. Movement is equal. A blow to one end of the machine resounds on the other end. /18/ In ancient times there was more difference between an inhabitant of Byzantium and an Athenian than now exists between an Englishman and an Iroquois, because in the end the two nations communicate and know each other more. An inhabitant of Scandinavia dresses like a Parisian, and a Lapp thinks and talks like us; at the ends of Asia they live as they do in the center of Europe. Travel, and you will almost see no difference between their customs.

Today there are currutacos everywhere in the world, and at bottom nothing distinguishes them. On Carmen Street they manufacture two identical scarves. One flies to the ends of Asia, the other goes to the main room across the street.

Two fashion doll-models leave the delicate hands of a designer on Montera Street, one of them travels to a corner of Galicia; Who would have said it! The other crosses the immense Ocean, and comes to rest in the court of the ancient Incas. A square dance [*contradanza*, the currutaco's favored pastime] starts up on Fuencarral Street, in the little Plaza of the Angel, in a thousand places; since in this favored town diversions swarm; they multiply to infinity. This happy square dance is repeated one field day on the banks of the mighty Amazon River. A currutaco has a conversation in the Puerta del Sol; it is in unison with another that takes place on the stroll ways of opulent Mexico. The same phrases, the same opinions. They cite the same books. (qtd. in [Fernández de Rojas] 1796, 16–19; my translation)

The author of this book was not mistaken about the effects of "globalization," since it is true that the global spread of empire and its commerce did indeed bring Madrid fashions in dress and dance rather quickly to Buenos Aires, Potosí, and La Plata, just as it delivered Chinese silks to the Americas on their way to London and Paris via Spanish ports. Such commerce may have seemed to those involved—those with the greatest stakes in remaining au courant, at least—the sense of living in an age of "simultaneous, empty time" (Anderson 1991), where, geographic distance no longer a barrier, the world might live as one. Such ideas nourished the dream of merging nation and state for those already imagining an empire-wide republic of citizens (of a kind that was briefly institutionalized in the constitution of the Cortes [parliament] of Cádiz of 1812). But let us remember that the *Book of Fashion* is a work of satire.

In some ways this fad itself involved an extreme form of self-parody, along the lines of twentieth-century *camp* (Newton 1972). No wonder *currutaquería*, the science of being a currutaco, was a parody of itself: It celebrated reason and aesthetic appreciation of the world in the most unhinged way, by asserting the superior intellect of those most able to perform aristocratic superiority over others, which is to say, members of the imperial administration. It was social hierarchy for the social climber, as is suggested by the *Book of Fashion*'s title phrase "of the newly minted kind" (*del nuevo cuño*), which in the Spanish of the time denoted "one who has recently entered a profession, guild, or social class." The book is not, after all, a celebration of currutaco trend, but a critique. "Bred, not born" (Amann 2015, 262), currutacos were here being denounced as social climbers and effeminized fops.

That is because it was the fashion of a recently reemboldened aristocracy, adopted by the then-growing bourgeoisie, "middling sorts" from among the plebeian social estate, now enriched through commerce or employment in Crown administration, and themselves emboldened by the crumbling of revolutionary ideas about rule by commoners, the reassertion of monarchical social hierarchy, and new trends in political economy that made wealth and ostentation itself (and not just honorable lineage) into a marker of high social standing.

In the French fad that emerged when Parisian aristocrats could finally come out of hiding, no longer terrorized by the guillotine, the female outfit and style that accompanied the incroyables was that of the *merveilleuses*, who wore gossamer, highly revealing togas modeled on those of ancient Rome or Greece. Spanish and French fashions for ladies prior to this moment had been quite different: a jacket-like bodice with poufed shoulders, fitting tightly to the waist, below which voluminous skirts reaching to the ankles were held away from the body by whalebone stays. In Spain the new fashion, on the

FIG. 16 Francisco de Goya y Lucientes, *Quién más rendido?*, 1797–99. Etching, aquatint, drypoint. Inventory G02115. © Museo Nacional del Prado, Madrid.

contrary, often referred to as a *camisa* for its nightshirt-like thinness and straight fall, was gathered directly under the bust, empire style; below, its lightweight fabric was layered into a series of fringed tiers.

Ladies who wore such things and on whom currutacos doted were known as *madamitas del nuevo cuño*, a rather vulgar interlingual expression, borrowed from the French *madame*, which when used in the Hispanicized diminutive *madamita* was a term for a prostitute. *Del nuevo cuño*, applied to women, would have resounded of the Spanish term for female genitals, *coño* (then as today it was simultaneously the most vulgar four-letter term for the vulva but was also quite commonly used, by both men and women, as an interjection of surprise or dismay).

The suggested vulgarity of the madamitas drew also on the newly fashionable form of mannered courtship in which such pairs engaged: *cortejo*. The husbands of elite women were supposed to allow their wives to be courted, in public and in private, by other men. In his engraving titled *Quién más rendido?*,

"Who has submitted more?," Goya depicts himself as a currutaco, obsequiously presenting himself to a haughty, *camisa*-clad Duchess of Alba (fig. 16).

The title is another play on words, where *rendido* applies both to Goya and the duchess, with Goya surrendering his dignity and masculinity, and the duchess in a style suggestive of slatternly sexual submission. For more conservative members of society, and for commoners, this form of cortejo, where effeminized currutacos dallied with elite married women, potentially cuckolding their purportedly aristocratic husbands, constituted a scandalous breach of the old honor code (Amann 2015; Martín Gaite [1972] 2000). That was particularly the case when the madamitas del nuevo cuño engaged in yet further play with dress codes that marked status and gender by wearing the outfits of the lower class, provincial maja (as depicted by Goya). Dressed either way, such women were as good as naked, something Goya also appreciated.[7]

So we may well imagine Don Antonio as a currutaco, accompanying a young Doña Martina in her stylish tiered and fringed dress, trotting out the renewed haughty pretensions of the (would-be) aristocracy in styles that flew as quickly to Buenos Aires, Potosí, and La Plata as it had from Paris to Madrid.[8] Their relationship, at least until Don Antonio's violent jealousy got in the way, may well have included attending soirees in Potosí and La Plata, where they almost certainly would have taken part in *contradanzas*, then all the rage in Potosí and Manila as well as in Madrid. Don Antonio's faddish currutaco outfit would have been just the ticket for such a courtship, no doubt also involving the elaborate, exaggerated mannerisms of French-inspired cortejo (Amann 2015). Among other things, these involved formal hand kissing, done while standing in a haughty but humbled posture, bent at the waist but head and chest high.

The outfit of the gender- and class-crossing, honor-transgressing dandy (for this was the Spanish version of that turn-of-the-nineteenth-century fashion and personal style) and the corresponding over-the-top impersonation of aristocratic privilege via an exaggerated performance of disdain for social inferiors was an excellent fashion choice for a bodily female, middling-class social climber who desperately needed to convincingly perform the manners of the male aristocrat. Currutacos appeared to be self-parodying, ultrasnobbish aristocrats, beset by mannered, even effeminate, affectations, while sustaining misogynist treatment of women and disdain for social inferiors, the performative bulwarks of white masculinity; the style was a peculiarly appropriate way for a woman to pass as a man and for a person of lower to middling origins to pass for an aristocrat.

Finding His White Privilege: Sex and Social Climbing in the Colonies

Potosí may have been a cold and harsh high-altitude city, but Governor Sanz's house was the center of its courtly social life. Potosí was famous for its theaters, with plays regularly performed by traveling theater companies (Beyersdorff 1999), and for the grandness of its festivals and processions (Voigt 2016). As a mining boomtown, it was also well known for the number of its taverns, gambling dens, brothels, and violent crimes. We might imagine the pair strolling around the plaza, chaperoned by Martina's parents, but we should also keep in mind the possibilities for subterfuge and secret meetings in secluded spots, carried out with the help of clerics, servants, and slaves in the governor's thrall. The chronicle of colonial life in Potosí written by Bartolomé Arzáns de Orsúa y Vela ([1735] 1965) is rife with descriptions of young women who cross-dressed as men to meet their lovers or to avenge themselves by sword on men who had killed a brother or father (Boyle 2010). A good deal of this infamy spilled over into neighboring La Plata, where well-to-do Potosínos kept a second home for their families, nearer to the judicial and executive powers of the audiencia and in a milder climate. One trial record for wife murder carried out in La Plata (involving members of the audiencia) describes how a married woman deceived her husband, likewise by stealing out of her house after dark in men's clothing and taking a stroll to a secluded garden with an obliging priest, acting as beard, who led her to her lover (Abercrombie 2000). But La Plata was by all accounts a courtlier and more genteel place than Potosí, which was better suited to those Spaniards interested in quick riches, gambling dens, and illicit affairs.

The central church of Potosí (where the city's minority of peninsular and Creole Spaniards heard mass) holds the record of Don Antonio's marriage to Doña Martina (see appendix B.5):

In Potosí in the year of our Lord seventeen ninety nine, on the thirtieth of the month of March: Having read the three proclamations or admonitions on three successive feast days at the time of the parish mass, and there having resulted no impediment whatever, I Don Juaquin Cevallos, lieutenant of the rector priest of this Holy Matrix Church, married and solemnly joined in matrimony through words in presence, their having first expressed their mutual consent, Don Antonio Yta, native of the Court of Madrid, legitimate son of Don José Yta and Doña Felipa Ybañes; residents of the Court, with Doña Martina Bilbado, legitimate daughter of Pedro Bilbado and Doña Justa Balberde. Attending the matrimony were Juan Manuel Solares, Don Baltasar Rodrigues, Don Pedro Antonio Domingues. Godparents were Don Juan Soto and Doña Rufina Torquemada. And in evidence of this I sign: [signature and rubric: Juaquin Cevallos]

The marriage certificate reveals that Doña Martina shared at least one thing in common with Don Antonio: both came from "mixed" marriages, where (in the contexts shared with people who knew them) only their mothers' status merited a "Doña." The prevalence of this marker of *hidalguía* among the witnesses and godparents also point to social-climbing upward mobility.

Aiming to excel also in a colonial career, Don Antonio early on had learned to play the peninsular card, to highlight that he was Spanish born, and to flaunt his familiarity with the most recent fashions of Madrid. That was how to curry the favor of the other Spanish-born figures who dominated the administration of empire. By doing so, he would also have been maximally foregrounding his distance from Indians, the natives and vast majority population of the territory. That is because Indies-born Spaniards, or Creoles, as they were called, were suspected of having been tainted through excessive intimacy with Indians. That taint was conceived, in those days, as more than metaphorical. A kind of Lamarckian understanding of biological inheritance held that one's bodily essence could be transformed by living in a tropical climate, consuming "indigenous" foods, and living in too much contact with non-Spaniards (Brading 1993; Earle 2014; Katzew 2004; Premo 2005b). Such prejudices limited Creoles' possibilities for advancement in the imperial administration, but it privileged peninsulars like Sanz and Antonio Yta.

The more efficient, modern, and "just" society envisioned by Sanz and Cañete did not translate into a critique of Spanish colonialism or a defense of the rights of the indigenous peoples who constituted a majority of the population, the African slaves who labored in fields and worked in Spanish kitchens, or the free blacks and mixed population of castas whose numbers swelled the streets of Spanish American cities but not its universities, seminaries, or administrative offices. Nor would such egalitarian projects be in the cards after Creoles gained independence from Spain to found their own new republics.

Don Antonio Yta was of the last generation of peninsular Spaniards to benefit from Crown prejudices against Creoles. The revolutionary era that from the middle of the nineteenth century had gripped the Audiencia de Charcas had begun in the 1730s with an abortive plot by Creoles and mestizos in Oruro to overthrow the Spanish king and install an Inca emperor. The revolutionary spirit then passed to Indians in the 1770s, leading in 1780–81 to a generalized indigenous rebellion against Spanish overlords (apart from the king himself) and hereditary indigenous nobility, the caciques, who had become increasingly abusive as the right-hand men of the colonial administration. Organized by the town council officers of the *repúblicas de indios*, the town-centered polities created by Spanish sixteenth-century resettlement policies, the great rebellion, in which thousands of Spaniards (and caciques) had perished, was sparked in part by the efforts of Enlightenment-era "Bourbon" reformers (to use the dynastic name for the era) to "secularize and rationalize" the empire (Penry 2000; forthcoming).

In the early nineteenth century, when Creole Spanish revolutionaries imagined a future without a king and a new American nation founded on the principles of popular sovereignty, they looked back at that indigenous rebellion while scheming how to exclude Indians from citizenship—and the exercise of the vote that from the point of view of the elite "Spanish" minority of the population would lead to their ruin. So in that new order, the only place for indigenous people was as administered and governed populations of persons who, in part because of their collective land titles and in part because of a newly forged racism, were regarded as insufficient for citizenship.

Don Antonio's favored status as a cosmopolitan peninsular hidalgo had bought him a quick rise in the colonial world, marriage to Doña Martina, and then appointment as an administrator of the town of La Magdalena in the distant, tropical province of Moxos. No doubt he was no more apt for the job than some hundreds of Creole Spaniards whose aspirations for advancement were crushed by the favoritism given to peninsulars like Don Antonio. Once in his post, he would serve under the governor of that ex-Jesuit province, now under military rule, Lieutenant Coronel Don Miguel de Zamora y Triviño, applying reforms to the governance of its indigenous population. But first he was to spend a year with his new wife in the refined capital city of La Plata, planning the reforms to be visited on the native population of the many indigenous towns of Moxos. His peregrinations from the port cities of Málaga and Montevideo and Buenos Aires to the rambunctious mining center of Potosí had led him finally into a position of power and a job in Crown administration that would begin in one of the empire's stateliest capitals. There his familiarity with the "high culture" of Madrid and the fashions of the nobility would come in very handy indeed.

CHAPTER 4

MEANS AND ENDS

Zenith and Nadir of a Social Climber

Antonio and Martina's Rise in the Courtly City of La Plata

Married to a young woman, hired into an administrative post in the colonial government that would provide a salary and (along with whatever dowry might have been forthcoming from his in-laws) the possibility of establishing an independent household, complete not only with the servants who helped aspiring aristocrats avoid demeaning labors but the threshold behind which to better maintain his secret and his wife's erstwhile virtue, on which his repute as a man, and particularly an aristocratic one, now also depended, it seems that Don Antonio was now fully in the pink.

La Plata was a much warmer and safer place to live than was Potosí, and as the capital of the Audiencia de Charcas, it was a cultured place too.[1] The expediente does not tell us where Antonio and his wife lived in La Plata during the year they spent together there, but we must imagine it to have been fairly humble, since at the time of his arrest Antonio had yet to receive his pay for the two years he worked as administrator of the Indian town of La Magdalena. Perhaps Don Antonio gained a dowry on marrying Doña Martina, and perhaps he had found other sources of income while working as bishop's page and living as the governor's protégé. We can't be sure. Possibly they rented humble digs on their own, though it is more likely that as putative hidalgos they lodged as guests or boarders in one of the great *casonas* (big houses) owned by the city's ruling elite, perhaps in the house of Don Miguel de Zamora y Triviño, governor of the Indian towns of the former

FIG. 17 Patio of a *casona* in La Plata from exterior doorway, Sucre, Bolivia. Photograph by author.

Jesuit district of Moxos and Antonio's supervisor in colonial government in his new job as administrator of the distant chocolate-producing town of La Magdalena, a former Jesuit mission in the province of Moxos. Such a *casona*, of which many still stand in today's Sucre, looked like that depicted in figure 17, a former home now converted into a private university.

Marrying Doña Martina gave Don Antonio important new ways to perform his masculinity, apart from the obvious but problematic sexual obligations of marriage. According to the law, he now held patria potestad over her, "the power of the father," and as Doña Martina argues in her reply to his lawsuit over clothing, he exercised that power with jealousy. We should take that to mean that he aimed to restrict her insofar as possible to the house, recogida from the gazes of other men. If masculinity was in part defined by engaging in agentive, outward projecting acts (sallying forth into the public, onto the streets and plazas and taverns in a desenvuelto manner), denying that agentivity to women through recogimiento was an important way of reinforcing and foregrounding that masculinity. Don Antonio, that is, had every reason to embrace the governing measures of misogyny so generalized among his male peers. Indeed, Antonio had reason to excel in them.[2]

How did women strive to escape the confines imposed by such patriarchalism and misogyny? The violence of controlling fathers and jealous husbands could be escaped by fleeing to the homosocial space of the convent, but that move required a vocation and a renunciation of marriage and motherhood, as well as a calling to the inward, spiritual life rather than an outwardly oriented, active one. As a wife, the new fashions of the period provided some relief from wifely enclosure.

Doña Martina's wardrobe shows us that she dressed on occasion in the women's style that complemented the male currutaco outfit, the tiered gossamer empire-style camisa. The flirtatious exposure to men other than her husband that such costume implied would have been a hard pill for Don Antonio to swallow. It is clear from Doña Martina's response to Don Antonio's demand for the return of his (and her) clothing and possessions that she chafed under the restrictions that her husband's jealousy imposed on her. Possibly she would have had recourse, in his absence from the household, to another fashion popular among women who challenged the ideal of recogimiento, seeking greater freedom of movement and communication with others outside of the house. Obtaining such freedom was the goal of the new dress style and associated *cortejo*, by which married women got out from under their husbands' thumbs.

That style was itself associated with an early form of feminism sparked by the French Revolution and the reemergence of the notion of popular sovereignty, which raised the issue of eligibility for full citizenship and the vote. But the "woman question," as it was called, had been decided (against full female emancipation) by the execution by the Jacobins in 1793 of Olympe de Gouges, for her *Declaration of the Rights of Women* (1791). Suffrage for women would take another century to advance, although after the reactionary victory and the execution of the Jacobin Maximilien Robespierre in 1794, aristocrats generally were freed to strut the streets once again. As a consequence, what remained of rebellion against recogimiento for elite women were their fashions, now also taken up by the rising bourgeoisie. For Doña Martina, for example, that meant empire-style dresses and participation in cortejo, through which they might accompany male currutaco flaneurs in their haughty strolls and be accompanied to high-society soirees. Some elite women held their own tertulias to discuss matters of science and philosophy (sometimes invited to present their works at men's societies), and others took to the arts. But freedom of independent movement outside of the home was still restricted, especially by husbands' jealousy and fathers' and brothers' prickliness over virtue and honor.

Bartolomé Arzáns de Orsúa y Vela's ([1735] 1965) history of Potosí is replete with references to female cross-dressers, generally cases of women who slipped out of their homes into the night under a man's cape and hat to carry out one or another secret plan (revenge, with sword, of an offense or more amorous or adulterous ends), and the archival record of La Plata does not lack such cases (Abercrombie 2000). Such cases required the darkness of night to obscure faces that might be recognized by family or acquaintances, leading to discovery and punishment. Fortunately for women with secret business in the streets or with a desire to be in the streets, even just for a stroll, without their familial male escorts, there was another fashionable alternative in the last quarter of the eighteenth and first half of the nineteenth century that did not involve risky cross-dressing. That fashion involved a regular item of female clothing, of which Doña Martina had three in her wardrobe: the *mantilla*.

A large shawl with lace or embroidered or fringed corners, sometimes of Chinese silk (imported by the Manila Galleon), the mantilla was worn over the dress and could be pulled up to cover the head to go properly to mass. Women in the cities of Spain and the Indies, however, had taken to doubling the mantilla over the head and around the face, covering all but one eye. Those who wore this controversial fashion, denounced by traditionalist men, were called *tapadas*, "the concealed" (Poole 1988; Bass and Wunder 2009). Using perfectly respectable items of clothing and covering their faces in a sort of "new traditionalism" that referenced the still-current veiling of cloistered nuns, women attending mass, and brides (and the Muslim and converted *moriscas* of Spain), such women's freedom-producing anonymity scandalized moralizing traditionalists. Heavily commented on and depicted in countless works of theater, this form of "the veil functioned, to quote Joan Wallach Scott's work on modern-day France, as 'a screen onto which were projected images of strangeness and fantasies of danger'" (Scott 2007, 10, qtd. in Bass and Wunder 2009, 101).[3] That strangeness and danger, argue Laura Bass and Amanda Wunder, was a product of the rise of Spanish urbanism and migration and the opportunities

FIG. 18 Francisco Javier Cortés, *Tapada*, ca. 1827–38. Watercolor on paper, 24.3 × 18.2 cm. Donated by Juan Carlos Verme. Museo de Arte de Lima. Photo: Daniel Giannoni / Archi. 03.001308.001. Archivo Digital de Arte Peruano.

therein for social mobility, consumerism, and changes in status resulting from wealth rather than birth, combined with the consequent difficulty of identifying "one another through established signs of rank, gender, and race" (2009, 101). As a result, the veil (like the currutaco and, in places like Potosí and La Plata, the members of castas of ambiguous social estate or "race") became an emblem of a crisis of social recognition. No doubt the improvements to urban life carried out by figures such as Don Francisco de Paula Sanz (in Buenos Aires and Potosí)—adding sidewalks, tree-lined stroll ways and streetlights—only encouraged the flaneur to consume the city as spectacle while making a spectacle of himself, and the tapada, of herself (see fig. 18).

In a discussion of the dandy as flaneur, Janet Wolff (1985, 41) has argued that there was no possibility of a *flâneuse*, since even in the known case of a cross-dressing female dandy, George Sand, it was done disguised as a man.

But although they did so through anonymity, the tapadas of the Spanish Atlantic, I suggest, were *flâneuses*, in the absence of the term, even if, like George Sand, they were not in a position to take personal credit for their artistically rendered self-presentation, something that the currutacos and madamitas del nuevo cuño would not have wanted to miss. Although anonymous, the tapadas made themselves free to walk about, like those haughty male flaneurs, gazing directly (though with a "one-eyed gaze") at what they wished. In some ways it was analogous to the veiling of Muslim women, for whom the *almalafa* of Andalusia until the sixteenth century, and today the *burka* or *hijab*, provides a possibility of movement in public with the same kind of anonymity.[4] But tapadas, like dandies, also presented themselves as a fashionable and oftentimes sexually provocative spectacle to be *looked at*.[5] The costume did not hide, but often exaggerated, the curves of the body.

Since the tapada fashion covered all the face but the eyes, often just one, one wonders how many cross-dressing men found it a convenient disguise. Surely many who otherwise (with facial hair and such) had no possibility of "passing" for a woman in ordinary women's dress would have taken note of the freedom of anonymity it offered. Of course, to get away with it they would also have needed some skill at stylizing the body and practice at walking and fanning themselves in a feminine manner.

If Goya's portrait of *La maja desnuda* scandalized the elite Madrid salon, not so much for its full-frontal nudity but for the fearless forward gaze of its "wanton" subject, the tapadas scandalized not for their all-concealing clothing but for their free-because-anonymous *looking*. As Augustine had explained to the nuns of his order, the danger was what they could communicate with their eye(s) even when their tongue remained silent (which in this case, they did not). The record does not tell us whether Doña Martina availed herself of this fashion to freely go about town (to denounce her husband, for instance) without being recognized. But if she did, she made use of a direct analogue of Don Antonio's disguise: the use of clothing to conceal an aspect of individual identity that if revealed would produce stigma (in this case, a report of a woman's unvirtuous behavior to her father, husband, or brother, and to society at large). In Don Antonio's case the stigma being concealed was the female body and the prior name, María, while in Doña Martina's case, if she walked out tapada, "covered," the stigma being covered would have been being an unvirtuous *mujer libre*, should she be recognized as Doña Martina, Don

Antonio's wife. All the same, the use of disguise avoided problematic exposure and enabled the disguised to inhabit a livable, if opaque, identity. It turns out that such ruses were one of the social elite's most useful tools in life, if also, when engaged in by others, perceived as the worst threats to their existence.

Don Antonio and Colonial Governance in the "White City"

When we envision Don Antonio's preparation for carrying out his job as administrator of an ex-Jesuit mission town, we should imagine him deeply influenced by some, but not all, of the new ideas of that revolutionary era. Promoting equality and liberty was not to be his calling. Instead, he needed to enforce new strictures against the concealment of others' identities, including that of his wife. Along with other members of the Spanish elite, he would join in with the general condemnation of social climbing and passing, aiming to unmask others even while keeping his own firmly in place. And to fully occupy his new station in life, Don Antonio needed to strut his Madrid fashions and to highlight his peninsular superiority, as he strolled through the new, lighted and paved paseo around the plaza (see fig. 19).

No doubt Don Antonio latched onto the idea of "whiteness" as his prerogative, though it is doubtful that it produced much "fraternity" with Creoles. Like Don Pedro Vicente Cañete and Sanz, he would likely have supported the right of the Crown to coerce Indians to labor in Potosí's mines. Perhaps he would have agreed with Sanz, as Sanz put it at length in his defense of the coerced labor regime known as the mita, that Indians had not progressed since the days of the conquest and were generally lazy and that such coerced labor served as a way of teaching layabouts the value of work and of putting them in contact with civilized society (Sanz [1794] 1970). In any case, Don Antonio's new job as administrator of the mission town of La Magdalena required him to make Indian labor maximally useful to the Crown and to himself, since administrators like him earned far more from their private commercial activities using Indian labor than from their relatively measly salaries. He was also to deliver a "secular catechism" that aimed to teach Indians that the king had received his sovereignty directly from God, so as to overwrite for these rebellious Indians the teachings of Jesuits that God had granted sovereignty directly to the people. Ironically, another of his tasks was also to

FIG. 19 The plaza of La Plata, Sucre, Bolivia. Photograph by author.

impose a new sumptuary code on Indians, prohibiting them from dressing in the Spanish manner as a means of forestalling the social climbing and passing that Spanish elites, a tiny minority of the population here, feared as a threat to their privileged position and safety. But before he would travel there, he spent a year in La Plata with Doña Martina, while helping the governor of Moxos prepare their new administrative strategy.

It must have been quite a year for him. A new young wife, both of them decked out in the fancy and fashionable wardrobes of privileged peninsular Spaniards, enjoying the high life while rubbing elbows with the colonial elite in the genteel "White City," given over to sumptuous public festivals and paseos along newly paved boulevards and lording it over the Indians and Africans and castas while on their way to masked balls or tertulias, and now with a proper imperialist's job and salary! It must have seemed to Don Antonio that he had not only rescued himself from certain infamy and disgrace back in Spain but reached the pinnacle of success that all Spaniards who emigrated to América hoped for. But it was not to be so easily, or endlessly, enjoyed.

Capital of the vast district known as the Audiencia de Charcas, the city of La Plata held a university, a hospital, and the offices of the appeals court and administrative offices of the district, also called the "audiencia," a set of buildings located near the central plaza of this genteel town, long a residence for the families of Spaniards who enriched themselves in the rough-and-tumble mining center of nearby Potosí. As an appeals court district, the Audiencia de Charcas had formed part of the Viceroyalty of Peru (and its audiencias of Santa Fe, Quito, Lima, and Cuzco and the governorship of Chile) until 1776, when in a general reorganization of imperial administration the Audiencia de Charcas was detached from the Viceroyalty of Peru and joined with the Audiencia de Buenos Aires to form a new viceroyalty of the Río de La Plata, under the leadership of a new viceroy headquartered in Buenos Aires. The reorganization in part responded to a new economic reality—increased trade, much of it smuggled goods, between highland commercial centers like Potosí and La Plata and, through Buenos Aires, the Atlantic port of Montevideo.

Another reform, in 1778, divided the audiencias into intendancies, something like new provinces governed by Crown appointees directly under the viceroy's authority. Powerful figures like the intendant governor Francisco de Paula Sanz of the intendancy of Potosí now gathered circles of criados and employees around them to help impose further administrative reforms, creating openings for newcomers like Antonio Yta.

As an institution with an architectural home, the audiencia consisted of administrative offices, a courtroom, a jail, an archive, and living space for the audiencia president's household, including his slaves, servants, and criados.[6] An immense structure the size of one fourth of a city block, the buildings comprised three sections, each one a two- or three-story building constructed around a central patio, with a central passage leading from the first patio, where the audiencia offices were located, to the second, which the president (and his family and criados) called home, to the third, site of the living space of the president's indigenous servants and African slaves, as well as the men's and women's jails (the former in pitiful and barely habitable condition, the latter a roofless and collapsed structure). Not far away the city's main square, its *plaza mayor*, was the site for evening strolls of the wealthy elites and for public gossiping about shocking matters, such as that revealed in the proceedings against Don Antonio. On one side of the plaza sat the city's imposing cathedral; about a block away were to be found the impressive buildings of the Universidad Mayor Real y Pontificia San Francisco Xavier de Chuquisaca, founded in 1624, where the lawyers and judges of the case sometimes met with law students in the Colegio Carolino, essentially La Plata's bar association.

Today a city of 280,000 and still the judicial capital of the country (the legislative and executive capital having moved to La Paz in 1899), La Plata, in 1803, held a scarce few tens of thousands. Most of that population was made up of indigenous peoples, settled in separate parishes on the city's periphery, plus African slaves, free blacks, and a significant contingent of biologically and culturally "mixed" people.[7] Only one indigenous individual appears in the Yta case—the *pongo* (from Quechua *punku*, "doorway") who guarded the jail door at night, who disappeared with Yta on the night of his escape—but of course the president's house held numerous indigenous workers along with African-origin slaves and servants. Spaniards, whether peninsulars (born in Spain) or Creoles (born in the Indies), made up only a small fraction of the city's population. But as an audiencia capital, the seat of an archbishopric, and a university town with its own publishing houses, cadres of lawyers, bankers, and those engaged in large-scale commerce, it was a particularly "noble" city for its size. Alonso Carrió de la Vandera waxed at length on the ruinous and filthy state of Potosí and by contrast describes the city of La Plata in more glowing terms:

The city of La Plata is situated on a bubble or swelling of the earth surrounded by a ravine of little depth, which is narrow, barren, and encompassed by a chain of hills perfect in its orbicular form, thus seeming like a work of art. Its climate is mild; its streets, wide. The palace in which the president lives is a large house, falling apart in many places—which shows its great antiquity—as is likewise the house of the council or secular government. There are many large houses that may be considered palaces, and the inspector believes it is the best-planned city of all he has seen; with respect to the fairer sex, it has as many polished ladies as can be found in Potosí, Oruro, La Paz, Cuzco, and Guamanga. It is true that the climate is beneficial to the complexion. The communication with men of letters makes the ladies well informed, and the gatherings of litigants and rich priests bring the best statues and engravings from the surrounding areas, and frequently from great distances. We did not go into the archbishop's palace because the abodes of the ecclesiastics are not as manifest as those of the seculars. The former, being more somber, instill a sacred fear; the latter invite mortals with their gaiety. (Concolorcorvo [1773] 1965, 178)

The Enlightenment-era modernization of the city was not yet complete. The city council itself lamented the presence of pigs that owners allowed to roam in the very plaza and central city streets and published an ordinance prohibiting pigs within three city blocks of the plaza, "subject to the punishment of removing to the public jail any *cerdo* or *marrano* [pigs] entering into them" (Querejazu Calvo 1987, 449, my translation; see also Bridikhina 2001, 29). A great campaign to render the city more hygienic and orderly was underway precisely during the years of Don Antonio's presence there, and although he might have had to share the jail with confiscated pigs, the efforts of city officials, following orders issued from Madrid for the entire empire, had begun to bring greater order and "decency" to the streets, as well as to move human remains from churches and churchyards into a new cemetery on the edge of town.

The president of the audiencia and intendant governor, Ramón García Pizarro, argued that they city should be the "most beautiful . . . that being among those first order [cities] of America, it should be the first in ornamentation, cleanliness, and in all that might contribute to making it superior to the others." To this end he ordered that the thirty-six central blocks of the city be paved and, along with repairs to the supply of water for fountains throughout the city, took special care in constructing the public paseo, a broad walkway through principal streets and the central plaza along which leading citizens might stroll. Inhabitants who walked the streets on dark nights were ordered to carry lanterns (Querejazu Calvo 1987, 462; Bridikhina 2001, 33).

Generations of social-climbing Spaniards had come to the American colonies to better their station in life and to leave behind stigma such as belonging to the lowly pechero or commoner social estate or being descended from Jews or Muslims, from persons tried by the Inquisition for heresy, or to get away from a bad reputation resulting from other well-known criminal or debasing activities that hindered their prospects back in Spain. Peninsular Spaniards migrated to these American cities to rise to the very top of the social hierarchy, bettering what they had been in Spain itself. Just behind them in the scale of prestige and power were the American-born Creole Spaniards, chomping at the bit while being held back from the top by the peninsulars. The urban interstitial peoples, known as castas, carried out most of the petty commerce and trades, and they were social climbers too, whose blurring of formerly clear and fixed social boundaries the Spaniards experienced as an existential threat.

"Passing" was both the rule of the day and one of the Spaniards' (especially the now-downwardly mobile Creole Spaniards') greatest worries.[8]

Social mobility in the cities of the Indies was a worrisome if inescapable phenomenon. It was well known, of course, that many of the Spaniards arriving from the Iberian Peninsula, whatever their pretensions now, had undertaken the journey precisely, as had Antonio Yta, to leave behind social stigma. Those Spaniards with commoner, criminal, heretic, or illegitimate pasts or suspected Jewish or Muslim origins could remake themselves on this side of the Atlantic. The same logic made physical mobility into social mobility in Spanish America, enabling indigenous people who in their home territories owed tribute and the coerced labor known as *mita* to dodge such duties when they settled in cities, there becoming *indios criollos* (Abercrombie 1996; Graubart 2009; Lavallé 1993; Pagden 1987; Tandeter 1993). Another change of location and dress, with or without "mixed" ancestry, made their Spanish-speaking children into tribute-free mestizos. Indeed, all knew that the Crown itself was happy to remove the social stigma of illegitimate birth or "blackness" through payment for a certificate of legitimacy or "whiteness" called *gracias al sacar* (Twinam 1999, 18–19).

The general awareness that a good part of the population of the Audiencia de Charcas displayed in their clothing and manner statuses that, as far as elites were concerned, they did not merit, induced a certain panic among the ruling Spaniards. In the 1770s the elites of Potosí had petitioned the Crown to allow them to sort out the Spaniards, Indians, and Africans once and for all, dividing the "mixed" castas (who by now were becoming an urban majority) among these three primal categories, deciding which unmixed category they fit best and sending those most "Indian" back into their peasant territories and those most "black" into slavery (Abercrombie 1996). Requests from colonial Spaniards also led to the 1778 promulgation of the Royal Pragmatic on Marriage, enabling fathers to prohibit the marriage of their children to social inferiors (Twinam 1999, 18; Seed 1988; Socolow 1992). By the end of the eighteenth century, new ideas about the acquisition by Spaniards in the Americas of undesirable social and physical traits by contamination from their social inferiors, for example, from the use by Spaniards of Indian or African wet-nurses (see Premo 2005b) were added to concerns about contagion from the miasmas of corpses in church tombs or of animals and fecal matter in the streets, producing an understanding of hygiene and contamination that was social as well as corporeal.

And so it was at about the time that Antonio Yta arrived in Potosí and La Plata that Spaniards there, both Creole and peninsular, had begun to label themselves with the "pure" color term, *blanco*, "white," to differentiate themselves from the other, non-Spanish and now "nonwhite" castas. Something close to the "modern" concept of race was under construction, awaiting only the call to independence, liberty, and popular sovereignty to make whiteness necessary as a means by which former Spaniards (like former Englishmen in the thirteen North American colonies) could ditch their former ties to the master nation of empire while still retaining a claim to deserved privilege in a country where they were neither as "native" as the Indians nor in the majority (Abercrombie 2003).[9]

To halt or at least slow the flood of passing, new sumptuary codes forbid non-Spaniards from wearing Spanish-style clothing (indeed, this was one of the new rules that Antonio Yta was supposed to enforce as administrator of the Indian town of La Magdalena [Block 1994]). But such measures did not prevent contagion from the seething urban multitudes, whether in the pursuit of everyday life, such as purchasing food in the marketplace dominated by indigenous and "mixed" casta women, or seeking a meal or drink from a public tavern, most of them indigenous women–run chicherías (corn-beer taverns) (Mangan 2005; Gotkowitz 2003).

Patrolling the Colonial Frontiers of Social and Sexual Difference

In such chicherías beakers of *chicha* were served with spicy foods, mainly by indigenous women who operated their businesses, and their lives, without the control of the male patria potestas who guarded the decency of Spanish women and the honor of Spanish households.[10] The chicherías (and also the brothels) were frequented by Spanish men, usually, we must assume, without their wives, and were notorious for the kinds of cross-caste mixing that moral reformers despised (Gotkowitz 2003). The early nineteenth century saw reform efforts aimed at curtailing the chicherías (though some still operate today in today's Sucre) and replacing them, at least in the "decent" center of town, with cafés run by white men, and that French invention, the restaurant, from which nonwhite castas could be banned (Chambers 1999).

Colonial administrators were concerned with cross-caste mixing, social climbing, and passing, by which "nonwhites" posed as such. They were also deeply concerned about the possibility of sexual acts between persons of the same sex and, in very different ways depending on whether offenders were men or women, with transvestism. Men who had sex with other men or who dressed in women's clothing could expect the swiftest and most violent of punishments, while women who dressed as men (only with difficulty could they be imagined to "have sex" with other women) were much less problematic. Unlike men, who debased themselves by dressing as or taking a woman's role in sex, *mujeres varoniles*, or manly women, were at least aiming to improve themselves by becoming manly. Such prejudices stemmed from the esteem in which men held themselves and were justified by reference to the old conceit that nature tends to move toward perfection, which is to say, masculinity (Velasco 2011, 27–28). Yet in spite of the era's allergies to homosexual practices or to the blurring of performed sex (what we now call gender), homosocial contexts abounded.

Homosocial contexts (Sedgwick 1990) are easy to spot in the records. Some examples are convents, monasteries, military barracks, and Crown offices. Women were not to be found in official roles in the audiencia or town council offices or even among the artisans admitted to guilds; their special place was work making and vending foodstuffs in markets and the chicherías and *pulperías* (small stores selling provisions) as well as in elite households. With all those settings of homosociality, in which one or the other sex was excluded, it may be surprising that one does not find in the archival record of La Plata or Potosí any places of homo*sexual* encounter, something that today is referred to as "el ambiente"; taverns or street corners or brothels where men seek sex with other men, such as those that Serge Gruzinski (1985) and Zeb Tortorici (2007) have described finding in certain *pulquerías* in Mexico (*pulque* being an agave-based "beer" and *pulquería* the Mexican equivalent of the Peruvian chichería). Of course, homosociality in those contexts was mediated by the symbolic centrality of the opposite sex: Christ and a priest confessor in the convents, the virgin in the monasteries, the *chichera* in the chichería, and the symbolic presence of opposite-sex partners in the back-slapping, heterosexual joking typical of the bro-mance of military, fraternity, and all-male workplace contexts.[11]

While it is doubtful that well-known places of encounter for men who had sex with men could have survived for any length of time in an era when the punishment for sodomy was harsh and swift, it is likely enough that such men knew one another and met, in clandestine circumstances, and constituted

FIG. 20   Francisco Javier Cortés, *Juan José Cabezudo y amigo*, ca. 1827. Watercolor and tempera on paper, 23.5 × 34.2 cm. Donated by Juan Carlos Verme. Museo de Arte de Lima. Photo: Daniel Giannoni / Archi. 03.01214.001. Archivo Digital de Arte Peruano.

what Tortorici has termed "sodomitical subcultures" (see also Sigal 2003). A few decades later, and in the cosmopolitan port city of Lima rather than in conservative little La Plata, there certainly was such a thing as well-known and public *maricones* (a slang insult term akin to the English "queer"), such as the chef Juan José Cabezudo (see fig. 20), depicted in nonbinary clothing (pants but frilly blouse) by two different *costumbrista* painters (Pamo Reyna 2015). This would not have been possible in La Plata, and in any case, even though contexts for public homosociality for men were relatively abundant, making a colonial homosexual "ambiente" imaginable, the same cannot be said for public homosociality for women. Such contexts surely existed (the marketplace, for instance), but they were subject to a great deal of surveillance by male authority and at the same time were not semiclosed and darkened spaces of play, as were the taverns.

The stigma associated with chicherías, which were cited by elites as places of drunken lasciviousness, and also of sodomy and incest, can be best understood as an extension to indigenous-dominated social settings (fiestas and chicherías) of Spanish stereotypes of Indians more generally as ignorant, lazy, and idolatrous, with a proclivity to drunkenness and to every kind of vice, including criminal sexuality. In this, Spanish men engaged in what Hayden White (1978, 151–52) termed "ostensive self-definition by negation," projecting the most abhorrent and feared impulses, which have been rigorously suppressed, onto traditional enemies and stigmatized, non-Spanish "others," in the Spanish case, Muslims and Jews (long since expelled from Spanish realms) and, in the colonies, Africans and Indians. And so contexts dominated by these others or where Spaniards came most into contact with them, such as markets, chicherías, and public festivities, were themselves stigmatized and subject to surveillance and efforts at suppression.

In 1803 the convent and the cloistered space of the home (and in it the *estrada*, or sitting room) continued to be the places of homosocial mingling for Spanish and Creole women, whose Spanishness or whiteness was policed, in this colonial context, by the spatiality that in Spain had structured the division between plebeian women and aristocratic ones. Plebeians are defined by manual labor, and that was as true of women as of men. Back in Spain laboring plebeian women who sold food in market stalls, worked in the fields, or entered the service of men other than their husbands or fathers as domestics or factory workers were the very definition of *mujeres mundanas*, "worldly" women whose lack of recogimiento and freedom from a restraining patria potestad stained their virtue and their father's and husband's honor. But in Spanish America such laboring roles were for non-Spaniards, for Indians, blacks, and mestizos.

Mary Weismantel (2001) has written extensively of the dangerous androgyny attributed by Spaniards and Creoles to the *cholas* (descendants of urbanized *indias criollas*) who tended their kitchens, served them in chicherías, and sold them their foodstuffs in the marketplace. Indigenous workers of Spanish cities adopted Spanish dress styles (following edicts outlawing indigenous dress after the rebellions of 1780–81) in the era just prior to the French Revolution. As Spanish women abandoned the pollera, the ankle-length pleated skirt worn over hoops or *paneras* and layers of petticoats in favor of the form-fitting camisa in the mid-1790s, the pollera became the exclusive costume of the chola. Occupying public space in a manly way and controlling their own purse strings, the chola was the indigenized androgynous working woman in the colony's racialized form.

Chicherías and public markets were semipublic and ludic spaces, generally operated and dominated by indigenous and Afro-descended women wearing polleras (Mangan 2005). They were perceived by Spaniards or whites as insolent and indecent threats to decency rather than as obedient servants. No doubt the bad reputation of the chichería, the marketplace, and the public festival made them even more attractive to Spanish men, even for those who most condemned them, for their ludic and "world upside down" carnivalesque possibilities (Bakhtin 1984), including the possibility of finding "women on top" (Davis 1975). In such spaces and moments, that which is most "*socially* peripheral" can become "*symbolically* central" (Stallybrass and White 1986, 5–6).[12] But that does not mean an end to their marginalization and suppression once the festival, fair, party, or theatrical performance is over.

During his sojourn in La Plata with Doña Martina, Don Antonio would no doubt have tried to keep his wife away from such contexts and to reign in whatever transgressive impulses the new cortejo personal styles, accompanying the revealing camisa fashions, might have inspired in her. Perhaps Don Antonio and Doña Martina participated in gatherings of refined ladies and secular men of letters within the grand old palaces of the central city blocks that were now being "up-graded" as hygienic spaces of decency (Chambers 1999). Living there for a full year before heading to Moxos, they would have witnessed and perhaps have participated in some of the elaborate public spectacles that accompanied celebration of the king's birthday and the main Christian holidays, foremost among them the festival of Corpus Christi.[13] Perhaps they bristled, like the president of the audiencia, Don Ramón García Pizarro, at the indignities decent persons suffered at the hands of the vulgar rabble that crowded into the plaza during events organized by the city's elites. Such indignities led García Pizarro to ban from the plaza during such celebrations all *gente de poncho*, "people of the poncho," a metonymic euphemism for the "Indians" who characteristically wore this item of clothing, while Spaniards preferred morning coats and capes (Querejazu Calvo 1987, 462).[14]

Enforcing Absolutism, Social Estate, and Patria Potestad in Moxos and Cochabamba

The reformist monarch Charles III (intendant governor of Potosí Sanz's patron and perhaps, illegitimate, father) had sought to end the public celebrations at which the vulgar masses sometimes caused trouble and attempted to replace bullfights and elaborate dramatic dances of indigenous and mestizo artisans with more somber processions and more stately exhibitions of the urban militia. Fearful of the growing insolence of the urban plebes since the French Revolution and, in South America, the general indigenous rebellion of 1780–81, which had brought an Indian army to the very outskirts of La Plata, this was an effort to engineer proper public order, meaning respect by the masses of their social superiors. Like García Pizarro, his legal adviser Cañete and the intendant governor of Potosí Sanz had also railed against the disorder of festival processions. Efforts at suppressing them had also been accompanied by a shift in political philosophy, where it concerned the popular masses.

Where Habsburg kings had endorsed the theory of popular sovereignty and had based citizen rights on membership in municipal "republics" whose charters kings were forced to respect (Nader 1993), indigenous insistence on those rights during their rebellion (Penry 2000; forthcoming) and their assertion in the American Revolution of 1776, the French one of 1789, and the Haitian Revolution, still ongoing in 1803, had led to a shift toward royal absolutism. That shift had begun with the expulsion of the Jesuits in 1767 and the prohibition of books and writings they had championed that made popular sovereignty a product of natural law, that is, God's will (Stoetzer 1979).

Against such movements, the Bourbon king Charles III had aimed to impose a new understanding, that the sovereignty of kings, not of "the people," was God's will. Now the population at large was to learn a new, *royal* catechism, the *cartilla real*. The version that circulated in the Audiencia de Charcas was written by the archbishop San Alberto (in retired reclusion by 1803, his duties taken over by ecclesiastical prosecutor Méndez de la Parra). Along with other duties, imposing it in the indigenous mission towns of the tropical ex-Jesuit province of Moxos became Don Antonio's task when he gained employment as administrator of the town of La Magdalena.

Among the question-and-answer style passages of the cartilla real are the following:

Question: Who are you?
Answer: I am a loyal vassal of the king of Spain.
Q: Who is the king of Spain?
A: He is a lord so absolute that he recognizes no greater temporal authority.

Q: And where does the king derive his royal power?
A: From God himself.
Q: Was the king anointed by Christ?
A: Yes, father, as is seen in the Holy Scriptures.[15]

The missions of Moxos had become the Crown's responsibility in 1767, when the Jesuits were expelled from the Spanish Empire. Quickly transformed from the Jesuit's planned utopian communities, each self-governed by a town council and cacique (indigenous governor) and each with well-developed local industries, into potential sources of wealth for new secular governors and administrators, those towns had been ruinously administered prior to Zamora's appointment as governor of the province.

Zamora himself, and administrators such as Antonio Yta, would travel to Moxos at the end of 1801 to impose the *cartilla real* along with a new sumptuary code prohibiting indios from dressing in the hábitos of Spaniards (fig. 21). They also imposed a new fiscal regime; they reduced the number of indios exempted from tributes by service to the priest or in festivals, increased the production of manufactures and agricultural products, and more directly controlled the sales of such products to direct profits into Crown coffers (or their own pockets). In La Magdalena that meant cotton grown in the town's fields and cloth woven on its looms and also cacao, the seedpods that are transformed into chocolate. Already in the eighteenth century La Magdalena was known as a source of high-quality cacao, processed into chocolate in the city of La Plata, where chocolatiers still draw on the source today.

Traveling to La Magdalena de Moxos at the end of 1801, Don Antonio and Doña Martina would have entered the territory via Cochabamba, Martina's hometown (appendix A.7, fol. 8v). Overland, upriver, and overland again in these tropical lowlands, they no doubt constituted a truly colonial spectacle. We have no record of their trip, but Governor Zamora had his aristocratic wife, the Countess of Argelejo, Doña María Josefa Fontao y Losada, carried by Indians in a litter, accompanied by hundreds of others carrying the couple's personal baggage of fifty trunks full of goods, including fashionable clothing.

As one might have expected, things did not go well. At the end of 1802, about a year after they arrived, Don Antonio and Doña Martina, like the administrators of the other towns of the region and Governor Zamora himself, were suddenly sent packing, for the province's powerful cacique (the

FIG. 21 Alcide D'Orbigny and Émile Lassalle (drawing); Lassalle (engraving), *Musique et danse religieuse a Moxos (Bolivia)*, 1844. Lithograph on paper, 20 × 28 cm. Paris: Levrault; lithograph Roger et Cía. From D'Orbigny (1844). Inventory 80535. Biblioteca Nacional de España.

indigenous Canichana cacique governor, Juan Maraza) led a successful if bloodless rebellion against them.[16] Removing the governor's and administrators' belongings and having all the baggage carried to the other side of the border, they forced the Spanish officials to follow their clothing out of the province (Roca 2007, 261–62).

End of a Colonial Career?

After the debacle and back in Cochabamba, Don Antonio and Doña Martina must have settled into an uncomfortable life, apparently in his in-laws' house, though both continued to dress themselves like aristocrats, as Antonio's inventory of their possessions demonstrates. Don Antonio traveled to La Plata on his own in 1803 a few months before Doña Martina arrived there with her denunciation, to strive to recover his unpaid salary (which, given the failure of their mission to reform Moxos administration, may not have been forthcoming).

And then, denunciation, arrest, confession, jail for a year, and, finally, escape, into the blue, during a turbulent time that would soon erupt into revolution.

For his first seven years in Spanish America, Don Antonio had served powerful peninsular Spaniards in the humble role of criado. Such service had paid off with marriage to an aristocratic lady and appointment to a Crown post, promising a fruitful colonial career—a man's career—such a great leap from the conventual life that Doña María Yta had led back in Spain. Now that Crown post simply disappeared. Things went from bad to worse: no more job, no pay, and now his wife's accusation, a devastating act of marital betrayal. One might wonder if that accusation was connected in some way to the loss of the job or the absence of the pay or something else that came undone in the couple's mobile life together—a year's courtship in Potosí, a year in La Plata, another one in what must have been trying circumstances in La Magdalena, and then the long return trip from Moxos, via Martina's home-town of Cochabamba. Four years into a highly unconventional marriage, Martina found herself in Cochabamba with a now penniless, and apparently violently jealous, Antonio. And so she traveled to La Plata to denounce him to the authorities, imagining another life for herself.

Like many before him, Don Antonio had traveled from Spain to the Indies to make his fortune in a successful colonial career. Such careers were built on the exploitation of Indians, and the clothing on his back, the *hábito de español*, the particular currutaco sort of aristocratic "Spaniard's clothing" that he proudly wore, signaled a form of high status that was a mark of superiority of sex, social estate, nation, and race. Settling well into society as a married man in La Plata while holding a Crown post with its nice salary and other possibilities for personal enrichment would have made it possible to achieve the respectability that most fully marked a Spanish, hidalgo, white, and male social standing. That, perhaps, was Antonio's aim, though neither wealth nor respectability nor unquestioned maleness were to be his fate. All of Antonio's social climbing had been successful, including the transformation from María into Antonio that made the rest possible. But instead of respectability, Don Antonio's decade of labor reaped only Doña Martina's denunciation, arrest, a humiliating medical inspection, and jail, while investigating magistrates searched for a crime they could peg on their now androgynous prisoner.

As the audiencia considered transferring Don Antonio's case to the church, and Antonio to an ecclesiastical jail, where the complicating matter of such ambiguous sexuality would no doubt have been more vigorously pursued, Don Antonio brought the matter to a close. Ankles swollen from many months of shackles, and health broken, he gained the sympathy of a prison guard—the *indio pongo* who kept the door on nights and weekends—and with his collusion, and him, escaped from jail, disappearing into the turbulent flow of life in the late colonial era.

At least escape is what the warden of the jail reported. It is certainly possible, though there is no evidence to support the idea, that the jailbreak was orchestrated by an attorney or even a sympathetic judge in the audiencia, eager to make the impossible case go away. It was only after Antonio escaped that the original file, now including Felipa's letter and some wrenching arguments by Antonio's lawyer, was turned over to ecclesiastical prosecutor Bernardino Méndez de la Parra. Had the original documents been turned over sooner, Antonio might well have been subjected to further examinations and much more detailed questioning. In any case, there is no trace of the file in the archive of the archbishopric of La Plata. Only the copy made for the audiencia has survived.

Aftermaths

Within four years of Antonio's escape from jail, the audiencia itself was in turmoil: as the administrative center of one of the first districts of Spanish America to declare independence from Spain, its high officials and university-trained lawyers found themselves on opposite sides of a war fought between revolutionaries and royalists. Antonio's attorney was among the leaders of the revolutionary movement, organized within the bar association and following many of the ideas forwarded by the radical manuscripts of Victorián de Villava ([1797] 1822), developing the idea of popular sovereignty while advocating an imperial parliament with representation from the colonies (Levene 1946). The Creole and royalist legal adviser Cañete had desperately coveted Villava's job, but now that Villava was dead, his ideas lived on: Cañete was forced aside during the uproar that ensued when a group of lawyers (including Yta's attorney, Dr. Esteban Agustín Gascón) and law students stormed the audiencia buildings and forced the president of the audiencia, a proxy for the king himself, to resign in 1809 (Roca 2007).

Sanz would be executed by a firing squad of revolutionaries in the plaza of Potosí in 1810, while Gascón, siding with the revolutionaries, would be appointed to a judgeship in the revolutionary audiencia and become governor of the independent city of Salta in 1813 and representative of Buenos Aires in the constitutional convention of Tucumán, where he was a signer of the Argentine declaration of independence (Muzzio 1920, 202). Don Antonio would then (in 1816) have been forty-five years old.

Of Don Antonio Yta, there is no more to tell. Assuming that he survived the initial jailbreak and recuperated from his edema, it appears that he survived without being recaptured, since he managed to disappear from public records. Perhaps he was healthy and lucky enough to get cleanly away from La Plata, to begin life anew in those changing times. Having changed names once before, he most likely did so again, taking on a new identity. It is hard to image Don Antonio relinquishing his hard-fought maleness to return to female hábitos. That is because Doña María's efforts to "pass" as a woman and as a nun had themselves failed so badly, in contrast to Don Antonio's decade of success living as a man. I, for one, choose to believe that Don Antonio continued to live as a man and continued to master his fungible body. His currutaco outfit, along with his peninsular birth, would have to be ditched to survive in the world now dominated by patriotic and anti-Spanish Creoles. But as the latter struggled to make themselves natives of their new nations, his familiarity with transgressive romance would serve him well. And as those new patriots, beset by the leveling possibilities of their new constitutions, initially promising equality to all natives of the new nation (after 1825, in this region the nation was the Republic of Bolivia), fell back on the superiority of their lineage as justification for denying the vote to Indians, his practice at the performance of "whiteness" would bolster his chances.

Whatever his fate, we can certainly conclude that carrying off his transformation from Doña María into Don Antonio, a shift in hábitos made possible by passage from one context to another and by learning new codes of social distinction in which previous forms of pretense could be refurbished, and successfully sustaining this constant motion for a decade, was remarkable in itself. The life of Don Antonio Yta is a tribute to the human capacity for being many things and leading many lives in a world that much prefers more straightforward binaries.

CHAPTER 5

AFTERLIVES

Alternative Emplotments of Don
Antonio's Literary Lives

The Dilemma of Biographical Writing

Up until now, this book has been written in the genre of the social and historical biography, putting a life into its historical context. It has been colored by treatments of the texts that are its sources as kinds of narrative (drawing on literary theorists) and of the sociologic of performed statuses, roles, and individual "identities" (drawing on the ideas of social theorists). Such efforts do not entirely rescue this work from the faults generally attributed to biography as a genre of parasitic or even "colonialist" writing, aiming to "capture" historical personages or attributing to them intentionality they have not themselves expressed, to hang their portraits in a gallery of morally evaluated kinds of character. I have taken care with the use of gendering pronouns and tried to avoid pigeonholing Don Antonio by classifying him according to our contemporary identity categories. But at the same time I have not avoided describing how his acts were judged by others in his own day. For better or worse, this book not only is itself about narrative but *is* narrative, thereby also emplotting Don Antonio's life in ways that offer up his possible intentions and motives as judgeable guides to his character. That mea culpa is required, since this chapter now turns to critique of a handful of biographical treatments of Don Antonio's life written well after his lifetime. The aim is to illustrate how the attribution of particular intentionality to him; to his alter ego, Doña María; and to his wife, Doña Martina, in relation to conclusions about his "true sex" and sexuality have been produced by writers from the late nineteenth century to the near present. We begin, however, with the unofficial report by Mariano Taborga, presented in this book's introduction, which sets the stage for many later writers.

Impacts of the Taborga Letter and the Unidentified Lima Source

The legal proceedings suffered through by Don Antonio Yta were rumor fodder of the first magnitude, given the obvious prurient interest of the case, which hinged on identifying genitals and what kind of sex acts they performed. Given his well-known ties with powerful men, the potential for scandal was enormous. We can be sure that stories and rumors about the case ran rampant through the salons of La Plata's Spanish and Creole elite and engendered many a spicy joke among friends strolling the city's new paseo.

We cannot go back in time to eavesdrop on those conversations. The city's lettered elite, however, was also prone to written correspondence and made heavy use of the colonial mail system, in which indigenous conscripts to the mail service carried bundles of letters and documents with great efficiency and speed from one post house to the next. As we saw in the introduction, a short version of Don Antonio's confession left the nib of Taborga's pen very soon after it was also taken down by the scribe. The scribal version went into the expediente, but Taborga's letter was delivered by post to an unidentified correspondent in Buenos Aires. It ended up being copied into a notebook titled "curious notes," in the private collection of one Juan Manuel Beruti, who had access to the correspondence of an unnamed Buenos Aires official. Taborga had added several details (either in proof of his memory or of his talent for embellishment) that the scribe had not recorded in the official record, such as the penance that the pope had assigned to Doña María of climbing the Jerusalem steps thirty times, applying self-scourging on Fridays for a year, and staying away from convents. Taborga further adds the detail that the female actors with whom Don Antonio had traveled to Rome were Italians from Genoa, that Don Antonio had been *amancebado* (living and sleeping) with Martina prior to their marriage, and that Martina had been vexed by Antonio's jealousy. Taborga ends his epistle by moralizing: Antonio Yta's claim to having a male body was nothing but a lie. Not Antonio, *María* Yta is merely a woman who "hates her clothing" (that is, we may conclude, both her *hábito*, clothing; and *hábitos*, feminine ways of being) and prefers the life of a (male) rascal. In his condemnation, the author focuses on the act of deceit and supposes that María Yta engages in it to indulge *her* "bad" character.

If Taborga wrote another letter some months later, we might have seen how he also judged Doña Martina. For it was Taborga who had been forced to recuse himself from Don Antonio's case and who, in his capacity as legal adviser to the audiencia president, took up as a separate case Don Antonio's lawsuit against Doña Martina for return of his clothing (appendix B.8). In the exchange between Don Antonio and Doña Martina (and their lawyers), each accused the other of being the "gold digger," an impoverished parasite on the other's wealth. In spite of his earlier dismissal of Don Antonio as a warped Doña María, he stood up for Don Antonio's claim to his husbandly rights over marital property and forced Doña Martina to comply with his demands. Apparently the rights of a married "man," while the marriage was not yet annulled, outweighed Don Antonio's flaw of femaleness. Misogyny trumped homophobia, we might say.

A second version of the story, perhaps a copy of Taborga's letter, or another, later one, now missing, seems to have made its way to Lima, where near the end of the nineteenth century it became fodder for the composition of one of Peruvian folklorist Ricardo Palma's fictionalized *Tradiciones peruanas* ([1896] 2007). This celebrated Victorian-era author scoured the national archives of Peru for interesting source material, collecting them into what became a separate section, Papeles Varios, of the Biblioteca de Lima. He identifies his source for the story he titles "Mujer-hombre" (Woman-man) as "Papeles Varios, vol. 613." No longer extant in this form, Palma's source, if it still exists, has eluded this researcher. Palma's source might have been another copy of Taborga's letter or an unknown source.[1] In any case, this Victorian-era author transformed the story, particularly savaging Martina's character to suit his age and audience.

Ricardo Palma's Chaste and Obedient "Mujer-hombre" and Martina as Jezebel

Palma's version of the story of Don Antonio (see appendix B.9) is anything but faithful to the expediente (or even to Taborga's gossipy letter), though it shares similarities to the arguments of Don Antonio's public defenders, José Manuel Malavia and José Pimentel, in the lawsuit over clothing. Pimentel argued successfully that it was Martina, not Don Antonio, who deserved punishment for her excessive "liberty," that is, for failure to obey her husband. Having risen from a poor and wretched condition only through Don Antonio's aid, Pimentel's Martina is a faithless, vengeful, and heartless gold digger (B.8, fols. 4r, 8r–v). Whether or not Palma had access to a report containing such arguments, he adopted such a conclusion as to Martina's character to suit his literary purposes and his prejudices, as well as the misogyny of his day. Demands by women for suffrage and the full rights of citizenship, particularly the writings of Olympe de Gouges, the Jacobin activist herself guillotined during the Terror in Paris, had raised the "woman question" in the late eighteenth century.[2] It had been definitively answered, by both French philosophers and husbands throughout Spain, with a resounding "no." Palma writes in an era of renewed demands by women for suffrage and citizen rights, and his story reflects his own misogynist position on such issues.

Palma presents his version of Don Antonio's story as a case of "Mujer-hombre," which he juxtaposes with another case, "Hombre-mujer" (an equally misogynist treatment of independence hero Simón Bolívar's mistress, Manuela Sáenz). He makes his Antonio into a chaste and devout nun (a Clarisa from a nonexistent monastery of the Villa de Agreda in Spain) who disguises herself as a man exclusively for a life of adventure; taken in by the bishop, she is about to be consecrated as a priest when she escapes to Potosí. There, in the employ of Intendant Francisco de Paula Sanz, she is drawn into the web spun by Martina Bilbao, treated by Palma as a mestiza of sinful ways who has been locked up in the convent of Santa Mónica for her scandalous behavior. In service to the poor and destitute, Antonio visits her weekly at the convent's turnstile, providing her an allowance of six pesos for her subsistence. Out of the goodness of this female Antonio's heart, Antonio marries the mestiza Martina to win her release from imprisonment and then reveals his secrets to her. Traveling together to Chuquisaca after some bad investments in Potosí, Antonio gets a job in Moxos and there works lassoing wild bulls and such. After saving up for five years, the couple moves to Cochabamba, where the double-dealing Martina is courted by a *real* man, and to marry him she denounces Antonio to the audiencia president, García Pizarro. Returned to female costume, Antonio gains asylum in the convent of La Merced but is finally arrested and examined by the surgeon and two midwives, to whom he reveals his true sex and name, María Leocadia Álvarez.

Palma reports that the little nun María Leocadia was then sent to Lima and, from there, back to her convent in Spain. As for the ungrateful and perfidious, and not incidentally mestiza, Martina Bilbao, her new husband, only a few months after marrying her, gave her the punishment that her villainy called for. Palma concludes, "He beat her to death. It seems to me that you will feel no pain for the dead woman, and nor will I."

Adapting the story for Victorian-era sensibilities, Palma desexes Don Antonio, making *her* a chaste and devout nun guilty only of desire for a life of adventure and of having the courage and strength to carry it off. Same-sex desires or acts are banished from the interpretation. This is the idealized form of the *mujer varonil*, or "manly woman," inherited from Golden Age theater, and Palma's desexing of his Antonio/María repeats the desexing of the "lieutenant nun" Catalina de Erauso in Juan Pérez de Montalbán's ([1626] 1839) often-performed seventeenth-century play (Velasco 2003a) and the twentieth-century movie treatment of Erauso's life (see Velasco 2000), in which the disguise serves not only for reasons of adventure (and not sexual desire or unseemly ambiguity of sex) but to carry out honorable deeds.

Unhappy with the Spanish aristocrat of the real story, Dona Martina, Palma transforms her into the classic racialized temptress of nineteenth-century "foundational fictions," the earthy but untrustworthy female natives, blacks, or mixed-bloods who are the transgressive love interests to Creole, white male suitors in so many of the national romances analyzed by Doris Sommer (1993; see also Abercrombie 2003). A judge's sentence that restores the little nun to her convent back in Spain provides the virginal closure that makes this Yta (or Álvarez, in Palma's rewritten version) comparable to Palma's own interpretation of Catalina de Erauso, by his day known through the publication of the ersatz Erauso autobiography, and a well-known historical manly woman whose virginity particularly suited the times.

In Palma's interpretation Don Antonio becomes a sympathetic protagonist by valuing and performing masculinity and its virtues, carried out for motives untarnished by the stigma of sexual desire. Homosexuality and lesbianism were well known in Palma's day but were criminalized as deviant. An Antonio/María with same-sex desires would not have been a sympathetic figure to Palma's readers, nor was same-sex desire a suitable literary topic for publication. Instead, his Antonio becomes a vehicle for a paean to (hetero-sexual but desexed) masculinity. To underscore what is admirable about such manliness, which appears as a set of moral attributes rather than as a product of bodily impulses, Palma then leans on the classical repertoire of misogyny: feminine wiles and deceitfulness inherited from Eve. Being a Victorian writer, Palma does not also make reference to women's supposedly poor control of sexual impulses, as did writers in previous centuries (such as Rodríguez Freyle [1636] 1979, in *El carnero*). Palma's Antonio is in the end redeemed by submission: adventure over, manly virtues taught to her male audience, she returns to the cloister as a good little nun, while the devious mixed-blood Martina gets her "just deserts," killed by the violence of the misogynist masculinity that the story justifies and idealizes.

A Don Antonio for the Twenty-First Century

Drawing on the copy of Taborga's letter in Beruti's Buenos Aires notebook, on Palma's story, or on the expediente (or a combination of these), a number of early twenty-first-century authors, including historians writing for popular audiences and a playwright, have produced interpretations of Don Antonio's story for our time.

A trio of Argentine scholars, in works treating colonial transgressive sexuality (D'Aloia Criado 2003; Bazán 2004; Andahazi 2008), have drawn (and elaborated) on the Taborga's letter. None cite the expediente in the Archivo Nacional de Bolivia, which they apparently did not see. Walter D'Aloia Criado (2003) was the first to draw on the published version of the Beruti notebook to publish a short, stand-alone essay, while Osvaldo Bazán (2004) and Federico Andahazi (2008) cite D'Aloia Criado as their source for the case, each inserting a version into books treating a much larger gallery of cases of transgressive sex.

Drawing on the D'Aloia Criado essay, Bazán (2004) imagines the life of luxury and privilege achieved by Antonio Yta while serving as bishop Azamor's page: "There the young Antonio moved easily between the viceroy Nicolás Arredondo, the bishop, the town authorities, and the wealthy families. There was no act, solemn Te Deum, procession, or mass in which Antonio did not accompany the bishop. In the comfortable residence Antonio learned of the arrival of the new viceroy, Melo de Portugal y Villena, of the installation of the Royal consulate, always rubbing elbows with the best of colonial society in candlelit *tertulias* ended only by the voice of the night watchman" (Bazán 2004, 64; my translation).

Moving on to the house of Francisco de Paula Sanz in Potosí, Bazán imagines Antonio Yta surrounded by extreme luxury, with "ten black servants walking from here to there with trays of silver or gold. Not bad for a *polizón* [stowaway or tramp] who had done little or nothing in life" (2004, 64). Taking us through Moxos, the arrest in Chuquisaca, the medical examination, and the confession, all following Taborga's account, Bazán then brings us back to the bishop, who he imagines (contrafactually) to have been a supporter of illiberal absolutism and torture, so we might guess what he would have done had he uncovered Antonio's transvestism. Noting that Antonio's treatment by the church can best be understood through San Ignacio de Loyola's dictum that "if the church defined as black that which seems to us white, we must agree that it is black," he concludes that because "she was a woman, she felt like a woman but was attracted to other women," the Catholic Church decided that she should be a man. "The bishop," ends Bazán, "must have turned over in his grave" (Bazán 2004, 65).

D'Aloia, Bazán, and Andahazi regard Don Antonio as a lesbian living a life in disguise to enable her to fulfill her bodily desires and perhaps also enjoy some adventure. Don Antonio's role in their retellings of the story is to help to ridicule the bishop, judges, church, and law of the day for their inadequate understanding of the gap between sex and gender and of science and medicine. Don Antonio's use of male clothing in these accounts provides the external appearance matching an internal "trans" gender identity and same-sex sexual orientation. His long-term "masquerade" is excused as a means to an end that we (in the postmodern present) recognize as right and proper. Such anachronistic, transhistorical readings of the case make the stigma (the potential humiliation of discovery) that Don Antonio's costume covered disappear for us more cosmopolitan and modern judges.

A play performed in Mexico in 2012 and 2013 also takes up Don Antonio's story. Citing a newspaper account of the story (which I have been unable to find) as his original source, Mexican playwright Octavio Salazar-Villalba also found Palma's version (the only one to make Antonio Yta an invention of María Leocadia Álvarez) and used some combination of these sources as inspiration for a one-act play, *Los Extraños Hábitos de Don Antonio* (The Strange Habits of Don Antonio). The play was performed to quite good reviews during years that the legalization of gay marriage in Mexico City was a matter of national discussion. A cast of three engage in a series of dialogues among a priest, Don Antonio/Doña María (as both nun and husband), and Martina, laying out the moral quandaries and inner struggles involved, hoping that audiences might concur in supporting "the right of every person to choose their own route through life."[3]

The most recent treatment of Don Antonio's case is one among an impressively large array of brief case studies involving "love and loathing" in the colonial-era Audiencia de Charcas (today's Bolivia). Bolivianist historian Nicholas Robins (2015) offers an interpretation that draws on the case file itself but also on the litigation between Don Antonio and Doña Martina over clothing. His is the only one of these nineteenth- to twenty-first-century male renarrators of the case who has seized on the ambiguity of sex in his analysis.

Robins accepts Don Antonio's claim of having a functional member, and Felipa's statement on the impregnation of two women. He suggests that Don Antonio was both intersexed and bisexual. "[A] man by day, and a woman by night," Robins's Don Antonio made use of his female body to ingratiate herself with men (Bishop Azamor and Intendant Sanz) and her male one to have sex with women, such as Doña Martina. Robins's Yta possesses a *fully* androgynous body; both men's and women's clothing and gender performance are appropriate, because they are driven by natural, heterosexual bodily desire of both kinds (2015, 162). In Robins's interpretation, whether having sex with men or with women, a doubled Don Antonio and Doña María remain hetero. Robins's account thus retains the *frissón* of transvestism, while finessing the question of disjunction between gender and bodily sex. There is no disguise or deceit, and if judges see stigma, it is only because of their laughably poor scientific knowledge and inability to recognize an intersex condition.

Confession, the Archive, and Regimes of Truth

Each of these nineteenth- and twenty-first-century treatments narrates Don Antonio's story from the point of view of its author's contemporary, analytic context, something I have tried to avoid. Each figures the motives and character of Don Antonio and Doña Martina to serve the way they emplot the sequence of interactions that lead to the story's denouement and their own, moralizing conclusions, whether to impugn the character or competence of Don Antonio/Doña María, Martina, the secular judges, the church, the physicians, or the bad old Spaniards of the Black Legend past, prior to our supposedly more cosmopolitan and enlightened present. Together, especially when compared with Don Antonio's own self-emplotment and the emplotted explanations of Antonio or María's actions given by judges, lawyers, wife, and mother, they point to the importance of narrative form to the shaping of social personhood and to the judgment of sex/gender, as well as the character and potential criminality of those who perform it. Yet let us remember that not even Don Antonio's story was freely produced to speak to the ages. It was a "coerced autobiography," that is, a confession. Michel Foucault argued that confession is "one of the main rituals we rely on for the production of truth" ([1976] 1990, 58). As Marta Vicente points out, "Foucault sees confession as a form of disciplinary power: church, criminal justice, and the medicalized body, all work at obtaining 'the truth' out of the individual" (2016a).

It is true that secular courts had co-opted the ritual-sacramental framing of religious confession, producing a context where self-narration is turned toward the production of ordered knowledge. It is also the case that the courts in this era called on "expert witnesses" such as physicians to make "determinations of sex" and that such physicians were then engaged in an Enlightenment project to describe a rigidly binary understanding of sex in relation to natural, reproductive function. But as Vicente goes on to point out, the confessions of "trans" individuals, such as Don Antonio, often enough contradict, rather than submit to, the anatomical verdicts of physicians.

In addition to producing data wrested from him by a "truth regime" intent on ordering knowledge and producing orderly subjects, Don Antonio, like other confessants, has produced an elaborate narrative, drawing on widely circulated models of storytelling, such as those produced in relaciones and picaresque novels or those rehearsed bit by bit in everyday social interaction.[4] They draw on such shared narrative conventions to characterize themselves and to offer motive and justification for acts in ways that conform to social understandings of life's possible emplotments but also describe their individual positions and stakes in ways that demand recognition of their own stance toward the world. In Don Antonio's case that stance involves having a functional male member. His bodily sex, it turns out, is in service to the performative "sex" of his hábitos (or, as we now call that, his gender).

To have a gender, we might argue, is far more than the "stylization of the body" (Butler 1990, 25). It is to have "social being" in relation to others, for us defined in contrast to a "biologized" understanding of sex. Sex/gender, that is to say, is produced not by organic processes (though it is always understood in relation to them) but through socialization as a social being whose life is composed of enactments of habituated, status, and role-bound positions in relation to others and whose life-course and its transitions among kinds of status or role can be recounted, and lived, in the form of a story. Finding such stories and reading them along the grain (revealing the structures and institutions of imperial, colonial, and patriarchal power) and against it (discovering what has fallen through the cracks of, or failed to submit to, that regime), the historian can perhaps get past the "truth regime" and reveal how persons fashioned *themselves*.

Many scholars have argued that we should treat the "archive" as an object of study rather than as a "source" of objective information. Historians in the vein of social, cultural, and colonial history have been doing so for a few generations now. More recently scholars influenced by Foucault have called for renewed attention to the archive's "classificatory" service to governmentality, particularly in the regulation of sexuality (Stoler 2009; see also Steedman 2002). A queer-history perspective has promoted renewed focus on archives in an effort to recover from them evidence of gender and sex-nonconforming persons who appear there only in the written traces of legal processes aiming to erase them from the social body (Martínez 2016; Tortorici 2016b). Like clothing and the performative "social skin," archives conceal as much as they reveal. Sometimes archival documents seem to have recorded only the voice of authority. But when we have access to accused subjects' own accounts (as we do through Don Antonio's confession, even if coercively produced), other readings are possible. As Vicente has recently concluded, "Contrasting the authorities' narrative with the queer subject's own telling of the story allows us to enrich our understanding of how sex and gender were negotiated in the eighteenth-century Spanish world" (2016a).

Taborga's letter supposes that the confessant, María Leocadia to him, is simply a woman who despises her own sex and prefers to live the life of a male scoundrel. For him, Doña María Yta's deceit of dress points to other unknown secrets (she is a woman of many closets, he says), requiring investigation. Clothing, which ought, as a social skin, to reveal or tell the truth about what it covers, lies about that body to conceal other secrets. Ricardo Palma's fictionalized version of the story desexes María, treating her as a virginal nun who dresses as a man solely in search of adventure and who marries Martina as an act of charity to rescue a fallen woman from jail. Many treatments of the story of Catalina/Antonio de Erauso have also stressed (as did the king and pope) her virginity and the adventuresome and manly life in service to the king that they determined to be his or her motive (rather than the satisfaction of same-sex desires). Most of our more contemporary interpreters of Don Antonio/Doña María are quick to place *her* into the genealogy of lesbianism, apart from Robins, whose Don Antonio/Doña María is a fully "intersexed" person, a hermaphrodite (of the kind that does not, in fact, exist among mammals [see Fausto-Sterling 2012]), with functional male and female genitals, motivated to disguise one or the other sex to enjoy heterosexual relations with both men and women.

Disguise and deception about the body beneath the clothing are at the heart of the original accusation. It leads to investigation of Don Antonio's past life and crimes, motives, or character flaws. If Doña María was a woman masquerading as a man and no prior crimes were discovered, then emplotting a narrative about that masquerade was simplified. Either this was a chaste and honorable woman seeking a life of manly adventure and professional service (something easy for judges to sympathize with), or it was a lust-driven woman engaged in a contemptible ruse to satisfy perverse, same-sex desires. Either way, judges first needed to prove that there had been deceit, and that depended on the secure determination of Don Antonio's "true sex."

Physicians are mostly certain that Antonio is a woman, although they leave themselves a bit of wiggle room (they have not "seen it [the clitoris] in the action that he describes," which is to say, in a state of excitation). At the same time, they continue to pronominally gender Don Antonio as a man. As time passes, what thickens in the plot of Don Antonio's life story for most participants in the trial is his masculinity. Deception fades to the background as the aura of performed sex expands to bring Antonio's virile member back into mind. Don Antonio's performed masculinity is powerful enough to transform his body, in his own mind and in the minds of others.

With the medical findings (breasts, clitoris, vagina, menstruation), the vision of that male member leads some to conclude that Don Antonio was a her-maphrodite. Reaching such a conclusion not only resolved the otherwise baffling contradiction of body and performance but also exculpated Don Antonio, who would not then have been engaged in disguise or deceit, the act on which all possible criminal charges were predicated. Someone with a penis cannot be said to be masquerading as or "passing" for a man. What, then, was Don Antonio's true sex? Can he have been a hermaphrodite? Can a reconsideration of his sex erase the issue of deception?

CHAPTER 6

TRUTH

"True Sex," Passing, and the Consequences of Deception

Determining Don Antonio's "True Sex" and the Question of Hermaphrodism

Throughout this book I have tried to avoid in my discussions of Don Antonio's life the use of our own era's terminology for those whose bodies, desires, and performative realizations of social roles and categories in some way violate established notions of what it is to have a sex and live as one. I have justified my refusal to consider Doña María to have been a lesbian or Don Antonio a transgendered person largely through recourse to the historians' dodge: it would be anachronistic to do so when writing about an era when such categories had yet to be invented and institutionalized. This is not to say that there were not women who had sex with women, conscious of their systematically counternormative (transgressive) desires (what we now call sexual orientation) or that some of these women did so within a heteronormative framework, that is, in a masculine way or while feeling like a man. But no one in these documents applies terms like *homosexual* or *lesbian* to Doña María. These were not yet thinkable or livable "identities" in 1803, and Doña María could not have claimed them.

For the same reasons Don Antonio could not have claimed to be or have been labeled as transgendered. None of the words represented in the acronym LGBTQIA yet existed as habitable "identities." I recognize that failing to categorize Don Antonio/Doña María as a (transvestite) lesbian or "butch-dyke," female-to-male transgender, queer, or intersexed person might frustrate those searching for historical ancestors of contemporary forms of identification. Others have applied such terms to historical figures and have justified their choices (Brown 1986; Delgado and Saint-Saens 2000; Gruzinski 1985; Sigal 2003; Velasco 2003a), but for me this is problematic anachronism, where contemporary categories are read into the past in a way that both naturalizes the categories as transhistorical ones and obfuscates that past, making it more difficult to understand.

As more scholars over the past decade have delved into historical, archival traces of nonnormative gender, sexual orientation, or sexual practices, the debate has heated up (see Menon 2009; Martínez 2014; Marshall, Murphy, and Tortorici 2015; see also Traub 2013). Yet understanding past moments and constructing genealogies of sex, gender, class, and race hinge on tracking the social and cultural transformations of those shifting categories. As Kathryn Burns (2008, 202) puts it for the construct called "race," "upstreaming contemporary notions of race to interpret colonial racism can lead us to gloss over the very dynamics of difference and discrimination we most want to understand." The same holds for both sex and gender.

One term that is used in the case documents, however, deserves particular consideration. Don Antonio himself, along with his mother, lawyer, and certain judges (particularly Méndez de la Parra, the ecclesiastical judge) are ready to apply the term *hermaphrodite*. Don Antonio had asserted having a male member that appeared when needed, though physicians did not see it. The ecclesiastical prosecutor Parra had assumed that Don Antonio was a hermaphrodite, "in whom prevails the female sex." Don Antonio's mother's letter then convinced his attorneys of his hermaphrodism: "In the detailed reports given to me by Rita Benedicto and Vicenta Arias, they stated that in *his* construction *he* had qualities of a woman, but in the act a virile member manifests itself, with all the full functions of a man. Even from childhood, **his** character /29v/ was always rebellious, and in later years **he** was very strongly inclined toward the feminine sex, which resulted in giving us, *his* parents, many sorrows" (appendix A.21, fol. 29r–v). Continuing her account, she relates the paternity suits launched against Don Antonio, one in Madrid dating to before his change of hábitos, and one in Cádiz afterward, emplotting his trip to the Vatican and his departure for Málaga and South America not, as Don Antonio had said, to resolve a matter of conscience but as a flight from the effects of his functional, Don Juan–style maleness (fols. 28v–29r). It is more than likely that María, and then Antonio, convinced his lovers that he could perform sexually like a man; they seem to have convinced Doña Felipa that he had fully functional male parts, which she asserts as her reason for using masculine gender for him in her letter ("I refer to him as such because of the circumstances that I will relate" [fol. 28r]). Let us assume that she was so convinced, though we should also be cautious in reading this letter, after all written to exculpate her son by proving his hermaphrodism. But can *we* accept a determination of fully functional hermaphrodism (a woman who menstruates and a man who engenders children in a single body) in Don Antonio's case?

Prior to the rise of objectivist, scientific anatomy during the last half of the eighteenth century, hermaphrodism had been a frequent conclusion (of self-attribution and attribution by others, including physicians, priests, and secular judges) to identify the sex of persons whose body or behavior was mismatched with presumed qualities of male or female sex, as well as cases of anatomical androgyny. Such conclusions rested on Galenic or Aristotelian theories of biological sex, which viewed the male sex as the perfected type and female sex as an imperfect or incomplete version of it. Humoral theories suggested that the sex of infants was a product of a "hot" (for male) or "cold" (for female) womb. Hermaphrodism was thus intelligible as an intermediate condition and biological sex as subject to change over an individual's lifetime.[1]

The Eighteenth-Century Science of Sex

Principals in the case were divided on the hermaphrodism question, because a revolution in theorizing biological sex was just then in the works, but not yet complete. During the last quarter of the eighteenth century and the first quarter of the nineteenth, "sex" was in the process of being "medicalized," as physicians and surgeons with governmental standing in Spain began to think of themselves as working in the interests of science, refining categories simultaneously of the "natural" world and the legal, governmental one (Haidt 1998; Hirschauer 1997; Mak 2013; Soyer 2012; Vicente 2017).

Where in prior centuries determination of sex fell to the church for its critical implication in the moral realm of sin and salvation, the church now sometimes turned to physicians before issuing an opinion with moral ramifications. Doña María went to her priest and then the Vatican for advice, and the Vatican had indeed in earlier cases adjudicated sex, deciding in cases of intersexed individuals, then called hermaphrodites, which sex "predominated" to assign the correct one for sacramental and social purposes (baptism and marriage or its annulment). Failing to assign a person to one of the two sexes was unthinkable. Vatican records from the sixteenth century on reveal a familiarity with hermaphrodism (and also with apparently biologically female persons deserving of male status, such as both Don Antonio/Doña María and Catalina/Antonio de Erauso, though not the reverse, apparently male persons deserving of female status). A determination of sex was what the La Plata ecclesiastical prosecutor had sought from the audiencia when he sent Doña Martina there. On the basis of Martina's denunciation (and word of the physicians' findings and Don Antonio's statement), he expected a determination of hermaphrodism. This was a relatively common conclusion that in prior centuries explained the existence of "manly women" (McKendrick 1974; Perry 1987), regardless of the failure to find both kinds of genitalia in a single person.

Perhaps the most detailed case file is that of the sixteenth-century Spaniard known as Eleno or Elena Céspedes, daughter of a converted Muslim slave and a Christian mother, who had a child of her own before passing as a man for many years, taking a wife and taking up men's occupations (and becoming a practicing surgeon in the process). Philip II's physician declared Eleno to be a man, but later examinations reversed that finding, determining that Eleno was a woman in disguise, who had surgically manipulated her own genitals to produce the appearance of a phallus, which later disappeared (Burshatin 1996, 1998, 1999).

Chapter 2 of this book treated the case from 1617 of the young Spanish nun Magdalena Muñoz. When she jumped over a ditch, male genitals emerged from her body from the heat of the exertion. This was the end of Magdalena's career as a nun, about which she, now he, was relieved, now being free of "that jail" and of teasing by other nuns who had called her *marimacho*. The account suggests that Magdalena was an intersexed person, of a relatively rare type that makes it appear that a spontaneous sex change has taken place (see Vicente 2017, 29).

Like Eleno/Elena Céspedes (who does not appear to have actually been intersexed but who had sought permission to continue to pass as a man under the license of hermaphrodism), Magdalena Muñoz's case was in the hands of the church. By the later eighteenth century, most such cases ended up in civil courts, influenced by Enlightenment ideas and struggling to keep secular jurisdiction over the "determination of sex."

By the eighteenth century such cases of doubtful sex required a medical examination conducted by official physicians and surgeons, such as those who examined Don Antonio. Such physicians acted under the authority of the *protomedicato real*, a hierarchy of certifiers of medical training with branches in viceregal capitals, formed as a kind of public health service (see Lanning 1985). Providing medical texts and circulating journals, which detailed new medical approaches in fields including gynecology, they aimed to safeguard and improve medicine as a science and to implement its use in governance of the bodies of the king's subjects (Martínez 2014 provides an example). They were the institutions and agents of Michel Foucault's ([1976] 1990) biopower.

The institutional framework of the protomedicato, which governed physicians and surgeons appointed by the city councils of all Spanish towns, was the vehicle through which the Spanish Crown endeavored to vaccinate all its subjects (using Edward Jenner's technique pioneered only a few years earlier) against smallpox in the Balmís Expedition (Franco-Paredes, Lammoglia, and Santos-Preciado 2005), carried out with the help of detailed population censuses the Crown had initiated in the sixteenth century. The protomedicato and its successor institutions was also the institution to which fell not only the determination of sex in doubtful cases but its medicalization, through the objective definition of bodily sex. By the end of the nineteenth century, their work, now examining psyches as well as bodies, transformed same-sex activities from sin into a consequence of mental disease. Considering two eighteenth-century cases of suspected hermaphrodism will help to put Don Antonio's case into proper context.

Near Mexico City in 1759, Mariano Aguilera approached his priest, asking to have his sex officially determined so that he could be declared a man to marry the woman with whom he had been involved. Aguilera needed that determination because although he had been raised as a girl and was reputed to be one in his hometown, he now found himself *en su conciencia ser del sexo masculine*, "in his conscience to be of the masculine sex" (Martínez 2016, 428). Finding his women's attire to be repugnant to him and having "no inclination" to act as woman, he had always engaged in men's work. He was also perturbed by the *importunaciones* (solicitations or harassment) from men. His priest advised him to switch to male clothing. To be licensed to wear that clothing, live as a man, and now marry a woman, he asked the judge to have him examined by expert surgeons (431). María Elena Martínez points to the disjuncture Aguilera expresses between assigned sex and his feelings about being treated as a woman and to the centrality of occupation and clothing in the performative realization of gender. Aguilera also defined himself as *andrógino*, "androgynous," arguing that he had the virile equipment to "deflower" virgins (432–33).

Examined by a physician and surgeon, Aguilera proved to be intersexed, with the female parts prevailing and without a penis capable of penetration or insemination. Since they found him inapt for being penetrated as well, they then determined that there would be fewer complications were he to be allowed to live as a man. The ecclesiastical judge overseeing the case did not agree, declaring Aguilera to be a woman and "ineligible to contract matrimony not only as a man but as a woman," separating Aguilera from his betrothed and from his home community (Martínez 2016, 434).

In Madrid a few years later, in 1769, physicians were also called on to make a determination of sex in the case of Sebastián or María Leirado, a sometime amateur actor and singer who occasionally performed, on stage and for less formal audiences, in woman's dress. Of slight build and with a beardless, feminine face, Leirado had learned acting skills, first from age twelve as a servant for the actor María Teresa Garrido and then while working as an assistant to actor María Ladvenant. In the course of a string of service positions in various Spanish cities, Leirado was arrested for vagrancy and for wearing women's clothes. Examined by a physician on suspicion of being a hermaphrodite, Leirado was declared to be a male and returned to his parents in Madrid.

Over these years Leirado had apparently helped foster rumors of actually *being* the actor María Teresa Garrido, who had been banned from Madrid and was suspected of living disguised as a man. In Madrid Leirado opened a tavern, where the cooking, sewing, and ironing skills learned in service to actors may have been useful but also increased the suspicion of being, instead, a cross-dressed woman. Obtaining a part as a woman-dressed-as-a-man on the Madrid stage from actor friends, Leirado went home in male costume with a man. They had sex. That man, complaining that Leirado had given him a venereal disease, denounced Leirado to authorities as a female-to-male transvestite! Leirado was then arrested for a seventh time in four years and once again subjected to a medical examination, front and rear.

The examination once again revealed male genitals, along with a widened anus (plus venereal sores and genital warts), but the rest of Leirado's female presentation-of-self left room for doubts. The first physician referred the case to another, with similar results. The third physician to enter the fray was known as the foremost anatomist of Madrid at that time, but even he could not be fully convinced that Leirado might not in some way be a hermaphrodite. Nonetheless, Leirado was convicted of sodomy (which constituted penetration of either a man's or a woman's anus or being so penetrated) and sent into prison.[2]

Thirty-three years later, now in the era of "enlightened" medicine, one Juana Aguilar went on trial in the Real Audiencia de Guatemala for committing the "abominable sin" with women. In July 1803 (not long before Don Antonio's arrest) the colonial protomedicato commissioned the surgeon Narciso Esparragosa y Gallardo to study Aguilar's anatomy, since she was suspected of being a hermaphrodite (Martínez 2014; Few 2007). Most of the documentary record of the audiencia's proceedings has been lost, or not yet found, so we have no access to Aguilar as a person (acts, feelings, etc.), but the *protomédico's* report was published in *La Gazeta de Guatemala* as an essay in anatomical science. "Although Juana 'la Larga' (the Long)—as she had been nicknamed by townspeople presumably because of her genitalia—did have an enlarged clitoris, the protomédico (protomedic, or royal physician) asserted that she did not have a 'union of the two sexes' and therefore was not both a man and a woman" (Martínez 2014, 159).

But since Aguilar's vagina lacked an opening, and her clitoris, although enlarged, could not become erect or emit semen, Esparragosa concluded that "she was sexually 'neutral,' "like some bees." He "ended his report by noting that because the law (and in particular the crime of *pecado nefando*, or 'sodomy') required that the parties involved be of one or another sex, the court should exonerate Aguilar" (Martínez 2014, 160). Because the court documents are missing, we have no way of knowing the outcome of the case for Aguilar, apart from the mortifications of Esparragosa's "examination," which could only have reached the conclusion that Aguilar's clitoris could not become erect by masturbating her (something that Don Antonio likely avoided not because his doctors were squeamish but because of respect for his *Don*). But it was another step forward in the "enlightened" medicalization of sex, taking over from the church and defining it not in terms of sinfulness but of conformity or disconformity with mammalian reproductive function.[3]

The development of such knowledge of intersex conditions and the more scientifically "certain" determination that a person was male or female rather than hermaphrodite came at a price for those who formerly were labeled hermaphrodites or who hoped to be so labeled. They were now assigned a legal and social sex, punished if found to have violated the law and sent out into the world. That price resulted from what we might call the emergence of compulsorily heterosexed bodies. Hermaphrodism (the condition of a person with the functioning body of both the Greek sexual ideals, Hermes and Aphrodite) was now derided as a medieval myth, along with the notion that sex was malleable. The classification of two fully distinct sexes was now a mandate of "nature" understood as something other than God's will, something with its own organizing principles. The key to understanding sex was to determine its role in reproductive function. There was to be no room left for marvelous ambiguity and acceptable "exceptions." The published anatomical report of the *protomédico* of Guatemala was one of the infrequent cases of medically documented intersex conditions produced during the era of the "invention of sex." For Aguilar the consequences were unhappy. To be intermediate between male and female, for Esparragosa, was to have no sex at all.

The enlightened anatomical classification of sex was the precondition, or first step, on the way to the medicalization and institutionalization of homosexuality as a form of deviance, a mental illness without acceptable justification or possibility of normalization by assigning to them the "opposite" of their originally assigned sex to resolve the contradiction. Homosexuality and lesbianism were then understood to be deviant aberrations of persons suffering from "hermaphrodism of the soul" in Foucault's phrase, requiring corrective reversion to heterosexual orientation and activity to serve the natural and social purpose of reproduction.

That was the Enlightenment-era view, at any rate. It has persisted in the popular and religious imagination. The "science of sex," however, has marched on and has developed new ways to attempt to determine it. How would present-day physicians approach Don Antonio if asked to do so?

Don Antonio and Twenty-First-Century Sex Science

First of all, present-day physicians would discard the idea of hermaphrodism. The modern scientific use of this term is restricted to those creatures (among them worms, mollusks, and certain fishes) that possess two sexes, and both fertilize the eggs of others of their species and have their eggs fertilized by those others, as part of their normal functioning. Since possession of both functional sexes has never been recorded in mammals, much less in humans, hermaphrodism is not now considered a human possibility (Fausto-Sterling 2012). A condition in which some aspects of both sexes are present in one body is now termed *intersex*.

Asked to determine Don Antonio's sex, modern physicians would turn to a series of tests and procedures that were not available in 1803. After an exterior examination, they would then check the internal sex organs, aiming to see uterus and ovaries or the possible existence of undescended testicles or chimeric testes. They would do a DNA test to examine Don Antonio's sex chromosomes, to see if they were a female XX, a male XY, or something more ambiguous (XXY, for example). They would draw blood to identify the workings of Don Antonio's endocrine system for signs that estrogen or androgen were being improperly produced or taken up by the body.

The biology of sex in mammals, including humans, is complex, consisting of chromosomal sex (XX or XY, but also the ambiguous X and XXY), gonadal sex (ovaries or testes or tissues of both), infantile hormonal sex (involving the production and uptake of estrogen and testosterone), and pubescent hormonal sex, in which the gonads are activated by a developing brain. There is internal reproductive sex (uterus, ovaries, and vagina versus vas deferens and prostate), external genital sex (penis and scrotum or clitoris and labia), and possibly "brain sex," where certain parts of the brain may or may not be stimulated by genetic or endocrinological factors to diverge in male or female ways. At every stage there are possibilities for ambiguity, sometimes producing the recognizably ambiguous external genitals that used to be called hermaphroditic.[4]

Each of those tests, along with inspection of the external sex characteristics, marks a present-day method of determining sex as a property exclusive to the body. None of the tests are in themselves conclusive, and together so many factors are involved that in many cases it is impossible for scientists to make a determination or agree on one, at least if they have to choose between "male" and "female." But Don Antonio did report having regular menses, which suggests that his internal organs functioned in the female way, itself telling us that fathering children was no more than a fantasy. It is true that certain endocrinological conditions, such as androgen reuptake syndrome, can lead to a chromosomally (and gonadally) male child who will appear to be female until the endocrinological consequences of puberty suddenly cause a penis (and sometimes testes) to emerge, as is the likely cause of Magdalena Muñoz's transformation. But those penises do not then disappear until needed for a sex act. No, what Don Antonio and Doña Felipa report cannot have been the case, in biological terms. So Don Antonio's purported spurious children, born of Doña Rita Benedicto in Madrid or Doña Vicenta Arias de Reyna in Cádiz, according to Doña Felipa, are just that: spurious. Don Antonio's phallus is best understood as an apparition in the minds of those (including Don Antonio and those two women, if indeed they reported a functional virile member as Doña Felipa relates) who are unable to imagine heterosexual male social personhood without a penetrating phallus.

No doubt if the case had continued in ecclesiastical courts, judges like Bernardino Méndez de la Parra would have looked again for that phallus or alleged into existence a mechanical one, the dildo that would have marked Don Antonio, in the laws of the day, as a sodomite. Indeed, although "frica-trisses," women who sexually pleased one another without penetration, were sometimes, in some jurisdictions, denounced and brought to court (Tortorici and Vainfas 2016), such acts did not constitute sodomy for most judges or members of the general public. For most (as for Bill Clinton) there was no sex act, and thus no correct or incorrect one, without penile penetration. Don Antonio might have insisted that he "had sex with that woman," but, without penetration, the general consensus would have been that he did not and that he had neither consummated his marriage nor engaged in an act of sodomy.

Clitoral sexuality was, for most men at least, almost unimaginable, or at least unspeakable and unlegislatable, though it is also possible that lack of references to it result from the fact that it was not a crime, even if it was sometimes named and denounced as sinful (Velasco 2011). François Soyer (2012, 46) suggests that this archival absence results from ignorance of female sexuality, while Judith Halberstam (1998) argues that this conceptual failure owed to a chauvinist refusal to believe that the female sexual partners of people like Antonio might achieve sexual fulfillment without penetration. But we should not doubt that women, and plenty of their sexual partners, of whatever sex, knew otherwise.

Although modern techniques might have diagnosed some kind of hormonal intersexed condition not then appreciable, given his breasts, appearance of his genitalia, and menses (pointing to uterus and functioning ovaries) Don Antonio was a "biological" woman, assigned to the female sex at baptism and raised as a girl. Attracted to women and intent on satisfying those desires, first (as far as we know) in a nun's habit, Doña María had begun to try on male costume and customs while doing so, even before fully becoming Antonio the man. As far as we can tell, Doña María did not want to revel in her female body and femininity while making love to women but hoped that those women, even in the convent, would "think" and feel that she was a man. That is the gist of the reports from convents, what Doña Felipa reports María's lovers, Rita Benedicto and Doña Vicenta Arias de Reyna, as having concluded, and what Doña Martina also suggests. We do not have here, then, a straightforward case of same-sex (and same-gender) desire. Doña María and Don Antonio quite clearly wanted to have sex with women, *as a man*. That might lead us to conclude that the asserted "male member" and the persona of Antonio were the manifestation of transgender in the era before "gender" was divorced from bodily sex. And yet we are also left with doubts, since being or passing as a man was also then the only way to live *openly* as a person who loves women. At the same time, a more complex and also likely conclusion is that Doña María wanted to be freed from "the jail" of convents and from pressure to marry a man and also free to enjoy an active life, including sexual pleasure, rather than remaining a chaste and virginal, homebound, and impoverished lace-making spinster, which was indeed another alternative for some nonconforming women, if not for Doña María.

Living openly as a nonheterosexually oriented person was to remain impossible until the late twentieth century. That left only three options for those who either wished to perform the gender role not conforming to their assigned sex or who wished to engage in sexual acts with persons of the same assigned sex, or a combination of such desires. One was complete suppression or denial of such desires and submission to heteronormativity, whether by finding a homosocial context for a chaste life where lack of heterosexual relations was at least nominally expected or acceptable, such as the priesthood, a convent, or the military or by marrying and carrying out a full heterosexual life. The second was the closet (perhaps aided by one of the foregoing as "covers") and furtive, secretive, hidden expression of nonheterosexual orientation. The third option, available to those with amenable performative abilities and bodies, was passing, publicly expressing same-sex desire but concealing assigned sex.

Catalina/Antonio de Erauso chose a combination of these three: to pass as a man, but a military one in service to the king, while avoiding marriage and its complications. More than a century later, Doña María, who seems to have had both same-sex desires and an inclination toward masculine ways, also strove to pass as a person of male sex but fell into marriage along the way, whether as a covering tactic or for lust and love, or for a combination of these. In doing so, at the tail end of the era when Don Antonio might have been awarded male identity and sent on his way, he repeated the strategy of Sebastián/María Leirado and others who had gone before. As we shall see, Don Antonio's strategy, to "pass" as a man and to conceal the aspects of his body that indicated "female," has also been employed by many others since that time who were born or baptized as women while hoping to live and love as men. The strategy involves cross-dressing and successful impersonation of the performative gender of the sex (and sexual orientation) they wish to be taken for. Cross-dressing, or transvestism, has a long history and considerable social visibility, then in the theater, and now, within the LGBTQIA communities.

Carnivalesque Inversions, Theatrical Cross-Dressed Impersonation, and Drag

Don Antonio was not a hermaphrodite in the objectivist, scientific sense. Some sort of intersex condition that eighteenth-century physicians could not yet diagnose remains a possibility, but one we should not assume, since we cannot know. Can we then conclude that Doña María was a transvestite, lesbian woman, "posing" as a man? At the heart of the case is an apparent contradiction between Don Antonio's social identity and his bodily sex. The social identity was that of what we would now call a heterosexual man, but his bodily sex, as determined by physicians, made him, potentially, a woman flawed not only by masculinity but also by same-sex desire. Don Antonio's legal maleness, his name, his clothing, manners, and assertions prevented those physicians from referring to him as her, just as it prevented the judges from concluding that they were faced with a woman of deviant sexual orientation. Such facts should be a warning to those readers who might be tempted to pithily classify Don Antonio/Doña María (as so many have classified Catalina/Antonio de Erauso, the "lieutenant nun") as a "transvestite nun." That is especially so because all those involved in the case were familiar with cross-dressing on the stage and in masquerades, where it was a staple of "world upside-down" social inversions, particularly during carnival.

What is wrong with using the term *transvestite* to describe Don Antonio, now that we have concluded that he was essentially a "biological female"? Transvestism today is generally understood to be a form of temporary or secret or festive play. When undertaken as performance in a parade or a cabaret, it is called drag. In the vast majority of cases, historical and contemporary, cross-dressing as staged or ritual performance has involved men (whether homosexual or heterosexual) dressing and vamping it up as women, not women as men (with the exception of Spanish theater). Historically, "biological" women have been more successful at *passing* for men than "biological" men have been at passing for women. Theatrical or carnivalesque male-to-female transvestism has been regarded as making much more of a travesty of social conventions than the female-to-male kind, explaining its virtual absence from the Spanish stage (where it was often forbidden) while remaining a core feature of popular carnivalesque festivities.

Explaining this imbalance is not easy. It no doubt has something to do with ranking of the sexes, so for a woman to make herself appear to be a man was explicable as an act of social climbing, while a male presenting himself as a woman seemed a demeaning act of self-abjection. Also involved is patriarchalism's objectification of the woman, reduced to a body on display but also elevated to the status of an aesthetic object of an evaluative gaze. That objectification, which makes the female body a superior vehicle for the representation of bodily excess and incarnate desire, along with the resulting broader availability of "masking" props (wigs, clothes that exaggerate the body's curves, makeup), might also help to account for the abundance of male-to-female drag and the relative lack of female-to-male drag nowadays in the cabaret. Finally, of course, there is the matter of being able to perform the "other" sex convincingly. Men's bodies are statistically larger and often covered in hair. Adam's apples, larger jaws, broad shoulders, and narrow hips (and balding heads and beer bellies) do not mesh well with stereotypical images of female beauty. Likewise, the tradition of the objectified female body on display (including Don Antonio's era of the *madamitas del nuevo cuño*) requires showing some skin. For the average man without hormone treatment, and even with it, *passing* as a woman is not so easy. Too many "clues" give away the secret. That is no problem, however, with drag, since key to such performances is letting the audience in on the deception through "reveals," subtle or not.

Drag is a form of entertainment and also a political act, a commentary on the relationship between biological sex and performed gender. As Marjorie Garber has suggested, "One of the most important aspects of cross-dressing is the way in which it offers a challenge to easy notions of binarity, putting into question the categories of 'female and 'male,' whether they are considered essential or constructed, biological or cultural" (1992, 10).

Drawing on Esther Newton's (1972) study of camp and drag, Judith Butler focuses on the way that the disjunction between the performer's body and the performed gender is highlighted in the form of parody. "In imitating gender, drag implicitly reveals the imitative structure of gender itself—as well as its contingency, . . . part of the pleasure, the giddiness of the performance is in the recognition of a radical contingency in the relation between sex and gender" (1990, 137–38). For Butler, this is the source of its revolutionary potential.

And yet drag, like theater and the "carnivalesque," is constrained to a "bracketed" time and space, in service of the "poetic function" of practice, to borrow a concept from Roman Jakobson's (1960) analysis of the poetic function in language. In brief, such bracketed activity is much more than play, but at the same time much less than disruptive in a revolutionary manner. It is the means by which iterated actions, constrained by control of context and actors, can become metacommentaries (Jakobson's metalinguistic or reflexive function [1960]) on other everyday actions, whether merely to "define" them or to index new relationships between certain typified embodied and clothed actions and *particular* persons or the social relations between such persons and others with whom they interact inside or outside of the ritual frame. But whatever is being transformed, renewed, or negated, the acts, persons, and relationships within the ritual frame remain insulated from everyday or "real" life: "what happens in Vegas, stays in Vegas," so to speak.

In theatrical or ritual space-time, persons are licensed to systematically violate strictures that, offstage, remain firmly in place. Ritual masquerades and inversions may teach us that "all the world is a stage," but the theatrical license expires at the door of the theater, the arrival of Ash Wednesday, and the cold light of dawn in the street outside of the cabaret. Ritual inversions of social hierarchy are well known to reveal the radical contingency of that hierarchy, that is, that such hierarchy and the "roles" it ranks are social constructs. But they are also known to clarify and indeed reinforce that social hierarchy (V. Turner 1969; Bristol 1985; Schechner 1985). To continue the "act" beyond those ritual confines is either to engage not in permitted forms of transvestism or drag but in transgressive or even revolutionary activities (challenging power by inverting its structures and hierarchies) or to engage in passing, which requires the appearance of submission to the hegemonic order and, indeed, expression of support for it.

Of course resistance is not always futile: carnival inversions have often enough become rebellions. Likewise, drawing public attention (say, through news reports or by use of cell phone videos) to overzealous suppression of transgressive acts or stigmatized kinds of person can lead to larger social movements intent on redefinition of what constitutes transgression, stigma, proper use of force, and justice. Stonewall and Black Lives Matter are recent examples of such processes. Ritual transgression can indeed lead to transformation of social worlds (Bristol 1985).

Some post-structuralist scholars would find problematic the emphasis here on the social skin as boundary, to the degree that it makes analytic use of such play with distinctions between inside and outside, external appearances, and inner truth or reality. Such approaches to cultural form insist that all is discourse and aim to undo the Cartesian distinction between mind and matter and to dissolve the subject by revealing how discourse produces it as an effect. Full understanding of phenomena like drag, however, must focus on the deployment and interactional interpretation of such semiotic activity and thus depends precisely on analyzing how its elements, binaries or not, are deployed by persons as poetic and metacommunicative forms. These are the means by which actual, embodied persons come not only to enter and depart from socially established identities but also to challenge and sometimes to socially establish new identity arrangements. Without the binaries of surface and depth, exterior and interior, or appearance and reality, activities involving the social skin, such as masquerade, and the elaborate changes of clothing so important in life-crisis rites (putting on the nun's habit, the wedding dress, the academic gown, the police uniform and badge for the swearing in ceremony, etc.) would make no sense to those who engage in them or would cease to be effective. Consider Newton's (1972) analysis of drag.

Newton argues that drag conveys "two somewhat conflicting statements concerning the sex-role system." The first statement it symbolizes is that the sex-role system is truly natural and that homosexuals are thus unnatural. The second statement symbolized by drag *questions* this supposed "naturalness" of the sex-role system. If sex-role behavior can be adequately performed by the "wrong" sex, then that behavior is also an achieved performance, not an inherited one, when it is done by the "right" sex. "The gay world, via drag, says that sex-role behavior is an appearance; it is 'outside.' It can be manipulated at will." How it does so is complex, beginning with the straightforward assertion, by the wearing of drag, that the wearer is a homosexual, a man who in relation to other men places himself as a woman. Newton continues, "In this sense it signifies stigma. At the most complex, it is a double inversion that says 'appearance is an illusion.' Drag says, 'my "outside" appearance is feminine, but my essence "inside" [the body] is masculine.' At the same time it symbolizes the opposite inversion: 'my appearance "outside" [my body, my gender] is masculine but my essence "inside" [myself] is feminine.'" Newton goes on to declare the drag queen to be the very personification of stigma, accounting for the profound ambivalence toward drag in the gay world (1972, 107–8).

Newton's arguments hinge on close attention to the surface of the body as a boundary. Clothing (and signifying behavior related to it) draws attention to and asks us the audience to speculate on what lies beneath, what the "real body" might be like. But the skin itself then conceals something else, something "deeper," which is to say, identity and sexual orientation. Such play with surfaces is not limited to drag (and its close cousin, camp) but proceeds, as we must do, directly to the closet, to passing. In describing what is involved, Newton focuses on the world of male homosexuals:

The homosexual is stigmatized, but his stigma can be hidden. In Erving Goffman's terminology, information about his stigma can be managed. . . . The covert . . . homosexual community is engaged in "impersonating" respectable citizenry, at least some of the time. What is being impersonated? . . . The covert homosexual must in fact impersonate a man, that is, he must appear to the "straight" world to be fulfilling (or not violating) all the requisites of the male role as defined by the "straight" world. . . . Homosexuals "passing" are playing men; they are in drag. This is the larger implication of drag and camp. In fact, gay people often use the word "drag" in this broader sense, even to include role playing, which most people simply take for granted: role playing in school, at the office, at parties, and so on. (1972, 107–8)[5]

When Doña María, of assigned female sex, became Don Antonio, she engaged in an effort to pass as he, to quell her conscience (or to act in accordance with the sex of her self-image, which is what the term *conscience* then suggested) and to make the sin or shame of transgression and the stigma of same-sex desire disappear. That effort required constant self-monitoring and the ever-present danger of discovery, reduced considerably by traveling far from his own hometown and country, though increased again by courting and marrying Doña Martina. The effort paid off for a decade, though undoubtedly there were many close calls and moments of extreme danger. Yet it appears to have been more difficult for Doña María to convincingly perform femininity or a nun's exaggerated form of femininity in her recogida and chaste renunciation of the world, sexuality, and will. The decade or so after puberty and before becoming Don Antonio are replete with "troubles" for Doña María's parents and untold scoldings, punishments, penitential acts, ejection from convents, and brushes with the law. We have no images or descriptions of Doña María to know how closely she fit the idealized image of femininity in her days or ours, but it is clear that she found it untenable to continue to try to "pass" as both feminine and heterosexual. In spite of a lack of "male socialization" in childhood or as a young adult (apart from having incorporated the practiced schemas organizing female hábitos, the structural antitheses of male ones), interacting, speaking, dressing, and living as a man may have been an easier set of performances, perhaps resonating more completely with Doña María's embodied sense of self even before becoming Don Antonio.

Passing and the Closet

We have passed from transvestism and drag to the closet, in which Doña María had lived before becoming a man while struggling to get by, to live in the world into which she was born as a perhaps not so "feminine," overly assertive woman attracted to other women. Like the "closeted" homosexual in Newton's analysis, she had concealed (though not very successfully) same-sex desire, while being forced to wear and perform the hábitos of heterosexual womanhood, aiming to pass as heterosexual. She failed at that stressful, disaster-filled attempt, undone by her sexual appetites and tendency to act on them. From the perspective of twenty-first-century transgender theory we might conclude that stepping into the role of Don Antonio was to be freed from the closet and from the drag of women's hábitos during efforts to pass as a heterosexual woman, allowing Don Antonio not to pass artfully as woman but to be himself, to give expression to the inner truth that had been hidden under women's dress.[6]

Yet we cannot really know whether Doña María experienced her desire for women from a securely male "inner self" or instead if adopting that self was a way of resolving the double problem of conscience (awareness of engaging in "misdeeds") and social reprobation of same-sex acts, since performing maleness seems both to have erased the sense of sin and the barriers of social reprobation. If Don Antonio's self-consciousness became male to satisfy his conscience, making his desire heterosexual and thus not sinful or shameful, we might conclude that he became a hermaphrodite in the sense that term was still being used, a combination of a "hermaphrodism of the soul" with convincing performance of male hábitos. But bringing off that transformation to step out of a closet (Taborga's "trastiendas") of concealed same-sex desires, he entered a different closet that required him to engage in covering strategies to conceal his naked body and its functioning.

Don Antonio was much more successful passing for a masculine, heterosexual man than Doña María had been passing for a feminine, heterosexual woman. But unlike the experience of the casual transvestite (like George Sand in Paris), there would for Don Antonio be no offstage or downtime. Passing required habitual and sustained stylization of the body, adoption of masculine misogyny, and disdain for every sort of ambiguous sex. It required participation in the teasing or scorning of effeminate men and masculine women. It may have led Don Antonio to gossip about suspected sodomites, particularly men who had no publicly visible relations with women. Passing even required Don Antonio to court and then marry Doña Martina, then to be subject to her scrutiny in the intimacy of the house and bedroom. The constant self-monitoring that Don Antonio must have perfected had then to be redoubled. The degree of secretive self-monitoring required to pass, enforced by the terrible consequences of exposure, made passing into another sort of closet. But Don Antonio's closet cannot have been as difficult to sustain as what is usually meant by the term *closet* today, when a man or woman conceal same-sex desires and possible transgender identifications when in public, at work, or even with an opposite-sex spouse, enacting those desires only furtively and secretly. Don Antonio, at least, only had to conceal (always) his inconveniently female body parts, while living a privileged life in the male "sex" (or as we would say, gender) he chose to embody. Even though he did insist to physicians and the court that he had a functional member that appeared at the proper moment, it is difficult to imagine that he relished the role of hermaphrodite, a sex-ambiguous "freak of nature" that his mother and his attorney invoked as a legal escape hatch. Instead, he seems merely to have been assertively doubling down on the performance of his maleness.

Whether or not they systematically distinguish biological sex from "performative" or social gender and regardless of their conclusions as to Don Antonio's genitalia, all those involved in the case imply or specify performative attributes of ideal types of maleness versus femaleness. The success of Don Antonio's performative embodiment of masculinity depended on the strength of such indexes of "sex." Then, as now, men (like women) exhibited a broad range of sex- and gender-marking behaviors, from the hypermasculine, muscle-bound roughneck kind through the haughty but labor-avoiding, sometimes effeminate elites in their frilly shirts or tightly constraining currutaco jackets and slippers, and everything in between. Masculinity, like femininity, was branded for social estate, for free or slave, Spanish versus Indian nation, religion, and the emerging systems of classification called race.

To pass as a man, Don Antonio chose the aristocratic, peninsular Spanish variety (which offered the greatest social power and the least likelihood of losing control in social encounters). He would have wanted to play it up in the most stereotypical of ways to avoid detection for "lack of fit." For aristocrats and for the rising bourgeoisie, wearing class- and status-appropriate male clothing and sallying forth into the world indicated maleness, as long as the wearer could avoid unintentionally revealing something to the contrary, whether bodily facts or notably "female" behaviors. Don Antonio's name and profession (his work as a criado and later employment with the Crown as administrator of La Magdalena) was also indicative of maleness, as were his marital status, his manner (ways of walking, looking, and speaking), and his assertions about his sex. To this Doña Martina adds the matter of touching. Don Antonio refused to let himself *be touched* (by her and, we assume, anyone else). *He* was the one doing the touching.

These indicators of assertiveness add up to a key element of masculinity then termed *desenvoltura*, amounting to unconstrained, forward, immodest, confident ease of speech and action. The term is of course used to describe a fluidity of action as well as speech. Such a stance toward the world and others in it, which we might translate into social-science jargon as *agentivity*, practically defined masculinity.[7] It was the opposite of the inward-focused, recogida submission and subordination, what could be called *patientivity*, expected of stereotypical females of aristocratic or bourgeois standing. Failure to follow such norms risked stigmatization as an effeminate, sodomitical man or as a manly, public, and free woman (prostitute).

Other non–aristocrat-conforming behaviors would be expected of common laboring Spaniards back in Spain or of the indigenous, African, and biologically or culturally mixed in-between castas, who occupied the laboring and tribute-paying social estate in Spanish America. The men among them were expected to defer to "white" Spaniards, and the women among them expected to labor in public markets or the homes of unrelated elite men. The attributes of sex/gender, which take form through specific ways of dressing, speaking, looking, and behaving, cannot be understood in isolation from those of social estate or class, nation or race. Like sex/gender, those distinctions are also social constructs, produced performatively, in spite of being assumed, like sex, to have a basis in nature (blood, lineage, *calidad*, etc.).

As we have seen, clothing, and the associated stylized movements to which it sometimes contributes, serves (along with modification to hair and other aspects of the surface of the body) as a social skin, transforming the natural body of an individual natural being into the bearer of certain kinds of social being. At the boundary between the inside of the embodied person and the outside world and between experiential subjectivity and the interpretive gaze of others, it is understood to be a social surface that reveals as well as it conceals and potentiates or attenuates capacities or proclivities of the natural body. Likewise, ways of speaking, looking, and doing that mark specific roles or identities within the developmental sequence of socialization, the hierarchies of social estate or class, or distinctions of nation or race are also experienced by both individual actor and audience as an interactional boundary with the world of others, and such performative acts are similarly understood to be capable of both concealing and revealing, of identifying persons or misidentifying them.

Passing Fashions and Individualist Self-Fashioning

Changes of types of clothing (putting on a novice's habit when entering the convent, taking it off when thrown out of one, dressing as a married woman rather than as a single one, a widow in black, or a corpse in white linen wrap) were universally understood to be constitutive of changes in status. Some centuries of experience with the theater, with ludic masquerade in festivals, and with personal experience of deception by dress perpetrated by or against oneself and widely circulating stories of one or another kind of passing by criminals or social climbers had made it clear to all that *el hábito no hace el monje*. Having the *oficio* (profession or trade) of tavern keeper or bootblack, jeweler or stonemason, in itself reputed one as both a commoner and as a male. Dressing the part cemented the assumption. But everyone understood the possibility that others might be passing, convincingly playing a role, not on the stage but in real life. The epidemic of passing in the age of the rising, modern, individualist, and fashion-conscious bourgeoisie raised the stakes for surveillance of others and for ceaseless self-monitoring for those who indeed *were* engaged in passing, whether in the domain of social estate or class, nation, religion, or sex.

Such concerns were certainly heightened in the era of individualism and rapidly changing fashions made affordable to social-climbing commoners, aping the aristocracy, by industrial cloth production, particularly the cotton calicos manufactured in Europe from cotton grown in Spanish, Portuguese, Dutch, and English colonies in South Asia and the Americas, produced by African slaves on plantations and by indigenous people in missions such as those of Moxos. It is worth considering fashion's impact.

We have seen the both the attraction of the currutaco and *madamita del nuevo cuño* fads to consumers at the turn of the nineteenth century and the disdain for such fashions by traditionalists who saw not only an epidemic of passing along lines of social estate but a contagion of sex, whereby men were effeminized and women seemed no longer to know their place or worry about their reputations. These particular fashions, constituting the Spanish version of dandyism, which we might define as the effort through attention to fashion of making oneself into a work of art and of being looked at as one while confidently returning the audience's gaze, were but one particular, recurring version of the broader field of consumerist fashion, of the sort that Roland Barthes distinguishes with a capital F. The appeal of "Fashion" is that of no longer being tied to a single clothing-marked identity but to be freed to become someone else. For Barthes, "the multiplication of persons in a single being is always considered by Fashion an index of power; . . . herein lies the ancestral theme of disguise, the essential attribute of gods, police, and bandits. Yet, in the vision of Fashion, the ludic motif does not involve what might be called a vertigo effect: it multiplies the person without any risk to her of losing herself" (1983, 256–57).

All these modern dress styles were taken up particularly by the new bourgeoisie, the social-climbing middling class composed of those without formal membership in the aristocracy but with all the latter's ambition. In a challenge to the aristocracy's aim to more clearly mark their exalted station by imposing rigid sumptuary codes, the new fashions were adopted by these middling sorts in the manner of self-fashioning, in ways that always involved a degree of self-conscious performance. Adopting such fashions was serious play, of a kind that revealed the fungibility of the body, the individual, and, indeed, the distinctions of social estate. Both wearers or onlookers of these cross-class fashions, whether dressing *up*, as with currutacos, or *down*, as with aristocrats who adopted *majo* or *maja* styles or bourgeois who dressed in "radical" proplebeian sansculotte style, were made reflexively aware of the performative dimensions of social estate. The excitement of choosing to wear clothes that made a statement, rather than those that naturally belonged to a person's true underlying identity derived in part from the fact that such changes in clothing revealed the social constructedness of such class or *calidad* (quality).

Wearing clothing in this way created a new kind of spectacle, where one had always to suppose a possible contradiction between the class position indexed by the costume and the class membership of its wearer. These were not *passing* fashions, meant to enable their wearers to pass as something they were not. Instead their appeal, perhaps generated by avant-garde creators and early adopters, lay in the reveal, on the *frissón* created by an obvious appearance and reality gap, whether the gap resulted from a suspected effort at passing through the wearing of extremely class-marked styles or, for those wearing the costume as self-parody, between appearance and the wearer's ironic stance toward it. In these fashions clothing is a semiotic device deployed as a social skin, at the boundary between individual bodily being and social being, by which to play on the binary of appearance and reality in the registers of nation or race, social estate or class, sex or gender.

Quite beyond being an enactment of social class, the self-conscious play with the performative power of costume that we see in the currutaco was a commentary on a formerly rigid expression of social distinction, meant to reveal the conventions by which social distinctions were made to appear natural. This was the essence of modernity's shift from social estate, now revealed to be mere convention, to social class, now alleged to be a product of individual self-fashioning. But it was also a form of counterrevolutionary commentary on more egalitarian sartorial conventions of gender, momentarily fair play in what was, after all, a revolutionary era. Such sartorial styles drew on the ability of the wealthy colonial elite (its Spaniards) to acquire the latest indexes of cosmopolitan panache, whether the *currutaquería* that marked the (still dangerous) delicacy and currency of its men or the tapada fashion by which elite women, perhaps inspired by Benito Jerónimo Feijoo y Montenegro's eighteenth-century feminist tract ([1726] 1997), could venture anonymously into the streets in a virtual parody of nuns' recogimiento while preserving their privileges as Spanish women. They fit right in to the broader theatricality of social hierarchy, a vestige of the colonial baroque's theater of power in this audiencia capital. Playing only to a small, ruling fraction of the population, such fashions were adopted more widely among that fraction than they were in Madrid itself, as they came to mark distinctions between governing elites and the governed increasingly regarded as differences of substance and human capacities (that is, differences attributed to race) rather than those produced by schemes of governance that limited those called Indians to bare subsistence.[8]

It is difficult to imagine that Don Antonio relished the effeminizing currutaco fashions of his day (the peacock colors, delicate shoes, wasp-waist effect of the cutback of the coat), though that effeminization was also a marker of continental reason and was tempered by the presence of accoutrements of violence such as a club-like walking stick or sabre and dagger. Such outfits seem to have dared the hoi polloi (the Indians and blacks and castas) to laugh, only to get their just deserts. On the other hand, he may have preferred the hobnail boots for the surety of their stride and their horse-back-riding-warrior aristocratic implications. Possibly, the currutaco outfit in fact belonged to Doña Martina, as a cross-dressing uptake of the male fashion (although I have found no suggestion of such a fashion in documents or the literature of the era) or perhaps that was what Don Antonio hoped to imply. Whether it was his or hers, this sartorial choice approached the revealed cross-dressing conventions of drag.

Consequences: Revolutionary Potential of Drag and Transgender

Perhaps Butler is right about the revolutionary potential of drag. Of all our cases, Sebastián/María Leirado's doubled cross-dressing seems to be the closest to the drag performance in its adoption of theatrical frames and playful use of reveal: the sex/gender rebel Leirado let *their* audiences and *their* lovers (whom he instructed to write to him as "María") in on the secret of a woman under a man's clothes but not the secret of the man's body behind the womanly performance. Sebastián/María's rebellion ended in a prison sentence. Revolutionary potential was given shape in constitutions of the era, which promised certain kinds of equality to the citizen-subjects of the new nation-states, who were to be free to remake themselves in certain ways. Revolutionary women took up the banner of equality in the name of feminism, but even nominal equality of citizenship for women was not to be on offer for another century, and in the meantime revolutionary challenges to hegemonic standards were treated as criminal acts.

This remained true even after the independence of the Americas' new republics, with their egalitarian constitutions. From that time men in general doubled down on their monopolization of power over women, pushing the *madamitas del nuevo cuño*, for instance, back into more decent sorts of behavior, until, after another century and much struggle, the right to vote, to purchase contraceptives, and to gain education and professional employment began to pay off during the twentieth century. Female-suffrage movements at the beginning of the twentieth century, the civil rights movement starting in the 1960s, second-wave feminism in the 1970s, and, after all that, in the 1980s gay and lesbian rights in the wake of the Stonewall riots and activist work in the HIV-AIDS crisis led to the promise of equality under the banners of race, class, gender, and sexual orientation. And yet ongoing struggles, backsliding in social relations and in law, and the upsurge in racist, homophobic, misogynist, and xenophobic opposition to "political correctness" teach us that rights hard won and taken for granted can be stripped away in short order by those who feel their "free, white (male), and twenty-one" privileges threatened.[9]

It is tempting to regard Don Antonio Yta as a transgender warrior, fighting for the right to be different, a forerunner of today's queer- and trans-gender-rights activists, whose "trans" activities challenged his (authoritative male) judges to recognize the constructedness of gender and therefore the changeable conventionality of their own heteronormative privileges. But like seventeenth-century Catalina/Antonio de Erauso and the other historical "trans" subjects we have surveyed, Don Antonio worked hard to present, be taken, and pass for a stereotypical exemplar of one of the two sexes in a rigidly heteronormative, two-sex world. There was of course then no possibility of coming out of the closet as a person of same-sex desire. Passing in these cases covered both the womanly sex beneath the clothing and the potentially stigmatizing desire to have sex with persons of the same assigned sex.

Passing here also appears to have been a way of living a life conforming more closely to what they seem to have regarded as their inner "sex," Foucault's "hermaphrodism of the soul," as an aspect of embodied conscience and consciousness, which we would call their gender identity, irrespective of their actual genitals. In most of these cases, the sex of choice was male, which as the "superior" and rights-bearing sort made their efforts to pass understandable to their judges.

Erauso and Yta had no intention of engaging in rebellion against heteronormativity. Both of them fully embraced it and made use of the power of others' heteronormative assumptions to help construct their own cultural genitals in the minds of others, granting them the authorization to enact masculine performatives that emplotted properly male protagonists in their own and others' narrations of their lives. Of course, they wanted to have what LGBTQIA activists struggle for: the right to live and love in the sex and gender of their choice and to love the sex and gender of their choosing, without stigmatization, harassment by authorities, prosecution, social shunning, or the violence of the disapproving. They claimed the right to a habitable, dignified, and secure identity, protected, not persecuted, by law and social convention. The vast majority of the women of the eighteenth century who had same-sex desires lived closeted in convents, in unhappy marriages, or in other secretive and solitary covers; their same-sex acts likewise had to be hidden. They could not publicly embrace a lesbian identity, though had it been available and habitable, they *might* have done so. Many of them, too, would have preferred to have greater social power, to be free to walk the streets without fear, and to take up professions that were then monopolized by men. Doing so would have made them "masculine" in the language of the day. But it is unlikely that many of them could have passed as men, if they had wanted to.

Don Antonio, like Sebastián/María Leirado and Catalina/Antonio de Erauso, had what nowadays has been termed *passing privilege*, the body and habituated ways of behaving with it that convinced others of their maleness. If today some transgender activists strive for acceptance *as* transgender, hoping to eliminate stigma through social acceptance and a revolutionary upending of heteronormativity, that is not by any means a universal aim of transgendered persons. Heteronormativity has not been abolished, and being "read" as trans by unsuspecting persons who have emotionally invested in a relationship with the person passing leads to accusations of deception, feelings of betrayal, and potential acts of revenge, including not just legal complaints but murderous violence.

Tangled Webs: Betrayal in the Narrative Emplotment of Transgender Passing

Don Antonio's adult life was a long time ago now. Our documentary sources do not conclusively answer the question of the motive(s) for his adoption of performative hábitos of his specific kinds of maleness. Was it for the life of adventure and career and freedom to move about in the world that was the "birthright" of maleness, especially the white, patrician kind? Was it for the romantic or sexual affordances that came with such maleness, the possibility of publicly wooing women? Or was it to obey the pope's command and to reconcile Don Antonio's conscience? Such questions arise as we attempt to understand passing by turning to our mental archive of narrative plot and character development. It is unfortunate for those we too harshly judge, but perhaps inevitable and analytically productive that when we turn to that archive to evaluate a case of revealed passing, we are swept into a deep and broad narrative stream associated with deception and entailed moral evaluations of the deceiver's character that tie matters of sex/gender to deception and to the very core of what it is to be human.

Don Antonio/Doña María's life was about midway between the Golden Age Catalina/Antonio de Erauso and another much-written-about crossdresser, already in our own time: the piano-playing jazz band leader Billy Tipton. Controversies surrounding the Billy Tipton story may help to bring Don Antonio into the focus of contemporary theoretical debates.

Billy Tipton, born female in 1914 and raised as Dorothy Lucille Tipton, adopted the name Billy and used his newfound public maleness to help advance a career in a profession that then, as now, was dominated by men. But, like Don Antonio, he also used that male identity in pursuit of women. Tipton, who never formally married, nonetheless had three "Mrs. Tiptons" in his life and three adopted sons. He had a relatively successful career as a musician and recorded some records but ultimately settled down in Spokane, Washington, where he played local venues and, with his third partner, Kitty, raised his three adopted sons. The children and the three women in his intimate life have claimed never to have realized what became apparent when Billy, long since retired and suffering from an untreated bleeding ulcer, collapsed in his trailer in 1989. One of his sons was by his side and called 911. Undoing Tipton's clothing, the paramedic revealed his female body. He had refused medical treatment to conceal it. Tipton died at age seventy-four (Cromwell 2010).

The story hit the papers and then the works of theorists. Virtually all the accounts focus on the acts of deception—on the woman's body beneath male clothing and persona. His family members and "wives" regarded Tipton as a good husband and father, who was also a good lover—that is, they accepted him as a man on all counts (Halberstam 2005), if the women's accounts are to be believed and one or all of them are not themselves covering the potential stigma of same-sex desire.

But many accounts of Billy's life and death nonetheless foreground the deception as an act of betrayal, the unforgiveable result of what otherwise could be understood as a ruse necessary for the achievement of professional success (Middlebrook 1998, 177, cited by Halberstam 2005, 57). Other readings, backgrounding the notion of deception, prefer to see Tipton's work of passing as a result of the era's unfriendliness to same-sex desire. Most likely all these things are true. The discovery of Tipton's female body might have made his passing for a man into an act of betrayal for family members and colleagues had it happened during his life. To the women he was involved with Tipton told covering stories to explain the unusual genitalia—that he had suffered a disfiguring accident, for example—and those women might well have chosen to believe such stories and accept Tipton as a "normal" husband, which is to say a male one, rather than to face the possibility of lesbianism. In any case Tipton presented himself as a man, not as a woman. He would not have wanted to call himself a woman with same-sex desires and would have been unwelcome in the lesbian community of his time.[10]

Betrayal is also a theme in much of the reportage of the life and death of Brandon Teena, a "biologically" female person who sometimes passed for a young man in small-town Nebraska, best known by the public through the "Brandon" character played by Hillary Swank in the film *Boys Don't Cry*. Brandon Teena's girlfriends found him to be the ideal man, a perfect gentleman, unlike the other boys in their lives (Halberstam 2005, 64). But two of Brandon's male "friends," discovering his secret, responded to the discovery of Brandon's female genitals (revealed when they ripped off his clothes) with violence: they raped him. He reported the crime to the local police, who refused to act, and was then murdered by his rapists a few days later. Halberstam criticizes the incessant focus on deception in much of the reportage of Billy Tipton's and Brandon Teena's efforts to pass, which ultimately becomes an excuse for violence and murder: "When we read transgender lives, complex and contradictory as they may seem, it is necessary to read for the life and not for the lie. Dishonesty, after all, is just another word for narrative" (2005, 74).

While surely correct that it behooves us as authors and as readers to attempt to understand the complex lives of Catalina/Antonio, Don Antonio/Doña María, Billy Tipton, or Brandon Teena rather than to focus always on the matter of deception, on the "counterfeit" sex they portrayed through passing, it is also important to understand why deception is so often at the heart of treatments of passing in archival sources and popularized versions of passing lives. All of us have engaged in deception of some kind, and all of us well understand why Walter Scott's line, "Oh, what a tangled web we weave, when first we practice to deceive," is so widely resonant that it is usually misattributed to Shakespeare. Deception, and its product, betrayal, is a key narrative theme in all of our lives and in much of our literature.

While deception is central to accounts of Billy Tipton or Brandon Teena, it has been read into their lives by others, since neither produced their own autobiographical account. Halberstam summarizes the cumulative effect of such narrations: "After his murder, Brandon's life—the jumbled desires and deeds—becomes frozen into either a heroic narrative of derring-do or a reprehensible story of deception and denial." The strands of narrative incoherence of his life are rewoven into a "fantasy of moral order." The resulting false coherence then attributed to his life make him a "lost" soul. What "remains to queer archivists is to render Brandon 'unlost'" (2005, 74).

Billy Tipton and Brandon Teena did not tell their own stories; traces of their lives are embedded in others' accounts that emplot the action and ascribe to them one or another kind of morally judgeable character. But Don Antonio and Catalina de Erauso *did* tell their own stories. Both of them were induced to explain their own lives and in particular to account for their motives for passing deception, discovery of which led to their arrests.

Both Yta and Erauso make reference to their "particular inclinations": In Erauso's *probanza de méritos y servicios*, he accounts for his cross-dressing as follows: "[I] passed to the Provinces of Peru in a male habit, due to a particular inclination for taking up arms in defense of the Catholic faith and in service of your majesty."[11] Matthew Goldmark explains, "When this passage describes the hábito as gendered dress, it gives gender professional form and imperial justification. The hábito becomes a necessary precondition for service rather than a transgressive choice; the term and its gendered attachment—'ábito de baron'—is immediately followed by an explanation of Erauso's inclination towards wielding arms in defense of god and king. Hábitos provide Erauso's *pedimento* with a pre-established mold to detail service to the Crown" (2015, 218).

Don Antonio did so with an equally compelling argument; his change of dress and life obeyed the pope's command and served his own conscience. It is safe to assume that the papal dispensation would have imposed perpetual chastity; it is also the case that failing to be chaste would be entirely consistent with that era's understanding of manly behavior.[12]

Of course, the narrative of each aims to provide a positive spin on the generally disapproved act in which they have been caught: deception. The work of concealing their bodily sex required a great deal of self-monitoring. Don Antonio was well aware that others would not be able to see the phallus that he may well have experienced as "real." Both must have repeatedly rehearsed to themselves the stories they might tell if caught out (like Billy Tipton's explanation to Kitty that he had suffered a disfiguring accident). But these explanatory narratives are also coerced. Discovering that deceit, authorities have attempted to identify its motivation, that is, to understand the intentions behind it. Yta and Erauso are asked to produce narratives that explain those intentions, but judges are already at work, drawing on their understanding of conventions for the narration of character, whether of the canonically meritorious sort or of the transgressive kind deserving only contempt.

It happens that such narrative conventions have a deep history, starting well before romances of chivalry and *relaciones de méritos y servicios*, picaresque novels, and confesiónes. If we look back far enough, we find the sources of moralizing judgments about sex/gender embedded in the West's foundational narratives, those that undergird patriarchalism and misogyny.

The Bible's book of Genesis explains the origin of mortality and heterosexuality as a consequence of deception and betrayal. God forbids Adam and Eve to taste of the fruit of knowledge. But the "great deceiver," who exists precisely to test the obedience of Adam and Eve, tempts Eve to disobey God. Eve then convinces Adam to have a taste. Deception leads to betrayal, and Eve is the most culpable, leading Adam astray. As a result, both are exiled from Eden, now forced into sexual relations to have the children that in some way substitute for their lost immortality and to labor and sweat to produce their sustenance. The power of the patriarch rests on his role in containing easily misled and misleading women and in consolidating the transmission of a hierarchically ordered human households across the generations through patterns of patrilineal inheritance.

Coming out of a different but related narrative tradition is the Greek story of the origin of human reproductive sexuality, sex roles, and the travails of human life, which also result from deception. Hesiod recounts the deceptions of Prometheus, who first stealthily steals fire from Zeus by hiding it in a fennel stalk and then, once required to sacrifice animals to Zeus and to share the resulting feast, tricks Zeus again by giving him a choice of two portions—the roast meat hidden in the ox's unappealing stomach or the bones covered in a layer of gleaming, attractive fat. Zeus chooses the tricked-up bones. He conceals his anger to get his vengeance cold: in payback for the deceptions of Prometheus, all humans must fall from the Golden Age of plenty. Zeus gives Prometheus the gift of a beautiful woman, Pandora, whose evil and untrustworthy character has been concealed beneath the most beautiful clothing and jewelry (and veil) the gods can muster. The masquerade of her social skin replies to the veil of tasty fat over the dry white bones Zeus has received. Beguiled by Pandora's enticements, Prometheus also accepts the further gifts in the jar she carries. From now on, wives will be the bane of men, who must slavishly work to grow food from the seeds in the jar. Men (as well as women) will die miserable deaths from the diseases it contains and will also lack the solace of hope, which Zeus prevents from escaping the jar. The only satisfaction for men is being able to "cheat death" by producing children who will inherit their hard-won homes and fields but who will not be in the least grateful for their fathers' work in raising them.[13]

Both the Greek and Judaic foundational narratives are told from a male perspective. Each both institutes and explains the necessity for socially organized patriarchalist misogyny, an unequal distribution of power and powers between two sexes, to contain betrayal and ameliorate its unhappy results. But deception is not the exclusive property of womankind.

Deception is a gender-blind relational transgression, although one that is particularly tied to the satisfaction of individual desires and in particular to sexual desire. Its discovery by those who have been deceived leads to feelings of betrayal and escalating distrust and, as in Don Antonio's case, a search for antecedent crimes and desire for revenge. It can also be a crime in itself (in current tort and contract law in the United States, it can be fraudulent misrepresentation). But exculpation is possible, if the deceiver can convince the deceived, or other judges, through apposite narration, that their intentions were good ones. Motives are bad when they are self-serving—such as enhancing their own reputation or saving "face" or achieving some kind of personal satisfaction. They are good when they are "selfless," done to protect or serve others, such as Erauso's "service to the king," Yta's obedience to the pope, and perhaps Billy Tipton's efforts to avoid disappointing or shaming his long-term partners or children. Either way, as narrating animals, we are almost unable to avoid imputing judgeable motives for deception when we discover it. Not far below the surface, as we calculate the moral weight of deceivers' intentions, is our awareness that what motivates deception is the desire to exclusively possess (fire, knowledge, food, others' bodies). In the manner of circular reasoning, our deeply seated cultural misogyny also tells us that the incessant, unsatisfiable kinds of hunger that drive such desires are in one way or another the fault of women. Desire and deception are themselves gendered within our narrative genealogy of morals. Yet to focus exclusively on the narrative emplotment of adult human folly is to miss the other kind of narrative that ensues from our existence in mortal bodies with a trajectory of birth, socialization, and travails to satisfy bodily desires and to accumulate, reproduce, and finally die. Women's bodies are the bane of mortals because we came from them, whatever the deceptions of patrilineage and patriarchy might say. Such conclusions may lead us to oppose telling and doing, narrativity and performativity, as the antagonists in a battle of theories between discursive lies and enacted bodily truths capable of disrupting those lies. Let us see why that cannot be.

CONCLUSION

*Narrations, Enactments,
and Bodily Pleasure*

Narrativity and Performativity

Throughout this book I have repeatedly made reference to the usefulness of the Spanish concept of hábitos (and Bourdieu's habitus) for thinking about the clothed and embodied performance of sex/gender statuses and roles, themselves always intersectionally bound up with other regimes of performed distinction operative in Don Antonio's day, such as social estate, *nación*, religious versus secular roles, and so forth and their later recombined derivatives, class and race. We recognize the hábitos of a cloistered nun, an aristocratic man, or a criado because the elements of the hábitos of any one of these are bundled together in a stereotypical and recognizable pattern of costume; bodily motion and practices; stances toward others and ways of looking at, speaking, or listening to them (or not doing so); and attending expectantly and compliantly or commanding or ignoring them (or not doing those things). The resulting pattern is meaningful (and summed up in a named status and role) because it exists, through the organizing schemas of hábitos, in systemic relation to other patterned hábitos marking different statuses and roles.

In chapters 2 and 3 I aimed to show that the organizing schemas are made to stand out, their structural "bones" becoming clarified, through the bracketing they undergo in special ways of performing hábitos. Those include formal training, rites of passage such as confirmation or marriage ceremonies, and initiation rites in convents or as criados and criadas in noble households. They also include theatrical performances, which (like legal procedures in the courtroom) draw on ritual techniques to create a time-out-of-time, space-out-of-space context for bracketed "action about action" or metapragmatic action-commentary that, in spite of the suspension of disbelief or perhaps through tension between appearances and underlying reality that such always-partial suspension heightens, makes graspable as if from without, and knowable in a reflexive way, the logics of hábitos that may sometimes feel transparent or natural to those who inhabit them.

To the degree that such ritualized practices make the systematicity of hábitos apparent, they also relativize and denaturalize hábitos, revealing their constructedness. It is that effect that Butler seizes on when promoting the "revolutionary potential" of drag. That same effect leads performance-studies scholar Diana Taylor (2003) to take "the repertoire" of embodied performance as a potent antidote, or means of resistance to, the prison house of Foucauldian discourse, condensed in the figure of "the archive" as the location of inscription and constriction of persons into the state's classificatory system. One might put it this way: Doña María was ascribed a sex and inscribed as a female in the discursive registers of power, by which she would be constrained through the very structures of narrativity as a pronominal female; when she succeeded at performatively becoming Don Antonio, she began to break the bonds that had thus confined her.

The work of performance-studies scholars, crossing the disciplinary boundaries that had kept studies of narrative separate from studies of living social interaction, has been key to rethinking both how specific kinds of situated identities are constrained and narratively judged and how such strictures are challenged by certain kinds of performance. Yet certain of the theoretical frames deployed in the humanistic study of narratives and archives as well as those developed for the study of social interaction (and its repertoires) have perhaps obscured the systemic relation between narrativity and performativity. Postmodernist theoretical approaches, in which individuals or subjects are mere effects of "discourse" understood as language-driven logics through which power is deployed, have been one obstacle to recognizing this relation.

Gender theorists writing about performativity cite Butler's *Gender Trouble* (1990) and its follow-up book, *Bodies That Matter* (1993). Butler's approach is embedded in a post-structuralist, Foucauldian understanding of discourse as a meaning system preexisting and transcending individual subjects, whose qualities are therefore epiphenomenal and illusory. For Butler in these works, drag or transgender performativity are admirable to the degree that they are potentially revolutionary, revealing the "constructedness" of an oppressive, patriarchal heteronormativity and thus undermining the usual experience of such constructions as "natural" givens. But of course such disruption occurs only when the drag performer reveals the gap between the performance and the body beneath it or the transgendered person fails to pass, in some way revealing that same gap. As Jay Prosser points out, "Butler's essay locates transgressive value in that which makes the subject's life most unsafe" (1998, 49). Butler's work constituted one of the foundations of what has been termed "queer studies," the uptake of performative antiheteronormativity as an in-your-face form of political praxis. Prosser's response, not a critique of performativity per se, aimed at the culture of outing that made gender transgression into an admirable political act and condemned the desire of transgenders or transsexuals to pass as (or to become) heterosexual men or women into an act of complicity with heterosexist, patriarchal power.

As Halberstam summarizes (2005, 50), Prosser argues that the "gender trouble" that Butler writes of is particularly notable in the transgender or transsexual subject, which highlights the split between sex and gender through reveals of that split, thereby also revealing the constructedness of all sex and gender. For Prosser, when a queer movement holds up trans subjects as heroic banner-bearers advertising this split against the "straight" world's certainties of the naturalness of cis and hetero sex/gender alignment, it denies the legitimacy of some transgender trajectories, "in particular transsexual trajectories, that aspire to what this scheme devalues. Namely, there are transsexuals who seek very pointedly to be non-performative, to be constative, quite simply to be" (1998, 32).[1]

Here Prosser misinterprets Butler's concept of performativity, taking it to mean "something performed," mere play, as opposed to something "real." Butler's 1993 book aims to correct such misunderstandings.[2] Instead of performativity, Prosser takes up narrativity, foregrounding how transsexual and transgender self-narrations serve such persons' desire *to pass*, aiding them in the self-construction of desired gendered and sexed identities by invoking well-worn tropes of masculinity or femininity within emplotted action that can support, rather than disrupt, a binary sex and gender system.

From my point of view, while the dispute between a queer-studies celebration of public transgression and a transgender hope to pass as "normal" is quite
real, the theoretical debate between a purportedly postmodern performativity
and a humanist narrativity takes us nowhere. As Butler (1999) has also argued,
in her critique of Bourdieu's concept of habitus, they are mutually necessary
in human communicative life, as important to the construction of normative
and hegemonic moral orders as they are to their disruption to build new,
perhaps more just, social worlds (see also Namaste 1996).

Both *performativity* (as I use that term here, the schema-defined embodied communicative enactments of habitus) and narrativity (spoken and
written accounts of a plot-driven succession of episodes in a chronological
sequence illustrating the shaping or revelation of character) are mutually
constitutive and necessary parts of the relational, communicative construction
of situated identity. They are systematically related; both depend on sequence
and temporality, and both construct aspects of social protagonists within
particular kinds of spatial frames. Performatives depend for their efficacy on
iteration, repeating or referring to already-established, prior performatives,
handed down to current actors both through the socialization of experience
(habitus embedded in social relations) or through narrations that provide
explicit commentary on such things. Narrative, oral and written, recounts key
bits of performatives ("and when he said, 'I now pronounce you husband and
wife,' I was like, 'Wow!' [exuberant gesture to index intensity of emotion]")
or names them ("They were married in the cathedral, by bishop so-and-so"),
so as to execute them imaginatively in the mind's eye. Of course, narrated
performatives do not actually do the work of enacted ones, but their repeated
narration gives them more flesh when they are indeed performed in living
social contexts. It is not necessary to choose between Butler's theory of gender
performativity and, say, Prosser's alternative insistence (drawing especially on
Bruner 1991) on the centrality of narrative to the shaping of the trans life and
to the establishment of its "realness."

Butler's use of John Austin's (1975) theory of performatives exceeds the
limitations of a postmodernist understanding of discourse as something
always prior and external to individuals' entry into communicative relations
with others. Following Austin (and scholarship in the vein of pragmatic
linguistics), performatives can be felicitous or infelicitous—they can work
or they can fail. When they work, they bring something, and someone, into

relational existence: and the clothes *do* make the man, who is recognized and treated as one by others. When they fail, the desired outcome evaporates, and the man is revealed not to be one, or the marriage is declared not to have taken place.

Performatives, which like all acts of semiosis (and all signs) have both a material and a conceptual side, cannot even be described as effects of language (Ferdinand de Saussure's *langue*) in the abstract. They are exclusively interactional, producing effects in the very context of speech and of semiotic acts of communication. They are indicative of the lability, the changeability of language and discourse itself, through communicative interaction. Performative effects also require persons to make assumptions and reach conclusions about others' intentions, motives, and character. Without narrative there can be no performatives. At the same time, performatives are crucial elements of the narrative construction of social reality, which also index (point to) the materiality of social worlds, to the bodies that are stylized and the body parts beneath the presumptively gendered social skin.

Hábitos, Schemas, Reflexivity, Deception, Travel, and Narrative Redemption

In chapter 2, "Habits," I develop Pierre Bourdieu's concept of habitus through the Spanish "natural language" term *hábitos*, to begin to approach how different sorts of clothing, disposition, and signifying action are grouped together in patterned ways, called schemas, that can be analogized across distinct fields or arenas of social life. The registers of the social skin (body adornment and clothing) and stylization of the body account for some, but not all, of gender, while they also index the thing called sex. Distinguishably different habituated ways of speaking, looking, and acting toward others that we might label as indicative of class, and the practical abilities and certifications thereof that we associate with profession, are also inextricably bound up with the sex/gender complex, as are distinctions of race, religion, and nation. At the same time, as chapter 3, "Passages," argues, the sequence of episodes in narrative expresses transitions from one state to another through movement in space as well as time, as well they should, since all of us progress from one kind of state (say, son or daughter) to another (adult, or spouse and perhaps parent) in part through moving from one home to another. The fraught business of maturation, perhaps involving becoming independent, requires not only aging but motion and new life contexts and kinds of social relationships. Sometimes we don't like the limitations of what is on offer and choose another path. On occasion it requires concealment of information about oneself, perhaps known to others earlier or elsewhere, to not be excluded from a chosen new persona. For Doña María, becoming independent required becoming Don Antonio, free to have a career in the world as a single person and to love women without being censured and punished.

Is it unfair of us to consider those acts of self-transformation requiring acquisition of new hábitos far away from his life as María, as passing? Within the rights framework of contemporary identity politics, calling his efforts "passing" would be to deny the reality of the inner true self that was revealed, not concealed, by putting on male hábitos, just as, if he were alive or could have claimed a transgender identity, for us to refer to his past as "María" would be to thwart his efforts by "dead-naming" him. But failing to address the accusations made against him of imposture and deception of sex would make it impossible to understand the force of narrative conventions and the kinds of character and morally freighted action they entailed, by which he judged himself and was judged by others. Without the concepts of passing or deception, we would be blind to how Don Antonio had to shape his actions to avoid "tells" that might lead to ruin and would not be able to read his confession as an effort to recast his character, for his judges, as the morally admirable kind.

Perhaps, as Butler argued, Prosser had misinterpreted performativity as "mere performance," something indicative of inauthentic or feigned "identity." Reflexive understanding of the schemas organizing hábitos, however, do make for the possibility of stage performance, of "enmasked" actions aiming to deceive and for unproductive consciousness of gaps between what we hope to be taken for and what (in self-doubting mode) we think our actual capacities might be, in the shape of anxiety such as the "imposter syndrome." Goffman's (1959) approach to understanding the "presentation of self in everyday life" led him to Shakespearean reflections on performance "on-stage" and off, regarded by fellow players and audience members, and of set-like "frames" for particular kinds of action that is analytically useful, demanding neither classifying all performance as "faked" nor assuming all of it to be transparent and ingenuous.

Likewise Goffman's (1963) treatment of stigma, damaging information about self, and of the "covering strategies" employed to conceal it have been useful in thinking through Don Antonio's work of self-monitoring to avoid exposure of what he hid behind the closet of his clothing, work that eventually included a typically masculine "jealous" control of Doña Martina, whether to keep her for himself or to keep her from divulging secrets she had discovered.

The discovery of deception causes certain indexes or performatives to fail and undermines readings of an individual's status, character, or sex that are required for them to serve proper roles in canonical narratives that also support the performative self-identification of others within shared social worlds. When interlocutors recognize a protagonist's deception, the protagonist's character undergoes a transformation. Interlocutors begin to figure the protagonist in another kind of narrative, with very deep roots as a genre. Then come the explanations and excuses and perhaps a protagonist's redemption.

Don Antonio Yta's explanations of his "imposture," apart from obeying the pope and resolving a problem of conscience, involved *actually being a man and having a penis* and thus not having really engaged in deception. We, who perhaps don't think the material effects of performing maleness extend quite so far as to change the body in ways that persons other than Don Antonio could see, might hope that Don Antonio's motives had been loftier than that. Caring for and protecting Doña Martina and hoping not to hurt her and sustaining his acceptance as a man to enable him to actually have a career by which to do so might today constitute such motives. Empathy and selflessness make little appearance, however, in Don Antonio's narrated character, except perhaps for those instances where he "cannot recall" the names of co-conspirators, possibly to save them from the law.

Such motives are easier to see, however, in the case of Billy Tipton, who refused medical treatment, it seems, not to save himself from embarrassment or keep a lucrative job but to cushion others from embarrassment and harm and also, perhaps, simply to continue to be a man. He had retired due to illness that interfered with his piano playing, was separated from his third "wife," and his children were grown; his sisters, who knew all along of his passing life, had invited him to change back into her and move in with them. What prevented him from doing so? Love, perhaps? Or a degree of comfort in his male skin and the life he had made with it, not now to be thrown aside, even at the cost of his life?

Don Antonio in the Light of LGBTQIA Politics

In recovering sympathetic treatments of the lives of these transgender persons who began as female and became men (and about whom we know only because they were exposed), the question remains as to how such retellings square with contemporary LGBTQIA politics. We have seen that the rise of queer studies in the 1990s produced a certain antipathy toward the heteronormative tendencies of transgenders and transsexuals, particularly those who pass as heterosexuals and who may be regarded as insufficiently antiheteronormative and thus complicit with hegemonic sex and gender norms. Antiheteronormativity can also become *homonormativity*, expressed as an antipathy for those within homosexual and lesbian communities whose gender or sexual expression embraces, rather than challenges, the "ideal types" of masculinity and femininity of the hetero world. Writing in 1992, before the rise of the term *transgender* displaced part of the semantic territory formerly belonging to *transsexual*, Gayle Rubin ([1992] 2006) characterized the commonalities of passing female-to-male transgenders and butchness within the lesbian community:

Although important discontinuities separate lesbian butch experience and female-to-male transsexual experience, there are also significant points of connection. Some butches are psychologically indistinguishable from female-to-male transsexuals, except for the identities they choose and the extent to which they are willing or able to alter their bodies. Many FTMs live as butches before adopting transsexual or male identities. Some individuals explore each identity before choosing one that is more meaningful for them, and others use both categories to interpret and organize their experience. The boundaries between the categories of butch and transsexual are permeable.

Many of the passing women and diesel butches so venerated as lesbian ancestors are also claimed in the historical lineages of female-to-male transsexuals. There is a deep-rooted appreciation in lesbian culture for the beauty and heroism of manly women. Accounts of butch exploits form a substantial part of lesbian fiction and history; images of butches and passing women are among our most striking ancestral portraits. . . . It is interesting to ponder what other venerable lesbian forebears might be considered transsexuals; if testosterone had been available, some would undoubtedly have seized the opportunity to take it.

Perhaps, indeed, Don Antonio Yta would have done so. He certainly aimed to pass as a man and to take advantage of every privilege that corresponded not only to maleness but to the aristocratic, Spanish, and white kind. The option of living as a butch lesbian accepted or tolerated within a broader community was not open to María; if it had been, we must assume it would have been as an aristocratic and white butch lesbian. At any rate becoming Antonio was the only way toward loving women while having a career. His particular sort of passing, embedded in its special historical and colonial context, might seem especially noxious to contemporary LGBTQIA activists, whose work is about the achievement of recognition, toleration, and equality for those formerly socially excluded. Those three things are conspicuously absent in Don Antonio's particular form of intersectional passing, which was complicit with the powerful side of every kind of social distinction. Accusations of such complicity have been directed at contemporary transgenders as well and particularly against female-to-male transgender, the kind that reads as "passing up."

Writing about an earlier time, Rubin described the antipathy once commonly heard within the lesbian community toward female-to-male persons, "treating male-to-female transsexuals as menacing intruders and female-to-male transsexuals as treasonous deserters" ([1992] 2006, 476). Partly at fault was the perception of an excessive devotion to heteronormativity. Since then, transgender studies has pushed back against such opposition, arguing for adoption of a politics that does not depend on the transgressiveness of queer antiheteronormativity. But it remains the case that the masculine presentation of female-to-male transgenders does not sit well, particularly with feminist scholars in the ranks of queer activism. One response has been a renewed focus on the study of masculinity and the emergence of arguments that masculinity may well be expressed through gentleness, nurturance, and empathy rather than self-absorption, muscles, and violence.[3] But everyday experience and the statistics of gender-based violence do not allow such possibilities to be accepted as general conditions, to say the least.

Equally problematic in the institutionalization of transgender as a form of knowledge and governmentality is that it has been adopted in its most heteronormative-friendly form, demanding clear expressions of the masculine-feminine binary matched to medically and aesthetically sexed bodies. Media-celebrated cases (lately, Caitlyn Jenner) are those that best conform in appearance to a hypersexualized version of heteronormative standards. It is in such cases that *anti*-antiheteronormativity threatens to become just heteronormativity in the double negative.[4] Gender and sex ambiguity, or the cases of apparently M-to-F persons who perform publicly as trans but identify as men, are not well served by the term or the institutions dedicated to the phenomenon. This is especially true where trans intersects race and class (Valentine 2007). At the same time, heteronormativity and the homophobia or "gender panic" it generates when "straight" is faced with queer or trans is still a feature of contemporary American life, if somewhat alleviated by the successes on the legal and public recognition front of the LGBTQIA rights movements, which have made such identities visible and institutionalized them as rights-bearing kinds of difference.

Fungible Bodies: The Experience of "Gendered" Sexual Performativity and Pleasure

Since the 1970s we have thoroughly disentangled gender, a social and cultural construct, from sex, a material, bodily fact. We have perhaps done it too well, making "sex" an entirely medicalized fact in the hands of physicians, notwithstanding their profound disagreements about its definition (chromosomes? external sex characteristics? gonadal sex? endocrinological sex? brain sex?). We cannot now be convinced that Don Antonio might, during the sex act, have a penis we can't otherwise see. Billy Tipton was capable of sexually satisfying, with some kind of penetration, at least two of his three long-term sexual partners, without tipping them off that he was a she. It is quite likely that Don Antonio attempted to do the same, though without as much success. Tipton's sexual partners, and Doña Martina's blushing account of Don Antonio's refusal to be touched, suggest that both strove to have sex in a manly, which is to say an agentive, way. They did the touching with the lights out. Both may well have experienced Don Antonio's sex acts as those of men. For Don Antonio, living at the end of the era when spontaneous "changes of sex" without surgery and hermaphrodism were still imaginable, it was enough to convince him, and those to whom he told his story, that he had "the male thing." Bodily sex was then more fluid and more a product of performative gender in part because gender was taken to be inextricable from bodily sex. One thing implied the other. Now that we have successfully distinguished bodies from performances, there is less room for imagination, cultivated by narrative and sparked by performativity, to complete the picture. Apparently only hormone treatments and surgery can now do that, according to the medical establishment and much of the heterosexual public.

Even before the diagnosis of "gender dysphoria" entered the official annals of medicine, "problematic sex," which is to say, intersex conditions where external genitalia have appeared to be too androgynous to fit into the sex binary of everyday life, was the object of corrective surgery. The clinic at Johns Hopkins University hospital run by Dr. John Money specialized in such surgeries, most or all of which entailed turning insufficiently feminine infants into proper girls by reducing the size of the clitorises or turning infant boys born with micropenises, or those who through an accident of circumcision lost their penises, into girls by removing testes, supplying hormone treatments, and later performing surgeries to construct a vagina. The treatment rested on the 1970s separation of sex and gender and the supposition that gender, a cultural construct, was an entirely malleable product of socialization. Parents seem to have been very happy to find a solution that would keep their child from living a life as a "freak" with unacceptably different or unclear sex characteristics. In the long run, however, it turned out that some of the infant boys who were thus "transformed into girls," came to have a male gender identity as they matured, a gender now at odds with the sexed body the surgeons and endocrinologists had given them.[5] Those tragic results, in some cases leading to suicide, have raised the theory of "brain sex," some kind of "brain and mind" predisposition toward gender identification produced already, perhaps, during fetal development (Fausto-Sterling 2012). They point to just how little we actually know about the interaction of body and mind in the emergence of gender identification and of the bodily experience of sex. Both clitoral reduction or penectomy and vaginoplasty interfere with future sexual pleasure, leading adult intersex activists to vehemently oppose such "corrective" surgeries and to militate for broader social acceptance of intersex conditions and for greater freedom in the legal assignment of sex.

On another front, the inclusion of gender-identity disorder (GID) in the *DSM*-4 in 1973 (replaced in 2013 by the term *gender dysphoria*) at the same time that homosexuality was removed from the list of psychiatric disorders made it possible for persons who could convince doctors that they were "born into the wrong body," as it were, to get counseling and hormone therapy, as long as it appeared that they were so repelled by their bodily sex that changing it was the only option. To get treatment, it was necessary for such transgendered persons to convince doctors that their ultimate goal was construction of a missing penis or removal of one and surgical construction of a vagina. Unfortunately, the results of such surgeries, which have been performed now for several decades, are often unsatisfactory when it comes to the pleasurability of sex acts. Indeed, "adequate sex" in the medical literature on intersex and transsexuality seems to be defined, as was sodomy, in functional or hydraulic terms (penile penetration of a vagina or, in the case of sodomy, penetration of some other orifice or by some other penis-like object) rather than in the terms of sexual pleasure. Transgender activists who opt for cross-gender performativity, with or without hormone treatments that make the body feel and look more masculine or feminine, now push for a broader range of treatments and for recognition that it is possible to be sufficiently female with a penis or male without one or to enjoy sexual pleasure without penetration of one body by another.

Is it also possible to experience the body of the sex we are not through performative gender, self-narration, and sexual activity informed by the imagination? There is strikingly little work on sexual practices within the transgender world (though see Kulick 1998), but it would seem a fertile topic along the lines of certain new approaches to the materiality of meaningful experience, whether informed by phenomenological, ontological, or science and technology studies' frameworks (see Latham [2016] for one such effort). Gender may be a social construct, but it is a construct that takes material form. Our bodies and our experience of them are shaped by modifications to our social skins, undertaken always in embodied communicative interactions. Sexual activities, whether performed solo or with others, are themselves as social as they are physical and draw us into relations or, at any rate, narrative fantasies that shape even sexual pleasure in tune with the social identities we inhabit.

Final Thoughts on Don Antonio Yta

And so we reach the end of this study. A good ending point is perhaps to look back at what a good attorney had to say in defense of his client over two centuries ago, just prior to Don Antonio's escape from jail and from the archives: "Up to the present, as I understand it, my client has been accused of no crime other than having been discovered, at the petition of his consort Doña Martina and by virtue of the examination ordered by Your Excellency, that he has the womanly sex with all its qualities, while his manner, his clothing, his reputation, and his assertions were to the contrary. By no manner whatsoever do our law books contain dispositions demonstrating how this might be considered a crime" (plea of José Manuel Malavia, *procurador de los pobres*, Audiencia de Charcas, 1804, expediente, appendix A.11).

Here manner, clothing, reputation, and assertion—or what today we might call performance, in this case of gender—are contrasted with "sex with all its qualities," or the natural or biological facts from which, the judges of the audiencia presume, everything else should have flowed. But it was not yet possible entirely to separate sex from gender. Their entanglement, and the uncertainty produced by a conflict between so-called biological facts and gendered performance, once had a name, *hermaphrodite*, which perhaps opened up more possibilities than it foreclosed.

The concept of gender has been critical for launching feminist critiques of patriarchal or masculine oppression of women and has opened up important rights-based avenues of redress. Yet separating sex from gender, insisting on the biological "realness" of the former and the cultural constructedness of the latter, is an analytic act with sometimes deeply fraught medical and social consequences, as Butler (2004) and Eve Sedgwick (1990, 41–43) have made clear. If, unlike sex (regarded as a fact of nature), gender is a construct, it may be a matter of choice or something that can be changed through proper "nurture." Such ideas underlay lesbian and gay critiques of transgender as "treasonous" capitulation to heteronormativity and were central to the problematic sex-reassignment surgeries of Dr. John Money. Misapplication of the same logic to sexual orientation has led to the proliferation of "therapies" to reheterosexualize those who have gone astray.

The performance and evaluation of embodied, classed, raced, and gendered personhood is astoundingly complex. Having a particular sexual physiology has in no society been sufficient to mark gender. The case of Don Antonio Yta shows us, indeed, that male genitals can be called into *experiential* existence for others by successfully performing gender-patterned behavior while wearing the right clothing. It is no doubt also true that the penis was experientially *real* for Don Antonio, by the kinds of pleasure derived from his manly sexual interactions with women.

Don Antonio's skill in deploying proper costume, body stylization, gait, vocal timbre, and, we must suppose, specific vocabulary and habitual conversational topoi began the work of providing him with presumptive male genitals. But there was much more to it than that. Convincing performances of gender required culturally specific and time-dependent settings. Criminal trials involving honor, virtue, or their nineteenth-century derivative, decency (such as those for injury to honor and repute, such as the kind that precipitated and justified wife murder[6]) set those scenes for us, often in great detail. That is because saying or doing something, or simply being somewhere, had different consequences if it took place in the house or on the street, in the plaza or on the disreputable outskirts of town (the *arrabal*), in the church or chichería, at the marketplace or sewage ditch and also whether it was morning, noon, or night, at *horas* or at *deshoras*. Narratives about character and identity such as those we read in criminal trials or those we tell about famous persons, friends, or colleagues invariably judge the quality of persons in tune with their gender and do so by the same kind of scene setting and characterization used by novelists and playwrights. Effective historical analysis of gender, class, and race requires us not so much to copy these performance and narrative strategies (by returning to narrative history, for example) but to analyze them with empathy and skeptical reflection. Needing special attention, it seems, is our overly certain use of analytic distinctions, such as sex versus gender, material fact versus cultural elaboration, through which our judgments of others may do them harm in service to our own narrative self-fashioning.

APPENDIX A: THE EXPEDIENTE

The Documents and Spanish-to-English Translation

In the Spanish original, transcribed with the help of Julieta Judith Terán and the late Marcela Inch of the Archivo y Biblioteca Nacional de Bolivia, I have completed standard abbreviations and regularized the spelling of names. In the English translation, completed with the help of Susana Rosenbaum, Rachel Lears, and Kahlil Chaar-Pérez, I have indicated the attribution of gender to Antonio/María in the original Spanish text (through third-person pronouns and that language's gendered adjectives and gendered personal nouns), with boldface and square brackets. Added gendered pronouns required by English are italicized. When choice of gender for added pronouns was arbitrary, I have aimed to follow the apparent choice of the writer. I have divided the case record into twenty-seven items and labeled them with numbers, dates, and brief topical descriptions. Separate acts of writing are divided by dashes (—) and ellipses in the translation by dots (. . .). Folio numbers of the original manuscript are included, at page-break points, between forward slashes (/1r/). A manuscript folio consists of a sheet of paper, with recto (r) and verso (v) sides, so /1v/, in our standard page-numbering system, would be page 2. I refer to these folio numbers and the item numbers when referring to the expediente in the interpretive essay. They are useful for comparing the English translation to the transcription of the Spanish text. The full transcription and translation of the expediente is found at the PTA website, https://wp.nyu.edu/passingtoamerica/.

Source: "Case Presented by Doña Martina Vilvado y Balverde Against Don Antonio de Yta for Marrying Doña Martina in Spite of Being a Woman," EC 1805.96, 39 folios, ABNB.

Yta Expediente, English Translation

[A.1 October 7, 1803: Written, first-person denunciation by Doña Martina Vilvado y Balverde. Note: this is the second denunciation—the first is item 9.]

/1r/ Most Excellent Lord President [referring to Don Ramón García Pizarro, president of the Audiencia de Charcas]:

I, Doña Martina Vilvado y Balverde, native of the city of Cochabamba, in the most proper manner within the law before the wisdom of Your Excellency, do appear and state:

More than four years ago in the Villa de Potosí, I contracted matrimony with Don Antonio de Yta, native of the kingdoms of Spain, in the good faith and belief that **he** was male [*era **baron***], since *he* wore the clothing of such. But with the passage of time it has become clear that in reality *he* was a woman dressed as a man, through a group of evident signs such as monthly menstruation, making water in the same manner as do women, and, in a word, for not having consummated with me the supposed matrimony, with the pretext that *he* had taken a vow of chastity. Because of this *he* almost always slept away from the conjugal bed, and when *he* slept in my company, *he* took the precaution of putting on underwear. There were also many other signs that honor will not allow me to specify.

I understand that I should bring my demand for marriage annulment to the ecclesiastic judge, to whom it is appropriate to bring such purely spiritual matters. Without prejudice to such a demand, I should and do denounce the grave crime of disguise by costume of the cited Yta, for this is a point of public, secular, and profane law, whose jurisdiction belongs to magistrates and secular judges, given that the very act of using manly costume throws the most vehement presumption that this individual has committed other crimes and has come to this kingdom clandestinely without the corresponding pass or license.

In this regard I appeal to Your Excellency's rectitude to order a judicial determination of that Yta's sex so that by its results the penalties required by the law are applied and, when the facts are sufficiently clarified, that you hand over to me the original proceedings or a copy to use, as is my right, before the ecclesiastical judge. Therefore:

I ask and plead to Your Excellency to decide and order what will be just and to that end, etc. By plea from the presenting party, Martina Vilvado y Balverde. [Signature and rubric:] Luiz de Alcozer y Guerra.

[A.2, 3, 4 October 7, 1803: Expediente begun; Vilvado y Balverde ratifies writ but does not sign because does not know how; physician and surgeon notified of need for examination. All signed and rubricked by Valda, Rodríguez Romano, and García Pizarro.]

[A.5 October 7, 1803: Medical examination of Antonio Yta to determine his sex.]

/3v/ In La Plata on the seventh day of the month of October 1803:

Having conducted a thorough inspection and examination of the person named Antonio Yta, the titular physician, Don Joséf Gregorio Salas, and the surgeon of the city, Don Diego Juano, in my presence certify under the oath celebrated upon entrance into their offices: that this person is a true woman, whose nature is complete in all the generative external parts. And although this person says that in certain indecent moments a kind of fleshiness similar to the virile member protrudes over the pudenda, this is, in such case, the clitoris, a proper part of a woman's pudenda and nothing foreign to its nature, although the certifiers have not seen it in the action that **he** [él] describes. In addition to the aforementioned, this person's configuration is that of the feminine sex: the inferior extremities, rotund; the pelvic bones, long unlike those of men; the complete breasts that in no way differ from the sex except that they are somewhat flattened through constant compression and rigid from no secretion. Along with all this, **he** [él] assures us of having had regular menstruation. /4r/ And to certify this they signed it, to which I attest—[signatures and rubrics:] José Gregorio de Salas, Diego Sáenz de Juano, Calixto de Valda, public and town council scribe for His Majesty.

[A.6 October 7, 1803: Rodríguez Romano orders confession be taken, to clarify why "**she** who until now has been known as Antonio Yta" . . . "has disguised *her* sex," etc. (see the PTA website).]

[A.7 October 7, 1803: Confession of Antonio Yta]

In La Plata on the stated day, month, and year:

The person who is called Antonio Yta found **himself** present before His Excellency so that *his* confession might be taken: I, the scribe, received the oath /5r/ in the name of God Our Lord and made the sign of the cross, under which *she* promised to tell the truth about what **she** knew and was to be asked and being in accordance with the preceding decree for *her* true name, age, country, and state, *she* said that,

Her proper name is María Leocadia Yta; that *she* is thirty-two years old; that *she* is a native of Colmenar de Oreja, seven leagues away from Madrid in Spain; that **she** is single [*es soltera*].

Asked with what license **she** came to America, which she should show if *she* has it at hand, s*he* said that,

She sailed without license from the Port of Málaga on a commercial vessel traveling to Montevideo in the year 1794 but did not remember the season in which *she* set sail or landed in Montevideo or the name of the ship's captain or of the passengers in *her* company.

In view of the previous responses regarding the vehement suspicion thrown on *her* about the origin of *her* irregular behavior in disguising *her* sex and resolving /5v/ to set sail without license and in men's clothing, **she** was asked [*preguntada*] if it results [crossed out: viene = originates] from a crime worthy of examination and punishment by the government and whose hiding has animated its proceedings and to speak and give an account of what was *her* occupation in Spain before setting sail and what caused *her* to take these steps. And the witness said that,

Her parents put **her** [*la pucieron*] in an Augustinian convent in Colmenar de Oreja, where *she* took the habit. But *she* did not take her vows before they threw **her** out [*la sacaron*], because the nuns said it was more suitable this way. Right away, thinking they would make **her** a nun [*meterla religiosa*] under the protection of the Lady Duchess Widow of Medinacelli, *her* parents placed **her** [*la pucieron*] in the Franciscan convent called Santa Juana de la Cruz, near Illescas, four or five leagues away from Madrid, where *she* stayed eleven months without ever taking *her* vows. They sent **her** away [*la despidieron*] after catching **her** [*haverla sorprehendido*] with a nun and because they were convinced *she* was a man. They confirmed this opinion by news from the town of Colmenar de Oreja, where one thing or another had happened since the age of fourteen, when *she* took the habit in the Augustinian convent of Colmenar. About a year and a half passed between leaving that convent and entering /6r/ that of Santa Juana de la Cruz, and *she* does not remember now the years in which this happened. *She* was returned to the power of *her* parents, residents, and neighbors of Colmenar de Oreja; one year, more or less, passed, and they stipulated that *she* take the habit in Segovia in the convent of the Bernardas, which **she** did [*la tomó*]. Having stayed there some four or five months, **he** left or was thrown out [*salido o despedido*] by the nuns, although in precaution, for the same reason that caused *her* to leave the convent of Santa Juana.

She was taken [*haviendo sido conducida*] next to Madrid to the house of a married sister, and from there *her* parents led **her** (*la condujieron*), within the space of a year, more or less, to the Franciscan convent of Guet, where *she* again took the habit without ever taking vows, remaining there about six months (*she* does not remember the year). They threw **her** out [*la despidieron*] and gave *her* to *her* sister [crossed out: parents] for the reasons already stated by disposition of the nuns [between the lines: or of the chaplains who directed them].

She then found *herself* in Madrid in the house of *her* aforementioned sister, named Leocadia Yta, married to Don Eugenio, whose last name at the time *she* does not remember, employed in the customs house of Madrid. On the advice of *her* confessor *she* decided to go to Rome, and to execute this *she* went by /6v/ carriage to the city of Valencia unaccompanied and with help only from the money that *she* had with *her*, having left with the previously mentioned sister a letter for *her* father, in which *she* announced *her* resolution to go to Rome, this having occurred some twelve years ago.

Once **she** arrived [*llegada*] in Valencia, with help from a friend of *her* father, whose last name was Marzas, *she* traveled by land to Barcelona, where *she* set sail on a mail ship from that port to Genoa without passport or license from the government, in the company of two operantas, mother and daughter who also set sail in the same mail ship, not having stayed in the port of Barcelona even fifteen days, having traveled on the sea to Genoa for twenty or twenty-five days and staying in Genoa about two months. Afterward *she* set sail again in the company of the same operantas for Civitavecchia [Rome's port], and from there *she* traveled, again in the company /7r/ of the same women, all the way to Rome, having constantly worn women's clothing up until that point.

Finding *herself* in Rome and practicing the formalities *she* judged pertinent to quiet *her* conscience, it resulted from these that it was communicated to *her* through the Spanish-language penitentiary, Fray Pedro Ramos Aragones, of the Order of San Francisco, that by order of His Holiness *she* should dress from then on in men's costume. After having explained to the major penitentiary the difficulty that would arise in returning to *her* country, where they had known **her** [*la havian conocido*] since childhood as a woman, he told **her** [*la dijo*] that *she* should head wherever *she* pleased and that in any case *she* should dress as a man, which *she* did from that moment on before leaving Rome, where she remained about seven months, calculating the time from *her* arrival through *her* departure; for now, she does not remember in which year.

She left for Civitavecchia, where *she* set sail for Genoa and from that port to Barcelona, from which **she** went to Málaga and made all these trips alone [*sola*] and in men's clothing. And, finally, in the said port of Málaga, *she* set sail about nine years ago for the port where the ship was headed, Montevideo, not having waited in this last port but three days, after which *she* passed without license on a boat from that river to the capital of Buenos Aires.

Here *she* sought after Don Juan Antonio Pintos, a merchant from Cádiz and an acquaintance of *her* father. Not having found him, *she* presented *herself* to the illustrious lord Azamor, bishop of that city, telling him that *she* was destitute of help because *she* had not found the said Don Juan Antonio Pintos, from whom *she* had hoped to receive aid. With such motive *she* implored his protection, telling him *she* was a native **son** of Madrid [*hijo de Madrid*]. As a result of the conversation *she* had for this reason with the said illustrious lord, he remembered a cousin of **hers**, a barefoot Carmelite monk named Fray Julián de San Gerónimo, an acquaintance of the lord bishop, who then told **her** [*la dijo*] that *she* might have room and board in his palace. And that is how it came to be that *she* stayed in the bishop's house about three years until the death of the same lord bishop, having made *himself* /8r/ known in this time and afterward by the name Antonio Yta.

Finally, **he** decided to leave alone [*solo*] and without a passport for Potosí, and after being accidentally detained for about four months because of a broken leg, *he* continued *his* voyage to the expressed destination and found *himself* near Jujuy with a man from Buenos Aires [*porteño*] whose last name was Pazos and one of his servants, with whom *he* arrived to Potosí six years ago. And presenting *himself* to the lord governor of that town using the recommendations that *he* brought from Buenos Aires, the latter kept **him** [*le mantubo*] in his house about two years, at the end of which *he* left to arrange to marry Doña Martina Vilvado y Balverde, who was in Potosí at the time.

And with license from the lord governor for being from overseas [*ultramarino*], *he* married the said lady, having announced marriage banns in the matrix church of that town and celebrated the formal promise of marriage by the Franciscan priest Friar Angel So-and-So, today the ecclesiastical attorney of the convent of the city of Tarija, after having been granted the license by the priest of the central church, Dr. Guzmán. Afterward, *he* stayed (with *his* wife, living as a married couple) for two years in the said town, working in what /8v/ was offered *him*.

And having arrived in this city [referring to La Plata] to solicit a post, **he** was given the opportunity [*se le proporcionó*] to go to the province of Moxos to take up the duties of administrator of the town called La Madalena, where *he* stayed for a year in the capital, exercising the orders of the lord governor Zamora. And the next [year] **he** worked as administrator in the aforementioned town, at the end of which *he* came to this court to ask for *his* wages, which record is found in the Royal Audiencia.

Finally, in answer to the question before *him*, *he* adds that the reason that has motivated *his* attempt to hide and disguise *his* womanly sex has been to obey the order of His Holiness communicated by the major penitentiary as stated, as a result of the formalities *she* practiced in Rome to quiet *his* conscience.

Asked [*preguntada*] if before the major penitentiary in Rome communicated the stated order from His Holiness /9r/ any proceedings of examination to verify **her** sex had been carried out,

She said that there had been no action of this type.

For convenience, given the difficulties offered by the answer of *her* previous declaration, *she* was asked with more precision about the identity of *her* person; **she** was asked [*preguntada*] for the name of *her* parents and their place of residence [*vezindario*], and *she* said that,

Her father was named Don Joséf Yta and *her* mother Doña Felipa Ybáñez, natives and inhabitants of the town of Colmenar de Oreja, who were living at the time when the [**female**] witness [*la declarante*] set sail, but that today *she* does not know, for lack of news, whether they are alive or dead.

With His Excellency's orders this proceeding is suspended for now and will be continued when it is convenient, ordering that in the meantime *she* should remain in custody with the proper decency of *her* sex. Having read to the confessant the content of **her** confession,

She declared that it was well written, adding only that with Doña Martina Vilvado, before having celebrated what is called matrimony, *she* maintained an illicit friendship for the duration of a year in the said Villa de Potosí.

And *she* signed, and His Excellency added his rubric, to which I attest. [Signature:] María Leocadia Yta. [Rubric and signature:] Calixto de Valda.

[A.8 October 10, II, and 13, 1803: Transmission of these audiencia proceedings to the ecclesiastical judge of the archbishopric and request for information about any annulment proceedings there (see the PTA website).]

[A.9 October 4, 1803: Martina Vilvado y Balverde's petition to the church for annulment; ecclesiastical judge asks audience to order medical determination of sex.]

/IIr/ [In the margin:] Petition.

Lord Ecclesiastical Judge and Vicar General:

I, Doña Martina Vilvado y Balverde, native of the city of Cochabamba, in the best way within the law and through this representation before Your Lordship, do appear and state that more than four years ago, in the Villa de Potosí, I contracted marriage with Don Antonio de Yta, native of the kingdoms of Spain, with the purpose of avoiding the dangers of the world and to better serve God. From that time until now, I have devoted all my will and care to pleasing the said person, putting in **his** hand my modest decency and all my will at **his** disposal, and none of this has been enough to fulfill the consummation of the marriage, since to this date, in spite of my affections and insinuations, it has been impossible to attain this primary end of the matrimonial contract, for *he* has said to me through various insinuations that *he* has taken a solemn vow of chastity and that if by chance *he* married me it was only with the purpose of my personal service. I have recognized on the one hand *his* resistance toward such a necessary obligation and on the other have noticed that **he** has never let his body be touched, even when **he** was sick, that *he* makes water the way that women are accustomed to and, at the same time, is accustomed to sit like them and also has very grown breasts. Since I have been with **him**, I have recently observed the aforementioned circumstances, as well as releasing blood in the way that women do.

To know and to clarify if my marriage is legitimate and if I can obligate **him** to satisfy the conjugal duties, I appeal to Your Lordship's zealous sense of justice so /IIv/ that with the necessary precautions you may mandate that, through the person or expert of your choosing, it be determined if effectively *he* is a man or if *he* has some vice or defect that impedes matrimonial practice, without **his** suspecting any of this, because I am distrustful that if this reaches *his* notice *he* could flee, and I would be left in a hurtful state, without knowing if I am indeed married or not or at least abandoned by the one who should justly support me. Therefore, I ask and beg Your Lordship that in the event that the aforementioned indicators prove true, you declare null and insubstantial the said marriage and if they are not true, you obligate **him** to unite with me accommodating in what is just, for if I take this recourse, I have been stimulated by *his* inaction and to better save my conscience, which will be just. I swear that I do not proceed with malice and to that end, etc. Martina Vilbao.

[Margin: Ruling (*Auto*)] Plata, October 4, 1803. Rulings and hearings [*vistos*]:
     With respect to the fact that the sued in this case, Don Antonio de Yta, comes under royal jurisdiction: the official letter, with the testimony and this resolution, should be directed to the Most Excellent Lord President of this Royal Audiencia and Intendent Governor so that in the service of justice and with respect to the author of the sacraments, he will order the said Yta to appear before two physicians to determine **his** sex or if *he* suffers from some notable vice that annuls the sacrament of marriage so that in light of what results this court may make the appropriate /12r/ resolutions. Dr. Parra. Before me, Manuel Esteban Montero, Notary Public.
     I attest that this transcript matches the writ and original act of the context from which it was taken. [Signature and rubric:] Manuel Esteban Montero, Notary Public.

[A.10 October 17, 18, 21, 1803: Letter from Parra (ecclesiastical judge) to García Pizarro (audiencia president), asking latter to determine if "the other party to the suit is a hermaphrodite in whom prevails /13v/ the manly sex"; and reply.]

[A.11 (October 19, 1803?): Statement and plea for improved jail conditions from Malavia, Yta's state-appointed attorney.]

     /15r/ Most Excellent Lord President,
     Prompt resolution requested.
     I, José Manuel Malavia, criminal attorney to the poor in this audiencia on behalf of Don Antonio Yta, held in this audiencia's jail, in the most proper way within the law before Your Excellency do appear and state, . . . I omit also the declaration until the most opportune moment of the impertinence of Doña Martina in resorting to troubling Your Excellency's superior attention without the discretion appropriate to the matter or the case, nor the circumstances, consequences, and grave harms and humiliations that it has caused my party. I limit myself only to present to Your Excellency that the prison in /15v/ which Don Antonio finds **himself** is too hard, painful, and full of affliction, which has **him** at the point of the greatest desperation. . . .
     Up to the present, Most Excellent Sir, as I understand it, my client has been accused of no crime other than having been discovered, at the petition of *his* consort, Doña Martina, and by virtue of the examination ordered by Your Excellency, that he has the womanly sex with all its qualities, while *his* manner, *his* clothing, *his* reputation, and *his* assertions were to the contrary. By no manner whatsoever do our law books contain dispositions demonstrating how this might be considered a crime, requiring *him* to be condemned to prison and to enormous suffering. . . . /16r/ . . .
     [Signatures and rubrics:] Dr. Esteban Agustín Gascón and José Manuel Malavia.

[A.12 October 19, 1803: Order for improvements in Yta's treatment in jail, that "she be put in custody with the proper decency of her sex"; Warden's reply; specific orders for better treatment.]

[A.13 October 19 and 26, 1803 (*sic*): Letter from ecclesiastical judge to president of the audiencia asking for copies of determinations to add to his own annulment file.]

[A.14 July 20, 1804: Plea from Yta's lawyer, Malavia, requesting further humane relief in "that miserable man's" jail conditions.]

[A.15 August 1, 1804: Notice from second lieutenant of militia grenadiers of inspection of jail and evidence of Doña María Leocadia Yta's attempt to escape by making a hole in the wall.]

[A.16 August 3, 1804: Recusation from case of General Adviser Mariano Taborga, for having taken original denunciation from Martina Vilvado y Balverde prior to his appointment to the post; appointment in his place of Dr. Don Francisco de Paula Moscoso.]

Most Excellent Lord President,
Having reviewed the present case records, the general adviser of this government wishes to inform Your Excellency that he finds in them that, before obtaining the post of adviser, he made the writ at the head of this document in favor of the plaintiff, and therefore he finds himself legally impeded from continuing to lend his counsel on this matter in order to avoid incurring a grave breach of official duty [*prevaricato*]. In this regard he begs Your Excellency to excuse him and name another adviser, with the brevity demanded by the incredible delay of this case, the privileged recommendation of the law, and the humanity deserved by a woman imprisoned for so long. Plata, August 3, 1804. [Signature and rubric:] Dr. Mariano Taborga.

[A.17 August 22, 1804: Martina Vilvado ordered to put her accusation in proper form within three days.]

[A.18 August 22, 27, and 30 and September 6 and 7, 1804: Plea from José Pimentel, Yta's lawyer, asking for a medical evaluation of Don Antonio Yta and for removal of his shackles; physician's report of severe edema, order to comply with physician's recommendation; physician Salas's report of Don Antonio Yta's swollen legs, deteriorating medical condition, use of shackles; Cañete order for removal of shackles from his feet, orders visit from physician and treatment from hospital's apothecary.]

[A.19 September 24, October 3, 5, 16, 17, 18, 1804: Warden reports Don Antonio Yta's escape from jail, with the aid of (and with) the indigenous guard; related proceedings.]

/251/ Most Excellent Sir: [Margin: Please note (*Sirbase*)]
I, Don Feliz Cardozo, warden of this Royal Court Jail, before the honest and just wisdom of Your Highness do appear and state that on Friday the twenty-first of this month, Don Antonio Yta escaped, at nine thirty or ten at night, more or less. From what is inferred *he* left with a counterfeit key or through the window of the jail cell *he* was in, and with help from the Indian servant [*pongo*] *he* took off the shackles and went to the dwelling where the said servant was. They pulled up a board from the floor and with a short rope they both descended to the part between the bars. *He* then put the servant as a guard so that he could keep watch over and warn of what he could. Since I already was very suspicious, I went to guard **him** day and night, observing all of his moves. If I watched **him** [él] at night from six until seven thirty or eight, I left the three doors closed, taking this precaution because *he* had first planned to flee

through the hole *he* made in the wall that faces the ruins of the women's jail, which I fixed at my own cost and of whose occurrence I gave verbal account to the Most Excellent Lord President, as well as of the little or no security that this jail had for the accused of the state.

It is impossible to guard against predatory robbers. This is as much as I can report to the wise comprehension of Your Highness in compliance with my obligation. I beg and plead that Your Highness decide and mandate what you believe to be to your liking and just, and I swear to God Our Lord that I do not proceed with malice. [Signature and rubric:] Feliz Cardozo. . . .

[A.20 October 18, 30, 31, 1804: Effort to retrieve documents of original proceedings, in power of attorney for Vilvado y Balverde.]

[A.21 Testimony of Yta's mother, sent (with the following certifications, item 22) to Yta's lawyer Gascón and delivered by him to audiencia on November 28, 1804 (see item 24).]

/28r/ Madrid, 7 August 1804:
My Dear Lord, with all my respect,
I have received news of the benefits that Your Mercy has dispensed on **that son of mine** [ése *mi hijo*], and I refer to **him** as such [*así lo graduo*] because of the circumstances that I will relate to Your Mercy. In short, it is very true that at the age of nine *she* moved to the house of a powerful woman from the town of *his* birth, in whose company *she* stayed until the age of seventeen, when the said woman proposed that **she** [*la proporiciono*] take the habit in a Franciscan convent, where *she* did not take her vows. In a short time, *she* passed through three other convents, in the towns of Huete, Colmenar de Oreja, Santa Juana, five leagues from this court, and the last one in Segovia, in none of which *she* took vows. This is evidenced by the certificates of the prioresses that I remit to Your Mercy for confirmation. *She* has not committed the crime of apostasy, which I understand is applied to *her* case. After **she** was not admitted [*admitida*] in any /28v/ of the aforementioned convents, *she* resolved to go to Rome, where *she* stayed for some months; and on *her* return, *she* took up men's clothes, which according to the orders of Holy See *she* had to wear *her* whole life. On **her** return to Spain, **she** was discovered [*descubierta*] in Barcelona by sailors who were looking through *his* luggage and found women's clothes. For this, the last bishop kept **him** [*le tubo*] in seclusion and *he* was freed upon his death.

He then traveled to Cádiz, where *he* remained for four months, and after an incident occurred (which I will relate later) [margin: attention (*ojo*)], *he* set sail from Málaga for Montevideo, where *he* traveled to Buenos Aires to the home of the lord bishop Azamor, where, from what I learned, *he* had given them nothing to complain about concerning *his* conduct. Your Mercy, do not wonder that a mother should take an interest in a matter in which it is necessary to declare what happened.

After **she** was not admitted [*no fue admitida*] to take *her* vows in any of the convents, *she* remained in the company of *her* sister for a few months with the pretext that *she* worked in sewing in the house of Doña Rita Benedicto, inhabitant of this court [that is, the Royal Court in Madrid]. We heard the complaint that the latter was pregnant [margin: attention (*ojo*)] by **him** [*de este*], which surprised *his* father, my now-dead husband, and me. We heard this complaint from the aforesaid Rita when *he* [Yta] fled to Rome without our consent and without our knowing about any of this. We later learned from her relatives that Rita died /29r/ in childbirth, as did her baby. In the meantime, *he* stayed in Rome and upon arriving in Barcelona wrote to us from that city, telling us about dressing in men's clothes by order from His Holiness. From Barcelona *he* traveled to Cádiz, where **he** was involved [*andubo enredado*] with Doña Vicenta Arias de Reyna, who, declaring that *he* had gotten her pregnant, demanded that it was **his** duty to marry her. *He* immediately disappeared and headed to Málaga, where *he* set sail for these regions, and after *he* wrote from Buenos Aires from the house of the illustrious lord Azamor, I have not known *his* whereabouts until this occurrence, which has been announced to *his* brothers from that city, which thus shows that Your Mercy looks after **my wretched son** [ése *desgraciado mi hijo*] with interest. And with true mother's love, I am interested that you have the kindness to make use of all imaginable means to ensure that *his* case be attended by the lord president and that he look upon **her** [*ella*] with interest, as he who is in possession of *her* destiny with respect to its good development.

In the detailed reports given to me by Rita Benedicto and Vicenta Arias, they stated that in *his* construction *he* had qualities of a woman, but in the act a virile member manifests itself, with all the full functions of a man. Even from childhood, **his** character /29v/ was always rebellious, and in later years **he** was very strongly inclined toward the feminine sex, which resulted in giving us, *his* parents, many sorrows. **He** [*este*] was reprehensible in *his* interaction with Rita Benedicto and at the same time with another in the street of Los Remedios, this one a Valencian woman with whom *her* brother-in-law caught **her** [*la cogio*] in the act itself and in men's clothes.

All of this I communicate to Your Mercy for your government, even as it is painful to me to declare the weaknesses committed by **that son** [*ese hijo*] who has caused us so much anxiety. But amid all these circumstances I plead to Your Mercy with all my heart to interpose all good services with the lord governor in the case pending before him, hoping that Your Mercy's goodness will attend to the request of a mother who will always be your most attentive and faithful servant. She who kisses your hands, Felipa Ybáñez. Señor Dr. Don Esteban Agustín Gascón.

[A.22 July 29, August 3, 5, and 7, 1804: Certifications from convents, addressed to Yta's lawyer Gascón of Yta's presence there as novitiate and that she did not profess as a nun (see the PTA website).]

[A.23 May 7 and June 10, 1805: Order to make copy of complete file for the audiencia to keep and to forward originals to the ecclesiastical judge.]

[A.24 November 28, 1804(?): Yta's lawyer Gascón explains that he has just received Don Antonio Yta's mother's testimony (item 21) and convent certifications (item 22) and considers what they add to the case.]

. . . /32r/ . . . I, Dr. Don Esteban Agustín Gascón, lawyer of this Royal Audiencia, in the most proper way within the law, before Your Excellency do appear and state, . . .

After the [**male**] aforementioned escaped from the prison in which *he* suffered, when /34v/ Your Excellency's respectable judgment considered *him* perhaps a delinquent and apostate of one of the religious monasteries that *he* confessed to have inhabited, and after the ecclesiastical court considered the annulment of the marriage an incontrovertible point beyond all dispute, I received in hand the attached letter by maritime mail and swear by God Our Lord and make the sign of [a cross] that it has just arrived. It is dated in Madrid on August 7 of this year and sent by the mother of the aforementioned, Doña Felipa Ybáñez, and was accompanied by the three certifications and a letter from Don Eugenio Sánchez.

From this context it results that, contrary to what was believed, this unfortunate person did not lie in his expositions, that *he* has not committed any public crime that would have made **him** worthy of imprisonment, punishment, or other injurious and degrading condemnations, such as those that *he* has suffered. Furthermore, there is nothing worthy of attention to this magistrate in *him*, but *his* miseries and the defects with which nature wished to ridicule **him** [*de él*], and finally the case of the annulment of marriage is a much more serious consideration and demands a much more circumspect and maturely thought-out decision than it appeared at first by virtue of the first examinations. . . .

/33r/ I beg and plead that Your Excellency decide and determine as I have exposed to be just. I swear the necessary in law, etc. [Signature and rubric:] Don Esteban Agustín Gascón.

[A.25 November 28 and December 18 and 19, 1804: Order to add Yta's lawyer's letter and Yta's mother's testimony and convent certifications to case file and to produce it for the next hearing; scribe's report that rest of case file in possession of Vilvado y Balverde lawyer since August 31, 1803; order to retrieve the file urgently.]

[A.26 January 8, 16, 18, and 24, 1805: Demand for report on whether or not Yta has returned or been found; reports in the negative.]

[A.27 February 13, 1805: Prosecutor asks for original case documents to be sent to ecclesiastical judge, keeping a copy for the audiencia; February 15, 1805: order sent by audiencia's legal adviser; February 28, March 14, 1805: copy ordered on folio 9 sent to Curia; May 4, 5, 1805: ecclesiastical judge requests originals of entire expediente; May 6, 1805: notary public confirms authenticity of copy (the present document).]

[end of document]

Yta Expediente, Spanish Transcription of Original Document

Transcription by Thomas Abercrombie, corrected by Julieta Judith Terán and the late Marcela Inch of the Archivo y Biblioteca Nacional de Bolivia. It was previously published with an essay by the author in Abercrombie (2009).

Source: "Expediente seguido por doña Martina Vilvado y Balverde con don Antonio de Yta por casarse con doña Martina siendo muger," EC 1805.96, fs. 39, ABNB.

[A.1 7 de octubre, 1803: Escritura de la denuncia, en primera persona, de doña Martina Vilvado y Balverde.]

/1r/ Excelentísimo Señor Presidente:
Doña Martina Vilvado y Balverde, natural de la ciudad de Cochabamba, en la mejor forma que haya lugar en derecho ante la justificazión de Vuestra Excelencia paresco y digo:

Que hacen más de quatro años que en la Villa de Potosí contrajé matrimonio con don Antonio de Yta, natural de los Reynos de España, bajo la buena fe y creencia de que era barón, porque estaba en el traje de tal, pero con el discurso del tiempo se ha llegado a exclareser que en realidad era muguer vestida de hombre, por un conjunto de señales evidentes quales son mestrual cada mes, hacer aguas del mismo modo y forma que las mugueres [sic], y en una palabra por no haber consumado conmigo el supuesto matrimonio, con el presteto de que tenía hecho voto de castidad, de aquí provenía que casi siempre dormía separado del lecho conyugal, y quando lo hacía en mi consorcio, tenía la precaución de ponerse calsoncillos, y otras muchas que el pundonor no permite individualizar.
Bien veo que la demanda de nulidad de matrimonio la debo entablar ante el ecleciástico, a quien es peculiar conoser de esta causa como puramente espi/1v/ritual; pero sin perjuicio de ello, hago y debo hazer denuncia del grave delito del disfraz del traje del citado Yta por ser este un punto de derecho público temporal y profano cuyo conosimiento toca y pertenese a los Magistrados y juezes ceculares, principalmente quando el mismo hecho de usar el traje varonil, arroja de sí la vehementísima presunción de que este individuo há cometido algunos otros delitos, y ha venido al Reyno clandestinamente sin el pase y licencia que corresponde.

En esta atención ocurro a la rectitud de Vuestra Excelencia a fin de que se sirba mandar de que se haga el reconosimiento judicial del sexo de tal Yta, para que con lo que de él resultare se le aplinquen las penas fulminadas por las leyes, y esclarecido el hecho en la forma que baste, se me entreguen las diligencias original o el testimonio, para usar de mi derecho ante el juez ecleciástico. Por tanto:

A Vuestra Excelencia pido y suplico así lo provéa y mande que será justicia y para ella etc. A ruego de la presentante, Martina Vilvado y Balverde. [firma y rúbrica:] Luiz de Alcozer y Guerra.

[A.2, 3, 4 7 de octubre, 1803: Empieza expediente con los documentos precedentes, y ordena afirmación por Vilvado y Balverde de su denuncia; Médico y cirujano notificado. Firmados por Valda, Rodríguez Romano, García Pizarro.]

[A.5 7 de octubre, 1803: Examinación médica de Antonio Yta para determinar su sexo.]

/3v/ En la Plata en siete días del mes de octubre de mil ochocientos, y tres años:

El médico, y cirujano titulares de la ciudad don Joséf Gregorio Salas, y don Diego Juano, haviendo hecho inspección, y reconocimiento prolijo de la persona que nombra Antonio Yta en mi presencia certifican bajo del Juramento que tienen celevrado al ingreso de sus oficios: Que es verdadera muger, cuya natura la tiene completa con todas las Partes de la generación externa, y aunque dize que en ciertos casos indecentes se sobrepuja a la parte pudenda una especie de carnocidad semejante al miembro viril este aún dado caso es el clitoris propio de la parte pudenda de la muger, pero no cosa extraña a su naturaleza; vien es que los certificantes no lo han visto en la acción que él dize; a más de todo lo referido su configuración es propia del sexo femenino, las extremidades inferiores rotundas, los huesos innominados, largos de ningún modo propio a los hombres, las mammas completas que no difieren en nada del sexo ecepto que estan algo aplanadas mediante la continua comprehención, y rígidas por la ninguna secreción; fuera de todo él acegura haver tenido su menstruación contante [*sic*] /4r/ Y para que conste lo firmaron de que doy fe. [firmas y rúbricas:] José Gregorio de Salas, Diego Sáenz de Juano, Calixto de Valda, escribano de Su Magestad Público y de Cabildo.

[A.6 7 de octubre, 1803: Ordena recepción de la confesión "a la que hasta aora se conoze por Antonio Yta, dirigida a exclarecer la causa que le ha motivado su irregular procedimiento en disfrasar su sexo."]

[A.7 7 de octubre, 1803: Confesión de Antonio Yta]

En la Plata en dicho día mes, y año:

Haviendose hallado presente ante Su Excelencia la persona que se denomina Antonio Yta para efecto de tomarle su confeción: Yo el escribano reciví juramento /5r/ que lo hizo por Dios Nuestro Señor y una señal de cruz, bajo del qual prometió dezir verdad de lo que supiere, y fuere preguntada, y siéndole al tenor del auto antecedente por su verdadero nombre, edad, patria, y estado dijo:

Que su propio nombre es María Leocadia Yta: Que es de edad de treinta, y dos años: Que es natural de Colmenar de Oreja, siete leguas distante de Madrid en España: Que ella es soltera, y responde.

Preguntada con que licencia ha venido a América que devera exibir si la tuviese a mano dijo:

Que se embarcó sin licencia en el puerto de Málaga en una embarcación de comercio que hazía viage á Montevideo el año pasado de noventa, y quatro, no acordandose de la estación en que se embarcó; y desembarcó en dicho Montevideo, ni tampoco el nombre del capitán de la embarcación, y así mesmo de los pasageros que venían en su compañía, y responde.

Preguntada con vista de lo que resulta de las respuestas antecedentes, que en atención a la vehemente sospecha que arrojan de sí acerca de que el origen de su Irregular procedimiento en disfrazar su sexo, y resolverse /5v/ a embarcarse sin licencia, y en traje de hombre viene [tachado = trae origen] de algún delito digno del examen, y castigo del goviero cuya ocultación le ha animado a sus procedimientos diga, y dé razón qual fué su ocupación en España, antes de embarcarse, y qual fué la causa de tomar esta resolución, dijo:

Que sus padres la pucieron en un monasterio de Colmenar de Oreja que era de Agustinas en el que tomo el avito, y antes de profezar la sacaron, por haver dicho las monjas que así combenia. Que en ceguida llebando sus Padres el pensamiento adelante de meterla Religiosa con la protección de la Señora Duquesa viuda de Medina Zeli la pucieron religiosa en el comvento de Franciscas nombrado Santa Juana de la Cruz cerca de Illescas, quatro o cinco leguas de Madrid donde permaneciendo onze meses sin llegar a profezar, la despidieron de rezultas de haverla sorprehendido con una monja, y persuadídose que era hombre confirmandoze en esta opinión por noticias de esta clase que havían llegado a dicho comvento desde el Pueblo de Colmenar de Oreja haviendo sucedido uno y otro hallandose en la edad de catorze años, quando tomó el ávito en el comvento de Agustinos de Colmenar y pasado como año, y medio de Intermedio desde la salida de dicho comvento a la entrada /6r/ en él de Santa Juana de la Cruz, no acordándose por aora en los años en que sucedió: Que vuelta a poder de sus Padres, recidentes, y vezinos de Colmenar de Oreja, haviendo mediado el espacio de un año poco más o menos dispucieron que tomase el ávito en Segovia en el comvento de Bernardas, como en efecto la tomó, haviendo permanecido en él unos quatro, o cinco meses, y salido ó despedido por las Monjas aunque con precaución por la misma causa que ocacionó la salida del comvento de Santa Juana.

Haviendo sido conducida á Madrid a casa de una hermana suya casada, desde allí la condujeron sus Padres, mediando el espacio de un año poco más o menos al comvento de Franciscas de Guet, donde así mismo tomo el ávito sin llegar a profezar, permaneciendo como cosa de seis meses (sin acordarse tampoco el año) la despidieron, y entregaron a su [tachada = s padres] [entre renglones:] hermana por las mesmas causas ya referidas por dispocición de las monjas [entre renglones = o de los capellanes que las dirigían].

Que hallándose en Madrid en la casa de su Hermana yá citada nombrada Leocadia Yta, casada con don Eugenio cuyo apellido en el día no se acuerda, empleado en la aduana de Madrid, a rezultas del dictamen que le dió su confezor, se propuso ir a Roma, y para su execución se dirigió /6v/ en una caleza a la ciudad de Balencia sin acompañamiento alguno, y con solo el aucilio que le proporcionaba el dinero que llebaba suyo; haviendo antes dejado en Poder de dicha su Hermana una carta para su padre en la que le anoticiaba su resolución de ir a Roma, haviendo sucedido esto arán unos doze años poco más o menos.

Que llegada a Balencia con el aucilio que le proporcionó un Amigo de su padre apellidado Marzas, pasó por tierra a Barzelona en donde se embarcó en un correo procedente de aquel puerto para Genova sin pasaporte o licenzia del goviero, agregada a dos operantas madre e hija que se embarcaron ygualmente en el mismo correo no haviendose detenido en el expresado Puerto de Barcelona, ni quinze días, haviendo durado el viage de mar hasta Genova unos veinte o veinte y cinco días y detenidose en dicho Genova como cosa de dos meses, después de los quales se embarcó nuebamente en compañía de las mismas operantas con destino a Sivitabechia, y desde allí se dirijió siempre en compañía /7r/ de las mesmas mugeres hasta Roma, haviendo concerbado constantemente hasta este tiempo el traje de muger.

Que hallandose en Roma, y practicado las diligencias que juzgó conducentes a la quietud de su conciencia, rezultó de ellas havérsele comunicado por el penitenciario de la lengua española Fray Pedro Ramos Aragones, del Orden de San Francisco que de orden de Su Santidad devía vestir en lo sucecibo con traje de hombre y que sin embargo de haver expuesto al penitenciario la dificultad que se ofrecía desde luego para bolber a su país donde la havían conocido desde su primera niñez por muger, la dijo que tomase la ruta por donde gustase y que en todo caso se vistiese de hombre, como lo executó desde entonces antes de salir de Roma en cuya capital permaneció como cosa de siete meses, computando todo el tiempo desde su entrada hasta su salida, no acordandose por aora el año.

Y asi que salió para Sivitavechia donde se embarcó con destino a Genova, y de este puerto a Barcelona, desde el qual pasó a Málaga, haviendo hecho todos estos viages sola con traje de hombre: y ultimamente /7v/ que en dicho puerto de Málaga, se embarcó como lleba dicho hará como unos nueve años, con destino al puerto de Montevideo al que se dirigía la embarcación, no haviéndose detenido en este último puerto sino tres días, después de los quales pasó sin licencia en una lancha de aquel río a la capital de Buenos Ayres.

En la que solicitó a don Juan Antonio Pintos comerciante de Cádiz y conocido de su padre, y no haviendolo encontrado, se presentó al Yllustrísimo Señor Aramor obispo de aquella ciudad diciéndole que se hallaba destituido de aucilios por no haver encontrado al referido don Juan Antonio Pintos de quien esperaba le auciliase, con cuyo motibo imploró su amparo diciéndole era hijo de Madrid, y de resultas de la comversación que tubo con este motivo con dicho Señor Yllustrísimo se hizo memoria de un primo de la declarante religioso carmelita descalzo en Madrid llamado Fray Julián de San Gerónimo, conocido de dicho Señor Obispo, quien por último la dijo que tenía que comer, y quarto en su palacio, como así sucedió haviendo permanecido en la casa obispal como cosa de tres años, hasta el fallecimiento del mismo Señor Obispo, haviéndose hecho /8r/ a conoser en este intermedio tiempo, y posteriormente con el nombre de Antonio Yta.

Que por último se determinó salir solo, y sin pasaporte para Potosí, y después de la detención casual de unos quatro meses, ocacionada de una rotura de una pierna, ciguió su viaje con el destino ya expresado, y se encontró en las immediaciones de Jujuy con un porteño apellidado Pazos, y un criado suyo en compania de los quales llegó a Potosí aora seis años; y presentándose al Señor Governador de aquella Villa en uso de las recomendaciones que traía de Buenos Ayres le mantubo en su casa como cosa de dos años, al cabo de los quales salió de ella, con ocación de tratar boda con doña Martina Vilvao y Balberde que se hallaba a la sasón en Potosí.

Y con licenzia de dicho Señor Governador por ser ultramarino, trató de matrimonio con dicha Señora, haviendose corrido las amonestaciones en la Yglesia matriz de aquella Villa y celebrado desposorio el religioso de San Francisco Fray Ángel de tal, procurador en el día del convento de la ciudad de Tarija, después de haver concedido lizencia el cura de la Yglesia Matriz doctor Guzmán. Después de este tiempo permaneció dos años en dicha villa en concepto de casados trabajando en lo que /8v/ se le proporcionó.

Y haviendo venido a esta ciudad a solicitar algún destino se le proporcionó pasar a la Provincia de Moxos con cargo de Administrador del pueblo nombrado la Madalena donde se mantubo un año en la capital exercitándose en las ordenes del Señor Governador Zamora, y el otro en el expresado pueblo de la Magdalena donde estubo de Administrador, al cabo de los quales, se encaminó a esta corte en solicitud de su sueldo, cuyo expediente se halla en la Real Audiencia.

Finalmente en contestación de la pregunta a que responde añade: Que la causa que ha motibado su manejo en ocultar, y disfrazar su sexo de muger ha sido obedecer la orden de Su Santidad comunicada por el Penitenciario como tiene dicho, á resultas de las diligencias que practicó en Roma para quietud de su conciencia, y responde.

Preguntada si antes de comunicarle el Penitenciario en Roma la orden que expresa de Su Santidad precedió algún reconocimiento /9r/ de su sexo enterada de ello dijo:

Que no precedió diligencia alguna de esta clase y responde.

Con lo qual haviendose tenido por comveniente á vista de las dificultades que ofreze el contesto de su antecedente declaración inquirir con más puntualidad la identidad de su perzona, fue preguntada por el nombre de sus Padres, y su vezindario, y dijo:

Que su Padre se llamaba don Joséf Yta, y su Madre doña Felipa Ybáñez naturales, y vezinos de la Villa de Colmenar de Oreja, que vivian a la sason quando se embarcó la declarante, y que hoy en día ignora por falta de noticias si viben o mueren.

Con lo que ordenó Su Excelencia se suspendiese por aora esta diligencia que se continuara si se halle por combeniente, mandando que entre tanto permanezca en custodia con la desencia propia de su sexo, y haviendosele leido a la confesante su Tenor expuso:

Está vien escrita, y solo añadía que con doña Martina Bilbao, antes se haver celebrado el que llama matrimonio, mantubo ilícita amistad por el tiempo de un año /9v/ en la espresada Villa de Potosí.

Y lo firmó rúbricandolo Su Excelencia de que doy fe. [Scribe's notes on cross outs and between-the-lines additions follow:] Entre renglones = es = viene = hermana = o de los capellanes que las dirijian = v.e = testado = trae origen = padre = padres = y = sus = no v.e. [firma] María Leocadia Yta. [rúbrica y firma:] Calixto de Valda

[A.8 10, 11, y 13 de octubre, 1803: Transmisión de documentos al Provisor y Vicario General del Arzobispado, pidiendo de él información sobre cualquier juicio de nulidad allí.]

[A.9 4 de octubre, 1803: Petición a la Iglesia de Martina Vilvado y Balverde por nulidad del matrimonio.]

/11r/ [margen:] Petición

Señor Provisor y Vicario General. Doña Martina Bilbao, y Balverde, natural de la ciudad de Cochavamba en la mejor forma que há lugar en derecho, y por medio de esta representación ante Vuestra Señoria, paresco y digo. Que hacen más de quatro años, que en la Villa de Potosí, contrajé matrimonio, con don Antonio de Yta, natural de los Reynos de España, con el designio de evitar los peligros del Mundo, y de servir mejor a Dios. Desde dicho tiempo a esta parte, me he contraido con toda voluntad, y esmero a darle gusto al expresado, poniendo en su mano mi corta desencia, y toda mi boluntad, para que de ello disponga a su arvitrio; y nada desto ha sido suficiente, para que se verifique la consumación del Matrimonio, pues hasta el día, sin embargo de mis cariños e incinuaciones ha sido imposible conseguir el fin primario, que tiene el contrato matrimonial, por haverme dicho a varias incinuaciones, que tiene echo voto solemne de castidad, y que si acaso se casó conmigo, fue solo con el objeto de mi personal servicio. Conociendo por una parte la renuencia de una obligación tan presisa, y por otra advirtiendo que él, jamás se ha dejado tocar al cuerpo, aun estando enfermo, que en el uso de hacer aguas, es igual al que acostumbran las mugeres, y que al mismo tiempo acostumbra sentarse como estas, a demás de tener las tetas vien cresidas, y que ultimamente, por el mismo, que lo acompaño, se me han expresado las circunstancias referidas, como también de echar sangre al modo que las mugeres. Para saver y aclarar, si mi matrimonio es legitimo, y si puedo obligarlo a la satisfacción del devito, ocurro a la zelosa justificación de Vuestra Señoria; para /11v/ que vajo de las precauciones nesesarias se sirva mandar, que por la persona, o inteligente, que fuere de su agrado, se le reconosca, si efectivamente es hombre, o si tiene algún vicio, o defecto que se impida el uso matrimonial, sin que él llegue a translucir cosa alguna de estas, pues estoy reselosa de que si llega a su noticia, podrá profugar, y quedar yo en un estado lastimoso, sin saver si efectivamente soy casada, o no, o al menos desamparada de quien justamente deve sostenerme. Por tanto. A Vuestra Señoria pido y suplico, que en caso de salir ciertos los indicios incinuados, se cirva declarar, por nulo e insubsistente el matrimonio expresado, y quando no fuesen, obligarlo a que se una conmigo, condecendiendo en lo que es justo pues si hago este recurso, es estimulada de su inacción, y por salvar mejor mi conciencia que será justicia, juro no proceder de malicia y para ello etc. Martina Vilvado.

[margen: Auto] Plata y octubre quatro de mil ochocientos tres. Autos y vistos: Respecto a que el demandado en esta representación don Antonio de Yta, es de la jurisdicción real: Diríjase oficio, con testimonio de la representación, y esta providencia al Excelentísimo Señor Presidente de esta Real Audiencia, Governador Yntendente, para que en obsequio de la justicia, y respeto al autor de los Sacramentos, se sirva mandar de comparecer al expresado Yta, haga que por dos facultativos se reconosca el sexso que tiene, o si padese algún vicio notable que anule el valor del Sacramento del Matrimonio, a fin de que con inspección de lo que resultare se tomen en esta curia las pro/12r/videncias correspondientes—doctor Parra—Antemi Manuel Esteban Montero Notario Público.

Concuerda este traslado, con el escrito, y auto original de su contesto de donde se sacó de que doy fe. [firma y rúbrica:] Manuel Esteban Montero, Notario Público.

[A.10 17 de octubre, 1803: Carta de Parra (Provisor del Arzobispado) a García de Pizarro (Presidente de la Audiencia), pidiendo que el último hace examinación de Yta, para ver si es "hermafrorita (*sic*) y en quien prevalese /13v/ el sexo baronil."]

[A.11 Sin fecha (18 de octubre, 1803?): Pedido para mejoras en el trato de Yta en la cárcel del Procurador de Pobres.]

/15r/ Excelentísimo Señor Presidente.
Pide pronta providencia.
José Manuel Malavia, Procurador de pobres en lo criminal de esta Real Audiencia a nombre de don Antonio Yta, preso en esta Real Cárcel de Corte, según sea más conforme a derecho ante Vuestra Excelencia parezco, y digo: . . .
. . . y omitiendo también manifestar hasta el lance más oportuno la inpertinencia del recurso de dicha doña Martina, con que vino a molestar la superior atención de Vuestra Excelencia sin el correspondiente discernimiento del caso, de la causa, ni de sus circunstancias, y consequencias, y los gravísimos daños, y vegámenes, que le ha ocacionado, me contraigo solamente a representar a Vuestra Excelencia, que la prición en /15v/ que se halla el indicado don Antonio, es demaciado dura, penosa, y llena de aflicción, que lo tienen a punto de la mayor desesperación.
. . .
Ello es Señor Excelentísmo, que hasta la actualidad, según entiendo, no aparece contra mi representado otro delito, que él de haberse descubierto, a petición de su consorte doña Martina, y a virtud de los reconocimientos mandados hacer por Vuestra Excelencia, que tiene todas las qualidades, y sexo mugeril, quando su manejo, su trage, su reputación, y sus ascerciones eran contrarias; y de qualesquier modo que sea no se encuentran en nuestros cuerpos Diplomaticos unas disposiciones que demuestren los quilates de este delito para reputarlo en la prisión, que sufre por uno, de los más enormes, y de más alto grado. . . . /16r/ . . . Juro lo necessario en derecho etc.
[firmas y rúbricas] doctor Esteban Agustín Gascón. José Manuel Malavia.

[A.12 19 de octubre, 1803: Orden para mejoramiento de las condiciones carceleras de María Leocadia Yta, y que "custodiésela con la decencia propria de su sexo"; respuesta del Alcaide del cárcel; ordenes específicas para tal mejoramiento.]

[A.13 19 y 26 de octubre, 1803 (*sic*): Carta del Provisor Parra del Arzobispado al Presidente de la Audiencia.]

[A.14 20 de julio, 1804: Pedido del defensor de Yta, José Manuel Malavia, para más piedad humano en el trato "de este miserable" don Antonio Yta.]

[A.15 1 de agosto, 1804: Reportaje sobre una inspección a la cárcel, y evidencia que doña María Leocadia Yta ha intentado escapar haciendo aujero en la pared.]

[A.16 3 de agosto, 1804: Recusación del Asesor General Mariano Taborga, por haver tomado la denuncia original antes de su nombramiento formal como Asesor; en su lugar nombra a Doctor Don Francisco de Paula Moscoso.]

Excelentísimo Señor Presidente:
El Asesor General de este Govierno hase presente á Vuestra Excelencia haviendo reconosido los presentes Autos, encuentra en ellos, que antes de obtener el nombramiento de Azesor, hiso el escrito que está por cabesa, á fabor de la Denunciante, y por lo tanto se halla legalmente inpedido de seguir prestando sus dictámenes en este ásumpto, para no incurrir en un grave prevaricato. En esta atención suplica a Vuestra Excelencia que escusado se sirva nombrar otro Asesor, con la brevedad que demanda la increible retardasión de esta causa, y la pribilegiada recomendasión á que por las leyes, y la humanidad es aceedora [sic] una muger encarselada tanta tiempo. Plata y Agosto 3 de 1804. [firma y rúbrica:] doctor Mariano Taborga.
/21r/ Plata y Agosto 4 de 1804.
Vista la escusa antecedente de su asesor general interino, nombrase en su lugar al doctor don Francisco de Paula Moscoso, a quien se pasarán los presentes autos. [firma y rúbrica:] García Pizarro.
Proveyó y firmo el Decreto de suso el Excelentísimo Señor don Ramón García Pizarro caballero del Orden de Calatrava Teniente General de los Reales Exércitos Presidente de esta Real Audiencia de Charcas Capitán General Governador Yntendente de esta Provincia de la Plata, en el día mes y año de su fecha [rayado = con dictamen de su asesor general interino de que doy] fe. [firma y rúbrica:] Vicente José Marin, escribano de S. M. Público de real hasienda y yntendencia.
En La Plata en dicho día mes y año; Yo el escribano hise saver el nombramiento anterior al /21v/ procurador José Manuel Malavia, en su persona á nombre de su parte, doy fe. [firma y rúbrica:] Marin.

[A.17 22 de agosto, 1804: Orden a doña Martina Vilvado a poner en forma correcta su acusación contra Yta dentro de tres dias.]

[A.18 22, 27, 30 de agosto, y 6 y 7 de septiembre, 1804: Pedido de José Pimentel, abogado de don Antonio Yta, pidiendo evaluación médica del estado de su salud, retiro de la carlanca; la evaluación médica de Salas, reconociendo echimosis de los pies de don Antonio Yta, etc; orden a cumplir los requisitos del médico.]

[A.19 24 septiembre, 3, 5, 16, y 18 de octubre, 1804: Alcaide del cárcel escribe sobre el escape de Yta, con la ayuda del indio pongo; y items relacionados.]

/25r/ Muy Poderoso Señor: [margen: Sirbase]
Don Feliz Cardozo, Alcaide de esta Real Carzel de Corte ante el rexto [sic] y justificado selo de Vuestra Alteza paresco, y digo, que el biernes día 21 de este mes que rije, á profugado don Antonio Yta, a las nuebe y media ó dies de la noche, poco más o menos, del que se ynfiere salió con llabe falsa o por la bentanilla del calabozo, donde estaba, y con la ayuda del Yndio pongo, se quitó los Grillos, y pasó a la vivienda don estaba el dicho pongo, y arancaron una tabla del piso, y por un corto laso: Se descolgaron los dos, a la parte de la entrereja siendo así que ha este lo puso, como de sentinela, para que este al cuidado de lo que pueda, ha, caheren, y dar aviso, por hallarme ya mui sospechoso, de suerte que por día y noche yba aberlo, obserbando por todas

partes, si de noche me estaba con él desde las seis asta las siete y media o las ocho, dejando las tres puertas seradas; me hallaba con este cuidado por la primera fuga que yba a haser por un orado, que yso en la pared, que coresponde a la carzel caida de las Mujeres, lo que a mi costa, lo remedie, de cuio suseso di cuenta berbal al Excelentísimo Señor Presidente y de la poca o ninga [*sic*] seguridad que tenía esta carzel para, reos de Estado;

Siendo los ladrones de caza, no es posible precaberse de ellos. Es quanto puedo ynformar, a la sabia conprejención de Vuestra Altesa. En cumplimiento de mi obligasión, por tanto, etc. A Vuesa Altesa pido y suplico probéa y mande, lo que conseptuare ser de su agrado, y Justisia, y juro a Dios Nuestro Señor no proseder de malisia. Etc. [firma y rúbrica:] Feliz Cardozo.

[A.20 18, 30, y 31 de octubre, 1804: Intentos a recuperar del abogado de doña Martina Vilvado y Balverde los originales del expediente.]

[A.21 7 de agosto, 1804: Testimonio de la madre de Yta, enviado desde Madrid al abogado Doctor don Agustín Gascón.]

/28r/ Madrid siete de agosto de mil ochocientos quatro
Muy Señor mio y de todo mi mayor respeto:
Por noticias que he recivido de esa he sido sabedora de los beneficios que Vuesamerced ha dispensado a ése mi hijo, que así lo graduo por las circunstancias ocurridas que referiré a Vuesamerced, en breve compendio es muy cierto que á la edad de nueve años pasó a casa de una señora poderosa del Pueblo de su nacimiento, en cuya compañía permaneció hasta los diez y siete años en que dicha señora la proporcionó el tomar el Avito en convento de Franciscas donde no profesó, á poco tiempo, pasó a otros tres conventos que son en los Pueblos de Huete, Colmenar de Oreja, Santa Juana cinco leguas de esta Corte, y el último en Segovia, en ninguno de los quales profesó como consta de los certificados de las Prioras, que remito a Vuesamerced para que haga constar, que no tiene delito de Apostacía como tengo entendido se le aplica en su causa. Después de no ser admitida en nin/28v/guno de los referidos conventos, resolvió pasar á Roma donde permaneció algunos meses, y á su buelta tomó el trage de hombre que se mando por la Santa Sede, y que lo usase toda su vida. A su embarque para España fue descubierta en Barcelona por los marineros que al registrar su equipage hallaron ropas de muger por lo que el último obispo, le tubo en reclución, y a su fallecimiento le dieron livertad:

Pasó á Cádiz donde estubo quatro meses, y por un incidente ocurrido (que referire) [marg: ojo] se embarcó en Málaga para Montivedeo [*sic*] de donde paso a Buenos Ayres a casa del Señor obispo Asamor donde supe no había dado que decir respecto a su conducta. No extrañe Vuesa Merced que una Madre tome interés en un asunto en que es nesesario manifestar lo ocurrido.

Después que no fue admitida en ninguno de los conventos en la profeción permaneció en esta en compañía de su hermana pocos meses, y que con pretexto de que trabajava en costura en casa de doña Rita Benedicto vecina de esta corte, supimos por queja de esta hallarse embarazada [marg: ojo] de este lo que extrañamos mi difunto marido su padre. Esta queja nos dió la expresada Rita quando hizo su fuga a Roma, sin consentimiento nuestro y de que ignorábamos todo. La citada Rita falle/29r/ció en el parto, y también la criatura, como se nos comunicó por sus parientes. En este intermedio permaneció en Roma, y a su venida a Barcelona nos escribió de esta ciudad, comunicándonos el trage en que se vestía de hombre por orden de Su Santidad, y desde Barcelona pasó a Cádiz donde andubo enredado con doña Vicenta Arias de Reyna, quien también le formó querella de casamiento manifestando la había hecho embarazada de que le exigía por obligación, y en seguida desapareció para Málaga donde se embarcó para esas regiones, y después que escribió desde Buenos Ayres de la casa del Ylustrísimo Señor Azamor, he ignorado su paradero hasta el hecho orurrido que se ha avisado a sus hermanos desde esa ciudad manifestando que Vuesamerced mira con interés a ése desgraciado mi hijo, y que con verdadero amor de madre me intereso a fin de que tenga la bondad de poner los medios imaginables para que se le atienda por ese Señor Presidente en su causa, y se le mire en ella con vivo interés, como también él que se le atienda en poseción de su destino respecto a su buen desempeño.

En quanto a los informes que en esta se me dieron pormenor de las referidas, Rita Benedicto, y la Vicenta Arias eran que en su construcción, tenía qualidades de muger pero en el acto se manifiesta miembro viril con todas las funciones completas de hombre: Su ca/29v/ racter siempre fué aún desde la niñes reboltoso, y en edad mayor sumamente inclinado al sexo femenino de que resultaron [tachada = de que resultaron] darnos muchos pesares á sus Padres. Este le reprehendió muchísimo en su trato con la Rita Benedicto, y al mismo tiempo con otra en la calle de los Remedios, de esta que era una valenciana con quien su cuñado la cogió en el mismo, y en el trage de hombre.

Todo lo qual comunico á Vuesamerced para su govierno en medio que me és doloroso manifestar las flaquezas cometidas por ese hijo que nos há causado bastantes desazones: Pero en medio de todas estas circunstancias suplico á Vuesamerced de todo corazón interponga todos los buenos oficios con ese Señor Yntendente en la causa que pende de él, esperando de la bondad de Vuesamerced atenderá la solicitud de una Madre que será siempre su más atenta y segura servidora. Que sus manos beza. Felipa Ybáñez. Señor doctor don Agustín Gascón.

[A.22 29 de julio, 3, 5, y 7 de agosto de 1804: Certificaciones de los conventos, dirigidas al abogado Gascón, en los cuales Yta entró y salió sin profesar.]

[A.23 7 de mayor, 10 de junio, 1805: Ordena hacer copia certificada del expediente completo para la Audiencia, y enviar originales al Provisor y Vicario General.]

[A.24 28 de noviembre, 1804(?): El abogado de Yta, Gascón, explica que sólo ahora ha recibido el testimonio de la madre de Yta y las certificaciónes; considera lo que añaden al caso.]

El doctor don Esteban Agustín Gascón Abogado de esta Real Audiencia en la más bastante forma de derrecho ante Vuesa Excelencia paresco, y Digo: . . .

En este estado, y haviendo hecho fuga de la prición que sufría él referido don Antonio Yta, quando en /34v/ el respetable Juzgado de Vuestra Excelencia se le reputava tal vez como delinquente, y apóstata de alguno de los monasterios religiosos, en que confesó haver estado; y quando en la Curia Eclesiastica se concideraba también como punto incontextable, y fuera de toda disputa él de la nulidad del Matrimonio, ha llegado a mis manos por el correo Marítimo que acaba de recibirse como lo juro por Dios Nuestro Señor, y cita señal de [una cruz], la adjunta carta fecha en Madrid a 7 de agosto del corriente año de doña Felipa Ybáñez, Madre del referido Yta, con las tres certificaciones, y otra carta más de don Eugenio Sánchez, que la acompañan.

De cuyo contexto resulta, que esta desventurada persona nó faltó á la verdad, como se creía, en sus exposiciones; que nó há cometido delito alguno público que lo hiciese digno de prición, de castigos, ó de otras demostraciones injuriosas, y Mortificantes, como las que ha sufrido; que en ella no hay otra cosa digna [entre renglones: de la] atención de esta Magistratura, sinó sus miserias, y los defectos con que la naturaleza quizo burlarse de él; y ultimamente que la causa de nulidad de matrimonio és de mucha más grave concideración, y exige una desición más circunspecta, y maduramente pensada, que lo que aparecia al principio por virtud de los primeros reconocimientos; . . .

/33r/ A Vuestra Excelencia pido y suplico se sirva proveer y determinar como llevo expuesto por ser de Justicia. Juro lo necessario en derecho etc. [firma y rúbrica] Don Esteban Agustín Gascón.

[A.25 28 de noviembre, y 18 y 19 de diciembre, 1804: Ordena añadir la carta del abogado de Yta, testimonio de la madre de Yta, y certificaciones de conventos, al expediente, y producirlo para la próxima audiencia; respuesta del escribano que no lo tiene desde 31 de agosto de 1803; orden a recuperarlo urgentamente.]

[A.26 8, 16, 18, 24 de enero, 1805: Demanda a los carceleros para saber si Yta ha reaparecido o no; respuestas negativas.]

[A.27 13, 15, 28 de febrero, 14 de marzo, 4, 5, y 6 de mayo, 1805: Fiscal pide el expediente original para enviar al Provisor y Vicario General del Arzobispado, guardando una copia certificada para la Audiencia; mandado hacer; Provisor pide todos los originales; notario público certifica la copia (el documento presente).]

[fin del documento]

APPENDIX B: AUXILIARY DOCUMENTS

Contents

An asterisk (*) indicates that the item can be accessed at the Passing to América (PTA) website, https://wp.nyu.edu/passingtoamerica/. A dagger (†) indicates that the English translation appears in this appendix or in the main text; the Spanish original is available on the website.

B.1 A Plebeian Joséf de Yta in the Catastro de la Ensenada of Colmenar de Oreja, 1751
Source: "Spain, Catastro of Ensenada" (n.d.), Toledo, Oreja, H-193, AHN, image 2321. For the text, see the PTA website.

B.2 Yta's Parents' Marriage Certificate, 1762
Source: "Matrimonios," 1762, fol. 342r, APCO; my translation. For the Spanish original, see the PTA website.

English translation
In the parish church of Santa María del Sagrario of this Villa de Colmenar de Oreja, on the twenty-sixth of September in the year 1762, having previously [carried out] the three cautions required by the Holy Council of Trent and the Sinodal Constitutions of this archbishopric, which were given on twelfth, nineteenth, and twenty-first of the said month and year, Sundays and holy days, and having resulted no canonical impediment, I Don Juan Antonio Delgado, with the license of the lord priest of the said church, joined *infazie ecclesie* [in the presence of the congregation] through words in presence, which make true matrimony, Joseph de Yta, widower of Cathalina Hernandez, native of this villa, with Phelipa Ybáñez, daughter of Dionisio Ybáñez and of María de Lara, natives of Pozuelo de la Soga. And, after this, having asked them and being given their mutual consent, I gave them during mass the nuptial benedictions according to the rite and form of the church. Alphonso Cuarista Cassero and Pedro Antonio Garzia were witnesses. And we signed [signatures and rubrics of Don Juan Antonio Delgado and Francisco Xavier Garraçon y Robles].

B.3 Joséf de Yta, Son-in-Law of Ybáñez, Buys His Childhood Home
Source: Manuel José Ayuso, "Venta de una casa, Pedro Pablo Laguna, y consortes, a favor de Joseph de Yta el Maior: En 29 de diciembre de 1770," Protocolos de Colmenar de Oreja, vol. 29604, AHPCM, fols. 319r–332r. For the text, see the PTA website.

B.4 Extracts from the Rule and Constitution of the Agustínas Recoletas
Source: Agustinas Recoletas (1648); my translation. For the text, see the PTA website.

B.5 Marriage Certificate of Don Antonio Yta and Doña Martina Vilvado y Balverde
Source: "Libro de matrimonios de españolas y mestizos," 1796–1806, Iglesia Matriz de Potosí, AODP, fol. 88v. My transcription and translation; the English translation appears in chapter 3 of this volume.

Spanish original
[Margin: Don Antonio Yta con Doña María Bilbao (*sic*)]
En Potosí en el año del señor de mil setessientos noventa y nuebe a treinta del mes de Marzo: Haviendo leido las tres proclamas o moniciones [*sic*] en tres dias festivos continuos a tiempo de la misa parroquial y no haviendo resultado impedimento alguno yo Don Juaquin Cevallos Theniente de los señores Curas Rectores de esta Santa Yglecia Matris, case y uni solemnemente en matrimonio por palabras de presente haviendo ellos antes espresado su mutuo consentimiento a Don Antonio Yta natural de la Corte de Madrid hijo legitimo de Don Jose Yta y de Doña Felipa Ybañes vesinos de la Corte, con Doña Martina Bilbado hija legitima de Pedro Bilbado y de Doña Justa Balberde hasistieron al matrimonio Juan Manuel Solares Don Baltasar Rodrigues Don Pedro Antonio Domingues fueron Padrinos Don Juan Soto y Doña Rufina Torquemada y para que coste [*sic*] lo firme. [Firma y rúbrica] Juaquin Cevallos.

B.6 Extracts from *Libro de moda en la feria*
Extracts from *Libro de moda en la feria* (1795), attributed to Juan Fernández de Rojas, an Agustinian cleric born in Colmenar de Oreja in 1750 [d. Convento de San Felipe el Real, Salamanca, 1819]. This work by the prolific poet, satirist, and regular newspaper contributor is written as a reply to a letter to the newspaper *Diario de Madrid* by Don Preciso, pen name of Juan Antonio de Iza Zamácola, possibly also collaborator with Fernández de Rojas in the *Libro de moda*. Under the pen name Alejandro Moya, Fernández de Rojas was also author of another satirical tract targeting the aristocratic uptake of fashions deemed *barriobajera* [neighborhoods of working-class plebeians or rustics], focusing on the use of castanets by *majos* and *majas* (1792). The latter, renaming Madrid as Crotalópolis [City of Rattlesnakes], was itself followed by several books written as replies under different pen names. It parodied the encyclopedists and Enlightenment philosophers, through characters named Locke, Voltaire, and so on, who are to be found wandering the streets of Madrid, which, because of the elite uptake of folk customs, is filled with viperous castanet players. An early folklorist and "nationalist," the basque de Iza Zamácola also published a work on *contradanza* (country dance or square dance) in this satirical vein (1796), as well as works on the history and grammar of the Basque language and a collection of regional folk music that is the earliest collection of flamenco (1805). *Libro de moda* was republished in several editions and spurred a voluminous literature, including works for the stage and many popular songs (Amann 2015; Fillin-Yeh 2001; Haidt 1998, 1999). Just prior to a chapter on the "natural history" of the currutaco, the author of this tongue-in-cheek little book on the fad treats its ancient history down to the present day. The English translation appears in chapter 4 of this volume.

Spanish original

Estamos ya en la historia del dia. Digamos de los Currutacos actuales. En ninguna época ha habido tantos. La Currutaquería jamás ha estado tan extendida. Las luces se propagan por toda la faz de nuestro globo terraqueo. Su fuerza, su viveza parece aumentarse en razon de su extension. Jamás se ha sabido tanto. Jamás la ciencia ha sido tan universal. Se derrama por todas las clases, por todos /17/ los Pueblos. Se propaga succesivamente hasta las regiones mas remotas.

¡O siglo ilustrado! Hasta ahora, aun en los tiempos mas felices, la ciencia existia en un solo pueblo, la luz iluminaba un solo orizonte. Sus rayos no reflexaban sobre los demás. Yacian todas las naciones en profundas tinieblas.

Actualmente el globo todo forma una sola nacion, un solo pueblo, una sola familia. Las luces tienen su centro ó foco, se sabe qual es, desde allí se extienden por toda la orbita del mundo sabio, y reflexan baxo diferentes direcciones sobre los rincones mas escondidos y remotos. Caen átomos de luz, sobre los incultos Groelandos, y los elados Siberitas.

Comparemos pues la Currutaquería á una máquina de resortes. Todo está enlazado. La rueda mas remota se comunica libremente con la del centro. Giran todas en una misma direccion. El movimiento es igual. Un golpe dado en una extremidad de la /18/ máquina resuena en la otra. Antiguamente habia mas diferencia entre un habitante de Bizancio y un Ateniense, que ahora entre un Inglés y un Yroqués, porque al cabo las dos Naciones se comunican y conocen mas. Un habitante de la antigue Scandinavia viste como un Parisien, un Lapon piensa y habla como nosotros; en la extremidad del Asia se vive como en el centro de la Europa. Viajad, y quasi no advertireis diferencia de costumbres.

Hay pues actualmente Currutacos en todo el mundo, y en el fondo nada se diferencian. En la calle del Carmen se fabrican dos Zorongos Gemelos. El uno vuela á la extremidad del Asia, el otro va al quarto principal de enfrente.

Dos muñecas[1] salen de las delicadas manos de una Modista de la ca/19/lle de la Montera, la una viaja á un rincon de Galicia; ¡quién lo diría! la otra atraviesa el inmenso Océano, y descansa en la Corte de los antiguos Yncas. Se pone una contradanza en la calle de Fuencarral, en la plazuela del Ángel, en mil partes; pues en esta Villa favorita las diversiones *pululan*, se multiplican infinito. Esta dichosa contradanza se repite un dia de campo en las riberas del caudaloso río de las Amazonas. Un Currutaco tiene una conversacion en la puerta del Sol; está al unisono con otra que se tiene en los paseos de la opulenta México. Las mismas frases, las mismas opiniones. Se citan los mismos libros. /20/

Libro III. *Descripcion filosófica y fisica del ente Currutaco. ¿Es hombre? Señales de separacion ó diferencia entre los dos seres. Analisis de la historia natural del Currutaco.*

¡Aqui, aqui os quiero estupidos y aridos nomencladores de historia natural! Ved el capitulo, el libro, todo es lo mismo, que os prometí, y en el qual os ofrecí enseñaros lo que necesitais saber.

No, no nos dexemos arrastrar por unos ligeros y superficiales signos de semejanza, las mas veces equívocos é inciertos. Profundicemos, analicemos, escudriñemos en los mas secretos resortes. Comparemos, experimentemos, observemos con escrupulosa exáctitud. Deduzcamos consequencias ciertas, establezcamos principios /21/ innegables. Asi sabremos algo.

B.7 The Taborga Letter to a Friend in Buenos Aires

Source: Beruti (1946). Original source of document: Archivo del Doctor Dardo Rocha, now in La Plata, Argentina. Page numbers from the publication are given between backslashes, folio numbers from the original notebook in square brackets. The English translation appears in the introduction to this volume.

---

1. Modelos de modas, estatuas pequeñas que representan al vivo los trages reynantes.

Spanish original from printed source

[fol. 188] Noticio a Vmd el caso mas estraño q.e hà sucedido desde q.e hay mundo, y és el haverse Casado dos mugeres aòra quatro años y meses, que por maior selo noticio p.a q.e se admire, y divierta, y ès como sesigue [*sic*].

Oct.e 15 de 1803:

El 7. del que sigue seme presentó una muger q.e acabava de llegar en compañia del Correo de Cochabamba, llamada d.a Martina Bilvao y Balverde, presentandome un escrito contra su marido d.n Ant.o Ita, exponiendo que és natural delos Reinos de España, y q.e hace que esta Casada con èl mas de quatro años, y que casó en esa Villa con lisencia de V. por ser ultramarino; y por no haver vsado del fin del matrimonio, pretestando voto de castidad, y otros disparates, y haverle observado q.e orinaba siempre en basenica, siempre con casoncillos, mestruacion, y otras observaciones , como abultam.to de pechos. &.a lo delatava, por el continuo disfras de hom.e y portodo lo demas.

Hice buscar al demandado: puesto en mi presencia observè un hom.e pequeñuelo, regordete, como de 40 años; y tomada su confn resulto llamarse Da María Leocadia de Ita, natural del Colmenar de Oreja, 7. leguas de Madrid, que vino sin ninguna lisencia à este Reino; que se embarcó en Málaga: que à estado quando tenia 14. años en un Comvento de Monjas; y por que enamorava àlas otras monjas, la sacaron de alli; se fuè à Confesar, y el Padre la dijo, que era menester que fuera à Roma: [/fol. 188vta./] que dejo escrito ásus Padres, y con su trage natural hizo los viages siguienetes. De Madrid à /p.100/ Valencia; de esta à Barcelona; que en este Puerto se embarcó en un Correo p.a Genova, en compañia deunas [*sic*] operantas Italiana [*sic*] de esta Ciudad: siguió su viaje con las mismas hasta Civita Vequia, y siguiendo conlas [*sic*] Italianas h.ta Roma por tierra donde confesó, y el Penitenciario que era un fraile Fran.co Español, la dijo, que bolviera al 3.o dia: lo q.e ejecuto, y recivio la absolucion, y penitencia de subir 30 veses la escala de Jerusalem; que tomara una disciplina todos los viernes deun año; q.e no oyese misa en comv.to de mugeres, y q.e se pusiera trage de hom.e; y replicandole la penitente, que como havia de ir con aquel trage asu tierra: que era menester q.e hiciese lo q.e le mandaba el S.to Padre mas q.e no bolviera àsu tierra. Con este motivo se vistió de hom.e estuvo porcion de tpo* [*sic*] en Roma: se bolvió á Civitabequia, à Genova, y se embarcó p.a Barcelona, y de alli p.a Málaga, y en aquel Puerto p.a Montevid.o Que estubo en Buenos Ayres 2 ó 3, [*sic*] años en casa del S.or Azamor obispo q.e era de dicha ciud.d hasta q.e murio, y entonces determino venirse al Perú: Que mas aca del Lujan tubo la aberia de quebrarse una pierna, q.e estubo detenido quatro meses. Vltimam.te llegò a Potosí, donde estubo una porcion de tiempo en Casa del S.or Sanz: que alli trato de amores, y estubo amancebado conla tal d.a Martina Bilvao: que despues se caso: que despues vivió con ella en acomodo, que sele facilitó en Mojos donde fueron [/fol. 189/] ambas; y haviendo buelto la Bilvao estubo en su pais de Cochabamba; y habra 3. ó 4. meses, que se vino à qui [*sic*] la d.a M.a Leocadia à litigar los sueldos que tenia vencidos dela Admin.on que havia servido: En todo este tiempo, confiesa la una y la otra el buen trato, que le daba sin faltarle àla desencia en lo posible; y q.e le era molesta con tantos celos ([con ella]) que le daba. A mi presencia se hizo el recono-[p. 101] cim.to de la tal María Leocadia, por decir ella, que tenia de hom.e ante el ESS.no El medico titutal [*sic*], y el Cirujano: p.o todo ès falcedad, pues és una muger como todas, y si que demuestra ser mui osada, sin tener otra señal de varon: Lo cierto és que toda la relac.n desu declaracion es un ato de mentiras: es muger de muchas trastiendas, malisima de caveza, y aborrese su trage, p.r estar echa àla vida bribona. La tengo sola en un Calavoso: veremos lo que bà dando la cosa de si.

Se continuara.

B.8 Extract from Lawsuit over Clothing, 1803–4

Source: "Expediente seguido por Antonio Yta, preso en la cárcel de La Plata por ocultación y simulación de sexo, contra su mujer Martina Bilvao Valverde por apropiación indebida de sus efectos de ropa; La Plata, noviembre 5, 1803," EC.179.1804, ABNB; my transcription and translation. For the Spanish original, see the PTA website.

English translation
/1r/ List of the clothing that I have and that is in my house in Cochabamba and remained in the power of my wife.
[Margin: Legajo 35, n. 88]
Firstly, a cape of chestnut-colored cloth, with its ribbons of silk;
Two new blue capes [*sortú*: a kind of cape (Leira Sánchez, 1991, 18)]
Three pairs of breeches, one blue and one striped, and another, striped, of *genero*, all new;
One new blue jacket;
Seven vests, three of black silk, two plain and one embroidered with silk;
One white satin underjacket [*chupezi*, a small or short *chupa*, a jacket worn under other clothing (Souza Congosto 2007, 452)] embroidered with silver, one striped, another of white cloth, another of black cloth, which makes seven;
Two new Brittany shirts with Dutch fronts;
One pair of chestnut-colored silk stockings, two pairs of cotton stockings;
/1v/ One pair of buckles of smooth silver;
A hat with peaks on its top;
A necktie;
A pair of new whole boots.
All of this is the truth, and I swear to God Our Lord and this sign of the cross + [a cross]; if she denies this, ask Don Francisco Ventora Valiente and the tailor who lives on Santo Domingo Street in front of the carpentry shop, also a large hand cloth. [Signature and rubric:] Antonio Yta.
/2r/ [margin: n. 2]. List of everything that my wife has, both here and what there is in Cochabamba, since it has cost me money.
First of all a large new bedstead;
A marriage-size [double] mattress;
Four sheets;
Two large blankets;
A bedspread of brocaded silk;
Five pillows with their pillowcases;
A canopy that covers the bed with forty-five varas of new linen;
Two *camisas*, one of silk cloth with tiers and another of *groditud* [? *gro* = cloth of heavy silk];
Three shawls for going to mass, one white, of muslin, another black with points, with its velvet ribbon like those that are used now, another of black silk with wide points all around;
Three white *polleras* [wide-pleated skirts], one of fine cotton, another of striped fine fustian, another of embroidered muslin with its trimming;
One whole currutaco [currutaco: a dandy, or a faddish outfit that distinguished a dandy at this time] of fine new *zaraza* [printed cotton cloth from China];
Another bodice with purple and white flowers, new;
Two white bodices, one plain, another of fine fustian;
Four or five slips [*camisas*], two with Dutch linen sleeves;
Two large scarves for the shoulders;
Two fine white and red handkerchiefs for the nose;
Three pairs of silk stockings and others of cotton;
Six pairs of shoes that I ordered two months ago;
One hat lined in blue satin with a large rose-colored ribbon;
One large rose-colored wrap with its ribbon all around;

One piece of jewelry of gold covered in diamond chips with two large topazes that she puts around her neck with a ribbon with its little pearls and wears here;
Two large carpets of painted cotton;
Two silver plates;
Three fashionably made silver table settings;
One rosary with its pearls and gold beads and a gold cross;
Two little trunks without locks, of jacaranda;
One ordinary little painted trunk with its lock and key;
Two large trunks lined with linen, with their ordinary locks and keys;
Three hand cloths, two plain and one entirely of tatting, that at its time I will tell of;
One set of tack and a sidesaddle;
One perfume pot, which at its time I will also tell about;
Two pillowcases and two blankets that without my license she gave to her mother when we went to Mojos;
One plated *mate* and two silver *bombillas* [silver trimmed gourd and silver straws for drinking maté];
One ring with French stones;
One bedroll carrier;
One leather suitcase lined with linen;
One little whip with its silver tip and other little pieces of silver that will be found;
One tablecloth with four or five napkins;
One candlestick and a metal candlestick;
One white hat with its ribbon [*zinta de fondo*]
One iron brazier [*pailita*]
One calico foot warmer [*arrimador de angaripola*];
One baseboard [*rodapié*] of painted cotton;
With other little things that will be found that I cannot recall [*no tengo presente*] and everything I say here exists and thus this and that, which does not exist, has cost me sweat and work, and because it is the truth I swear to God Our Lord, and this sign of + [a cross]. [Signature and rubric:] Antonio Yta.

/4r/ [seal of Carlos IV, *un quartillo*, 1802–3]
Most Excellent Lord President,
       With the documents I present I ask for providence.
       José Manuel Malavia, public defender of this Royal Audiencia, in the name of Don Antonio Yta, prisoner in this royal jail of the court, at the request of his wife Doña Martina Vilvado y Balverde, for the concealment and simulation of sex, of which she has accused him in the case file created over this matter. I say that from the moment that the aforesaid Balverde achieved the capture of my client at Your Excellency's order . . . she has believed herself to be absolutely free of the subjection and due bonds of the marriage of which my client is in possession, and contenting herself with the black satisfaction of seeing him in a jail cell has also thought to appropriate his scarce goods and the clothing he wears, which she retains in her power, also dissipating that which my client has bought for her for her decency at the cost of great expense and sweat. Both [his and her possessions] of not inconsiderable value are shown in the two sworn notes, which I present with all necessary solemnity. Apart from his afflictions /4v/ and inconveniences caused by the jail cell in which he finds himself, *he* also suffers from a lack of a change of clothing to wear, as a result suffering from a bad case of jaundice [*tericia* or *ictericia*] and other illnesses resulting from the lack of cleanliness; in virtue of this and to remedy these damages and at the same time to forestall the dissipation of the clothing contained in the two aforesaid notes, due to the Balverde's mistaken notion that she owes no subjection or

obligation to respond in the least way to her husband, I appeal to Your Excellency's superior justification and ask that you order the aforesaid Doña Martina to exhibit and deliver this very day the clothing contained in bill number 1 for my client's use, and making manifest everything described in bill number 2, and to account for it, guaranteeing its delivery or its value for the purposes of the pending judgments, at the same time ordering her to remain in this city and to deliver to me a copy of the case file and whatever petitions she has forwarded, as I have previously requested, such that everything needed for the defense of my client is prepared. As a result, I ask and supplicate that Your Excellency be served to decree and determine everything I have expressed, it being only just. I swear that which is legally necessary, etc. [Signatures and rubrics:] Don Esteban Agustín Gascón, José Manuel Malavia.
———

. . .
———

/6r/ Most Excellent Lord President,

Doña Martina Vilvado y Balverde, in the most appropriate manner possible in law, appear before Your Excellency and, responding to the copy that has been sent to me of the two notes presented by Doña María Leocadia Yta, do say that everything that **she** claims is pure falsehood, since the only things that *she* brought to my house, when *she* managed to deceive and contract the supposed and simulated matrimony with me, are the following items: one very worn broadcloth cape, one scarf, one jacket, two pairs of pants, two shirts, two pairs of socks, two underjackets, and one old mattress, that as such **she herself** sold to the tavern keeper for two pesos and four reales. Those are the goods, and all the decency that *she* had, and now it can be understood that of all that, not even relics, could remain for all the years that have passed. Everything else, or whatever clothing that has been acquired here since then, has been at the expense of my money. Properly speaking nothing is *hers*, nor can *she* allege the slightest right to anything; since *she* has held no profession or employment, *she* cannot have had the wherewithal to pay for any clothing or furniture. /6v/ To that end, *she* had recourse to a husband's authority to go around selling many of my things, pieces of worked silver, utensils, and much decent clothing, and I will justify all of this whenever it is appropriate. In such a manner **this woman** has been damaging to me, not only with the disguise and concealment of *her* sex and punishable simulation of matrimony but also by having nearly stripped me of all I had, in order to dress **herself** up, keeping me in check by being an angry and violent and very jealous husband; it is astonishing that *she* still appears in *her* note speaking as if *she* were a man, throwing on me in a dissimulated way many challenges and threats. In these terms, and aware that against the said Yta I have not laid charges other than for the nullity or simulation of marriage, before the ecclesiastical court, it may serve Your Excellency's justification to deny the petition of the aforesaid Doña Leocadia and in consequence order *her* to appear before the lord *provisor* to move forward the judgment of annulment. For this and reserving for a more opportune time or for when the cited annulment is decided, my actions and rights against the referred to [**female**] Yta, I ask and supplicate Your Excellency to thus order command that will be just and swear what is required by law and to this end, etc. [Signatures and rubrics:] Don Buenaventura Salinas; Martina Bilvao y Balberde.
———

/8r/ Most Excellent Lord President,

José Pimentel, attorney for the jailed poor, in the name of Don Antonio Yta, in the case with Doña Martina Bilbao over the delivery of clothing and other things, according to the document copy from the seventh of December, do say that marital relations between my party and the said Doña Martina have been delinquent cannot be doubted for many considerations, and this woman who tired of dealing with Yta is worthy of all the severity of the law, in spite of her puerile and despicable exculpations. But at the same time through the unpunished liberty that she has cleverly swindled for herself (in contrast with the doleful affliction of my party), she intends to end her misfortunes by usurping the very clothing he wears and other little things by which he might aid himself.

It is notorious that Doña Martina was poor and wretched, only later sorted out through the agency of Don Antonio, and even though, in order to avoid differences, he now desists from demanding from her all the clothing that pertains to her, his natural needs do not allow him to forget to implore that Your Excellency's rectitude be served to grant to her the most serious decree so that she should recognize under oath the memo /8v/ on folio 1, openly declaring where the items it contains exist, under the penalty of continuing to be in rebellion and in consequence without any posturing or other evasion to arrange for them to be promptly handed over, as an act of alimentary justice to alleviate a most miserable person, and to that end . . .

I ask and supplicate Your Excellency to thus determine and decree, because it is just and for that, etc. [Signatures and rubrics:] Dr. Joséf Eugenio de Portillo; José Pimentel. . . .

Plata, July 9, 1804:

That the person contained appear, swear, and declare as is asked and carry it out. [Signature and rubric:] Dr. Taborga.

In the City of La Plata on the eleventh of the said month and year:

In conformity with that which has been ordered and to carry out that which I have been commissioned, Doña Martina Vilvado appeared, from whom I, the present scribe, received the oath that she made to God Our Lord and a sign of the cross, according to law, under which she promised to tell the truth about that which she knows and is asked, and doing it according to the tenor of the preceding document and the note that is on the first folio of this expediente, said that the cape described there is in the city of Cochabamba, where it remained, with nearly all the rest of the items pertaining to the declarer. In the same way in Cochabamba exist the two capes, one of fine cotton, or Moxos-stuff dyed blue, that up until now is in possession of the tailor to whom he took it for repair, and the other /9v/ an old one, of blue wool. Also in Cochabamba are three pairs of pants, including one pair that Yta made **herself**, from a hand bath belonging to the declarer. The jacket mentioned in the note is in the power of the said tailor, given to him by the said [**female**] Yta to repair it. The declarer does not know how many vests there are, since they had been thrown out and put aside for being old, with the exception of one of solid black, in ordinary condition, which has remained in Cochabamba among the goods of the exponent. And with respect to the shirts, she has them here and manifested them in the *auto* of the declaration, but they are old, and mended, and only one of them with its shirtfront, which can be exhibited when it is so ordered. As for the stockings, all that is in Cochabamba are one pair of unusable silk stockings and another pair of ordinary cotton ones, and when a sure time comes along, she will have everything mentioned in this declaration sent from Cochabamba and will show it to the lord judge of this case, in proof of its truth. The buckles did not belong to Yta but are the property of a neighbor in Cochabamba named Don Manuel /10r/ Delgadillo, who asked this declarer to sell them to be melted down. The hat arrived from Cochabamba all in pieces and eaten by cockroaches, and because of its uselessness she gave it to the boy who serves her. The necktie or cloth that is mentioned is here in power of the exponent; it is a cloth split down the middle. And the boots remain in Cochabamba. And this is the truth of that about which was to be explained about the matter, under the oath that she has given, in which she affirmed and ratified, having read this declaration to her from beginning to end, and she is twenty-two years of age, a bit more. She did not sign because she said she does not know how, of which I attest. [Signature and rubric:] Vicente José Marin, His Majesty's scribe, public and of the Royal Hacienda and Intendancy.

B.9 Ricardo Palma's Version of the Story, 1896

Ricardo Palma (1833–1919) was a prolific Peruvian folklorist and author.

Source: Palma ([1896] 2007), 4:276–77. Palma cites as *his* source Papeles Varios, Biblioteca de Lima, vol. 613, now nonexistent. For the Spanish original, see the PTA website.

English translation

WOMAN-MAN

In America Doña Catalina de Erauzo, baptized in colonial history with the surname "Lieutenant Nun," was not the only daughter of Eve or the only nun to change the skirts of her sex for manly clothing and customs.

On October 25, 1803, news arrived from Cochabamba to the Royal Audiencia of Lima about the discovery that a gentleman, known in Buenos Aires and in Potosí by the name Don Antonio Ita, was not that man with all a man's rights but instead Doña María Leocadia Álvarez, a nun of Saint Claire from the monastery of the Villa de Agreda in Spain.

From the extract of the document that can be found in the section "Various Papers" of the Biblioteca de Lima, vol. 613, it turns out that the bishop of Buenos Aires, Don Manuel Azamor, had among his familiars the young Don Antonio Ita, and that on the eve of conferring on him priestly orders, the aspirant escaped with the destination of Potosí, where the intendent governor Don Francisco de Paula Sanz granted him modest employment.

Ita became close to Martina Bilbao, a mestiza of sinful life, who through her frequent scandals gave the authorities cause to lock her in the monastery of Santa Mónica. Don Antonio went weekly to visit her at the visiting booth and gave her six pesos to provide her comfortable subsistence.

After some months of reclusion and as the only way of ending it, the gentleman proposed matrimony, revealing to her his true sex and asking of her the greatest reserve. With the proposal Martinica [little Martina] saw blue skies; she accepted with the greatest pleasure, and the chaplain of the monastery blessed the marriage, of which the godfather was none other than the intendent.

With the intendent's protection, some businessmen set the young man up with merchandise worth more than two thousand pesos, but he was soon /p. 277/ bankrupt, and, fleeing from his creditors, he took his wife to Chuquisaca, where he obtained a lucrative occupation in the mountains of Moxos. There he disdained no work no matter how rough, and he competed with the most robust and spirited men. Whether it was roping wild bulls or getting into it with fists and clubs with whomever, he never backed down.

After five years of feigned and peaceful married life, and having acquired with his labor and privations some little cash, Ita and his wife decided to leave the mountains and establish themselves in Cochabamba, and so they did.

Once in Cochabamba, Martina was presented with a husband of the real sort. Forgetting everything she owed to her make-believe man, she went to denounce him to the lieutenant general Don Ramón García Pizarro.

Ita managed at first to gain asylum in the convent of the Merced, but once the comendador was told of the charges, he turned Ita over to the civil authority, who named a physician surgeon and two midwives to carry out a professional determination of sex.

Convinced of never having been male, Don Antonio Ita ended up spontaneously declaring his true name to be María Leocadia Álvarez and true condition that of escaped nun, not for carnal love but for the spirit of adventure, like Doña Catalina de Erauzo.

The process ended with a sentence, by virtue of which the little nun was sent to Lima and, as a register entry attests, was returned to the convent in Spain.

As for the ungrateful and perfidious Martina Bilbao, after a few months of matrimony the new husband gave her payment worthy of her villany.

He beat her to death with a stick.

It seems to me that you will not feel anything for her, and neither will I.

GLOSSARY

alcalde higher-ranking member of a municipal council

alcayde [alcaide] warden of a jail or a castle

asesor letrado legal adviser to the president of the audiencia

audiencia hearing and, by extension, the court and the territory of its jurisdiction

auto judicial decree, ruling, or decision

boticario pharmacist

cabildo municipal council

cacique member of indigenous aristocracy

cacique gobernador indigenous governor of an indigenous town, district, or urban neighborhood

cárcel de corte the audiencia's holding cells for the accused during trial

confesión testimony of an accused person, responses to questioning; does not imply an admission of guilt

criado literally, "one who is raised": servant, ward, or guest sheltered and protected within a nonkinsman's household, bound by patron-client ties

desenvoltura unconstrained, self-assured, natural, forward, fluid, and swift behavior (in speech and action); the idealized disposition of masculinity, particularly that of aristocratic males

desposorio formal act of betrothal

escribano clerk, scribe; alternatively called *notario* or, if the chief scribe of an audiencia, *secretario*

expediente docket, file, record, dossier

gobernador intendente governor of an intendency, an administrative district of the audiencia

hábito nun's habit, clothing or costume; disposition proper to a certain status or role; habit

información sworn statement provided by someone not accused of a crime (see, by contrast, *confesión*)

natural "native of" a particular place, that is, born there; in the Indies, indios were also called *naturales*, being native to the place

oidor literally, "hearer" or "one who hears"; a judge within the Spanish Crown district and appeals court, forming also part of the executive charged with carrying out and enforcing Crown policy

operantas term used to label a mother-and-daughter pair of Italian women with whom Doña María traveled from Barcelona to Rome; not in dictionaries of the era and not to be found in literary concordances; most likely, female opera singers or actors penitenciaría apostólica Vatican office where those seeking special papal dispensations seek counsel

penitenciario an apostolic confessor, belonging to the Vatican's *penitenciaría apostólica*, charged with counseling and confessing individuals, in their own language, who sought special dispensations from the pope

pongo (colonial Spanish, from the Quechua *punku*)indigenous servant, literally (in Quechua), "door" and, as *punkukamayu*, "doorkeeper"

procurador lawyer with standing in the audiencia

procurador de pobres lawyer assigned to represent the poor in cases brought before the audiencia

provincia (de La Plata, de Potosí, de Moxos) a province within the viceroyalty, governed from the late eighteenth century by a *gobernador intendente* (intendent governor)

provisor head ecclesiatical judge of a bishopric or archbishopric; governed in place of bishop or archbishop in periods of *sede vacante* (vacant see)

real audiencia high court and council of state under a viceroy or captain general; the territory of its jurisdiction

recogimiento to be gathered into oneself, withdrawn, retired, distanced from dealings with people; the proper disposition of the virtuous woman and nun, particularly of the aristocracy or a cloistered convent or house in which that attitude is promoted

relación similar to *información*; narrative curriculum vita, provided not at court's request but voluntarily, seeking reward from the Crown

sede vacante vacant see; bishopric or archbishopric governed, when no bishop or archbishop occupies the seat, by the head of the bishop's council, the vicar general, or the *provisor*

señor applied only to authorities and hidalgos, translated here as "lord"; later in the nineteenth century, its use becomes more ubiquitous—it could be translated as gentleman or mister

Su Santidad "His Holiness," the pope

teniente asesor lieutenant legal adviser to the president of the audiencia

testimonio certified copy, certified testimony

ultramarino from the other side of the sea; in Spain a Spaniard native to the overseas colonies; in the colonies a Spaniard native of Spain

vecino resident with full legal rights of citizenship, generally a person owning a house plot (service on the municipal council was limited to vecinos)

villa town with the right of self-governance through a municipal council, that is, an *ayuntamiento* (in Spain) or *cabildo* (in the Indies)

NOTES

Introduction

1. Selections from the case file compiled by the court scribe appear in appendix A. Notes and parenthetical references to appendixes often include item numbers (e.g., B.6 refers to appendix B, item 6) as well as folio numbers.

2. The expediente ANB EC 1805.96, "Case Presented by Doña Martina Vilvado y Balverde against Don Antonio de Yta for Marrying Doña Martina in Spite of Being a Woman [39 Folios]," comes from the Archivo y Biblioteca Nacionales de Bolivia, located in Sucre (formerly, La Plata or Chuquisaca), still the judicial capital of the country that emerged when this part of the Audiencia de Charcas separated from the Provincias Unidas del Río de la Plata, when it won its independence from Spain in wars lasting from 1810 to 1825. The term *audiencia* refers to several things: a "hearing," as in a formal proceeding presided over by a judge; a court of appeals and the building in which it is located; and the territorial jurisdiction of that court.

3. Taborga, *acting* as legal adviser to the president of the audiencia, had committed a double fault that he would later regret. Reporting the details of the case to someone outside of the audiencia was an indiscretion. But taking up official duties and taking sworn testimony, before he himself had been sworn in as legal adviser, was an illegal act, *prevaricato*, for which he would later be forced to recuse himself from the case. That recusal is what identifies the writer of the letter sent to Buenos Aires, which was copied (unsigned) into a collection of letters sent to an unidentified official of the viceroyalty. Nonetheless, it must be acknowledged that the writer could also have been Rodríguez Romano or even García Pizarro, neither likely to have been present, but, as official signatories with access to the legal record, they might have claimed to have been there.

4. On the registration and documentation required for travel to the Americas, see Siegert (2005).

5. "Woman of many secrets" here translates *mujer de muchas trastiendas*, literally "woman of many back rooms." The term *trastienda* suggests slyness but also backstage, dressing room, storeroom, and, appropriately for this case, closet.

6. Beruti (1946); see appendix B.7 for the Spanish original of the Buenos Aires letter. This unsigned letter was preserved in a copybook belonging to Juan Manuel Beruti (a Pablo Manuel Beruti is listed in Araujo's 1792 *Guía de forasteros* as the "Escribano of the Tribunal y Audiencia de Cuentas" under Viceroy Arredondo).

7. The entire corpus of sources is available online at the PTA website.

8. Jorge Juan and Antonio de Ulloa (1965) were members of the French Geodesic Mission (1735–42), aiming to precisely locate the equator; Baron von Nordenflycht's expedition (1788–98) of mining engineers from Poland spent time in Gov. Francisco de Paula Sanz's house in Potosí just prior to Don Antonio's arrival (Buechler 1973; Helmer 1993). Just after Don Antonio's arrest, the Balmís Expedition (1803–6), with a host of physicians, vaccinators, and a number of small boys alternately infected with cowpox to keep the vaccine's virus alive, traveled

through these regions vaccinating the king's subjects in the Americas against smallpox, using Edward Jenner's new technique (Franco-Paredes, Lammoglia, and Santos-Preciado 2005).

9. On Enlightenment reforms of governance, see Paquette (2008); on the "invention of nature" in the Spanish Enlightenment and the development of forms of scientific observation and classification, see Barrera-Osorio (2006), Cañizares-Esguerra (2006), Haidt (1998), and Vicente (2017). See Cañizares-Esguerra (2001), Kagan (1996), Premo (2017), and Silverblatt (2004) for treatments of the tendency of Anglophone scholars, influenced by Black Legend prejudices, to place Spain's empire before or outside "modernity" and for major advances in the understanding of a particularly Spanish modernity.

10. On the predicament of the Creole Spaniards and their role in revolution, see Brading (1993), Lavallé (1993), and Pagden (1987).

11. My analysis, of course, rests on the insights not only of gender theorists studying contemporary issues but on those from various strands of queer, lesbian, gay, or transgender history. See Blackmore and Hutcheson (1999), Boyd (2006), Bullough (1974), Bullough and Bullough (1993), Crompton (1980–81), Dekker and Van de Pol (1997), D'Emilio (1983), Donoghue (1993), Dreger (1998b), Duberman, Vicinus, and Chauncey (1989), Foucault ([1976] 1990), Laqueur (1990), Mak (2013), Marshall, Murphy, and Tortorici (2015), Sigal (2003), P. Smith (1989), Soyer (2012), Spurling (2000), Stryker (2008, 2017), Stryker and Whittle (2006), Tomás y Valiente (1990), Tortorici (2007, 2013, 2015, 2016b), Traub (2013), Velasco (2003a, 2011), and Vicente (2017).

12. On the medicalization of sex, a process that in part depended on defining it in biological terms, see Mak (2013), Vicente (2017), and chapter 6 of this volume.

13. Key works on the study of gender include Collier and Yanagisako (1987), Davis (1975), Reiter (1975), Rich (1980), Rubin (1975), Kessler and McKenna (1978), Scott (1986, 1988), Butler (1990), Ortner (1996), and Strathern (1990). Without being exhaustive, a list of works on gender in imperial Spain or the colonial Spanish Atlantic include Arrom (1985), Chambers (1999), Dopico-Black (2001), Gonzalbo Aizpuru and Ares Queija (2004), Jaffary (2007), Johnson and Lipsett-Rivera (1998), Lavrin (1992), Seed (1988), T. Smith (2006), Socolow (2000), Stern (1999), Twinam (2005), and Vollendorf (2001a, 2001b). Stoler (1995, 2002) usefully explores the intersection of gender and race in the colonial project.

14. The distinction between sex and gender, now naturalized in scholarly discourse in English, if not so among the general population, has not traveled well. Braidotti (2002, 292–93) treats the difficulty of reproducing the distinction in Romance and Scandinavian languages. There was particular resistance to adoption of the sex-gender distinction by the conservative Real Academia Española (Velando Casanova 2005).

15. On social estate in Spain, see Maravall (1979, 1984) and Thompson (1985). On sumptuary codes, see Sempere y Guarinos (1788). On honor and virtue, see Burkholder (1985) and Johnson and Lipsett-Rivera (1998). On recogimiento, see Pérez Baltasar (1984) and van Deusen (2001).

16. Demonstrating the relativity of phenotype in the era was the practice of *gracias al sacar*, by which legal "Spanishness" and legitimacy of birth could be purchased by persons "of color" (Twinam 2015, 1999).

17. On *raza* as flaw, see Hill (2005, 2006). On the purity of blood, see Martínez (2011). On race and *nación, calidad*, and so on, see Burns (2008) and Herzog (2012). On estate and race vis-à-vis property relations, see Herzog (2013) and the argument developed in Abercrombie (2000).

18. Doña Martina directed her statement, written by her attorney Luiz de Alcozer y Guerra, to the president of the audiencia. It was formally received by Taborga, the just-appointed (but not yet sworn-in) legal adviser to the president (and the president's son-in-law), though the document signature is that of Rodríguez Romano's (Doctor Don Vicente Rodríguez Romano).

19. On the church's laws regarding marriage, annulment, and nonconsummation, see *Code of Canon Law* (n.d.).

20. Even sodomy, never under the exclusive purview of the Inquisition (Tortorici 2016a, 11) had fallen completely under the jurisdiction of secular courts by this period (and while annulment fell to the church, it was not the concern of the Inquisition).

21. On the *protomedicato*, see Lanning (1985) and Martínez (2014).

22. On ambiguous sex, hermaphrodism, and the medicalization of sex, see Burshatin (1996, 1998, 1999); Cleminson and Vázquez García (2013); Daston and Park (1995), Dreger (1998a, 1998b); Few (2007); Haidt (1998); Hirschauer (1997); Jones and Stallybrass (1991); Mak (2013); Martínez (2014, 2016); Soyer (2012); Tortorici (2015); and Vicente (2017).

23. The large literature on Erauso includes Aresti (2007); Erauso ([1592] 1829, 1992, 1996, 2002); Goetz (2003); Goldmark (2015); Gunn (1999); McKendrick (1974); Merrim (1994); Miras (1992); Myers (2002); Pancrazio (2001); Perry (1987, 1999); Rocha (2003); Velasco (2000, 2003a, 2003b); and Vicente (2016b). The play about Erauso is Pérez de Montalbán ([1626] 1839).

24. On formal theater and festive drama in the region, see Beyersdorff (1999). On festive cross-dressing in Oruro's carnival, see Abercrombie (2003). On cross-dressing in the Spanish theater, see Bravo Villasante (1955), Bass (2008), Donnell (2003), Ekins and King (1996), Garber (1992), Heise (1992), McKendrick (1974), and citations in chapters 1 and 2 of this volume.

25. Both audiencia judges and ecclesiastical ones held jurisdiction over sodomy, which was removed from the purview of the Inquisition in 1509 in all Spanish realms except the Crown of Aragon (Martínez 2016, 424). On sodomy and its legal status and persecution, see Blackmore and Hutcheson (1999), Garza-Carvajal (2003), Gruzinski (1985), Sigal (2003), Spurling (1998, 2000), Tomás y Valiente (1990), and Tortorici (2016b).

26. Conflicts over marriage choice and petitions by American Spaniards to the Crown led to the Real Pragmática of 1776 (Lavrin 1992; Seed 1988; Socolow 1992), granting parents the possibility of blocking their children's marriages. On the *cuadros de castas*, see Carrera (2003) and Katzew (2004). Martínez's (2011) analysis is illustrative.

27. Goffman points out that *stigma* is a Greek term formerly referring to marks, brands, or tattoos applied to persons (slaves, criminals) as a sign they were to be avoided or shunned in public places. In later days think the "scarlet letter," yellow star, or pink triangle. Nowadays the term "is applied more to the disgrace itself than to the bodily evidence of it" (1963, 1–2).

28. Bakhtin's concept of the chronotope (1981) usefully charts the relationship between itineraries of travel and the episodes of character development in the kinds of narration treated here.

29. Key sources on narration and self-fashioning more generally are Bruner (1991), Greenblatt (1980), Ochs and Capps (1996), Schiffrin (1996), C. Taylor (1992), and White (1978, 1981). On self-fashioning in Iberia, see Delbrugge (2015). On legal testimony more generally, see Davis (1987), MacLeod (1998), and Scheppele (1989). On religious confession, see Bilinkoff (2006). On the confession as "involuntary autobiography," see Kagan (2005). On the legal genres of relación and información, sources for the picaresque novel, see Folger (2011), González Echevarría (1990), MacLeod (1998), and Spadaccini and Talens (1991).

30. On the Spanish concept of hábitos, applied to Catalina de Erauso, see Goldmark (2015). On the convent and its hábitos, see Burns (1999, 2003), Lehfeldt (2003, 2005), and van Deusen (2001).

31. On "clothing systems" generally, see Barthes (1983), Gaines (1990), Hendrickson (1996), Roach and Eicher (1965), Simmel (1971), and T. Turner (1980). On the status of the criado and criada, see Cañeque (2005) and Sarasua (1994). On Spanish clothing system more specifically, I draw on Amann (2015), Fillin-Yeh (2001), Haidt (1998, 1999, 2000), Landes (1988), Leira Sánchez (1991, 1997), Moers (1960), Souza Congosto (2007), Vicente (2006, 2016b), and Wolff (1985). On the South American tapada, see Bass and Wunder (2009), Peraita (2008), and Poole (1988).

32. The *Diccionario de la lengua española* defines *recogimiento* (masculine noun) as "1. Action and effect of gathering or gathering oneself; 2. house of recogidas" and *recogida* (feminine noun) as "1. Action and effect of gathering (to bring together dispersed persons or things);

2. Suspension of the use or course of something; 3. Action of withdrawing correspondence deposited in mailboxes by the mail service; and 5. The disused meaning, Action and effect of *recogerse* (retiring from, distancing oneself from dealings with people)" (n.d.; my translation). On gender in language, see Gal (1991) and Ochs (1992).

33. The tricentennial edition of the dictionary of the Real Academia Española gives the following definition of the feminine noun *desenvoltura*: "1. Desembarazo, despejo, desenfado; 2. Impudicia, liviandad; and 3. Despejo, facilidad y expedición en el decir [1. unburdened or easy, natural and self-assured, confident, forward, or uninhibited; 2. immodest or shameless, frivolous or trivial; and 3. self-confident, easy, fluent or swift in speech]" (*Diccionario*; my translation).

34. On the persecution of same-sex relations among women, see Crompton (1980–81), Delgado and Saint-Saens (2000), Garza-Carvajal (2003), Gruzinski (1985), Tortorici and Vainfas (2016), and Velasco (2011).

35. Travel narratives as autobiography and biography are treated by Siegert (2005). Passing per se has been treated by Gianoulis (2010), Ginsburg (1996), and Sánchez and Schlossberg (2001). For passing in early modern Spain as a generalized feature of "self-fashioning," see Fuchs (2003).

36. Spanish commentators attributed Creole Spaniards' "insufficient Spanishness" to "Lamarckian" effects on their bodies from having lived in the tropics among Indians. See, for examples, Brading (1993), Juan and Ulloa (1991, 65), Pagden (1987), and Premo (2005b).

37. On limitations on a wife's freedom of movement or agency, from recogimiento or patria potestad, and challenges to it posed by late eighteenth-century feminism, see Arrom (1985), Boyle (2010), Burns (2003), Dopico-Black (2001), Johnson and Lipsett-Rivera (1998), Landes (1988), Lavrin (1992, Lipsett-Rivera (2012), Mannarelli (1999), Peraita (2008), Pérez Baltasar (1984), Perry (1992), Poska (2004, 2013), Reher (1996), Rípodas Ardanaz (1977), Seed (1988), T. Smith (2006), Socolow (1990, 2000), Sponsler (1982), van Deusen (2001), and Vollendorf (2001b).

Chapter 1

1. The substitution of assistants for head scribes, yet another level of intervention between witness and text, in the head scribe's later production of clean copy, in spite of instructions to scribes to record witnesses' exact words, has received brilliant attention in Burns (2010, 88–89). Burns points to the scribal manual of Juan y Colom ([1736] 1993) for the rules concerning testimony taking and also to instances where such norms were breached.

2. See the discussion in this book's preface of pronominal and grammatical gendering pertinent to the translation of Don Antonio's confession.

3. Pronouns, like the terms *this* or *that*, are shifters (Silverstein 1976); they serve as semantic categories serving as subject or object in a sentence, while also serving as indexes, in Peirce's (1931–35) typology of the sign, which point to something outside of language, such as a particular person in the context of speech. When a third-person pronoun points to him or her, it also sexes them, attributing to them a kind of sexed body. Although languages like Spanish also sometimes attribute differential qualities through the distinction between formal and familiar second-person pronouns (*tú* versus the modern *usted*, a shortened version of the respectful or formal *vuestra merced*, your mercy, still in use in Don Antonio's day when addressing persons of higher social standing). Yet those terms are relative and fungible (one person's tu is another's usted) in a way that gendered third-person pronouns are not, since they obey a rigid binary into which persons are supposed invariably to be divided. This grants the pronouns a particularly forceful indexical effect.

4. González Echevarría (1990) points to the legal framework in which relaciones and *probanzas* were produced, addressed always to a distant authority, as the origin of the picaresque genre that lampoons those documents (along with romances of chivalry). I prefer to see the picaresque as the mirror of the confesión.

5. See extracts from the lawsuit in appendix B.8; the full text and Spanish original are available at the PTA website.

6. For the testimony by Don Antonio's mother, see appendix A.21; the convent certifications (item 22) are available at the PTA website.

7. Goldmark writes that "William Childers, for instance, has suggested that conquest produced an irreconcilable tension between 'the limited repertoire of exempla' and the individual variations produced by colonial bureaucracies' 'demand for narrative.' For Childers, such bureaucratic demands shifted the soldier from the chivalric type to individuated self" (2015, 230, referring to Childers 2010, 415).

8. The expediente is not a trial record, because criminal charges were never filed, and witnesses, other than the accusing party and the accused, were never called. The prosecutors of the case searched for a crime but could not find one.

9. I have consulted the *archivo arquidiocesano* Monseñor Taborga (Sucre, Bolivia) without success on this score.

Chapter 2

1. The Real Academia Española defines it thus:
Hábito:
  1. Special way of proceeding or conducting oneself acquired through repetition of identical or similar acts, or originating through instinctive tendencies.
  2. Clothing or suit that each person uses according to his or her state, profession, or nation, and especially that which is used by those of religious estate. (*Diccionario*; my translation)

2. Aquinas coined the term *habitus* to translate into Latin the concept of *hexis* as elaborated in Aristotle's *Nichomachean Ethics* (Wacquant 2016, 65).

3. As developed by Silverstein (1976), pragmatic linguistics draws, among others, on Peirce (1931–35) and (as does Butler in addressing performativity) Austin (1975). Useful elaborations are found in Hanks (1990), Harkness (2015), Keane (2018), Manning (2012), and Ochs (1992). The approach is especially useful in addressing materiality, since it does not presuppose, as does the Saussurean semiology taken up by most structuralist and poststructuralist analytics, an irreconcilability between concepts and things or acts.

4. At this time the distinction between hidalgos and pecheros was still important but was in the process of being undermined by instituting a new form of taxation based on the value of property owned and of labor performed rather than social estate. Thus transforming the tax structure was a central aim in the cadastral census of the Marques de la Ensenada.

5. The population figure is from Ayuntamiento (2018).

6. "Spain, Catastro of Ensenada" (n.d.), Toledo, Oreja, H-193, AHN, image 2321.

7. Manuel José Ayuso, "Venta de una casa, Pedro Pablo Laguna, y consortes, a favor de Joseph de Yta el Maior: En 29 de diciembre de 1770," Protocolos de Colmenar de Oreja, vol. 29604, AHPCM, fols. 319r –332r. See also appendix B.3.

8. Covarrubias Orozco ([1611] 1943, 790) defines *marimacho* as *la muger que tiene desembolturas de hombre*, "the woman who exhibits the unconstrained speech and acts of a man."

9. When Don Antonio said "sent to live with" rather than "I became a *criado/a*" he used a circumlocution of the sort that evaded the self-gendering that use of the personal noun would have accomplished.

10. The palace and its extensive complex of convents, gardens, and other dependencies, demolished (except for the church) in the mid-nineteenth century, is described in Mesonero Romanos (1861, 230–31).

11. Lope de Rueda, often referred to as Spain's first professional actor and founder of public theater, is said to have specialized in transvestite roles (playing female characters) in the mid-1500s (Donnell 2003, 65–68).

12. The saying is found in Mateo Alemán's *Primera parte de Guzmán de Alfarache* (Cátedra [1599] 1992) and has been heard by me uttered about certain persons passing by my skeptical friends in 2017 Spain. The phrase evokes Shakespeare's lines, uttered by Polonius while advising his son: "Costly thy habit as thy purse can buy, / But not express'd in fancy; rich, not gaudy; / For the apparel oft proclaims the man. . . . / This above all: to thine own self be true [*Hamlet* 1.3]). Such expressions point to a long tradition of skepticism about the efforts of persons to mark their statuses through clothing and habitual behavior.

13. It was the claim of Pedro de Benavente, eyewitness and cook, that Maríana "se quito el cabello" (she cut off all her hair) and that the duke "se holgaba mucho de vella estar en el abito de honbre" (took great pleasure in seeing her in men's attire) (Alonso Cortés 1903, 26).

14. The walls of the convent were not always experienced as the bars of a cage, but sometimes as a form of security. Spaces for intellectual freedom of a kind that produced writings by figures like Saint Teresa of Ávila or Sor Juana Inéz de la Cruz and administration of conventual wealth also gave abbesses and prioresses a good deal of power outside the convents' walls (Burns 1999). Lehfeldt (2003, 2005) argues that convents' walls were "permeable," particularly to access by powerful noble patrons.

15. See also appendix B.4. Proverbs 6:16–19 lists "haughty [or proud] eyes" as the first of the things that God hates. Here Augustine interprets "haughty eyes" as those that stare at others. The Spanish *enclavar los ojos*, translated here as "fix your eyes on," might also be translated as "nail your eyes into"; to stare is to penetrate another, an active rather than passive deed that incites and inflames.

16. Bass and Wunder (2009) trace the history of such veiling, which originates in both Christian and Muslim practices. Repeated outlawing of the custom owing to scandals ensuing from such women's freedom of action only exalted the custom (105–6).

17. Because of some elisions and disagreements between Don Antonio's recounting of these years and Doña Felipa's, it is difficult to piece together these years of puberty and adolescence.

18. As Surtz (1990, 10n13 and citations there) points out, Santa Juana's case was an important variant within the fairly common phenomenon of the "transvestite saint," some of whom (such as the early and possibly apocryphal martyr Saint Barbara or the well-known Jeanne d'Arc) take up not only men's clothing but weapons to become warriors in service of the true God.

19. The international community of transgender Catholics sees a patron saint of transgender in a future Santa Juana; see, for example, Cherry (2017). In March 2015 that hope was renewed when Pope Francis began beatification proceedings ("Servant of God"). See also Fernando Iwasaki, "El último milagro del barroco," *Pulso*, September 15, 2015.

20. González Marmolejo (2002) treats penitence ordered during confession for sexual sins.

21. The term *operantas* as used here is not found in dictionaries or concordances. It might be a variant either of *operista* (female opera singer or actor) or *operante* ("one who operates," as in medical practice). Given the context, it most likely here indicates female actor or singer, though the definition of *operante* is instructive. The *Diccionario enciclopédico de la lengua castellana* describes the action of *operantes*: "To execute upon the living animal body, by means of the hand or instruments, some work, such as to cut off a member, extract foreign bodies, replace missing organs, etc., with the purpose of curing an infirmity, supplementing the action of nature, or correcting a physical defect." (Spanish original: "Operante: que opera. Operar: Ejecutar sobre el cuerpo animal vivo, por medio de la mano o de instrumentos, algún trabajo, cómo cortar un miembro, extraer cuerpos extraños, reemplazar órganos que faltan, etc., con

objeto de curar una enfermedad, suplir la acción de la naturaleza ó corregir un defecto físico.")
(Zerolo et al. 1895, 2:423).

22. The *paenitentiaria apostolica* (in English, the apostolic penitentiary) is one of three tribunals of the Roman Curia. It is responsible for the absolution of excommunications, the dispensation of sacramental impediments, and the issuance and governance of indulgences. See "Apostolic Penitentiary" on the Vatican website.

23. See chapter 6 for a discussion of other cases of suspected or claimed hermaphrodism judged by the church or secular law in this period and before.

24. The Jerusalem steps, also called the Scala Sancta, are still a focus of activity for penitents in Rome. Brought to Rome by crusaders, they are held to be the original stairs leading to Pilate's chambers, climbed by Jesus Christ on his way to judgement. Penitents generally climb them on their knees (Lea 1896, 457–58).

Chapter 3

1. Potosí is well described not only in Cañete y Domínguez's contemporaneous *Guía* ([1787] 1952) and the voluminous and novelized history by Arzáns de Orsúa y Vela ([1735] 1965) but in numerous scholarly works, beginning with Hanke (1956) and including works focusing on the coerced labor system (Bakewell 1984; Buechler 1981; Tandeter 1993). Mangan (2005) describes the predominance of indigenous women in the retailing of foodstuffs and running of taverns. Most recently, Moore (2010), writing from a Marxist, political-ecology perspective, has identified the city and its mines as a critically important early example of extractive capitalism in colonized peripheries.

2. Sanz and Cañete's opponent in the ideological battle over indigenous labor (treated by Buechler 1981 and Lorandi 2012) was Victorián de Villava, who occupied a special judgeship in the audiencia as "protector of the Indians." Villava's lengthy condemnation of the *mita* de Potosí was answered by Sanz, though likely penned by Cañete, in defense of a coerced labor regime ("Escrito en defensa del servicio de la mita en respuesta a otro del fiscal Villava de 3 de enero de 1795," May 24, 1795, Potosí, vol. 38, fol. 335r, Colección Mata Linares, Real Academia de la Historia, Madrid). A tireless campaigner for equality, Villava was author of a tract ([1797] 1822) arguing for representation of American towns in the Spanish *cortes* (parliament), which circulated especially among members of the La Plata Bar Association.

3. Among the ceremonial staff of his house, Sanz kept "ten young negros dressed in strict etiquette: white cummerbund, short breeches, stockings with buckles, and full scarlet-colored frock coat" (my translation). The original is "diez negros jóvenes vestidos de rigurosa etiqueta, centro blanco, calzón corto, medias con hebillas y amplia casaca color de grana" (Fidel López 1911, 415).

4. Jorge Juan and Antonio de Ulloa, members of a midcentury expedition of geographers aiming to pinpoint the equator, had remarked on the Creoles' apparent divergence from Spanish norms in both mores and phenotype (Juan and Ulloa 1991, 65; Premo 2005b); claims of Creole degeneracy were countered by the thinker Benito Jerónomio Feijoo y Montenegro, known as the "Spanish Voltaire" ("Españoles Americanos," in Feijoo y Montenegro [1726–40] 2002, 109–25). Feijoo also defended the abilities of women ([1726] 1997).

5. My thanks to Ana María Presta for help identifying these items of cloth and clothing.

6. The Romantics would ultimately win the battle of fashion by identifying *majo* and *maja* styles with the body of the nation (think the matador's "suit of lights" and the flamenco dress).

7. Goya's famous *La maja desnuda* depicts a naked *maja*, gazing directly at the viewer. It was painted in the late 1790s, not for public exhibition but for the private *gabinete* (a cabinet, in English a private room known as a "closet") of Manuel Godoy, minister of King Carlos IV. The forthright stare might have been one mark of a maja (and of a *madamita del nuevo cuño*),

as women who transgressed the mandate that proper ladies keep their eyes downcast, but in this case the gaze was meant to inflame the viewer (the aristocrat or the male friend to whom he revealed his collection) in a private scandal (Ezquerra del Bayo 1959).

8. Vicente (2006) studies Catalan calico producers, showing that exports from Barcelona to Spanish colonies at the end of the eighteenth century accounted for half of all production and totaled millions of yards of that cloth per year. The relative cheapness, availability, and effective marketing of such textiles expanded fashion far beyond the moneyed elites.

Chapter 4

1. Sucre is sometimes called the "city of four names." It was founded as the Villa de la Plata, the "Town of Silver" by conquistadors in a place the Indians called Chuquisaca, still an alternative name for the city and also the name of the national department of which it is also capital. Besides "La Plata" and "Chuquisaca," the city is also called "La Ciudad de Charcas."

2. On married women's legal status, see Sponsler (1982).

3. Bass and Wunder (2009) trace the history of such veiling, which originates in both Christian and Muslim practices. In contrast to earlier centuries, when such veiling was recommended for Christian women, it was repeatedly banned from the sixteenth century onward (105–6). Repeated prohibition only served to exalt the custom (138).

4. It is for this reason, and also of course to please the men of their families and to remain virtuous, that many Muslim women are pleased to adopt the veil, contrary to the wishes of Christian Westerners who hope to save them from it (Abu-Lughod 1988; Scott 2007).

5. As Fillin-Yeh argues, "If I dwell on surveillance or escape from its purview it is because, in at least one important definition of a dandy's mode of behavior, the activity would seem to exclude women from dandyism, since they tend to be conventionally positioned as objects of male gaze. But dandies, though looked at (for, of course, it is being looked at that activates the private show and public spectacle of dandyism), look right back. They are looking subjects whose performative impact surrounds them like an aura; sartorial projection is protection. They are not simple (and not passive) recipients of a gaze. On the contrary. Looking goes in both directions" (2001, 20).

6. See Cañeque (2005) on paternalism and kinship-like relations that tied criados to their patrons, creating expectations of patrimonial rewards. Lomnitz (2001b, 2001c) highlights the continued role of such vertical ties after independence and how patron-client obligations have been relabeled as corruption.

7. On the use of the urban space of La Plata as a performative stage, see Bridikhina (2001).

8. On the predicament of Creole Spaniards posed by passing from below and prejudicial treatment from above, see Abercrombie (1996, 2003), Brading (1993), and Pagden (1987).

9. "Blanco" appears in parish registers and census lists in Potosí in the late 1770s, becoming generalized in place of "Spaniard" in the 1790s. Creoles adopted the color term at about the same time they began to militate for full rights and representation in the *cortes* of Spain. They similarly relabeled *indios criollos* (indigenous people acculturated to Spanish ways and dress in the cities) with the derogatory term, *cholos*. On the invention of "race" in Spanish America, see references in Abercrombie (1996) and also Burns (2008), Carrera (2003), Herzog (2012), Hill (2005, 2006), Martínez (2011), and Rappaport (2014). For a comparative case, see Stoler (2002).

10. Mangan (2005) studies indigenous women proprietors of Potosí's chicherías and *pulperías* (small general stores) and efforts by Spanish elites to control them. Gotkowitz (2003) depicts cross-caste tensions in the chicherías of Cochabamba. See Abercrombie (2003) and Weismantel (2001) on the centrality of the *chola chichera* to twentieth-century Creole-white fears of miscegenation and downward social mobility. Chambers (1999) describes the

transitional era that used hygienic policies to separate "decent" whites from contaminating castas, in part through the promotion of the café.

11. Colonial-era sodomy trials (examples from La Plata in Spurling 1998, 2000) illustrate how heteronormativity imposed heterosexual roles even on participants in male-on-male sex, wherein witnesses often describe one participant—the one on the bottom—as being "the woman" in the act (Tortorici 2007).

12. Stallybrass and White go on to explain, "The low-Other is despised, denied at the level of political organization and social being whilst it is instrumentally constitutive of the shared imaginary repertoire of the dominant culture" (1986, 5–6).

13. For accounts of late eighteenth-century festivals in the mining centers of Potosí and Oruro, and elite condemnations of them, see Abercrombie (1996, 2003) and Voigt (2016). Beyersdorff (1999) treats public festivals and their ritual dramas, as well as the theatrical performances of traveling players. Public spectacle, control of public space, and hygiene concerns in La Plata are covered by Bridikhina (2001). A history of its leading families is in Presta (2014). Bristol (1985) theorizes the intertwining of carnival and theater and plebian challenges to elites therein for Renaissance England.

14. The order reads as follows: "Given that experience has proven the continual misfortunes that occur in the bullfights when members of the plebe crowd into the middle of plaza, putting their lives at risk, and so that residents have the satisfaction of seeing masques, farces, and military maneuvers at their ease, I should and do order that no persons wearing ponchos enter the middle of the plaza, on penalty of twenty-five lashes for boys, to be given on the spot, and for others, in the jail" (Querejazu Calvo 1987, 462; my translation).

15. The *cartilla real* was composed by Governor Lázaro de Ribera in 1792, just prior to his departure and replacement by Zamora (Furlong Cardiff 1954, 16–17); de Ribera had drawn from a *cartilla* written by Bishop San Alberto. Imposing it then spawned a series of revolutionary *cartillas* (Irurozqui 2002).

16. After the rebellion the countess, Zamora's wife, settled in the city of Charcas, from whence she wrote many letters to the viceroy in Buenos Aires, informing him of picaresque doings in the audiencia (Vázquez Machicado 1988, 307–24, cited in Roca 2007, 261n12).

Chapter 5

1. It is also possible that the source was a more extensive and faithful summary of the expediente published by another folklorist three years before Palma's story saw print, the Bolivian Diez de Medina (1893).

2. See Olympe de Gouges's 1791 pamphlet, *Declaration of the Rights of Woman and the Female Citizen*, qtd. in Mousset (2007).

3. The play was reviewed in several Mexican newspapers, many presented in Salazar-Villava (n.d.) and "Extraños hábitos" (n.d.).

4. Records of judicial proceedings were not often consulted once cases were concluded; they did not constitute some kind of actively used "data bank," as did census or taxation documents. The judicial archive was colloquially called *el carnero*, as seventeenth-century author Juan Rodríguez Freyle ([1636] 1979) titled his satirical pseudochronicle. *El carnero* translates to "the boneyard" or "the trash heap" or, in more contemporary language, "the circular file," as Rodríguez Freyle's work reported; see also Abercrombie (2000) for, based on "dead" judicial expedientes, the errors and misdeeds of life in the Audiencia de Santa Fé (see Abercrombie [2000] for an analysis of an actual expediente—involving wife murder and the use of disguise to walk the streets without being recognized—drawn on by Rodríguez-Freyle).

It is unlikely that the Yta expediente was ever again officially consulted after the case was closed, apart from having been read by curious archivists, folklorists, and historians combing through the now-dead archive, associated with no-longer-existent judicial offices and state powers. At the same time, a large percentage of early modern archival documentation was not produced *by* "the state" at all. Civil litigation and criminal accusations such as Doña Martina's denunciation were addressed *to* courts of law envisaged as guarantor of rights (see Premo 2017). The shelves of notaries' archives were also filled with copies of contracts, last wills and testaments, powers of attorney, and other socially binding expressions of ritualized agreements that served the interests of the king's subjects (safeguarding rights to legal redress) rather than serving as a means of state surveillance.

Chapter 6

1. On medieval theories of sex and of hermaphrodism, see Vicente (2017), drawing on an extensive literature including Bullough (1974), Daston and Park (1995), Donoghue (1993), Dreger (1998b), Haidt (1998), and Soyer (2012). See also Cleminson and Vázquez García (2013) and Mak (2013).

2. My brief account of the case of Sebastián/María Leirado draws on Vicente (2017).

3. Further treatment of the medicalization of sex is to be found in Daston and Park (1995), Haidt (1998), Hirschauer (1997), Mak (2013), Soyer (2012), and Vicente (2017).

4. On the various ways of determining "biological" sex (chromosomal, gonadal, endocrinological, etc.) and varieties of intersex, see Dreger (1998a, 1998b), Fausto-Sterling (2012), Garber (1992), and Kessler (1998). Mak (2013) demonstrates how the assignment of one sex or another to "hermaphrodites" in nineteenth-century northern Europe depended more on gender performance than on genitals, while Martin (1991) shows how qualities of the dance of gender performance are attributed by "objective" scientists even to the egg and the sperm.

5. My own experience as a naive young undergraduate at the University of Michigan underscores this point. Invited to an Anthropology Department Halloween party in the early 1970s, I attended without costume and discovered a carnivalesque assortment of faculty and graduate students. Feeling somewhat out of place, I sat down next to an equally uncostumed young woman in skirt, hose, sweater, and makeup, looking as naive and untransformed by the world of anthropology as I was. As I tried to chat her up, she very quietly and kindly advised me that she was, in fact, attending the party in drag. It was Gayle Rubin, and I had my first lesson in transgressive queer politics.

6. On passing, I have drawn on Fuchs (2003), Goffman (1963), Gianoulis (2010), Ginsburg (1996), Halberstam (2005), Kroeger (2003), Newton (1972), Prosser (1998), Renfrow (2004), Sánchez and Schlossberg (2001), and Sullivan (1990). The closet, of course, is brilliantly treated in Sedgwick (1990).

7. On the question of agency, see also Ortner (2001).

8. On the theatricality of power in La Plata (and Potosí), see Abercrombie (1996), Arzáns de Orsúa y Vela ([1735] 1965), Bridikhina (2007), and Voigt (2016). On the differentiation of indigenous versus Spanish peoples through kinds of property they were assigned, see Herzog (2013). On the emergence of racial ideology in this context see, among others, Burns (2008), Graubart (2009), Herzog (2012), and Hill (2005).

9. "I'm free, white, and twenty-one" was an expression of unconstrained freedom used quite commonly among self-identified "white" people in the first half of the twentieth century by male and female characters as a line needing no gloss in dozens of films from the 1920s through the 1950s. A search on YouTube provides many nauseating examples.

10. As Gayle Rubin put it, writing in 1992 before *transgender* came to occupy much of the semantic field of *transsexual*: "In spite of the overlap and kinship between some areas of lesbian and transsexual experience, many lesbians are antagonistic toward transsexuals, treating male-to-female transsexuals as menacing intruders and female-to-male transsexuals

as treasonous deserters. Transsexuals of both genders are commonly perceived and described in contemptuous stereotypes: unhealthy, deluded, self-hating, enslaved to patriarchal gender roles, sick, antifeminist, antiwoman, and self-mutilating" ([1992] 2006, 476).

11. The Spanish original of this passage is "Pasó a las provincias del Perú en ábito de barón, por particular inclinación que tubo de ejercer las armas, en defensa de la fee católica y servicio de vuestra majestad" ("Documento No. 1," March 7, 1626, appendix to Ferrer, *Vida i sucesos*, 131, cited in Goldmark 2015, 218).

12. Reading relación against the picaresque novel, as did González Echevarría (1990) in formulating a general theory of the origin of the picaresque, is particularly instructive when applied to Catalina de Erauso's own texts: the official curriculum vitae–like relación submitted to the Crown by Erauso and the much more widely read "novelized" pseudoautobiography (Goldmark 2015). The former work is a tale of service to a liege lord, following the canonical conventions of the day. The latter work is full of swashbuckling plot developments and the well-developed antisocial protagonist characteristic of the picaresque novel. Don Antonio's confession, presenting as blasé the *pícaro*-like acts that led Doña María to become Don Antonio, reflects the uptake into popular consciousness of the picaresque as autobiographical narrative genre.

13. I take this summary of Hesiod's stories of the theft of fire, the deception of the meat, and the gift of Pandora from the wonderful analysis by Jean-Pierre Vernant (1989) and multiple readings with students of the pertinent sections of Hesiod's *Theogony* and *Works and Days* (2009).

Conclusion

1. In light of considerable misinterpretation of her use of "performative" to mean "mere" performance, Butler (1997) clarified her position. Halberstam summarizes this passage by Prosser: "Many transsexuals do not want to represent gender artifice; they actually aspire to the real, the natural, indeed the very condition that has been rejected by the queer theory of gender performance" (2005, 50).

2. In an interview with Sara Ahmed, Butler revised her position on the superiority of queer "destabilization" of hegemonic orders: "Some people very much require a clear name and gender, and struggle for recognition on the basis of that clear name and gender. It is a fundamental issue of how to establish and insist upon those forms of address that make life livable" (Ahmed 2016, 490).

3. See Edwards (2006). Califia (2006) provides such a defense of female-to-male masculinity.

4. Those most media-celebrated cases are male-to-female, while female-to-male appears to be much more unsettling to contemporary publics, perhaps because they are generally more convincing in their work or because male-to-female, when successfully convincing, is subject to so much more aesthetic scrutiny for their ultraheteronormative, hypersexualized, medicalized, and mediated bodies when their "realness" is evaluated.

5. On Money's work on intersexuality and the rise of intersex activism, see Dreger (1998a, 1998b), Kessler (1998), and Chase (1998a, 1998b).

6. See Abercrombie (2000). A whole genre of Golden Age plays also treated wife murder as a product of the requirements of male honor (Stroud 1990).

REFERENCES

Archival Documents

Archivo del Obispado de la Diócesis de Potosí, Bolivia (AODP)
Archivo Histórico de Protocolos, Comunidad de Madrid, Spain (AHPCM)
Archivo Histórico Provincial de Toledo, Catastro de Ensenada, Archivo Histórico Nacional, Madrid (AHN)
Archivo Parrochial, Iglesia de Santa María del Sagrario, Colmenar de Oreja, Spain (APCO)
Archivo y Biblioteca Nacionales de Bolivia, Sucre (ABNB)

Published Sources

Abercrombie, Thomas A. 1996. "Q'aqchas and La Plebe in Rebellion: Carnival vs. Lent in Eighteenth-Century Potosí." *Journal of Latin American Anthropology* 2 (1): 62–111.
———. 1998. "Tributes to Bad Conscience: Charity, Restitution, and Inheritance in Cacique and Encomendero Testaments of Sixteenth-Century Charcas." In *Dead Giveaways: Indigenous Testaments of Colonial Mesoamerica and the Andes*, edited by Susan Kellogg and Matthew Restall, 249–89. Salt Lake City: University of Utah Press.
———. 2000. "Affairs of the Courtroom: Fernando de Medina Confesses to Killing His Wife (Charcas, 1595)." In *Colonial Lives: Documents on Latin American History, 1550–1850*, edited by Richard Boyer and Geoffrey Spurling, 54–76. New York: Oxford University Press.
———. 2003. "Mothers and Mistresses of the Urban Bolivian Public Sphere: Postcolonial Predicament and National Imaginary in Oruro's Carnival." In *After Spanish Rule: Postcolonial Predicaments of the Americas*, edited by Andrés Guerrero and Mark Thurner, 176–222. Durham: Duke University Press.
———. 2009. "Una vida disfrazada en el Potosí y La Plata colonial: Antonio-nacido-María Yta ante la Audiencia de Charcas (un documento y una reflexión crítica)." *Anuario de Estudios Bolivianos, Archivísticos y Bibliográficos* 15:3–45.
Abu-Lughod, Leila. 1988. *Veiled Sentiments: Honor and Poetry in a Bedouin Society*. Berkeley: University of California Press.
Agustinas Recoletas. 1648. *Regla dada por nuestro Padre San Agustín a sus monjas, con las constituciones para la nueva recoleccion dellas, aprobadas por Nuestro Santisimo Padre Paulo V para el Real Convento de la Encarnacion de Madrid, y confirmadas por Nuestro Santisimo Padre Urbano VIII, y mandadas guardar en los demás Conventos de España de la misma recoleccion*. Madrid: Diego Diaz de la Carrera.
Ahmed, Sara. 2016. "Interview with Judith Butler." *Sexualities* 19 (4): 482–92.
Alemán, Mateo. (1599) 1992. *Primera parte de Guzmán de Alfarache*. Madrid: Cátedra.

Alonso Cortés, Narciso. 1903. *Un pleito de Lope de Rueda, nuevas noticias para su bibliografía.* Valladolid: Imprenta de Juan Hernando.

Amann, Elizabeth. 2015. *Dandyism in the Age of Revolution: The Art of the Cut.* Chicago: University of Chicago Press.

Andahazi, Federico. 2008. *Pecar como Dios manda.* Vol. 1 of *Historia sexual de los argentinos.* Buenos Aires: Planeta.

Anderson, Benedict. 1991. *Imagined Communities: Reflections on the Origin and Spread of Nationalism.* New York: Verso.

"Apostolic Penitentiary." Vatican. Accessed March 18, 2018. www.vatican.va/roman_curia /tribunals/apost_penit/index.htm.

Araujo, José Joaquín de. 1792. *Guía de forasteros en la ciudad y Virreynato de Buenos-Ayres para el año 1792.* Buenos Aires: La Real Imprenta de Niños Expósitos.

———. (1803) 1908. *Guía de forasteros del virreinato de Buenos Aires.* Vol. 4 of *Biblioteca de la Junta de Historia y Numismática Americana.* Buenos Aires: Compañía Sud-Americana de Billetes de Banco.

Aresti, Nerea. 2007. "The Gendered Identities of the 'Lieutenant Nun': Rethinking the Story of a Female Warrior in Early Modern Spain." *Gender and History* 19 (3): 401–18.

Arrom, Silvia Marina. 1985. *The Women of Mexico City, 1790–1857.* Stanford: Stanford University Press.

Arzáns de Orsúa y Vela, Bartolomé. (1735) 1965. *Historia de la Villa Imperial de Potosí.* Providence: Carter Brown Library.

Austin, John L. 1975. *How to Do Things with Words.* 2nd ed. Edited by James O. Urmsonand and Marina Sbisà. Cambridge, Mass.: Harvard University Press.

Ayuntamiento de Colmenar de Oreja. 2018. "Información." aytocdo.com.

Bakewell, Peter J. 1984. *Miners of the Red Mountain: Indian Labor in Potosí, 1545–1650.* Albuquerque: University of New Mexico Press.

Bakhtin, Mikhail. 1981. *The Dialogic Imagination: Four Essays by M. M. Bakhtin.* Translated by Caryl Emerson and Michael Holquist. Austin: University of Texas Press.

———. 1984. *Rabelais and His World.* Bloomington: Indiana University Press.

Barrera-Osorio, Antonio. 2006. *Experiencing Nature: The Spanish American Empire and the Early Scientific Revolution.* Austin: University of Texas Press.

Barthes, Roland. 1983. *The Fashion System.* Translated by Matthew Ward and Richard Howard. Berkeley: University of California Press.

Bass, Laura R. 2008. *The Drama of the Portrait: Theater and Visual Culture in Early Modern Spain.* University Park: Pennsylvania State University Press.

Bass, Laura, and Amanda Wunder. 2009. "The Veiled Ladies of the Early Modern Spanish World: Seduction and Scandal in Seville, Madrid, and Lima." *Hispanic Review* 77 (1): 97–144.

Bazán, Osvaldo. 2004. *Historia de la homosexualidad en la Argentina: De la conquista de América al siglo XXI.* Buenos Aires: Marea.

Beruti, Juan Manuel. 1946. "'Memorias Curiosas' o 'Diario' de Juan Manuel Beruti (final del manuscrito)." *Revista de la Biblioteca Nacional* 14:17–134.

Beyersdorff, Margot. 1999. *Historia y drama ritual en los Andes bolivianos (siglos XVI–XX).* La Paz, Bolivia: Plural Editores.

Bilinkoff, Jodi. 2006. *Related Lives: Confessors and Their Female Penitents, 1450–1750.* Ithaca: Cornell University Press.

———. 2015. *The Avila of Santa Teresa: Religious Reform in a Sixteenth-Century City.* Ithaca: Cornell University Press.

Birdwhistell, Ray L. 1970. "Masculinity and Femininity as Display." Chap. 6 in *Kinesics and Context: Essays on Body Motion Communication.* Philadelphia: University of Pennsylvania Press.

Blackmore, Josiah, and Gregory S. Hutcheson, eds. 1999. *Queer Iberia: Sexualities, Cultures, and Crossings from the Middle Ages to the Renaissance*. Durham: Duke University Press.

Block, David. 1994. *Mission Culture on the Upper Amazon: Native Tradition, Jesuit Enterprise, and Secular Policy in Moxos, 1660–1880*. Lincoln: University of Nebraska Press.

Boon, Jessica A., and Ronald E. Surtz, eds. 2016. *Mother Juana de la Cruz, 1481–1534: Visionary Sermons*. Translated by Ronald E. Surtz and Nora Weinerth. The Other Voice in Early Modern Europe: The Toronto Series. Toronto: Iter Academic Press; Tempe: Arizona Center for Medieval and Renaissance Studies.

Bourdieu, Pierre. 1985. "The Genesis of the Concepts of Habitus and of Field." *Sociocriticism* 2:11–21.

———. 1990. *The Logic of Practice*. Translated by Richard Nice. Stanford: Stanford University Press.

Boyd, Nan Alamilla. 2006. "Bodies in Motion: Lesbian and Transsexual Histories." In Stryker and Whittle 2006, 420–33.

Boyer, Richard, and Keith Davies. 1983. *Urbanization in Nineteenth-Century Latin America, Statistics and Sources*. Los Angeles: University of California/Latin American Center.

Boyle, Margaret E. 2010. "Chronicling Women's Containment in Bartolomé Arzáns de Orsúa y Vela's History of Potosí." *Studies in Eighteenth-Century Culture* 39:279–96.

Brading, David A. 1993. *The First America: The Spanish Monarchy, Creole Patriots, and the Liberal State, 1492–1867*. Cambridge: Cambridge University Press.

Braidotti, Rosi. 2002. "The Uses and Abuses of the Sex/Gender Distinction in European Feminist Practices." In *Thinking Differently: A Reader in European Women's Studies*, edited by Gabriele Griffin and Rosi Braidotti, 285–310. New York: Zed Books.

Bravo Villasante, Carmen. 1955. *La mujer vestida de hombre en el teatro español (siglos XVI–XVII)*. Madrid: Revista de Occidente.

Bridikhina, Eugenia. 2001. *Sin temor a Dios ni la justicia real: Control social en Charcas a fines del siglo XVIII*. La Paz, Bolivia: Instituto de Estudios Bolivianos.

———. 2007. *Theatrum mundi: Entramados del poder en Charcas colonial*. La Paz, Bolivia: Plural Editores/Instituto Francés de Estudios Andinos.

Bristol, Michael D. 1985. *Carnival and Theater: Plebian Culture and the Structure of Authority in Renaissance England*. New York: Methuen.

Brown, Judith C. 1986. *Immodest Acts: The Life of a Lesbian Nun in Renaissance Italy*. New York: Oxford University Press.

Bruner, Jerome. 1991. "The Narrative Construction of Reality." *Critical Inquiry* 18:1–21.

Buechler, Rose Marie. 1973. "Technical Aid to Upper Peru: The Nordenflicht Expedition." *Journal of Latin American Studies* 5 (1): 37–77.

———. 1981. *The Mining Society of Potosí, 1776–1810*. Syracuse: Syracuse University Press.

Bullough, Vern L. 1974. "Transvestites in the Middle Ages." *American Journal of Sociology* 79 (6): 1381–94.

Bullough, Vern L., and Bonnie Bullough. 1993. *Cross Dressing, Sex, and Gender*. Philadelphia: University of Pennsylvania.

Burkholder, Mark A. 1985. "Honor and Honors in Colonial Spanish America." In Johnson and Lipsett-Rivera 1985, 18–44.

Burns, Kathryn. 1999. *Colonial Habits: Convents and the Spiritual Economy of Cuzco, Peru*. Durham: Duke University Press.

———. 2003. "Forms of Authority: Women's Legal Representations in Mid-Colonial Cuzco." In *Women, Texts, and Authority in the Early Modern Spanish World*, edited by Marta V. Vicente and Luis R. Corteguera, 149–64. Burlington, Vt.: Ashgate.

———. 2008. "Unfixing Race." In *Rereading the Black Legend: The Discourses of Religious and Racial Difference in the Renaissance Empires*, edited by Margaret R. Greer, Walter D. Mignolo, and Maureen Quilligan, 188–202. Chicago: University of Chicago Press.

————. 2010. *Into the Archive: Writing and Power in Colonial Peru.* Durham: Duke University Press.

Burshatin, Ira. 1996. "Eleno Alias Eleno: Genders, Sexualities, and 'Race' in the Mirror of Natural History in Sixteenth-Century Spain." In *Gender Reversals and Gender Cultures: Anthropological and Historical Perspectives*, edited by Sabina Petra Ramet, 105–22. London: Routledge.

————. 1998. "Interrogating Hermaphroditism in Sixteenth-Century Spain." In *Hispanisms and Homosexualities*, edited by Sylvia Molloy and Robert McKee Irwin, 3–18. Durham: Duke University Press.

————. 1999. "Written on the Body: Slave or Hermaphrodite in Sixteenth-Century Spain." In Blackmore and Hutcheson 1999, 420–56.

Butler, Judith. 1990. *Gender Trouble: Feminism and the Subversion of Identity.* New York: Routledge.

————. 1993. *Bodies That Matter: On the Discursive Limits of "Sex."* New York: Routledge.

————. 1997. *Excitable Speech: A Politics of the Performative.* New York: Routledge.

————. 1999. "Performativity's Social Magic." In *Bourdieu: A Critical Reader*, edited by Richard Shusterman, 113–28. Oxford: Blackwell.

————. 2004. *Undoing Gender.* New York: Routledge.

Califia, Patrick. 2006. "Manliness." In Stryker and Whittle 2006, 434–38.

Cañeque, Alejandro. 2005. "De parientes, criados, y gracias: Cultura del don y poder en el México colonial (siglos XVI–XVII)." *Historica* 29 (1): 7–42.

Cañete y Domínguez, Pedro Vicente. (1787) 1952. *Guía histórica, geográfica, política, civil y legal del gobierno e intendencia de Potosí.* Edited by Armando Alba. Potosí, Bolivia: Editorial Potosí.

————. (1794) 1973–74. *Código Carolino de Ordenanzas Reales de las Minas de Potosí y demás provincias del Río de la Plata.* Edited by Eduardo Martiré. 2 vols. Buenos Aires: Universidad de Buenos Aires.

————. 1810. *El clamor de la lealtad americana en defensa de la legitimidad del Supremo Concejo de Regencia, contra los atentados de la Junta Gubernativa de Buenos Aires.* Buenos Aires: Colegio de San Fernando.

————. 1812. *Carta consultiva sobre la obligación que tienen los eclesiásticos de denunciar a los traidores y exhortar en el confesionario y púlpito su descubrimiento y captura, sin temor de incurrir en irregularidades los que asistieren armados en los combates contra los insurgentes, ni los que promovieren y concurrieren a la prisión de sus caudillos prófugos, que sirve de apéndice a la Pastoral del Señor Arzobispo Moxó.* La Plata, Argentina: Imprenta de los Huérfanos.

————. 1973. *Sintagma de las resoluciones prácticas cotidianas del Real Patronazgo de las Indias según el orden y método establecido por las Leyes del Reino y Reales Cédulas.* Buenos Aires: Talleres Gráficas Mundial.

Cañizares-Esguerra, Jorge. 2001. *How to Write the History of the New World: Histories, Epistemologies, and Identities in the Eighteenth-Century Atlantic World.* Stanford: Stanford University Press.

————. 2006. *Nature, Empire, and Nation: Explorations of the History of Science in the Iberian World.* Stanford: Stanford University Press.

Carrera, Magali M. 2003. *Imagining Identity in New Spain: Race, Lineage, and the Colonial Body in Portraiture and Casta Paintings.* Austin: University of Texas Press.

Castejón, Antonio. N.d. "Taborga: De Villaescusa (Cantabria) a Bilbao (Bizkaia, s. XVI) y América." Accessed July 2017. www.euskalnet.net/laviana/gen_bascas/taborga.htm.

Chambers, Sarah. 1999. *From Subjects to Citizens: Honor, Gender, and Politics in Arequipa, Peru, 1780–1854.* University Park: Penn State University Press.

Chase, Cheryl. 1998a. "Affronting Reason." In *Looking Queer: Body Image and Identity in Lesbian, Bisexual, Gay, and Transgendered Communities*, edited by Dawn Atkins, 205–20. Binghamton: Haworth.

———. 1998b. "Hermaphrodites with Attitude: Mapping the Emergence of Intersex Political Activism." *GLQ* 4 (2): 189–211.

Cherry, Kittredge. 2017. "Madre Juana de la Cruz: Queer Saint of Sixteenth-Century Spain." *Q Spirit*. May 3, 2017. qspirit.net/madre-juana-de-la-cruz-queer-saint/.

Childers, William. 2010. "Baroque Quixote: New World Writing and the Collapse of the Heroic Ideal." In *Baroque New Worlds: Representations, Transculturation, Counterconquest*, edited by Lois Parkinson Zamora and Monika Kaup, 415–49. Durham: Duke University Press.

Christian, William A. 1989. *Apparitions in Late Medieval and Renaissance Spain*. Princeton: Princeton University Press.

Cleminson, Richard, and Francisco Vázquez García. 2013. *Sex, Identity, and Hermaphrodites in Iberia, 1500–1800*. New York: Routledge.

Code of Canon Law. N.d. Libreria Editrice Vaticana. Accessed June 22, 2016. www.vatican.va /archive/ENG1104/_P3Y.HTM.

Collier, Jane Fishburne, and Sylvia Junko Yanagisako, eds. 1987. *Gender and Kinship: Essays Toward a Unified Analysis*. Stanford: Stanford University Press.

Concolorcorvo (Alonso Carrió de la Vandera). (1773) 1908. *El lazarillo de ciegos caminantes*. Vol. 5 of *Biblioteca de la Junta de Historia y Numismática Americana*. Buenos Aires: Compañía Sud-Americana de Billetes de Banco.

———. (1773) 1965. *El Lazarillo: A Guide for Inexperienced Travelers Between Buenos Aires and Lima*. Translated by Walter D. Kline. Bloomington: Indiana University Press.

Covarrubias Orozco, Sebastián de. (1611) 1943. *Tesoro de la lengua castellana o española*. Edited by Martín de Riquer. Barcelona: Horta.

Crenshaw, Kimberlé Williams. 1989. "Demarginalizing the Intersection of Race and Sex: A Black Feminist Critique of Antidiscrimination Doctrine, Feminist Theory, and Antiracist Politics." *University of Chicago Legal Forum* 1989:139–67.

———. 1991. "Mapping the Margins: Intersectionality, Identity Politics, and Violence Against Women of Color." *Stanford Law Review* 43 (6): 1241–99.

Crompton, Louis. 1980–81. "The Myth of Lesbian Impunity: Capital Laws from 1270 to 1791." *Journal of Homosexuality* 6 (1–2): 11–25.

Cromwell, Jason. 2010. "Default Assumptions; or, The Billy Tipton Phenomenon." *FTM Newsletter* 28:4–5.

Cruz, Anne J. 2010. "Figuring Gender in the Picaresque Novel: From Lazarillo to Zayas." *Romance Notes* 50 (1): 7–20.

D'Aloia Criado, Walter. 2003. "Crónicas del Buenos Aires Virreinal: La pintoresca historia de Don Antonio de Ita; Paje que fue de un obispo de Buenos Aires." *Junta Sabatina de Especialidades Históricas* (Buenos Aires) 3:139–43.

Daston, Lorraine, and Katharine Park. 1995. "The Hermaphrodite and the Orders of Nature: Sexual Ambiguity in Early Modern France." *GLQ: A Journal of Lesbian and Gay Studies* 1 (4): 419–38.

Davis, Natalie Zemon. 1975. *Women on Top: Society and Culture in Early Modern France*. Stanford: Stanford University Press.

———. 1987. *Fiction in the Archives: Pardon Tales and Their Tellers in Sixteenth-Century France*. Stanford: Stanford University Press.

Daza, Antonio. 1613. *Historia, vida y milagros, éxtasis y revelaciones de la bienaventurada virgen Santa Juana de la Cruz*. Madrid: Sánchez.

Dekker, Rudolf M., and Lotte C. Van de Pol. 1997. *The Tradition of Female Transvestism in Early Modern Europe*. New York: St. Martin's Press.

Delbrugge, Laura, ed. 2015. *Self-Fashioning and Assumptions of Identity in Medieval and Early Modern Iberia.* Boston: Brill.

De León, Fray Luís. 1987. *La perfecta casada.* Edited by Mercedes Etreros. Madrid: Taurus.

Delgado, María José, and Alain Saint-Saens, eds. 2000. *Lesbianism and Homosexuality in Early Modern Spain.* New Orleans: University Press of the South.

D'Emilio, John. 1983. "Capitalism and Gay Identity." In *Powers of Desire: The Politics of Sexuality,* edited by Ann Snitow, Christine Stansell, and Sharan Thompson, 101–13. New York: Monthly Review Press.

Derrida, Jacques. (1972) 1999. "Signature Event Context." In *A Derrida Reader: Between the Blinds,* edited by Peggy Kamuf, 80–111. New York: Columbia University Press.

———. 1988. "Signature Event Context." In *Limited Inc,* translated by Samuel Weber and Jeffrey Mehlman, edited by Gerald Graff, 1–23. Evanston: Northwestern University Press.

Diccionario de la lengua española. N.d. S.vv. "desenvoltura," "hábito," "pícaro," "recogimiento." Real Academia Española. Accessed April 5, 2018. dle.rae.es.

Diez de Medina, Ángel. 1893. "Don Antonio de Ita." In *Crónicas potosinas: Notas históricas, estadísticas, biográficas, y políticas,* edited by Modesto Omiste, 3:560–66. 3 vols. Potosí, Bolivia: "El Tiempo."

Donnell, Sidney. 2003. *Feminizing the Enemy: Imperial Spain, Transvestite Drama, and the Crisis of Masculinity.* Lewisburg, Pa.: Bucknell University Press.

Donoghue, Emma. 1993. "Imagined More Than Women: Lesbians and Hermaphrodites, 1671–1766." *Women's History Review* 2 (2): 199–216.

Dopico-Black, Georgina. 2001. *Perfect Wives, Other Women: Adultery and Inquisition in Early Modern Spain.* Durham: Duke University Press.

D'Orbigny, Alcide. 1844. *Voyage dans L'Amérique méridionale.* Vol. 3. Paris: Bertrand; Strasbourg: Levrault.

Dreger, Alice Domurat. 1998a. "'Ambiguous Sex'—or Ambivalent Medicine?" *Hastings Center Report* 28 (3): 24–35.

———. 1998b. *Hermaphrodites and the Medical Invention of Sex.* Cambridge, Mass.: Harvard University Press.

Duberman, Martin, Martha Vicinus, and George Chauncey Jr., eds. 1989. *Hidden from History: Reclaiming the Gay and Lesbian Past.* New York: New American Library Books.

Earle, Rebecca. 2014. *The Body of the Conquistador: Food, Race, and the Colonial Experience in Spanish America, 1492–1700.* Cambridge: Cambridge University Press.

Edwards, Tim. 2006. *Cultures of Masculinity.* Routledge: New York.

Ekins, Richard, and Dave King, eds. 1996. *Blending Genders: Social Aspects of Cross-Dressing and Sex-Changing.* London: Routledge.

Erauso, Catalina de. (1592) 1829. *Historia de la Monja Alférez, doña Catalina de Erauso.* Edited by Joaquín María de Ferrer. Paris: Imprenta Julio de Didot.

———. 1992. *Vida i sucesos de la monja alférez, autobiografía atribuida a Doña Catalina de Erauso.* Edited by Rima de Vallboba. Tempe: Arizona State University.

———. 1996. *Lieutenant Nun: Memoir of a Basque Transvestite in the New World.* Translated by Michele Stepto and Gabriel Stepto. Boston: Beacon Press.

———. 2002. *Historia de la monja alférez, Catalina de Erauso, escrita por ella misma.* Madrid: Cátedra.

"Los extraños hábitos de Don Antonio." N.d. *EIDOS.* Accessed April 11, 2018. http://cartel eradeteatro.mx/2012/los-extranos-habitos-de-don-antonio/.

Ezquerra del Bayo, Joaquín. 1959. *La Duquesa de Alba y Goya: Estudio biográfico y artístico.* Madrid: Aguilar.

Fausto-Sterling, Anne. 2012. *Sex/Gender: Biology in a Social World.* New York: Routledge.

Feijoo y Montenegro, Benito Jerónimo. (1726) 1997. "Defensa de las mujeres." In *Teatro crítico universal.* Edited by Victoria Sau. Vol. 1. Barcelona: Icaria. (Translated as *An Essay on Women; or, Physiological and Historical Defense of the Fair Sex.* London: Bingley, 1765).

———. (1726–40) 2002. *Teatro crítico universal.* Edited by Ángel Raimundo Fernández González. 7th ed. Madrid: Cátedra.

[Fernández de Rojas, Juan]. 1795. *Libro de moda en la feria, que contiene un ensayo de la historia de los Currutacos, Pirracas, y Madamitas del nuevo Cuño, y los elementos, ó primeras nociones de la ciencia Currutaca: Escrito por un filosofo Currutaco, publicado, anotado, y comentado por un señorito Pirracas.* Madrid: Imprenta de la Viuda e Hijo de Marin.

———. 1796. *Libro de moda o ensayo de la historia de los Currutacos, Pirracas y Madamitas de nuevo cuño escrita por un filósofo Currutaco.* Madrid: Imprenta de Don Blas Román.

Few, Martha. 2007. "'That Monster of Nature': Gender, Sexuality, and the Medicalization of a 'Hermaphrodite' in Late Colonial Guatemala." *Ethnohistory* 54 (1): 159–76.

Fidel López, Vicente. 1911. *Historia de la República Argentina.* Vol. 1. Buenos Aires: Roldán.

Fillin-Yeh, Susan. 2001. "Introduction: New Strategies for a Theory of Dandies." In *Dandies: Fashion and Finesse in Art and Culture,* edited by Susan Fillin-Yeh, 1–34. New York: New York University Press.

Folger, Robert. 2011. *Writing as Poaching: Interpellation and Self-Fashioning in Colonial "Relaciones de Méritos y Servicios."* Leiden: Brill.

Foucault, Michel. (1976) 1990. *History of Sexuality.* Vol. 1. Translated by Robert Hurley. New York: Vintage.

Franco-Paredes, Carlos, Lorena Lammoglia, and José Ignacio Santos-Preciado. 2005. "The Spanish Royal Philanthropic Expedition to Bring Smallpox Vaccination to the New World and Asia in the Nineteenth Century." *Clinical Infectious Diseases* 41 (9): 1285–89.

Fuchs, Barbara. 2003. *Passing for Spain: Cervantes and the Fictions of Identity.* Urbana: University of Illinois Press.

Furlong Cardiff, Guillermo. 1954. "Lázaro de Ribera y su breve Cartilla Real." *Humanidades* 34:15–70.

Gaines, Jane. 1990. "Fabricating the Female Body." In *Fabrications: Costume and the Female Body,* edited by Jane Gaines and Charlotte Herzog, 1–27. New York: Routledge.

Gal, Susan. 1991. "Between Speech and Silence: The Problematics of Research on Language and Gender." In *Gender at the Crossroads of Knowledge: Feminist Anthropology in the Postmodern Era,* edited by Micaela di Leonardo, 175–203. Berkeley: University of California Press.

———. 2002. "A Semiotics of the Public/Private Distinction." *Differences: A Journal of Feminist Cultural Studies* 13 (1): 77–95.

Garber, Marjorie. 1992. *Vested Interests: Cross-Dressing and Culture Anxiety.* New York: Routledge.

Garfinkel, Harold. 1967. *Studies in Ethnomethodology.* Englewood Cliffs: Prentice-Hall.

Garza-Carvajal, Federico. 2003. *Butterflies Will Burn: Prosecuting Sodomites in Early Modern Spain and Mexico.* Austin: University of Texas Press.

Gianoulis, Tina. 2010. "Passing." *glbtq Encyclopedia.* Accessed August 2016. www.glbtqarchive.com/ssh/passing_S.pdf.

Ginsburg, Elaine. 1996. *Passing and the Fictions of Identity.* Durham: Duke University Press.

Goetz, Rainer H. 2003. "The Problematics of Gender/Genre in Vida i sucesos de la monja alférez." In *Women in the Discourse of Early Modern Spain,* edited by Joan F. Cammarata, 91–107. Gainesville: University Press of Florida.

Goffman, Erving. 1959. *The Presentation of Self in Everyday Life.* New York: Doubleday.

———. 1963. *Stigma: Notes on the Management of Spoiled Identity.* New York: Simon and Schuster.

Goldmark, Matthew. 2015. "Reading Habits: Catalina de Erauso and the Subjects of Early Modern Spanish Gender and Sexuality." *Colonial Latin American Review* 24 (2): 215–35.

Gómez, María Asunción. 2009. "El problemático 'feminismo' de *La monja alférez* de Domingo Miras." *Espéculo: Revista de Estudios Literarios* 41. www.ucm.es/info/especulo/numero41/monjalfe.html.

Gonzalbo Aizpuru, Pilar, and Berta Ares Queija, eds. 2004. *Las mujeres en la construcción de las sociedades iberoamericanas.* Mexico City: Centro de Estudios Históricos, Colegio de México.

González Echevarría, Roberto. 1990. *Myth and Archive: A Theory of Latin American Narrative.* New York: Cambridge University Press.

González Marmolejo, Jorge René. 2002. *Sexo y confesión: La iglesia y la penitencia en los siglos XVIII y XIX en la Nueva España.* Mexico City: Conaculta–Instituto Nacional de Antropología e Historia.

Gotkowitz, Laura. 2003. "Trading Insults: Honor, Violence, and the Gendered Culture of Commerce in Cochabamba, Bolivia, 1870s–1950s." *Hispanic American Historical Review* 83 (1): 83–118.

Graubart, Karen B. 2009. "The Creolization of the New World: Local Forms of Identification in Urban Colonial Peru, 1560–1640." *Hispanic American Historical Review* 89 (3): 471–99.

Greenblatt, Stephen J. 1980. *Renaissance Self-Fashioning: More to Shakespeare.* Chicago: University of Chicago Press.

Gruzinski, Serge. 1985. "Las cenizas del deseo: Homosexuales novohispanos a mediados del siglo XVII." In *De la santidad a la perversión, o de porqué no se cumplía la ley de Dios en la sociedad novohispana,* edited by Sergio Ortega, 255–83. Mexico City: Instituto Nacional de Antropología e Historia.

Guitarte Izquierdo, Vidal. 1992. *Episcopologio español (1700–1867): Españoles obispos en España, América, Filipinas y otros paises.* Castellón de la Plana, Spain: Ayuntamiento.

Gunn, Elizabeth. 1999. "Hábito y espada: Más allá del travestismo en *La monja alférez* de Domingo Miras." *Romance Languages Annual* 11:478–83.

Haidt, Rebecca. 1998. *Embodying Enlightenment: Knowing the Body in Eighteenth-Century Spanish Literature and Culture.* New York: St. Martin's Press.

———. 1999. "Fashion, Effeminacy, and Homoerotic Desires(?): The Question of the Petimetres." *Letras Peninsulares* 12:65–80.

———. 2000. "The Name of the Clothes: Petimetras and the Problems of Luxury's Refinements." *Dieciocho: Hispanic Enlightenment* 23 (1): 71–75.

Halberstam, Judith. 1998. *Female Masculinity.* Durham: Duke University Press.

———. 2005. *In a Queer Time and Place: Transgender Bodies, Subcultural Lives.* New York: New York University Press.

Hanke, Lewis. 1956. *The Imperial City of Potosí: An Unwritten Chapter in the History of Spanish America.* The Hague: Nijjoff.

Hanks, William F. 1990. *Referential Practice: Language and Lived Space Among the Maya.* Chicago: University of Chicago Press.

———. 2005. "Pierre Bourdieu and the Practices of Language." *Annual Review of Anthropology* 34:67–83.

Harkness, Nicholas. 2015. "The Pragmatics of Qualia in Practice." *Annual Review of Anthropology* 44:573–89.

Heise, K. Ursula. 1992. "Transvestism and the Stage Controversy in Spain and England, 1580–1680." *Theatre Journal* 44 (3): 357–74.

Helmer, Marie. 1993. "La mission Nordenflycht en Amérique espagnole (1788): Échec d'une technique nouvelle." In *Cantuta: Recueil d'articles parus entre 1949 et 1987,* 302–3, 310–11. Madrid: Casa de Velázquez.

Hendrickson, Hildi. 1996. Introduction to *Clothing and Difference: Embodied Identities in Colonial and Post-Colonial Africa,* edited by Hildi Hendrickson. Durham: Duke University Press.

Herzog, Tamar. 2012. "Beyond Race: Exclusion in Early Modern Spain and Spanish America." In *Race and Blood in the Iberian World*, edited by Max S. Hering Torres, María Elena Martínez, and David Nirenberg, 151–67. Berlin: Verlag.

———. 2013. "Colonial Law and 'Native Customs': Indigenous Land Rights in Colonial Spanish America." *Americas* 69 (3): 303–21.

Hesiod. 2009. *Theogony* and *Works and Days*. Translated by M. L. West. New York: Oxford University Press.

Hill, Ruth. 2005. *Hierarchy, Commerce, and Fraud in Bourbon Spanish America: A Postal Inspector's Exposé*. Nashville: Vanderbilt University Press.

———. 2006. "Towards an Eighteenth-Century Transatlantic Critical Race Theory." *Literature Compass* 3 (2): 53–64.

Hirschauer, Stefan. 1997. "The Medicalization of Gender Migration." *International Journal of Transgenderism* 1 (1). www.symposium.com/ijt/ijtc0104.htm.

Irurozqui, Marta. 2002. "El sueño del ciudadano: Sermones y catecismos politicos en Charcas tardocolonial." In *Elites intelectuales y modelos colectivos*, edited by Monica Quijada and Jesus Bustamante, 219–50. Madrid: Consejo Superior de Investigaciones Científicas.

Iza Zamácola, Juan Antonio de. 1796. *Elementos de la ciencia contradanzaria para que los curruta- cos, pirracas, y madamitas de nuevo cuño aprendan por principios a bailar las contradanzas por si solos o con las sillas de su casa*. Madrid: Viuda de Joseph García.

———. 1805. *Colección de las mejores seguidillas, tiranas, y polos que se han compuesto para cantar a la guitarra*. 3rd ed. Madrid: Hija de Joaquín Ibarra.

Jaffary, Nora E. 2007. *Gender, Race, and Religion in the Colonization of the Americas*. Burlington, Vt.: Ashgate.

Jakobson, Roman. 1960. "Closing Statements: Linguistics and Poetics." In *Style in Language*, edited by Thomas A. Sebeok, 350–77. New York: MIT Press.

Johnson, Lyman, and Sonya Lipsett-Rivera, eds. 1998. *The Faces of Honor: Sex, Shame, and Violence in Colonial Latin America*. Albuquerque: University of New Mexico Press.

Jones, Ann Rosalind, and Peter Stallybrass. 1991. "Fetishizing Gender: Constructing the Hermaphrodite in Renaissance Europe." In Epstein and Straub 1991, 80–111.

Juan, Jorge, and Antonio de Ulloa. 1991. *Noticias secretas de América*. Madrid: Historia 16.

Juana de la Cruz, Madre. (1509) 1982. *Libro del conorte*. Edited by Ronald E. Surtz. Barcelona: Puvill Libros.

Juan y Colom, José. (1736) 1993. *Instruccion de escribanos en orden a lo judicial*. Valladolid: Editorial Lex Nova.

Kagan, Richard. 1996. "Prescott's Paradigm: American Historical Scholarship and the Decline of Spain." *American Historical Review* 101 (2): 423–46.

———. 2005. "Autobiografía involuntaria o inquisitorial." *Cultura escrita y sociedad* 1:92–94.

Katzew, Ilona. 2004. *Casta Painting: Images of Race in Eighteenth-Century Mexico*. New Haven: Yale University Press.

Keane, Webb. 2003. "Semiotics and the Social Analysis of Material Things." *Language and Communication* 23:409–25.

———. 2018. "On Semiotic Ideology." *Signs and Society* 6 (1): 64–87.

Kessler, Suzanne J. 1998. *Lessons from the Intersexed*. New Brunswick: Rutgers University Press.

Kessler, Suzanne J., and Wendy McKenna. 1978. *Gender: An Ethnomethodological Approach*. Chicago: University of Chicago Press.

Kroeger, Brooke. 2003. *Passing: When People Can't Be Who They Are*. New York: Public Affairs.

Kulick, Don. 1998. *Travesti: Sex, Gender, and Culture Among Brazilian Transgendered Prostitutes*. Chicago: University of Chicago Press.

Landes, Joan B. 1988. *Women and the Public Sphere in the Age of the French Revolution*. Ithaca: Cornell University Press.

Lanning, John Tate. 1985. *The Royal Protomedicato: The Regulation of the Medical Professions in the Spanish Empire*. Durham: Duke University Press.

Laqueur, Thomas. 1990. *Making Sex: Body and Gender from the Greeks to Freud*. Cambridge, Mass.: Harvard University Press.

Latham, J. R. 2016. "Trans Men's Sexual Narrative-Practices: Introducing STS to Trans and Sexuality Studies." *Sexualities* 19 (3): 347–68.

Lavallé, Bernard. 1993. *Las promesas ambiguas: Ensayos sobre el criollismo colonial en los Andes*. Lima: Pontificia Universidad Católica del Perú.

Lavrin, Asunción. 1992. *Sexuality and Marriage in Colonial Latin America*. Lincoln: University of Nebraska Press.

Lea, Henry Charles. 1896. *A History of Auricular Confession and Indulgences in the Latin Church*. Philadelphia: Lea Bros.

Lehfeldt, Elizabeth A. 2003. "Spatial Discipline and Its Limits: Nuns and the Built Environment in Early Modern Spain." In *Gender, Architecture, and Power in Early Modern Europe*, edited by Helen M. Hills, 131–49. Aldershot: Ashgate.

———. 2005. *Religious Women in Golden Age Spain: The Permeable Cloister*. Aldershot: Ashgate.

Leira Sánchez, Amalia. 1991. "El traje en el reinado de Carlos III." In *Moda en sombras: Catálogo de la exposición*, 16–20. Madrid: Dirección General de Bellas Artes y Archivos.

———. 1997. "El vestido en tiempos de Goya." *Anales del Museo Nacional de Antropología* 4:157–88.

Levene, Ricardo. 1946. *Vida y escritos de Victorián de Villava*. Buenos Aires: Casa Peuser.

Linehan, Peter. 2004. *The Ladies of Zamora*. University Park: Penn State University Press.

Lipsett-Rivera, Sonya. 2012. *Gender and the Negotiation of Daily Life in Mexico, 1750–1856*. Lincoln: University of Nebraska Press.

Lomnitz, Claudio. 2001a. *Deep Mexico, Silent Mexico: An Anthropology of Nationalism*. Minneapolis: University of Minnesota Press.

———. 2001b. "Nationalism as a Practical System: Benedict Anderson's Theory of Nationalism from the Vantage Point of Spanish America." In Lomnitz 2001a, 3–34.

———. 2001c. "Ritual, Rumor and Corruption in the Formation of Mexican Politics." In Lomnitz 2001a, 145–64.

Lorandi, Ana María. 2012. "Heterogeneidad de los discursos ilustrados: Funcionarios reales y eclesiásticos en el ocaso del imperio." *Estudios Bolivianos* 17:75–105.

Lowenthal, David. 1999. *The Past Is a Foreign Country*. Cambridge: Cambridge University Press.

MacLeod, Murdo J. 1998. "Self-Promotion: The *Relaciones de méritos y dervicios* and Their Historical and Political Interpretation." *Colonial Latin American Historical Review* 7 (1): 25–42.

MacPherson, C. B. 1999. *Property: Mainstream and Critical Positions*. Toronto: University of Toronto Press.

———. 2011. *The Political Theory of Possessive Individualism: Hobbes to Locke*. New York: Oxford University Press.

Mak, Geertje. 2013. *Doubting Sex: Inscriptions, Bodies and Selves in Nineteenth-Century Hermaphrodite Case Histories*. Manchester: Manchester University Press.

Mangan, Jane. 2005. *Trading Roles: Gender, Ethnicity, and the Urban Economy in Colonial Potosí*. Durham: Duke University Press.

Mannarelli, María Emma. 1999. *Hechiceras, beatas, y expósitas: Mujeres y poder inquisitorial en Lima*. Lima: Ediciones del Congreso del Perú.

Manning, Paul. 2012. *The Semiotics of Drink and Drinking*. New York: Bloomsbury Academic.

Maravall, José Antonio. 1979. *Poder, honor, y elites en el siglo XVII*. Madrid: Siglo Veintiuno.

———. 1984. "Trabajo y exclusión: El trabajador manual en el sistema social de la primera modernidad." In *Estudios de historia del pensamiento español*, 363–92. Madrid: Ediciones Cultura Hispánica.

"María Petronila de Alcántara Pimentel y Cernesio." 2012. Fundación Casa Ducal de Medinaceli. Accessed March 19, 2018, http://en.fundacionmedinaceli.org/casaducal /fichaindividuo.aspx?id=215.

Marshall, Daniel, Kevin P. Murphy, and Zeb Tortorici, eds. 2015. "Queering Archives: Intimate Tracings." Special issue, *Radical History Review* 122:1–10.

Martin, Emily. 1991. "The Egg and the Sperm: How Science Has Constructed a Romance Based on Stereotypical Male-Female Roles." *Signs* 16 (3): 485–501.

Martínez, María Elena. 2011. *Genealogical Fictions: Limpieza de Sangre, Religion, and Gender in Colonial Mexico*. Stanford: Stanford University Press.

———. 2014. "Archives, Bodies, and Imagination: The Case of Juana Aguilar and Queer Approaches to History, Sexuality, and Politics." In *Queering Archives: Historical Unravelings*, edited by Daniel Marshall, Kevin P. Murphy, and Zeb Tortorici. Special Issue, *Radical History Review* 120:159–82.

———. 2016. "Sex and the Colonial Archive: The Case of 'Mariano' Aguilera." *Hispanic American Historical Review* 96 (3): 421–43.

Martín Gaite, Carmen. (1972) 2000. *Usos amorosos del dieciocho en España*. 6th ed. Madrid: Editorial Anagrama.

McKendrick, Melveena. 1974. *Women and Society in the Spanish Drama of the Golden Age: A Study of the "Mujer Varonil."* Cambridge: Cambridge University Press.

Mendoza, Gunnar. 1954. *El doctor don Pedro Vicente Cañete y su Historia Física y Política de Potosí*. Sucre, Bolivia: Universidad de San Francisco Xavier.

Menon, Madhavi. 2009. "Afterword: Period Cramps." In *Queer Renaissance Historiography: Backward Gaze*, edited by Vin Nardizzi, Stephen Guy-Bray, and Will Stockton, 229–35. Farnham, U.K.: Ashgate.

Merrim, Stephanie. 1994. "Catalina de Erauso: From Anomaly to Icon." In *Coded Encounters: Writing Gender and Ethnicity in Colonial Latin America*, edited by Francisco Javier Cevallos-Candau, Jeffrey A. Cole, Nina M. Scott, and Nicomedes Suárez Araúz, 177–205. Amherst: University of Massachusetts Press.

———. 1999. *Feminist Perspectives on Sor Juana Ines de la Cruz*. Detroit: Wayne State University Press.

Mesonero Romanos, Ramón de. 1861. *El antiguo Madrid: Paseos histórico-anecdóticos por las calles y casas de esta villa*. Madrid: Tipografía Mellado.

Middlebrook, Diane Wood. 1998. *Suits Me: The Double Life of Billy Tipton*. New York: Houghton Mifflin.

Miras, Domingo. 1992. *La monja alférez*. Murcia: Secretariado de Publicaciones y Servicio de Actividades Culturales de la Universidad de Murcia.

Moers, Ellen. 1960. *The Dandy: Brummell to Beerbohm*. Lincoln: University of Nebraska Press.

———. 2003. *Literary Women: The Great Writers*. New York: Doubleday.

Mol, Annemarie. 2003. *The Body Multiple: Ontology in Medical Practice*. Durham: Duke University Press.

Moore, Jason. 2010. "This Lofty Mountain of Silver Could Conquer the Whole World": Potosí and the Political Ecology of Underdevelopment, 1545–1800." *Journal of Philosophical Economics* 4: (1): 58–103.

Mousset, Sophie. 2007. *Women's Rights and the French Revolution: A Biography of Olympe de Gouges*. New Brunswick: Transaction.

Moya, Alejandro [Juan Fernández de Rojas]. 1792. *El triunfo de las castañuelas o mi viaje a Crotalópolis*. Madrid: Imprenta de González.

Muzzio, Julio A. 1920. *Diccionario histórico y biográfico de la República Argentina*. Buenos Aires: Libreria Juan Roldan. Accessed August 3, 2015. www.archive.org/stream/diccionari ohist12muzz/diccionariohist12muzz_djvu.txt.

Myers, Kathleen Ann. 2002. "Writing of the Frontier: Blurring Gender and Genre in the Monja Alférez's Account." In *Mapping Colonial Spanish America: Places and Commomplaces of Identity, Culture, and Experience*, edited by Santa Arias and Mariselle Meléndez, 181–201. Lewisburg, Pa.: Bucknell University Press.

Nader, Helen. 1993. *Liberty in Absolutist Spain: The Habsburg Sale of Towns, 1516–1700*. Baltimore: Johns Hopkins University Press.

Namaste, Ki. 1996. "'Tragic Misreadings': Queer Theory's Erasure of Transgender Subjectivity." In *Queer Studies: A Lesbian, Gay, Bisexual, and Transgender Anthology*, edited by Brett Beemyn and Michele Eliason, 183–203. New York: New York University Press.

Newton, Esther. 1972. *Mother Camp: Female Impersonators in America*. Chicago: University of Chicago Press.

Ochs, Elinor. 1992. "Indexing Gender." In *Rethinking Context: Language as an Interactive Phenomenon*, edited by Alessandro Duranti and Charles Goodwin, 335–58. New York: Cambridge University Press.

Ochs, Elinor, and Lisa Capps. 1996. "Narrating the Self." *Annual Reviews in Anthropology* 25:19–43.

Ortner, Sherry. 1996. *Making Gender: The Politics and Erotics of Culture*. Boston: Beacon Press.

———. 2001. "Specifying Agency: The Comaroffs and Their Critics." *Interventions* 3 (1): 76–84.

Pagden, Anthony. 1987. "Identity Formation in Spanish America." In *Colonial Identity in the Atlantic World, 1500–1800*, edited by Nicholas Canny and Anthony Pagden, 51–93. Princeton: Princeton University Press.

Palma, Ricardo. (1896) 2007. "Mujer-hombre." In *Tradiciones peruanas: Octava y ultima serie*, 276–77. Alicante: Biblioteca Virtual Miguel de Cervantes. www.cervantesvirtual.com /nd/ark:/59851/bmc15428.

Pamo Reyna, Oscar G. 2015. "El travestismo en Lima: De la colonia a la república." *Acta Herediana* 56:26–38.

Pancrazio, James J. 2001. "Transvested Autobiography: Apocrypha and the Monja Alférez." *Bulletin of Hispanic Studies* 78 (4): 455–73.

Paquette, Gabriel. 2008. *Enlightenment, Governance, and Reform in Spain and Its Empire, 1759–1808*. Basingstoke: Palgrave McMillan.

Peirce, Charles Sanders. 1931–35. *Collected Papers of Charles Sanders Peirce*, edited by Charles Hartshorne and Paul Weiss, vols. 1–6. Cambridge, Mass.: Harvard University Press.

Penry, S. Elizabeth. 2000. "The Rey Común: Indigenous Political Discourse in Eighteenth-Century Alto Perú." In *The Collective and the Public in Latin America*, edited by Luis Roniger and Tamar Herzog, 219–37. Brighton: Sussex Academic Press.

———. Forthcoming. *The People Are King: The Making of an Andean Politics*. New York: Oxford University Press.

Peraita, Carmen. 2008. "'Como una casa portátil': Cultura del tapado y politica del anonimato en el espacio urbano del siglo XVII." In *Dressing the Spanish Way: Prestige and Usage of Spanish Attire at the European Courts (Sixteenth–Seventeenth Centuries)*, edited by José Luis Coloner and Amalia Descalzo, 291–318. Madrid: Centro de Estudios de Europa Hispánica.

Pérez Baltasar, María Dolores. 1984. *Mujeres marginadas: Las casas de recogidas en Madrid*. Madrid: Gráficas Lormo.

Pérez de Montalbán, Juan. (1626) 1839. *La monja alférez: Comedia en tres jornadas*. Barcelona: Imprenta de José Tauló.

———. (1626) 2007. *La monja alférez*. Edited by Luzmila Camacho Platero. Newark, Del.: Cuesta.

Perry, Mary Elizabeth. 1987. "The Manly Woman: A Historical Case Study." *American Behavioural Scientist* 31 (1): 86–100.

———. 1992. "Magdalens and Jezebels in Counter-Reformation Spain." In *Culture and Control in Counter-Reformation Spain*, edited by Ann J. Cruz and Mary Elizabeth Perry, 145–70. Minneapolis: University of Minnesota Press.

———. 1999. "From Convent to Battlefield: Cross-Dressing and Gendering the Self in the New World of Imperial Spain." In Blackmore and Hutcheson 1999, 394–419.

Phillips, William D., and Carla Rahn Phillips. 2010. *A Concise History of Spain*. Cambridge: Cambridge University Press.

Poole, Deborah A. 1988. "A One-Eyed Gaze: Gender in Nineteenth-Century Illustration of Peru." *Dialectical Anthropology* 13 (4): 333–64.

Portillo Valdés, José María. 2007. *Victorián de Villava: Circunstancias e itinerarios*. Madrid: Doce Calles-Fundación Mapfre.

———. 2009. "Victorián de Villava, Fiscal de Charcas: *Reforma de España* y Nueva Moral Imperial." *Studia Histórica: Historia Contemporánea* 27:27–52.

Poska, Allyson M. 2004. "Elusive Virtue: Rethinking the Role of Female Chastity in Early Modern Spain." *Journal of Early Modern History* 8 (1–2): 135–46.

———. 2013. "Upending Patriarchy: Rethinking Marriage and Family in Early Modern Europe." In *The Ashgate Research Companion to Women and Gender in Early Modern Europe*, edited by Jane Couchman, Katherine A. McIver, and Allyson M. Poska, 195–212. New York: Ashgate.

Premo, Bianca. 2005a. *Children of the Father King: Youth, Authority, and Legal Minority in Colonial Lima*. Chapel Hill: University of North Carolina Press.

———. 2005b. "'Misunderstood Love': Children and Wet Nurses, Creoles and Kings in Lima's Enlightenment." *Colonial Latin American Review* 14 (2): 231–61.

———. 2017. *The Enlightenment on Trial: Ordinary Litigants and Colonialism in the Spanish Empire*. New York: Oxford University Press.

Presta, Ana María. 2014. *Encomienda, familia, y negocios en Charcas Colonial: Los encomenderos de La Plata, 1550–1600*. 2nd ed. Sucre, Bolivia: Archivo y Biblioteca Nacionales de Bolivia/Fundación Cultural del Banco Central de Bolivia.

Prosser, Jay. 1998. *Second Skins: The Body Narratives of Transsexuality*. New York: Columbia University Press.

Querejazu Calvo, Roberto. 1987. *Chuquisaca, 1539–1825*. Sucre, Bolivia: Imprenta Universitaria.

Rappaport, Joanne. 2014. *The Disappearing Mestizo: Configuring Difference in the Colonial New Kingdom of Granada*. Durham: Duke University Press.

Reher, David S. 1996. *La familia en España pasado y presente*. Madrid: Alianza Universidad.

Reiter, Rayna R, ed. 1975. *Toward an Anthropology of Women*. New York: Monthly Review Press.

Relación verdadera de una carta que embió el padre Prior de la orden de Santo Domingo, de la Ciudad de Úbeda, al Abbad mayor de San Salvador de la Ciudad de Granada, de un caso digno de ser avisado, como estuvo doze años una monja professa, la qual avía metido su padre por ser cerrada, y no ser para casada, y un día haziendo un exercicio de fuerza se le rompió una tela por donde le salio la naturaleza de hombre como los demás, y lo que se hizo para sacalla del convento: Agora sucedió en este año de mil y seys ciento y diez y siete. 1617. Granada: s.n.

Renfrow, Daniel G. 2004. "A Cartography of Passing in Everyday Life." *Symbolic Interaction* 27 (4): 485–506.

Restall, Matthew. 2003. *Seven Myths of the Spanish Conquest*. New York: Oxford University Press.

Rich, Adrienne. 1980. "Compulsory Heterosexuality and Lesbian Existence." *Signs: Journal of Women in Culture and Society* 5:631–60.

Rípodas Ardanaz, Daisy. 1977. *El matrimonio en Indias: Realidad social y regulación jurídica*. Buenos Aires: Fundación para la Educación, la Ciencia, y la Cultura.

———. 1982. *El obispo Azamor y Ramírez: Tradición cristiana y modernidad*. Buenos Aires: Universidad de Buenos Aires.

———. 2002. "Los libros de un burócrata de la ilustración: La biblioteca potosina de Francisco de Paula Sanz (1810)." In *Derecho y administración pública en las Indias hispánicas: Actas del Duodécimo Congreso Internacional de Historia del Derecho Indiano*, Toledo,

19–21 de octubre de 1998, coord. Feliciano Barrios Pintado, 2:1489–515. Cuenca, Spain: Ediciones de la Universidad de Castilla–La Mancha.

Roach, Joseph. 1996. *Cities of the Dead: Circum-Atlantic Performance*. New York: Columbia University Press.

Roach, Mary Ellen, and Joanne Bubolz Eicher. 1965. *Dress, Adornment, and the Social Order*. New York: Wiley and Sons.

Robins, Nicholas. 2015. *Of Love and Loathing: Marital Life, Strife, and Intimacy in the Colonial Andes, 1750–1825*. Lincoln: University of Nebraska Press.

Roca, José Luis. 2007. *Ni con Lima, ni con Buenos Aires: La formación de un estado nacional en Charcas*. La Paz, Bolivia: Plural.

Rocha, Víctor. 2003. "El poder del cuerpo y sus gestos. Travestismo e identidad de género en América Colonial: El caso de Catalina de Erauso." *Cyber Humanitatis* 27 (Universidad de Chile). Accessed June 2017. http://web.uchile.cl/vignette/cyberhumanitatis/CDA /texto_simple2/0,1255,SCID%253D7513%2526ISID%253D347,00.html.

Rodríguez Freyle, Juan. (1636) 1979. *El carnero*. Caracas: Biblioteca Ayacucho.

Rubin, Gayle. 1975. "The Traffic in Women: Notes on the 'Political Economy' of Sex." In *Toward an Anthropology of Women*, edited by Rayna R. Reiter, 157–210. New York: Monthly Review Press.

———. (1992) 2006. "Of Catamites and Kings: Reflections on Butch, Gender, and Boundaries." In Stryker and Whittle 2006, 471–81.

Salazar-Villava, Octavio. N.d. "Los extraños hábitos de Don Antonio." *Tema Fantástico*. Accessed April 11, 2018. http://extranoshabitos.blogspot.com.

Sánchez, María C, and Linda Schlossberg. 2001. *Passing: Identity and Interpretation in Sexuality, Race, and Religion*. New York: New York University Press.

Sanz, Francisco de Paula. (1779–80) 1977. *Viaje por el Virreinato del Río de la Plata: El camino del tabaco*. Buenos Aires: Centro de Estudios Interdisciplinarios de Hispanoamérica Colonial, Universidad de Buenos Aires.

———. (1794) 1970. *Contestación al discurso sobre la mita de Potosí escrito en la Plata a 9 de marzo de 1793 contra el servicio de ella*. Edited by María del Carmen Cortés Salinas. *Revista de Indias* 30: 199–22.

Sarasua, Carmen. 1994. *El servicio doméstico en la formación del trabajo madrileño, 1758–1868*. Madrid: Siglo Veintiuno Editores.

Saussure, Ferdinand de. 2011. *Course in General Linguistics*. Translated by Wade Baskin. Edited by Perry Meisel and Haun Saussy. New York: Columbia University Press.

Schechner, Richard. 1985. *Between Theater and Anthropology*. Philadelphia: University of Pennsylvania Press.

Scheppele, Kim Lane. 1989. "Telling Stories, Forward to Legal Storytelling." Special issue, *Michigan Law Review* 87:2073–98.

Schiffrin, Deborah. 1996. "Narrative as Self-Portrait: Sociolinguistic Constructions of Identity." *Language and Society* 25:167–203.

Scott, Joan Wallach. 1986. "Gender: A Useful Category of Historical Analysis." *American Historical Review* 91 (5): 1053–105.

———. 1988. *Gender and the Politics of History*. New York: Columbia University Press.

———. 2007. *The Politics of the Veil*. Princeton: Princeton University Press.

Sedgwick, Eve Kosofsky. 1990. *Epistemology of the Closet*. Berkeley: University of California Press.

Seed, Patricia. 1988. *To Love, Honor, and Obey in Colonial Mexico: Conflicts over Marriage Choice, 1574–1821*. Stanford: Stanford University Press.

Sempere y Guarinos, Juan. 1788. *Historia del luxo y de las leyes suntuarias de España*. 2 vols. Madrid: Imprenta Real.

"Servant of God: Juana de la Cruz." Ordo Fratrum Minorum. March 24, 2015. www.ofm.org /ofm/?p=9086&lang=en.

Siegert, Berhnard. 2005. "Pasajeros a Indias: Biographical Writing Between the Old World and the New." In *Talleres de la memoria: Revindicaciones y autoridad en la historiografía indiana de los siglos XVI y XVII*, edited by Robert Folger and Wulf Oesterreicher, 295–306. Hamburg: Lit Verlag.

Sigal, Pete, ed. 2003. *Infamous Desire: Male Homosexuality in Colonial Latin America*. Chicago: University of Chicago Press.

Silverblatt, Irene. 2004. *Modern Inquisitions: Peru and the Colonial Origins of the Civilized World*. Durham: Duke University Press.

Silverstein, Michael. 1976. "Shifters, Linguistic Categories, and Cultural Description." In *Meaning in Anthropology*, edited by Keith Basso and Henry Selby, 11–55. Albuquerque: University of New Mexico Press.

Simmel, Georg. 1971. *Fashion, Individuality, and Social Forms*. Chicago: University of Chicago Press.

Smith, Paul Julian. 1989. *The Body Hispanic: Gender and Sexuality in Spanish and Spanish American Literature*. Oxford: Clarendon Press.

Smith, Theresa Ann. 2006. *The Emerging Female Citizen: Gender and Enlightenment in Spain*. Berkeley: University of California Press.

Socolow, Susan M. 1990. "Women and Crime: Buenos Aires, 1757–1797." In *The Problem of Order in Changing Societies*, edited by Lyman L. Johnson, 1–18. Albuquerque: University of New Mexico Press.

———. 1992. "Acceptable Partners: Marriage Choice in Colonial Argentina, 1778–1810." In Lavrin 1992, 209–46.

———. 2000. *The Women of Colonial Latin America*. Cambridge: Cambridge University Press.

Sommer, Doris. 1993. *Foundational Fictions: The National Romances of Latin America*. Berkeley: University of California Press.

Soux, María Luisa. 2010. *El complejo proceso hacia la independencia de Charcas (1808–1826): Guerra, ciudadanía, conflictos locales, y participación indígena en Oruro*. La Paz, Bolivia: Institut français d'études andines/Plural/ASDI/Instituto de Estudios Bolivianos.

Souza Congosto, Francisco de. 2007. *Introducción a la historia de la indumentaria en España*. Madrid: Istmo.

Soyer, François. 2012. *Ambiguous Gender in Early Modern Spain and Portugal: Inquisitors, Doctors, and the Transgression of Gender Norms*. Boston: Brill.

Spadaccini, Nicholas, and Jenaro Talens, eds. 1991. *Autobiography in Early Modern Spain*. Minneapolis: University of Minnesota Press.

"Spain, Catastro de Ensenada, 1749–1756." N.d. *Bernardo de Yta, 1751*. Vol. 2 of *Relaciones del estado seglar*. *FamilySearch*. Accessed March 14, 2012. https://familysearch.org.

Sponsler, Lucy A. 1982. "The Status of Married Women Under the Legal System of Spain." *Journal of Legal History* 3:125–52.

Spurling, Geoffrey. 1998. "Honor, Sexuality, and the Colonial Church: The Sins of Dr. González, Cathedral Canon." In Johnson and Lipsett-Rivera 1985, 45–67.

———. 2000. "Under Investigation for the Abominable Sin: Damien de Morales Stands Accused of Attempting to Seduce Antón de Tierra de Congo (Charcas, 1611)." In *Colonial Lives: Documents on Latin American History, 1550–1850*, edited by Richard Boyer and Geoffrey Spurling, 112–29. New York: Oxford University Press.

Stallybrass, Peter. 1986. "Patriarchal Territories: The Body Enclosed." In *Rewriting the Renaissance: The Discourses of Sexual Difference in Early Modern Europe*, edited by Margaret W. Ferguson, Maureen Quilligan, and Nancy J. Vickers, 123–44. Chicago: University of Chicago Press.

Stallybrass, Peter, and Allon White. 1986. *The Politics and Poetics of Transgression*. Ithaca: Cornell University Press.

Steedman, Carolyn. 2002. *Dust: The Archive and Cultural History*. New Brunswick: Rutgers University Press.

Stein, Stanley J, and Barbara H. Stein. 2003. *Apogee of Empire: Spain and New Spain in the Age of Charles III, 1759–1789*. Baltimore: Johns Hopkins University Press.

Stern, Steve J. 1999. *La historia secreta del género: Mujeres, hombres y poder en México en las postrimerías del periodo colonial*. Mexico City: Fondo de Cultura Económica.

Stoetzer, O. Carlos.1979. *The Scholastic Roots of the Spanish American Revolution*. New York: Fordham University Press.

Stoler, Ann Laura. 1995. *Race and the Education of Desire: Foucault's History of Sexuality and the Colonial Order of Things*. Durham: Duke University Press.

———. 2002. *Carnal Knowledge and Imperial Power: Race and the Intimate in Colonial Rule*. Berkeley: University of California Press.

———. 2009. *Along the Archival Grain: Epistemic Anxieties and Colonial Common Sense*. Princeton: Princeton University Press.

Strathern, Marilyn. 1990. *The Gender of the Gift: Problems with Women and Problems with Society in Melanesia*. Berkeley: University of California Press.

Stroud, Michael D. 1990. *Fatal Union: A Pluralistic Approach to the Spanish Wife-Murder Comedias*. Lewisburg: Bucknell University Press.

Stryker, Susan. 2008. "Transgender History, Homonormativity, and Disciplinarity." *Radical History Review* 100:145–57.

———. 2017. *Transgender History: The Roots of Today's Revolution*. 2nd ed. New York: Seal Press.

Stryker, Susan, and Stephen Whittle. 2006. *The Transgender Studies Reader*. New York: Routledge.

Sullivan, Lou. 1990. *Information for the Female to Male Cross Dresser and Transsexual*, 3rd ed. Seattle: Ingersoll Gender Center.

Surtz, Ronald E. 1990. *The Guitar of God: Gender, Power, and Authority in the Visionary World of Mother Juana de la Cruz*. Philadelphia: University of Pennsylvania Press.

Tamburini, Filippo. 1995. *Santi e peccatori: Confessioni e suppliche dai registri della Penitenzieria dell'Archivio Segreto Vaticano (1451–1586)*. Vatican: Instituto de Propaganda Libraria.

Tandeter, Enrique. 1993. *Coercion and Market: Silver Mining in Colonial Potosí, 1692–1826*. Albuquerque: University of New Mexico Press.

Taylor, Charles. 1992. *Sources of the Self: The Making of the Modern Identity*. Cambridge, Mass: Harvard University Press.

Taylor, Diana. 2003. *The Archive and the Repertoire: Performing Cultural Memory in the Americas*. Durham: Duke University Press.

Temple, Edmond. 1830. *Travels in Various Parts of Peru: Including a Year's Residence in Potosi*. London: Colburn and Bentley.

Thompson, I. A. A. 1985. "Neo-noble Nobility: Concepts of Hidalguía in Early Modern Castile." *European History Quarterly* 15:379–406.

Tirso de Molina. (1613–14) 1948. *La Santa Juana: Trilogía hagiográfica (1613/1614)*. Madrid: Editorial Castilla.

Tomás y Valiente, Francisco. 1990. "El crimen y pecado contra natura." In *Sexo barroco y otras transgresiones premodernas*, edited by Francisco Tomás y Valiente, 33–55. Madrid: Alianza Editorial.

Tortorici, Zeb. 2007. "'Heran todos putos': Sodomitical Subcultures and Disordered Desire in Early Colonial Mexico." *Ethnohistory* 54 (1): 35–67.

———. 2013. "Agustina Ruiz: Sexuality and Religiosity in Colonial Mexico." In *The Human Tradition in Colonial Latin America*, edited by Kenneth J. Andrien, 117–32. 2nd ed. Lanham: Rowman and Littlefield.

———. 2015. "Sexual Violence, Predatory Masculinity, and Medical Testimony in New Spain." In *Scientific Masculinities*, special issue of *Osiris* 30, edited by Robert Nye and Erika Milam, 272–94. Chicago: University of Chicago Press.

———, ed. 2016a. "Introduction: Unnatural Bodies, Desires, and Devotions." In Tortorici 2016b, 1–22.

————. 2016b. *Sexuality and the Unnatural in Colonial Latin America*. Berkeley: University of California Press.

Tortorici, Zeb, and Ronaldo Vainfas. 2016. "Female Homoeroticism, Heresy, and the Holy Office in Colonial Brazil." In Tortorici 2016b, 77–92.

Traub, Valerie. 2013. "The New Unhistoricism in Queer Studies." *PMLA* 128 (1): 21–39.

Turner, Terence S. 1980. "The Social Skin." In *Not Work Alone: A Cross-Cultural View of Activities Superfluous to Survival*, edited by Jeremy Cherfas and Roger Lewin, 112–40. London: Temple Smith.

Turner, Victor. 1969. *The Ritual Process: Structure and Anti-Structure*. New York: Transaction.

————. 1982. *From Ritual to Theater: The Human Seriousness of Play*. New York: PAJ Books.

Twinam, Ann. 1999. *Public Lives, Private Secrets: Gender, Honor, Sexuality, and Illegitimacy in Colonial Spanish America*. Stanford: Stanford University Press.

————. 2005. "Women and Gender in Colonial Latin America." In *Women's History in Global Perspective*, edited by Bonnie G. Smith, 187–237. Vol. 2. Urbana: University of Illinois Press.

————. 2015. *Purchasing Whiteness: Pardos, Mulattos, and the Quest for Social Mobility in the Spanish Indies*. Stanford: Stanford University Press.

Uhagón, Francisco R. de. 1896. "Relación de cómo una monja de Ubeda se tornó hombre." In *Relaciones históricas de los siglos XVI y XVII*, 335–37. Madrid: Sociedad de Bibliófilos Españoles.

Uriburu, Damaso de. 1934. *Memorias de Damaso de Uriburu, 1794–1857*. Buenos Aires: La Facultad.

Valentine, David. 2007. *Imagining Transgender: An Ethnography of a Category*. Durham: Duke University Press.

Van Deusen, Nancy. 2001. *Between the Sacred and the Worldly: The Institution and Cultural Practice of Recogimiento in Colonial Lima*. Stanford: Stanford University Press.

Vázquez Machicado, Humberto. 1988. *Obras completas*. Vol. 3. Edited by Guillermo Ovando–Sanz and Alberto M. Vázquez. La Paz, Bolivia: Ediciones Don Bosco.

Velando Casanova, Mónica. 2005. "La RAE y la violencia de género: Reflexiones en torno al debate lingüístico sobre el título de una ley." *Cultura, Lenguaje, y Representación: Revista de Estudios Culturales de la Universitat Jaume I* 11:107–24.

Velasco, Sherry. 2000. *The Lieutenant Nun: Transgenderism, Lesbian Desire, and Catalina de Erauso*. Austin: University of Texas Press.

————. 2003a. "Interracial Lesbian Erotics in Early Modern Spain: Catalina de Erauso and Elena/o de Céspedes." In *Tortilleras: Hispanic and U.S. Latina Lesbian Expression*, edited by Lourdes Torres and Inmaculada Pertusa, 213–27. Philadelphia: Temple University Press.

————. 2003b. "La primera dama, el público y Catalina de Erauso: Colaboración teatral en la monja alférez de Pérez de Montalbán." *Bulletin of the Comediantes* 54 (1): 115–32.

————. 2011. *Lesbians in Early Modern Spain*. Nashville: Vanderbilt University Press.

Vernant, Jean-Pierre. 1989. "At Man's Table: Hesiod's Foundation Myth of Sacrifice." In *The Cuisine of Sacrifice Among the Greeks*, translated by Paula Wissing, edited by Marcel Detienne and Jean-Pierre Vernant, 21–86. Chicago: University of Chicago Press.

Vicente, Marta V. 2006. *Clothing the Spanish Empire: Families and the Calico Trade in the Early Modern Atlantic World*. New York: Palgrave.

————. 2016a. "Maria Elena Martínez's 'Sex and the Colonial Archive.'" *Sex and the Colonial Archive: The Case of 'Mariano' Aguilera* (open forum), posted by Sean Mannion. *Hispanic American Historical Review*, July 22, 2016. permalink: hahr-online.com /maria-elena-martinez/.

————. 2016b. "Staging Femininity in Early Modern Spain." In *Mapping the Early Modern Hispanic World Essays in Honor of Richard L. Kagan*, edited by Kimberly Lynn and Erin Rowe, 339–59. Cambridge: Cambridge University Press.

———. 2017. *Debating Sex and Gender in Eighteenth-Century Spain.* Cambridge: Cambridge University Press.

Vidal, Emeric Essex, Esq. 1820. *Picturesque Illustrations of Buenos Ayres and Monte Video, Consisting of Twenty-Four Views: Accompanied with Descriptions of the Scenery, and of the Costumes, Manners, &c., of the Inhabitants of those Cities and their Environs.* London: Ackermann.

Villava, Victorián de. (1797) 1822. *Apuntes para una reforma de España sin trastorno del gobierno monárquico ni la Religión: Por el Señor Don Victoriano de Villava, del Consejo de S. M. y su fiscal en la Real Audiencia y Chancillería de La Plata; Año de 1797.* Buenos Aires: Imprenta de Álvarez.

Vivas, Mario Carlos. 1997. "José Eugenio del Portillo, abogado y político cordobés." *Cuadernos de historia* 7:195–214.

Vives, Juan Luís. (1523) 2000. *The Education of a Christian Woman: A Sixteenth-Century Manual.* Translated and edited by Charles Fantazzi. Chicago: University of Chicago Press.

Voigt, Lisa. 2016. *Spectacular Wealth: The Festivals of Colonial South American Mining Towns.* Austin: University of Texas Press.

Vollendorf, Lisa. 2001a. "'Doubt It Will Amaze You': María de Zayas's Early Modern Feminism." In Vollendorf 2001b, 103–20.

———, ed. 2001b. *Recovering Spain's Feminist Tradition.* New York: Modern Language Association of America.

———. 2005. *The Lives of Women: A New History of Inquisitional Spain.* Nashville: Vanderbilt University Press.

Wacquant, Loïc. 2016. "A Concise Genealogy and Anatomy of Habitus." *Sociological Review* 64 (1): 64–72.

Wahrman, Dror. 2006. *The Making of the Modern Self: Identity and Culture in Eighteenth-Century England.* New Haven: Yale University Press.

Warner, Michael. 1991. "Fear of a Queer Planet." *Social Text* 29:3–17.

Weismantel, Mary. 2001. *Cholas and Pishtacos: Stories of Race and Sex in the Andes.* Chicago: University of Chicago Press.

White, Hayden. 1978. "The Forms of Wildness: The Archaeology of an Idea." In *Tropics of Discourse: Essays in Cultural Criticism,* 150–82. Baltimore: Johns Hopkins University Press.

———. 1981. "The Value of Narrativity in the Representation of Reality." In *On Narrative,* edited by W. J. T. Mitchell, 1–23. Chicago: University of Chicago Press.

Wolff, Janet. 1985. "The Invisible *Flâneuse*: Women and the Literature of Modernity." *Theory, Culture, and Society* 2 (3): 37–46.

Zayas y Sotomayor, María de. 1989. *Tres novelas amorosas y ejemplares, y tres desengaños amorosos.* Madrid: Castalia.

Zerolo, Elías, Miguel de Toro, Emiliano Isaza Gómez, y otros Escritores Españoles y Americanos. 1895. *Diccionario enciclopédico de la lengua castellana.* Vol. 2. Paris: Garnier Hermanos.

INDEX

www.ingramcontent.com/pod-product-compliance
Lightning Source LLC
Chambersburg PA
CBHW032118020426
42334CB00016B/998